Martin Luther

Gerhard Brendler

Martin Luther

—

Theology and Revolution

Translated by Claude R. Foster, Jr.

New York Oxford
Oxford University Press
1991

Oxford University Press

Oxford New York Toronto
Delhi Bombay Calcutta Madras Karachi
Petaling Jaya Singapore Hong Kong Tokyo
Nairobi Dar es Salaam Cape Town
Melbourne Auckland

and associated companies in
Berlin Ibadan

Library of Congress Cataloging-in-Publication Data

Brendler, Gerhard.
(Martin Luther. English)
Martin Luther: theology and revolution/Gerhard Brendler:
translated by Claude R. Foster, Jr.
p. cm.
Includes bibliographical references and index.
ISBN 0-19-505112-2
1. Luther, Martin, 1483–1546. 2. Reformers—Germany—Biography.
I. Title.
BR325.B69513 1989
284.1′092′4—dc 19
(B)
88-38881
CIP

Printing (last digit): 987654321
Printed in Germany

Gerhard Zschäbitz
1920–1970
In Memoriam

Preface

—

This book was written in the German Democratic Republic for the citizens of that republic. However, the themes that dominated the life of Martin Luther—faith, Bible, reformation, revolution—command universal attention.

The occasion for this biography of Martin Luther was the quincentennial celebration in 1983 of his birth. The reason for the writing of this book was to attempt to clarify my own personal relationship with Luther. The motive was patriotism. The aim was to appeal for tolerance and a strengthening of the awareness that we in the German Democratic Republic are erecting a socialist society not in a vacuum but in a baptized country.

Five hundred years from now, how will posterity regard us? This question repeatedly confronted me when, while writing this book, I was prompted to shake my head in disbelief at those questions raised as issues about which Luther and his opponents wrangled, and I was tempted to offer my hero somewhat belated advice or even censor him.

I believe many share my view that every present is merely the future of many pasts as well as the past of many futures. I do not know whether or not this observation is true, but I am certain that in the German Democratic Republic the increasing attraction for intellectuals to "heritage and tradition" is linked to a belief that there is a unity of present, past, and future. Thus the rediscovery of the past is the prerequisite for self-awareness. In this context, Martin Luther became for me a spiritual adventure. In the writing of this book, I was in my element.

A historical personality must be understood within the context of his time but must not be reduced to that context. Martin Luther was not just an echo of his time. With his own voice he addressed his century and thereby propelled it forward. Under the conditions of his time, which was characterized by the first revolution in German history, he thought as a theologian and acted as an intellectual in a princely dukedom. Theology, reformation, and the confrontation with revolution stamped his life so markedly that they stand at the center of this biography.

If we want to understand Martin Luther, then, we must believe that for him the problems that dominating his life were real and that his words truly stated his convictions. He was and remains a problematic and provocative symbolic figure of German and European history.

If you inquire of Martin Luther, dear reader, you must be prepared to accept his answer as a question directed to you concerning what it means to be human.

The translator, my friend Claude R. Foster, J., made several trips to East Berlin, where we together read the entire English manuscript. I am grateful to him for his congenial translation.

East Berlin

G. B.

Translator's Acknowledgements

I wish to thank Mrs. Mildred M. Van Sice for the incalculable assistance that she rendered in the preparation of the manuscript for the press. Furthermore, I express my warm appreciation to the author, Gerhard Brendler of the Academy of Sciences in the German Democratic Republic, and to his colleague Karl Drechsler, as well as to their staffs, for the generous hospitality and assistance extended during my visits to East Berlin to confer with the author.

A note of thanks for their generous advice is in order also to colleagues and friends in the Federal Republic of Germany and the German Democratic Republic and at West Chester University. Mr. Richard Schneider of West Chester University and Professor Horst Beintker of the Friedrich Schiller University in Jena offered especially helpful suggestions. In addition, my former professor, Walther Kirchner, also provided counsel.

I thank my wife, Lois Burns Foster, for her tolerance and forebearance in overlooking the many domestic chores left undone in order that I could remain riveted to my task.

Translator's Notes

—

The manuscript was completed before the German Democratic Republic autumn revolution of 1989.

Before the storm broke forces were at work which challenged rigid party orthodoxy. Brendler's Luther biography may be considered representative of that intellectual current which was helping to prepare the way for the November transformation.

With the approval of the author, some passages have been expanded while others have been revised to provide greater clarity for the English-language reader.

Contents

—

Introduction
—

Professor Faustus tells his attendant, Wagner, "The past, my friend, is a book with seven seals. What you call the spirit of the ages is in reality the spirit of those in whom the times are reflected." Thus the past becomes a mirror in which each age discovers its own reflection. The sixteenth century Reformation provides such a mirror, for "Luther was a genius of a very special mark. His stamp has already lasted a long time, and his influence on future centuries cannot be estimated" (Goethe, 1828). Until the nineteenth century, the historical interpretation of the Protestant Reformation was ordinarily based on what has been called classical Protestant and Catholic scholarship. Roman Catholic scholarship regarded the Reformation as a great misfortune that destroyed Catholic civilization and ruptured European unity. Luther was a rebel who opened the door to violent revolutions patterned after his own rebellious and irresponsible conduct. Protestant historians, on the other hand, saw the Reformation as the work of God purging His Church. Luther was God's chosen instrument; Rome was the whore of Babylon depicted in the Apocalypse, and the Reformation was the divinely ordained *kairos*, preparing the world for the final act of the historical drama. The modern ecumenical posture appears to have put an end to the old Protestant-Catholic Reformation polemic. The ecumenical spirit has discovered a different reflection in the mirror of the Reformation.

As this biography will illustrate, the East German Marxist interpretation of the life and career of Martin Luther also discovers in the Reformation — that period called by Friedrich Engels the pivot point of German history — historical forces and personalities that helped establish and stabilize the first socialistic state in German history, the German Democratic Republic (GDR). Marxist historians employ the works of Karl Marx and Friedrich Engels as a key in their interpretation of history. There are two aspects of the evaluation of Martin Luther in the writings of Marx and Engels.

1. The Reformation and Peasants' War constituted the first middle class revolution in European history. Thomas Müntzer, the leader of the peasants, was frustrated in his attempt to create, by revolution, a unified, democratic German state. Luther sided with the princes, opposed Müntzer and the peasants, and thereby postponed for centuries the realization of

this unified state. Engels regarded Luther's conduct as a betrayal of the masses; he saw Luther as the lackey of the princes in their effort to maintain the status quo. Marx considered Luther's theological conservatism the major factor in the defeat of the peasants: the revolution failed because of theology.

2. The Reformation and Peasants' War taken together are still regarded as the first middle-class revolution in European history, but it is acknowledged that the bourgeois revolutionary forces were too weak in the sixteenth century to realize immediately a new middle class political and social order, not to mention the popular socialist democracy for which Thomas Müntzer and the common people were striving. But the Reformation provided the bedrock on which all subsequent European revolutions were founded. The Reformation afforded the necessary historical breakthrough out of medieval feudalism and into the new capitalist society and the series of bourgeois revolutions—Dutch, Puritan, American, French— which were to lead Europe to the threshold of contemporary socialist societies. Seen from this perspective, the hammer-blows in Wittenberg in October 1517 posting the ninety-five theses that initiated the Reformation, were echoed exactly four centuries later in October 1917 by the salvos from the gunship *Aurora*, which signaled the beginning of the Bolshevik Revolution. In this particular of Marxist historical writing, there is a clear line from Luther to Lenin. Supplementing this second orientation of the Marxist evaluation of Luther, Marx wrote, "Germany's revolutionary past is theoretical; it is the Reformation. As at that time it was the monk, so it is now the philosopher in whose brain the revolution is born." In this second orientation, the reformer is depicted neither as a traitor to the masses nor as a lackey of the princes but rather as a herald of a new age. East German Marxist historians have been engaged since 1945 in a quest for the dialectical balance between Luther and Müntzer, reformation and revolution. The history of the GDR has determined to a great degree which aspect of the Marx-Engels evaluation is to prevail. Gerhard Brendler's Luther biography is the culmination of debate, dialogue, and dialectic within the East German Marxist historical collegium.

East German historians divide the history of the GDR into four stages:

1. the antifascist democratic revolution of 1945–1949 in the Soviet occupied zone in which demilitarization, denazification, and democratization took place;

2. the establishment of the foundation of socialism from 1949 to 1961 in the new state of the GDR;

3. the progress toward an advanced socialist society from 1961 to 1970;

4. the further development of an advanced socialistic society since 1970.

From about 1945–1961, East German Marxist historians regarded the reformer as the lackey of the princes and blamed his conservative theology for the failure of the Peasants' War. The reasons for this are to be found in the early history of the East German state. East German Marxist historians faced the monumental task of completely rewriting German history to conform to Marxist historical canons. Bourgeois historical interpretations were unacceptable, and the total discarding of the historical works of the Third Reich was necessary. The traditional rivalry between Christianity and Marxism, the perceived complicity or at least apolitical posture of the German Lutheran Church during the Nazi era helped to promote an antipathy toward Luther among Marxist historians.

From 1945-1961, claiming that the German bourgeoisie had supported Hitler and therefore had forfeited any right to political power, German Marxists called for a united postwar German socialist state. In order to combat the threat of partition and dismemberment originating in American, French, and British quarters, German Marxists turned to German history for examples of national union. They found in Thomas Müntzer and the Peasants' War the first attempt to unite the German people in a socialist democracy. Since Luther had opposed Thomas Müntzer and the peasants, and had supported the German princes, he was responsible, in the eyes of the Marxist historians, for the prolongation of German political particularism. Luther thus became associated with the divisive bourgeois forces, and those very forces, in the twentieth century as in the sixteenth, appeared to prevent the unification of the German nation in a socialist democracy. Thomas Müntzer, on the other hand, became the hero for East German Marxist historians. In some early East German Marxist studies of the Reformation, the postwar phenomenon of two rival German states was reduced to Luther versus Müntzer. Marxist historians in the GDR continued until 1961 to call for German unification under the banner of socialist society. As long as that call prevailed, the Marx-Engels evaluation of Luther as a traitor, lackey, and reactionary also prevailed. The international postwar political rivalry, the Cold War, the policy of rollback and containment of international communism, the Truman Doctrine, and the Marshall Plan prepared the way for the establishment of a West German state (the Federal Republic of Germany) under the supervision of the Western allies in 1949. When the Federal Republic of Germany (FRG), granted full sovereignty, was integrated into NATO and the Western economic community, and when it became clear that no unification of Germany within the boundaries of a socialist democracy as envisioned by East German Marxists would be possible, the GDR sealed its borders against the FRG on August 13, 1961, and turned its attention toward developing a separate and sovereign German socialist state.

The new emphasis on building socialist society within the boundaries of the GDR silenced the call for a unified German state and raised the appeal for a socialist patriotism and the integration of the first socialist state in German history into the broad stream of the international proletariat. Recognizing that no state can be born in a vacuum, and taking very seriously Engels' affirmation that the German Reformation is the pivot point of German history, the GDR emphasized the second orientation of the Marx-Engels evaluation of Luther: Luther was the herald of a new age. This facilitated the building of a socialist society by enabling the GDR to enlist in its efforts a broader spectrum of its citizens, many of whom are still associated with the Lutheran Church (7,700,000 in a population of 16,800,000, according to a 1983 census), and by incorporating the great heritage of the Reformation. (Most sites of the German Reformation are located in the GDR). By his revolt against the Roman Catholic Church, the bastion of medieval feudalism, Luther had liberated bourgeois ideology. Max Steinmetz, the mentor of this new emphasis in East German Marxist Reformation scholarship, spoke of a new theology as the necessary precondition for the birth of a new ideology. Thus, dialectically considered, the theology that caused the Peasants' Revolt to founder was the conduit through which bourgeois revolutionary ideology was channeled.

The current domestic and international concerns of the GDR are reflected in the sophisticated treatment of Luther here presented by Gerhard Brendler. The growing appreciation of the GDR for the contribution that the Lutheran Church is able to make in the building of socialist society has resulted in a more charitable evaluation of Martin Luther. The Wartburg meeting in August 1964 between Walter Ulbricht, the East German head of state, and Moritz Mitzenheim, the Bishop of Thuringia, inaugurated a new era in Church-State relations. In March 1978, Erich Honecker, the recent East German head of state, in a major policy address thanked the leadership of the Lutheran Church for the significant contribution that Christians in the GDR are making to the building of socialist society and to the maintenance of world peace. In the GDR a large corpus of literature concerning Christians who resisted Adolf Hitler is appearing. That the emphasis in this literature is no longer on the failure of the German churches to resist Hitler but rather on those Christians who were martyred because of their resistance suggests a certain attempt at rapprochement between state and church. The concentration camp, where Christians and communists were subjected to the same fate and where they learned to coexist and to cooperate, has become the catalyst for the current Christian-Marxist dialogue. Under these new conditions East German Marxist Reformation scholarship has evolved toward a more "mature" view of Luther and the Reformation. The spirit of those in whom the time are reflected was clearly seen in 1967 at the 450th celebration of the posting of Luther's ninety-five theses. On that occasion, Gerhard Zschäbitz, professor at the Karl Marx University in Leipzig, employed a Lenin quote to exonerate Luther from what

Zschäbitz considered unfair accusations made by some of his Marxist colleagues: Lenin had written that historical personalities may be judged by the present generation not on what they did not accomplish but rather, compared with their predecessors, on what they did accomplish. Zschäbitz then concluded that Luther was neither a traitor to the peasants nor a lackey of the princes. Luther was bound to his time and place on the historical stage, and he acted, as he had to, in conformity with his historical milieu.

On June 13, 1980, Erich Honecker, the East German head of state, accepted the nomination of his party to chair the State Luther Committee, charged with preparing celebrations to mark the five hundredth anniversary of Luther's birth in 1983. In preparation for the Luther quincentennial, the East German State invested millions of marks in the renovation of historical sites associated with Luther and the Reformation. A dramatization of Luther's life, depicting the new appreciation for the reformer, was broadcast in 1983 on national television. In his address to the State Luther Committee, Honecker emphasized Engels' depiction of Luther as the herald of the great transformations in European society at the demise of feudalism. Honecker pointed out that Luther's works stamped the ideas of the sixteenth century in a determinative manner; viewed from the threshold of the twenty-first century, his influence on the ideology of European civilization is beyond dispute. Professor Horst Bartel, director of the Central Institute for Historical Studies in the Academy of Sciences in East Berlin, convoked an international historical congress at the Halle-Wittenberg Martin Luther University to celebrate the Luther quincentennial. Before Director Bartel's untimely death in 1984, he had established an institute for the study of church history within the Academy of Sciences of the GDR. Gerhard Brendler was appointed director of this new institute. Despite occasional serious setbacks, the relationship between church and state—since the Ulbricht-Mitzenheim Wartburg colloquy (August 1964), the Honecker-Bishop Schönherr proclamations (March 1978), and the rapprochement cultivated for the Luther quincentennial—is decisively better today than it was in the 1950s, as reflected in the contemporary East German Marxist view of Luther.

The rehabilitation of Luther does not mean the neglect of Thomas Müntzer. Both figures are needed to represent reformation and revolution if the dialectical tensions of the sixteenth century, which gave birth to the first middle class revolution in European society, are to provide the reflection that the twentieth century seeks to discover. Luther is the herald of that new age, and Müntzer is its hero. The emphasis on the ideological foundation provided by Luther does not deprive Müntzer of his historic mission, for Müntzer's mission (popular socialist democracy), though not viable in the sixteenth century, nevertheless provided a paradigm for future socialist societies and also demonstrated the limitations of bourgeois revolutions. In the current East German Marxist view, Luther and Müntzer, reformation and revolution, are held in delicate juxtaposition: no Luther, no Müntzer. When a Luther spoke, could a Müntzer remain silent? In 1983, Erich Honecker expressed it thus: "It is important for the sense of history and tradition in our people, living as they are in a socialist society, that Luther and Müntzer should not be counterposed from the very outset as figures constituting irreconcilable opposites. They must be comprehended dialectically as the two great personalities of the first German revolution."

In 1989 the GDR will celebrate the quincentennial of the birth of Thomas Müntzer. In the Marxist interpretation of the GDR, Müntzer's rainbow banner, which was defeated on the hills of Frankenhausen in Thuringia on May 15, 1525, has at last been hoisted over the society where "power belongs to the common people." The Marxist dramatist Friedrich Wolf expressed this interpretation in his play *Thomas Müntzer: the Man with the Rainbow Banner*, as follows:

> Everything has its time
> And time brings forth from her womb only that which is ripe.
> Be consoled and tell my comrades
> That the grain which fell under the sickle
> Will, nevertheless, find root and one day bring forth fruit.

The GDR in competition with the FRG as the heir to German history and culture, has developed a broad basis of historical consciousness and has incorporated into its history all the great achievements in Germany's past. The German Reformation has become a major cultural and historical foundation for the East German State. Many East German Marxist historians now concur with Brendler's affirmation, "We must recognize that we are striving to build a socialist society in a baptized country."

In permitting Luther to remain a religious reformer, East German Marxist Reformation scholarship reaches its acme in Gerhard Brendler's biography of Luther, which reflects an image of Luther that may surprise many. Other surprises also await the reader: for example, the subtle parallels between the theological revolutionary ideology of the sixteenth century and the political revolutionary ideology of the twentieth century. In 1983, the quincentennial of Martin Luther's birth and the centennial of Karl Marx's death, these two great but long alienated sons of Germany finally were reconciled through the Luther-Müntzer relationship reflected in Brendler's grand synthesis of reformation and revolution.

West Chester, Pennsylvania
April 1989
C. R. F.

Martin Luther

Chapter 1

Child, Youth, Student, Monk, and Priest
1483–1512

In Eisleben on November 10, 1483, Margarethe Luder, wife of the miner Hans Luder, bore her husband a son. On the next day, November 11, St. Martin's Day, the boy was baptized and, according to custom, given the name of the saint on whose feast day the baptism took place. The Luder family was not originally from Eisleben; Möhra, south of Eisenach, was the family's ancestral home. Heine Luder, Martin's grandfather, was a farmer there; he owned a farm on which he paid taxes.

Not all farmers in the German feudal society of that day lived in the relative security of Heine Luder and the other farmers of western Thuringia. The inheritance tax required of the Luders was a feudal rent, but apart from this obligation they enjoyed an independence which could not be exercised where, as in southwest Germany, there were stricter conditions of feudal dependency, such as personal indenture.

However, this relatively secure social standing of the Thuringian farmers could be preserved only if the farms were not divided but passed on intact to the heir, and it was desirable that the farms be enlarged. This ancient custom which promoted agrarian stability in Thuringia found expression in the inheritance law. In this region it was the right of the youngest son to inherit the family farm because he lived under parental protection for the longest period; the period before the parents' ability to work diminished and they were forced to resign their patrimony was shortest for the youngest child. The Thuringian custom of assigning the patrimony to the youngest son reduced those conflicts and tensions which arise from the desire for land in an agrarian community, and was in another way advantageous and reasonable: since the older sons could not be expected, without unwillingness and resentment, to submit to the yoke of youth and to follow the directives of their younger brothers, a stimulus was created for the older brothers to search for an independent livelihood and to seek their fortunes in the wider world. The customary inheritance law made for progress and, in the long run, contributed to the division of labor in the society. The law also assisted in liberating younger heirs, physically weaker and less experienced, from subjection to their older, stronger, and more experienced brothers. Since the older brothers did not want to hire themselves out as menials, handymen, or day laborers in the village, or because of overpopulation were unable to do so, they were obliged to seek their fortunes elsewhere. Thus ancient Thuringian peasant wisdom concerning inheritance led to an increase in the urban population, and urban problems were thereby increased. On the one hand, this general increase in the urban population, especially in the lower working class, gave rise to social unrest and many other causes for conflict. On the other hand, a considerable labor force was formed to satisfy such needs of society as manpower for the mining industry and employees for early capitalistic enterprises.

Legal and social interconnections and the economic restraints associated with them prompted Hans Luder to move from Möhra to Eisleben. Heine Luder had fathered four sons: Hans the elder, Hans the younger, Veit, and Heinz. Heinz was the youngest son; he bore his father's name and he inherited the family farm. Hans the elder, Martin's father, took advantage of the copper and silver mining enterprises conducted in the Möhra region, became a miner, and in 1483, the same year in which he married Margarethe Lindemann, he migrated to Eisleben. The Eisleben-Mansfeld region was one of the more important mining centers of Germany—indeed, of Europe.

Hans Luder's hopes that Eisleben would offer greater possibilities for success than Möhra were not disappointed. His position improved after he moved from Eisleben to Mansfeld in 1484. Hans Luder was industrious, thrifty, circumspect, and goal-oriented, working his way up from miner to mine owner. In Mansfeld he was one of the four men elected to represent the interests of the mining community before the city council. He held investments in eight mines and three foundries. From time to time he borrowed money, and he was obliged to work hard to free himself from debt.

The social advancement of Hans Luder was not a steady, upward march. It was much more of a struggle for, with, and against money. No single individual could mine and refine copper ore or any other ore, for that matter. Shafts had to be dug, tunnels ventilated, and water drained. Mine platforms had to be built. The deeper the ore stratum, the more expensive were then drainage operation and the extraction "arts," as these techniques were named. As long as veins close to the surface of the shaft could be mined, the investment was relatively modest and the extraction of the ore could be carried out in so-called family enterprises, in which a miner alone or with his family members could perform the entire operation. This is how mining had started in the Middle Ages.

With the increased demand for ore and the increasing depths of the shafts, single miners were forced to form guilds in order to bear the higher cost of extracting the ore. But the ore had not only to be extracted and refined; it had also to be sold. The merchant entered the picture in a dual role, as purchaser and distributor of the mine products and also as financier for both the family-owned and the guild-operated mines. For the miners, dependency on the market gradually led to an economic and finally to a social dependency on the merchants.

The greater the demand for metal, the deeper the shafts had to be dug and, in turn, the greater the demand for capital to meet production costs. Thus an autonomous dynamic was developed from modest origins as economic and technical needs constituted a dialectical thrust. Capital flowed into production and the producers subjected themselves to the dominance of the capital. It was in mining that capitalism began to flower.

The so-called *Saigergesellschaften* dominated the copper mining industry. These investors bought up raw copper, separated silver from copper, and then brought both products to the market. Miners became indebted to the *Saigergesellschaften* by borrowing in accordance with the expected yield of raw copper. Nominally the mine owners remained independent. In reality they often were so deeply in debt that their mines hardly belonged to them. Some mine owners were entrepreneurs, others had lost their independence and were not much more than wage earners or foremen for investors. The social and economic position of Hans Luder hovered between the poles of independent entrepreneur and debtor.

The fate of Hans Luder was not his alone. In this stock and investment system an early form of capitalism was developing not only in mining enterprises but also in textile production, shipbuilding, printing, and many other areas. Capital brought improvement in production techniques and alterations in the society. Its most important social impact was that it rendered insecure the small entrepreneurs and producers, completely subjugated them to capital's demands, in some cases brought about their economic ruin, deprived them of their ownership in production, and reduced them to wage earning or to penury. On the other hand, large capital conglomerates that provided some few commercial societies with fantastic wealth were quick to appear. Among these societies the Fuggers have remained until this day a symbol for all that is associated with money, banks, commerce, interest, and wealth. The Fuggers also symbolize business efficiency, organizational talent, ambition, and unscrupulous conduct. To be sure, the large banking establishments not only exemplified the nature of budding capitalism but were also in a position to undermine the small, modest business enterprises.

Sometimes gradually, sometimes rapidly, with varying degrees of intensity, early capitalism everywhere in the several states caused a sharpening of social distinctions between rich and poor—distinctions which even without capitalism had already existed. It was to be sure an incipient and by no means a mature capitalism. Germany still needed 300 to 350 years before the essential features of capitalism—namely the bourgeoisie and the proletariat—would be fully developed and their class rivalry would become the pivot for all social action. But the foundation for such action was already laid in the sixteenth century, when the growth of capitalism was already sufficient to introduce unrest into society and to provide a powerful impetus to German history.

It was amidst these historical developments that Luther's parents made the transition from Thuringian peasant farmers to entrepreneurs in the emerging bourgeois society of the sixteenth century. These early bourgeois entrepreneurs worked hard, were thrifty, and took such great risks that their very existence was sometimes at stake. They are to be distinguished from the bourgeois class of several centuries later which shaped modern capitalism.

At the end of the fifteenth and the beginning of the sixteenth century the future clearly belonged to capitalistic enterprise. Capitalism provided the most modern social element in the society. Even the lives of great historical personalities cannot be explained entirely in terms of prevailing economic and social conditions. Such a one-sided attempt would be invalid because these conditions offer a multiplicity of possibilities from which the individual may more or less freely choose. Nevertheless, we should not lose sight of the fact that Martin Luther came out of the transitional milieu from agronomy to early capitalistic entrepreneurship. The climate of the parental home in which Martin grew up must be attributed primarily to the fact that the farm had been replaced by the city in the life of the family and, furthermore, that the necessary choice to abandon agriculture in favor of mining constituted a new point of departure for work life, and social advancement.

From Luther's occasional remarks, we know that sobriety and thrift prevailed in the climate of his parental home. It was a home with many children, where every penny was counted, and where corporal punishment was employed to discourage disobedience. Once when Martin took a nut without permission, his mother struck him so hard that his nose bled. His father once whipped him so severely that Martin harbored a grudge against his father and avoided him for days. Only gradually did the father regain the son's affection. Parental loss of temper and injustice made an indelible impression even on those children who were not exceptionally sensitive.

Martin's parents were persevering, industrious, and hard-working. In later years Luther recalled that in the early days in Mansfeld his mother had carried wood on her back from the forest and that she had loved to sing such popular ditties as "If folks are not kind to thee and me, the fault perhaps with us may be." Martin had three brothers and four sisters, and was particularly close to his brother Jacob.

At four and one-half years of age Martin had to be enrolled in school. Day in and day out, without vacation, school kept him occupied. Even on Sundays, school obligations had to be met because school children were required to sing at worship services. An older neighborhood youth, Nicholas Oemer, later to become Martin's brother-in-law, used to carry the child piggyback to school. Whoever could afford to pay the tuition deemed it necessary to send his children to school as soon as possible not only so that the children might begin to learn early but also because the discipline and supervision they received at school kept them out of the way at home when they were still too young to work. In most families one pregnancy followed another, so that the mothers, who were already fully occupied with domestic duties, had their hands full.

Martin attended the Mansfeld Latin School for nine years, learning first reading, then writing. Reading taught him an elementary Latin vocabulary which he was immediately required to use to the fullest extent possible. If a pupil employed German for words that he already should have learned in Latin, he was punished. One day Luther was given fifteen strokes with a cane or switch because he was unable to decline a Latin noun that the vindictive teacher had not yet taught him. Whipping was part of the pedagogical system, and this system created an instrument for informing: the so-called wolf (in Latin, lupus), the pupil informer with his wolf's notepad on which were inscribed the names of pupils to be reported to the teacher, saw himself as honorably serving the system. The teacher secretly assigned the wolf to observe the other pupils and to note how often the pupils spoke German instead of Latin. The guilty were then punished with cane or switch. Whether or not Martin rendered such lupus service is unknown. Such a possibility, however, is not to be excluded, for his later intellectual achievement indicates that he must have been a good pupil. We know, furthermore, that he benefited for nine years from the school system of his day. It is quite possible that during that period some teacher recruited Martin for lupus service. There was a twofold rationale behind the cruel pedagogy of the sixteenth century: to hammer Latin into the heads of the young pupils, whatever the cost, and to have the pupils become accustomed to informing and to being betrayed. Thus it was a primitive but effective method of training pupils to be submissive and at the same time goal-oriented: a pedagogy based on corporal punishment, apprehending offenders, forcing submission, and encouraging informing.

The curriculum was based primarily on rote learning and was designed to train the memory. The Latin grammar used in the classes was a text from the fourth century, the so-called *Donatus*. For rules of grammar there were memory verses, prayers, poems, fables, and quotations from the works of the great Latin writers. The lessons included nothing about German history or literature; the study of history was confined to Biblical and Roman history. Language, literature, and history—from which the pupils could select examples, models, and ideals whereby they could sharpen their thinking and feeling, create for themselves a subjective world of values,

and thus develop their own personalities—were borrowed from the ancient Roman authors and their successors as well as from the holy places
made familiar in Christendom through repetitive prayers. The national intellectual alienation found its strongest expression in the self-description
of that entity in which the several feudal German states were then united,
the "Holy Roman Empire." When, by the imperial diet's decision, "of the
German Nation" was added to this title in 1485, nothing German was added
to the curriculum or the grammar schools. On the contrary, in the schools
Latin was rewarded with praise, German with the switch.

Learning Latin had certain advantages because it was the scholarly, commercial, diplomatic, and ecclesiastical language of western Europe, that
part of Christendom which since 395 A.D. had segregated itself from Con-
stantinople, thus creating a schism within Christendom between the Latin
West and the Greek East. Whoever was proficient in Latin could participate in the international intellectual life which was spread like a thin var-
nish over the borders, peoples, and tribes of Europe. Whoever was proficient in Latin was distinguished from the masses, and could expect greater
prospects because Latin opened doors for employment and advancement in
the service of the powerful: princes, city councils, the Church, or the universities. The knowledge of Latin was a mark of prestige for one who belonged to the upper ranks of society or who was climbing the social ladder;
it placed one among the elite. Luther learned Latin well and was finally a
master of the language after many years of patient study and tenacious industry. The foundation of Luther's masterful achievements in Latin was
provided by the Mansfeld School with its punishment pedagogy and lupus
informers.

The school also promoted in Martin that for which he seems to have had
a natural inclination, perhaps inherited from his mother: his love of music
and song. In later years Luther reported that singing had been his favorite
subject at school. In the light of what we know about the curriculum of the
schools of that time—including schools of other cities where the curriculum
was similar to that at Mansfeld—it appears understandable that singing, especially outside the school in the church or at public places, was a welcomed variation to declension, conjugation, and memorization in the classroom. Along with singing and musical composition the pupils were
introduced to elementary arithmetic. Luther never had a formal course in
arithmetic, and he never mastered the science of mathematics, at least not
as the discipline might have applied to the domestic budget.

Because there were few books, the pupils learned what was written on
the classroom chalkboard. They copied the sentences from the chalkboard
onto their slate tablets and then by constant repetition learned the material
by heart. There were no homework assignments; everything had to be
learned was learned in the classroom. Because paper was still too expen-

sive for unrestricted usage, memory necessarily served as a supplement to notebooks and textbooks. The sparsity of materials vindicated the prevailing and accepted learning technique of hammering facts into one's head. The pupils did not meet in separate and distinct classes, but all together where the lessons were adapted to different age ranges.

Until he was fourteen years old, Martin spent the most beautiful hours of each day in the schoolroom. Then he met the same fate that his father had confronted in Möhra: as the eldest of many children he must be the first to go out into the world. By today's standards he did not go far, but by sixteenth century calculations, Magdeburg, the metropolis on the Elbe, was distant. The decision to send him to Magdeburg rather than to a city nearer Mansfeld—Halle or Leipzig, for example—was probably due to the fact that the Mansfeld foundry owner, Peter Reinicke, had sent his own son to Magdeburg. In addition, there was the possibility that Martin would find lodging with Paul Mosshauer, a highly respected Mansfelder, who was an official in the archiepiscopal see at Magdeburg.

But Martin's father had not sent him to Magdeburg to learn a trade or business. Hans Luder had more ambitious plans for his son; therefore, the lad was to continue his schooling. In Magdeburg Martin entered the school of the Brethren of the Common Life. This brotherhood was a religious fellowship which had originated in the Low Countries. The name indicates the nature of the alliance: an association of lay and clerical persons voluntarily living in a monastic-like community under the authority of a director but without having taken monastic vows. This community, with its emphasis on the education of youth, accomplished a great deal. In the houses of the Brethren there were always rooms set aside for scholars. The pedagogic techniques for instilling learning were to encourage and to set a good example rather than to wield a switch. For Martin, learning instilled by switch and cane had ended.

From his one-year stay in Magdeburg Martin retained two poignant memories: one of a singular penitent, the other of his own illness. Years later, in 1533, Luther reminisced about Wilhelm von Anhalt, the Franciscan monk from a noble house who had captured Martin's attention in Magdeburg. With his beggar's sack slung over his shoulder, his body punished by fasts and vigils, the young nobleman was regarded as a saint. The illness so clearly remembered was only a passing fever. For several days Martin had been obliged to remain in bed. When he had found himself alone, he had drunk by hasty draughts from a bucket of water, despite the physician's strict command that Luther was not to slake his thirst. He had then fallen into a deep sleep from which he had after several hours awakened, refreshed and well.

Panem propter Deum (bread for God's sake): by going with small groups from house to house and intoning this plea *(Kurrende)*. Martin earned his daily bread in Magdeburg. Such begging was common practice and had no negative or shameful connotations associated with it. Almsgiving, a Christian duty and an integral part of sixteenth-century society, was considered a good work. Charity honored the benefactor without disgracing the beneficiary. The *Kurrende* pupils were also called *Partekenhengst*, for they supplemented their main meal, which they ate at their lodging, with bread earned by singing. The bread morsels (called *parteken* from the Latin *pars*: part), which everyone who had any regard for his own social station kept in store, were dispensed to pupils and others in need of charity.

For Luther the next station on life's journey was Eisenach, where he remained a *Partekenhengst.* After one year in Magdeburg, he left for reasons unkown at Eastertime in 1498. Perhaps his parents thougt support for their eldest son would be more readily available in Eisenach, where the Luders had relatives.

Luther attended the St. George Latin School in Eisenach. He was already an advanced pupil: he spoke the language fluently, wrote essays, practiced versification, and advanced from his knowledge of Latin writers to proficiency in Latin rhetoric. He was thus progressing toward subject matter which was taught in the Arts curriculum, the introductory course of study at the universities. Luther took the main, midday meal with the Schalbes, a wealthy merchant family, and tutored their younger son. Martin probably lived in Kunz Cotta's house, but we cannot be certain that the house now designated as the "Luther House" is the house in which the Cottas resided.

In Eisenach Luther came into contact with respected middle-class families, not those who had risen out of the new forms of entrepreneurship but rather the representatives of the traditional urban middle class. Since the eleventh and twelfth centuries this group had played an increasingly important role in Germany. Their importance was linked to the expanding textile markets and the growing commercial enterprises of the late Middle Ages.

Members of the Schalbe family enjoyed a good reputation and had many contacts. They were well educated and pious. Prayer, family devotions, and church attendance were taken for granted by this family. The Schalbe family was especially attached to the Franciscans. Years later, at his table talks, Luther was to say that his Eisenach hosts were "captives" and "servants" of the Franciscans.

Luther's memories of Eisenach were pleasant: "my beloved city," he called it. Furthermore, he praised his Eisenach teachers, Tribonius and Wiegand Güldennapf from Fritzlar. He expressed gratitude for Vicar Braun at St. Mary's Church and for the Eisenach Franciscans. Martin was in Eisenach from age fifteen to eighteen. What next? His father decided that Martin should study law at the university in Erfurt.

The decision was not a bad one, and it demonstrated the determination, ambition and self-confidence of Luther's father and of the entire class to which he now, after almost two decades of successful mining, belonged. To study jurisprudence and become a master if not a doctor in both legal codes—Roman law which applied to imperial and civic life and canon law which applied to the Church—was to aspire to positions of decisive leadership in society, to create for oneself the possibility of admittance to higher public office, to influence policy, possess power, and be in a position to exercise it. The study of law provided the opportunity to gain recognition for oneself and for one's class, and it afforded the opportunity to advance one's offspring as well as to boost friends up the social ladder.

Hans Luder was able to pay the entire matriculation fee for his son at Erfurt University. Payment of tuition was not an unconditional prerequisite for admission because medieval universities did not make admission contingent on the parents' ability to pay. The matriculation fees could be reduced or occasionally, in the case of poverty *(propter pauperitatem)*, canceled. Naturally the upper classes enjoyed greater access to university education. But the Church was careful to ensure that gifted poor students also gained the opportunity to study and seek advancement. A solid foundation in the Latin language was the necessary prerequisite for study at the university since Latin was the vehicle of communication in lectures, exercises, and disputations. Thus knowledge of Latin was the capital of the poor which was recognized by the universities in lieu of money. A second prerequisite for admission to medieval universities was legitimate birth. Each newly matriculated student was obliged to swear an oath of loyalty to the university along with an oath of affirmation that he was of legitimate birth. To be born out of wedlock was to be illegitimate. However, this disadvantage could be removed by papal or episcopal dispensation if one's family had good connections. Illegitimacy was not the problem for the lower classes that it was for the feudal nobility whose lifestyle tended to promote it. The Luders needed no dispensation. Furthermore, Martin's knowledge of Latin must have been considered adequate for the university level; otherwise, he would have been assigned, as was the custom, to remedial study under a senior student.

Martin was equipped to begin his studies immediately. Of course, he did not immediately begin the study of law, as it might happen in modern European universities. Martin began his studies in the school of arts. The school of arts did not prescribe a course of study in the fine or performing arts, as the name might suggest to the modern reader; rather, it provided the initial university curriculum that each student was obliged to complete for the master's degree that would allow him to advance to the higher-level curricula of his major study. The arts curriculum took its name from the seven liberal arts included in this course of study: the trivium (grammar, logic, and rhetoric), and the quadrivium (geometry, arithmetic, music, and astronomy). The professional curricula, one of which the student would select to prepare himself for his vocation, comprised three fields of specialization: theology, law, and medicine.

In a certain humorous sense those educated in the school of arts were by modern definition indeed artists, artfully manipulating language and juggling concepts. They concerned themselves not with concrete objects in the physical world and not with experiments to demonstrate the relationship and properties of such objects but rather with definitions, names, and words employed to describe physical objects and the material world and with the manner in which such a world was to be conceptualized.

However, the Latin word *artes* which described this curriculum has another connotation which reflects something of the social essence of the medieval university; in the sources of that day *artes* often referred to handwork. The organization of the university was indeed a faithful reflection of the artisan guilds: the guild principle was applied to intellectual rather than to manual activity. As in the guilds advancement was from apprentice to journeyman to master, so in the university the progression was from bachelor to master. Just as the guilds had certain privileges which permitted the guild alone to craft specific products, engage in certain trades, and exercise, autonomous authority in all matters pertaining to the guild (as, for example, the admittance of apprentices, supervision of the tests for journeymen and masters, and the perpetuation of ceremonies, rites, and customs associated with the guild), so the universities and their respective schools also possessed their own rules and regulations which were anchored in their charters.

What distinguished the universities from the guilds, apart from specific intellectual activities, was the greater degree of independence that the universities enjoyed and expressed in the words "academic freedom." Academic freedom was a legal privilege. It provided that the members of the university community—the professors and other faculty together with their families, as well as the students— were not subject to the jurisdiction of the local civil authorities but possessed their own jurisdiction implemented by a legal proctor *(Pedell)* and prison *(Karcer)*, both under the immediate supervision of the university rector.

University traditions imitated those of the guilds. In his very first days at the university, the similarities between guild and university would have been clear to the young Luther. Just as the guild apprentice at initiation endured paddling and practical jokes so the student was subjected to certain initiation rites upon entrance to the academic world. A cap adorned with donkey ears or some other symbol from the animal world was placed on his head. With great pomp and ceremony these symbols of irrational and uncouth behavior were then removed from the student's head to demonstrate that the student now put such conduct behind him and embraced understanding and wisdom. As a sign that he had renounced irrational and crude behavior and had been endowed with new understanding and wisdom, the obligatory pail of water was emptied over the student's head. This initiation frolic was called deposition.

With such initiation and deposition, "Martinus Ludher ex Mansfeld" began his studies, which in the first weeks and months did not differ significantly from those already pursued at Latin school. Texts already familiar to him were quickly reviewed in order to ensure rapid advance and a more or less common starting point for all new students, especially with respect to their Latin language skills. *Repetitio mater studiorum est* (repetition is the mother of learning) was the motto not only for sharpening language skills; in a much larger sense was repetition the mother of learning. By continuous repetition the medieval era took great pains to assimilate the intellectual heritage which antiquity bequeathed to the victorious Church and which the Church in its turn channeled and transformed for its purposes. Such an ancient heritage was indeed vast in contrast to that which the Middle Ages themselves brought forth. However, the overall accomplishments of the Middle Ages are not to be regarded as being of little consequence. The medieval world built a new world on the ruins of the ancient slave societies, a new world which was the source of that powerful surge in science, technology, education, culture, and economy which characterize the modern age. Although these characteristics were present in European society before the sixteenth century, in retrospect it is during the sixteenth century that they became most recognizable.

The decline of the Roman Empire—its destruction by invading Germanic tribes during the great migrations of the fifth century (a destruction which was accelerated by slave revolts), the gradual political decentralization, and the transformation of society in a variety of ways—opened the way for historical progress and the formation of a feudal society. The Germans who made such a transformation of society possible (in the Balkans the Slavs played a similar role for Byzantium) were barbarian in every sense of the word and were culturally very inferior to the Romans. The Germanic victory brought Roman urban culture to a standstill. The Christian Church, especially its monasteries, preserved much from destruction during the period of collapse and migration. The most valuable cultural element preserved was the Latin language, far superior to the barbarian tongues in that it had served a world empire for a millenium, had absorbed a significant part of the cultural heritage of the ancient Orient and particularly of Greece, and had assimilated, integrated, and digested that heritage. The Latin language provided a voluminous wealth far exceeding that of the barbaric tongues not only quantitatively but also qualitatively. Above all it possessed many terms articulating abstract concepts without an awkward counting or parallel listing. The Latin language thus had attained an ability to describe the world in conceptual terms, a level of maturity the barbarian tongues had not yet acquired. Since Socrates, achieving a conceptual understanding of the world had been considered the fundamental task of knowledge.

The Church was enabled to preserve the cultural heritage of antiquity because it was not identified with the declining state authority, its organization was pan-European, and barbarian leaders and administrators depended on the Church. Its role as preserver and administrator guaranteed Church leadership for 1,000 years. Thus it happened that, among other responsibilities, the Church monopolized education and school administration until the rise of the cities. Even as the cities with their own schools gradually eroded the ecclesiastical monopoly, for many generations the Church continued to set the educational tone for subject matter, pedagogical techniques, and to a large degree educational goals. The Church was not merely integrated into the feudal system; it also contributed to the intellectual continuum, providing influences from Near Eastern and Mediterranean history. To some degree it hallowed and sanctioned the existing system.

This educational function of the Church, no less than those influences coming from the city and the bourgeoisie, also determined the university *habitus* as expressed in the action or spirit of the universities. Ecclesiastical influence found expression in dress, language, style, and the position of theology as the queen of the curricula. It was not without justification that the university population was described as "half priests." Monastic influence and discipline were echoed in the life of the universities. Luther experienced such monastic discipline in the student commune. Each pupil was required to live in a commune where strict surveillance was practiced to enforce the regulations: decreed hours for rising and for morning devotions, lecture attendance, supervised private study, recreation, curfew, and sleep. Only in exceptional cases was permission granted to move outside the student commune. The commune population constituted a fraternity, but no glorious fraternal fun was associated with these communes. The German fraternities, known for their carousing and drinking, first came into existence in the nineteenth century. Martin lived in the St. George Commune, also known as the "beer pocket." The name suggests a happy, libational fellowship, but this cannot be verified. To be sure, it was in Erfurt that Luther learned to play the lute, and he was considered "a right sociable fellow," but in general the St. George Commune was probably no more liberal or rigid than were the other student communes. Whatever the case, repetition and memorization of texts were pursued as zealously there and elsewhere. After just eighteen months, the shortest permissible time, Luther took his bachelor's examination.

Having earned the bachelor's degree, he was an associate on the arts faculty. Being an associate meant that he had mounted the first rung on the academic ladder. He was now permitted—yes, obliged—to lecture to the younger students, to conduct exercises for them in grammar and logic, and to consider himself something of a teacher. Before he received his bachelor's diploma, he was a student and note taker, and he remained so as far as the masters on the faculty were concerned. But in his capacity as teaching fellow he dictated to the younger students, who repeated his words, and he listened to and corrected their recitations.

At the same time, Luther continued his studies. The trivium was considered concluded on the successful completion of the bachelor's examination, but the quadrivium remained to be mastered. In the quadrivium Aristotle, that "old heathen" as Luther later called him, was the leading authority. Luther studied old and new logic, physics, ideas concerning the soul, and spherical astronomy in books by Aristotle, including the mysteriously titled *Metaphysics.* This book was so named simply because some ancient editor, in arranging Aristotle's writings, happened to place it after the works on physics. The Greek word for "after" being *meta,* the work was entitled *Metaphysics.* Aristotle's works became Luther's primary consideration. In preparation for his examinations Luther was required to read, annotate, learn, and master Aristotle's teaching on deduction, Luther was obliged to familiarize himself with Peter Hispanus' tractates on logic, which owed their ideas primarily to Aristotle. By such concentration on a prescribed authority the future masters of arts—that is, the masters of liberal arts—acquired a broad and thorough foundation in the various categories of study and in philosophical principles.

Completing his master's examination in February 1505, Luther again finished his course of study in the shortest possible period. Of the seventeen candidates taking the examination, Luther ranked second. He was now prepared to begin his professional studies in the school of law. He had hardly begun his new curriculum when an event ocurred which abruptly interrupted the academic program prescribed by his father, or which Luther at least decided to employ to liberate himself from paternal tutelage and pursue his own course. On his way from Mansfeld back to Erfurt he was overtaken near the village of Stotternheim by a thunderstorm. A lightning bolt struck so nearby that he was thrown to the earth. Luther cried out: "St. Anne, help me! I will become a monk."

According to canon law a vow taken under such circumstances was not binding. It was indeed questionable whether such a terrified cry of anguish could be certified as a vow. Thus neither by conscience nor by law was Luther obliged to enter a monastery. The fact that he actually did justifies the assumption that the question concerning the ultimate course of his life had preoccupied his mind, that what he had learned up to that point and the goals set for him by his father did not satisfy him, that he was wrestling with himself and with the world. When the conditions of the society of Luther's day are considered, the thought arises that his decision could have been influenced by his discontent with his world, that he had experienced frustrations inciting the desire to turn his back on that world and especially to flee from the study of law. To be sure, none of these assumptions can be substantiated conclusively. We could also assume that his decision to enter the monastery fell from heaven like that lightning bolt in Stotternheim. However, because people for centuries have entered monasteries with and without lightning bolts, we should be cautious in all speculations concerning Luther's motives to become a monk.

Whatever his motive, on Juli 17, 1505, Luther knocked on the door of the Erfurt Augustinian monastery and was admitted. At first he was received as a guest in order that he might be observed as to his sincerity. Next he was assigned to a monk responsible for guiding him through his novitiate. Then Brother Martin was robed in the garb worn by the Augustinian monks inside the monastery: a white tunic with hood and cape and a broad leather belt. For trips outside the monastery the Augustinians wore a black hooded cloak or cowl, a white scapular (which might also be worn inside at night), white stockings, and shoes.

The monastic orders are organizations within the Church, and are called orders because their members have obligated themselves for life to observe certain rules and orders, in Latin *ordines*. The historical roots of the religious orders lie in the rather loose and unstructured alliances of hermits in Egypt, North Africa, Palestine, Syria, and Asia Minor in the third century. The decision to form communities within a single house led to the foundation of the Christian monastery and to the necessity for communal rules. The most important of these rules, with certain variations still enforced today, originated with Basil (fourth century), Augustine (beginning of the fifth century), and Benedict of Nursia (sixth century). In addition to prescribing the vows of poverty, chastity, and obedience, the monastic rules governed dress, daily duties, the manner of procuring food, and especially prayer and meditation. While the rules of Basil found special authority within the Eastern Orthodox churches, Latin Christendom took up the rules prescribed by Augustine and Benedict. Many monastic orders, especially the Cistercian and the Praemonstratensian, played an important role in the Middle Ages in cultivating fallow land, reclaiming land, and lending stability to the feudal order.

The strict monastic spirit fought for centuries against mundane influence in the Church and against the complete integration of the Church into medieval society. The monastic orders sought independence from the bishops within whose dioceses their houses were located, and to be subject to the pope alone. Monasticism, with its ordered life, was one of the forces enabling the papacy in the eleventh century to engage in a power struggle with the emperor, the high point of which saw the German Emperor, Henry IV, in the famous "pilgrimage to Canossa" in 1077, humbled before Pope Gregory VII, a monk educated at the monastery of Cluny. With the establishment of new monastic orders during the thirteenth and fourteenth centuries, the papacy was successful in obstructing, isolating, and suppressing anticlerical and heretical movements and in channeling the energies of the religiously motivated—energies which easily could have found expression in anarchy and rebellion—into papal avenues. The most important of the newly established orders were the Franciscans and the Dominicans, whose members in the beginning lived only from begging; thus the Franciscan and Dominican orders were described as begging (or mendicant) orders. In 1244 the Augustinian eremite order was founded in Italy, adopting the Augustinian rule as its governing principle.

His counselor during his novitiate, "a fine old gentleman," as Luther remembered him, was responsible for introducing Luther to the domestic routine of the Augustinian Order and for instructing him in the proper deportment of an Augustinian: no laughing; walking with bowed head and measured step; focusing straight ahead and not glancing about; speaking to other monks only in the presence of the prior or the novice mentor; drinking only while seated and holding the cup in both hands; being silent in the church, the corridors, the refectory (dining hall), and the cells (sleeping cubicles). Silence surrounded the monk. Luther had escaped from the world. Kneeling, of course, was familiar to him from participation in divine worship. Now he learned to throw himself at the feet of his superiors and to lie with arms outstretched in the form of a cross until a gesture by his superiors permitted him to rise. At least once a week he confessed his sins and did penance. But the routine of the monastic schedule, every hour accounted for, hardly left room for sinful thoughts.

The monks were required daily to recite together in the church the Divine Office, a sequence of prayers, psalms, hymns, and readings spaced throughout the day at specified hours, and contained in a book called a breviary. At two A. M. the bell summoned the monks to the first office, Matins, followed by Lauds. At its conclusion the monks retired to a special room where they listened to a reading from the Augustinian Rule or to a chapter from Holy Scripture. (The room thus came to be called the chapter room.) They then returned to their cells until six A.M., when the bell once again summoned them to church. According to Roman reckoning (derived from that of the ancient Jews), six A.M. was the first hour of the day. Therefore the office to be prayed at six o'clock was called Prim. Subsequent offices were offered at three-hour intervals according to the breviary: at nine A.M. (the third hour), Terce, followed by Mass; at noon (the sixth hour), Sext; at three P.M. (the ninth hour), None. After Sext the midday meal—the first meal of the day—was eaten. At five P.M. vespers was said, followed at six by the evening meal. At seven o'clock the final prayer of the day, Compline, was offered, and at eight the monks retired for the evening. The furnishings in the unheated cells consisted of a wooden bed frame, a straw mattress, a blanket, a table with a Bible on it, a chair, and a crucifix on the wall. The cell door had no lock and was fitted with a small peephole which permitted observation of the cell inhabitant from the corridor. No visitation in the cells was permitted.

What occurred in the monastery during the three-hour intervals between the performance of the liturgical offices? The cells were cleaned, begging missions in the city were conducted, natural needs were satisfied, the kitchen was cleaned as well as the cloister, the refectory, the corridors, the chapter room, and the church. There were duties enough to occupy the novices with the menial tasks assigned to deflate their pride and teach humility. In addition, there was the prescribed searching of the conscience in preparation for weekly confession, and there were periods of meditation in order to discipline thought and feeling. The most important activity for the novice was to prepare himself for profession, the monk's vows of poverty, chastity, and obedience that finally and irrevocably made him a monk for life, vows from which only the pope or the vicar general of the monk's order could absolve him if deemed expedient to prevent his wrongdoing from disgracing the order.

The preparation of the novices for profession was the responsibility of the novice master—the older, more experienced, and absolutely trustworthy monk. The novice master advised his charges, helped them, and was responsible for testing their sincerity. He also made certain that they subjected their vocation to repeated examination, that they were persuaded of their calling, and that they were worthy of the order.

Luther's novitiate ended with the desired but not inevitable outcome: in September 1506, Brother Martin took his monastic vows. The period of menial service was now over for Luther because a monk holding the master of arts degree, as Luther did, would not be employed by his order, like the lay brothers, merely to execute the daily chores at the monastery. As a priest, a master of arts could be of much greater service to the order. Thus Luther, at the direction of his order, began to climb a new ladder; not an academic one but rather one which ascended into the ecclesiastical hierarchy.

The rungs of the new ladder were marked by ordinations. On December 19, 1506, Luther was ordained a subdeacon. On February 27, 1507, he was ordained deacon, and on April 4, 1507, the metropolitan bishop of Erfurt, Johann von Laasphe, ordained him a priest in the Erfurt cathedral. Now Luther was privileged and obliged to administer the sacraments—baptism; penance; marriage; extreme unction; and the sacrament of the altar, the Holy Communion or Eucharist—those holy signs under which the Church dispensed the grace of God. In contrast to many others for whom the priesthood not infrequently was simply regarded as a secure living, Luther was very serious about his priestly calling. This sincere desire to penetrate the mystery of the priesthood led him to a profound examination of the essence and idea of the priestly office.

To be a priest was something entirely different from being an academician. Academic success could be achieved by work, study, and discipline. One could make oneself an academician by one's own efforts and by demonstrated capability for which the community awarded recognition and a degree. The master of arts was recognized by all European universities and qualified the holder to teach within their walls.

But the priesthood was different. To become a priest required no academic preparation, no achievement for which one could claim the right to the title of priest. One did not make oneself a priest. One was selected for and ordained to the office. The ordination of the priest was regarded as an act of grace which was bestowed from above and from the community. The ordination of the priest was regarded as a transmission of the special power and spiritual authority which Jesus Christ had bestowed on his apostles, especially on Simon Peter. By the laying on of hands, the apostles had transmitted this power and authority to their successors, and thus the priestly authority was transmitted generation after generation by the laying on of hands until this same power entered the miner's son, the farmer's grandson, the master of arts and monk, Martin Luther. His ordination bestowed upon the young Luther the most important of all priestly gifts, namely, the power and the authority to stand before the altar and transform the eucharistic bread and wine into the body and blood of Christ, thus repeating the sacrifice of Christ on the cross at Golgatha.

This authority or power did not originate with man. It was not an authority or power which was concealed or which slumbered within man and needed only to be awakened. This authority and power came from without and had little to do with the specific person in whom it worked. The priest was only a temporal vessel of this spiritual power. The priest's acts were performed not by virtue of any human authority but by the Holy Spirit. The Spirit was immutable and immortal. The activity of the Spirit expressed through the priesthood lent the priest an inalienable character. A priest could be decapitated, drowned, burned at the stake, stoned, hanged, stabbed, beaten, strangled, imprisoned, hunted, but he could never be stripped of his priesthood. A priest remained a priest even though the human vessel of the priesthood was fragile, imperfect, frayed, or corrupt and marred by violation of moral or ecclesiastical laws. The priesthood created a consciousness of an elite and elect company. To be sure, a priest could be excommunicated: canon law made provision for such a possibility. But even in the state of excommunication a priest did not cease to be a priest and was still authorized to administer the sacraments to those in danger of dying. Even though administered by an excommunicated priest, the sacraments had full validity. The sacraments were effective *ex opere operato*—that is, on the basis of the completed act, independent of the worthiness of the dispenser or of the recipient. The priesthood and what it dispensed—namely, the sacraments—constituted a mystery. The administration of the sacraments remained forbidden to the laity.

The fact that the "unworthy priest" was one of the solemn themes of canon law and an obvious problem reveals a disparity between the idea and the practice of the priesthood. Among the reasons for the inability to harmonize ideal with practice was that in the late Middle Ages the number of priests increased disproportionately, to the detriment of other professions and vocations. Although new clerical and preaching positions were established, there continued to be more ordinations than positions to be filled. The modest education of priests often was in sharp contrast to the ideal qualifications for the office. Thus increasingly the clergy became symptomatically parasitical. Under the prevailing conditions, serious concern with the discrepancy between theory and practice in the priesthood was the stuff from which conflict erupts, as the next few years would demonstrate.

The mystery of the Mass awed the newly ordained Father Luther as, on May 2, 1507, he stepped before the altar of the Augustinian monastic church in Erfurt to read his first Mass, the *Primiz*. This moment, which after ordination itself is the most celebrated in the life of a priest, transpired in the circle of other priests, brother monks, and relatives.

With twenty horses and in esteemed company, the young priest's father, still known as Hans Luder, journeyed to Erfurt to participate in honoring his son. Now Hans had become the father of a priest. Now perhaps after all Hans Luder was somewhat compensated—not well, but in small measure—for his offspring's choice to become a monk rather than a lawyer. When Martin mentioned the subject for his calling to his father at the banquet table, Hans Luder responded with a sharp answer: "Do not the reverend gentlemen know that father and mother are to be honored?" To become a priest was certainly a respectable ambition, and Luther's father had spent a great deal of money for the banquet, thereby demonstrating that success could be achieved outside of the Church. Two years earlier he had explosively expressed the anger incited by his son's decision to enter the monastery. In a letter to his son, Hans Luder had again addressed Martin with the familiar second person pronoun, *Du*. (Formerly he had addressed the master of arts student with the more respectful and formal second person pronoun *Sie*.) At first the father had refused to consent to Luther's entering the monastery. This son for whom he had already selected a bride from an honorable family had robbed him of his highest hopes.

Finally the father had granted his permission for Martin to enter the monastery, although no paternal permission was required. The death of two of his children probably moved Hans to assent to Martin's decision, but the father still harbored resentment. Perhaps the disagreement with his father was still smoldering within the young priest fourteen years later when he abandoned the monastery in 1521, and even eighteen years later in 1525, when, by marrying a former nun, he entered into wedlock, which his father had originally planned for him.

These steps may have been a late attempt at reconciliation with his father and thus a rationalization of a quarrel with the Church. In terms of personal pain, not to mention the social repercussions, the quarrel with the Church far exceeded the father-son conflict. During the years following the *Primiz* nothing is heard suggesting that Luther suffered from his father's rancor or that he was torn between his filial and his priestly duties. That conflict—if there ever had been one, as the interpretation of modern psychoanalysts, reading more into the sources than exists, would have it— had long ago been resolved.

The twenty-three year-old priest was assigned new duties. His order instructed him to study theology. Now he was obliged to return to the academic ladder which he had abandoned when he entered the monastery and which, furthermore, he perhaps had wanted to leave forever. Now he must return to study, first for the baccalaureate in the school of theology and then for his new responsibility as a teacher who in that school was called the licentiate. To be sure, he had never really ceased studying after his entrance into the monastery. The Augustinian rule required the monk to read a chapter in the Bible each day, and each novice received a red leather-bound copy of the Scriptures. Since he had entered the monastery, the Bible had become Luther's spiritual nourishment. But with his new curriculum in theology, time for the Bible was curtailed. The curriculum, dominated by Aristotle, was based not so much on Aristotle's own writings, which Luther already had thoroughly studied in the school of liberal arts, but on that scholasticism which had evolved out of the various levels of interpretation of Aristotelian thought by the scholars of the Middle Ages. To return to Aristotle meant to go well beyond the patristic tradition and the Church Fathers, and to confront once again that pagan philosophy against which early Christianity had necessarily asserted itself. The primitive Church, as it progressed from simple faith to theology, partially borrowed from pagan philosophy and, in a transformed guise, assimilated it. The specific intellectual-historical function of the patristic period was, to some degree, the integration of reason with faith without eliminating faith from theology.

Aristotle represented the apex of Greek philosophy which had developed out of the ancient mythology and had finally liberated itself from divine sagas. Promoted by the free, slave-holding Greek citizens, Greek philosophy was an intellectual movement against the mythological tradition; this philosophy was an attempt at a rational explantation of the world.

The Middle Ages could borrow and revitalize Greek philosophy only after European feudalism had overcome its incipient barbarian stages and had brought forth many cities with distinct political independence. At any rate, the reception and revitalizing of Aristotelian philosophy primarily falls into the period of the eleventh, twelfth, and early thirteenth centuries, a period of urban growth when the large and more important cities wrested autonomy from their feudal lords, kings and bishops.

The dominance of Aristotelian philosophy and the development of urban indenpendence were, even if on different planes, symptoms of the profound transformation of feudal society which, in addition to undergoing other changes, became linked to a significant expansion of the civic administrative apparatus. It is justifiable to presume that in the mentality of both the late medieval feudal states and urban life, favorable condition existed for the increased (and increasing) interest in the original writings of ancient authors, made known to Europe through the Arabic civilization in Spain. Aristotle was among these authors. But there was also an interest in Aristotle nourished by the appeal of novelty and the contrast of his thought vis-à-vis the traditional intellectual categories of medieval Europe. With Aristotle, reason once again confronted revelation, philosophy confronted religion—the juxtaposition that had existed for primitive Christianity in the first century of its existence. The task that the Church fathers had earlier found it necessary to address—namely, the integration of reason and faith—reappeared for the thinkers of the late Middle Ages.

The task of reconciling reason with faith was mastered by the Italian, Thomas Aquinas. In his major work, *Summa Theologiae*, Thomas attempted to validate the assertions of Christians revelation by declaring them in agreement with the concept of "Being" in Aristotle's philosophy. Thomas succeeded in his task by a simple and ingenious device: he defined God as the highest Idea—a definition that was compatible with Aristotle's concept of absolute Being.

This absolute Being, Being in itself, is the last step in the process of abstraction. When the conception of a thing is abstracted from its concrete characteristic and identity, conception of the abstraction is produced. This conception in turn is abstracted, and thought runs through a series of such abstractions which become increasingly diminished in content and diminished in concrete concept. The higher the steps of abstraction are ascended, the more abstract, according to this method, the posited concept becomes. The process of abstracting can be continued until finally nothing can be said of an object except that it exists—that is, that it possesses *Being*. This *Being*, however, is always to a certain degree qualified; it is the "Being of the world" and not some other *Being*. It is still an attribute of something, but it is not that something itself. If the abstraction is carried out to the last station, it passes through this abstraction of the Being of the world to that profound and incommunicable being—namely, the Being of Being. The last station has been reached: a Being which cannot be brought by acrobatic abstraction to any other or higher Being. If we turn the matter upside down, as Aristotle learned to do from his master Plato, we no longer delude ourselves that we, from our environment, abstract absolute Being. Rather we boldly assume that this sublime Being is doubtlessly that Being which exists most absolutely—indeed, that it is that Being which existed before all other Being.

The concept has a dual advantage: among the available intellectual presuppositions it was attractive and productive; it integrated esthetics, faith, and reason into a well balanced intellectual structure. The concept appeared attractive because it was consoling to posit that the Being arrived at after such a strenuous quest really existed and that from the vantage point of that Being a wonderful panorama of all lesser Beings was afforded. The concept proved productive because now the world could be created intellectually from the highest idea of Being. Explaining creation was, moreover, the task of theology, which could now reverse the process of abstraction to derive reality from the idea by the process of emanation. What abstraction draws from the conrete, weakens to generalization, and dilutes to idea, emanation releases from the idea to reconstitute the generalization and particularize in the concrete. Being thus gives birth to the concrete world out of itself, and this creation appears as emanation of absolute Being. This explanation, although sterile and unattractive, is more or less what the Bible much more beautifully and in poetic pictures conveys as revelation concerning the creation of the world by the Spirit of God. Thus scholasticism consummated its work of art, the coordination of reason and revelation, the reconciliation of philosophy with ecclesiastical dogma, the garbing of Aristotle in a monk's cowl and securing him a place next to the Church fathers. Many scholars, the most tenacious being Anselm of Canterbury and Scotus Erigena, had promoted this synthesis of reason and revelation. As parallel examples in the history of philosophy have occasionally demonstrated, various intellectual concepts were amalgamated, and on this foundation was built an inspiring intellectual structure that could be considered the companion piece of the Gothic cathedrals.

No scholastic scholar ever held that reason and revelation are the same. The distinction between reason and revelation was not blurred but sharply delineated; faith took precedence over knowledge and revelation over reason. But the attempt was repeatedly made to reduce the tension between the explanation based on reason and that based on revelation and to harmonize these two explanations of the origin of the world so that the inevitable contradictions, never completely reconciled by scholasticism, might remain at a minimum. Every attempt at coordinating faith and knowledge was made because, after all, the theologians could not entirely forget what they had learned in the liberal arts curriculum, and they did not want to degrade that training too much. After all they were indebted to their liberal arts education for the intellectual advantage held over the nonacademic ecclesiastics who, not infrequently, became their ecclesiastical superiors.

Deviation from this trend to harmonize reason and revelation was bound to occur repeatedly and spontaneously in lectures and expository writing. When a professor spoke to his students from his lectern, from time to time, consciously or unconsciously, he would depart from his notes, interpreting them in words, sentences, and formulations for which his own personal and subjective thought was the basis. Or, more important, the professor might place his wisdom at the service of political goals; his persuasion, of course, was bound to find an echo in his philosophizing or theologizing, especially if his political goals were aimed against the claims of the papacy. Political confrontations regarding such matters were reflected in academic interpretations.

The school of thought that had emanated from such a political and intellectual confrontation and that was binding on Luther at the Erfurt Theological School was Occamism, which had originated two centuries earlier with the English philosopher and theologian, William of Occam (1300–1349). Occamism stood in sharp contrast to Thomism and, like Thomism, was an exceptionally multifaceted and complicated intellectual current. It was not so much the ramifications of the two schools that were relevant to Luther's future problems but rather the divergent fundamental concepts concerning the nature of God. These concepts must now be addressed.

While Thomism had interpreted God primarily with the help of the concept of Being from Aristotelian philosophy, Occamism conceived of God as the highest and absolute Will. The definition of highest Will did not necessarily contradict the view which considered God the highest form of Being; however, the emphasis shifted. This difference of emphasis on either Being or Will became a matter of prestige, because each university declared in its statutes which view was to be taught. For example, Erfurt was committed to teach the *via moderna* (new thinking) of Occam rather than the *via antiqua* (old thinking) of Thomas Aquinas, which was taught at Cologne.

The distinction between the *via moderna* and the *via antiqua* was sharp, and was not based only on differentiation between Will and Being. Each school sought to articulate various points, observations, and nuances; but the deepest difference was revealed in the question concerning general concepts, the so-called universals. This question was: Do general concepts exist essentially and independently before the things and their attributes which they define, or are the general concepts only names for existing things which can be apprehended by the physical senses? Those who posit that the universals exist in reality before the objects and independently of them and that they also exist in and after them (*ante rem, in re,* and *post rem*) are "realists". This was the characteristic *via antiqua,* or Thomistic interpretation. The opponents, rejecting a "real" existence of the universals and insisting that the name of the object, applied by reason to the given object, constitutes that object's "reality," are nominalists. Luther's Erfurt teachers were committed to the *via moderna,* nominalism.

The difference between nominalism and realism touches on a basic question in philosophy: What is the fundamental difference between idealism and materialism? The difference is demonstrated in the medieval scholastic concepts in which realism, contrary to what the name suggests, is akin to idealism, while nominalism suggests a tendency toward materialism. However, realism is not to be categorically identified with idealism, nor nominalism with materialism.

A simple comparison, originating with no less a sage than Albert Einstein, provides a clever illustration, to be understood in a allegorical rather than a literal sense, of course. The concepts did not correspond to the objects, Einstein once reflected, as the bouillon to the bone but rather as the claimcheck to the coat. To pursue this simile, the nominalists should be compared with those who think of concepts as a claimcheck; the realists should be compared with those who, when they contemplate concepts, anticipate a broth: a bouillon which, to be sure, can be prepared only from bone because the bouillon is brought forth from bone and is an emanation, derivitive, and objectification of that from which it has come.

That Luther's thought in Erfurt was forced into nominalistic channels was to prove significant for the future formulation of his independent opinions. We will return to this subject at a later point. Suffice it to say here that nominalism promotes and encourages the work of translation. Nominalism treats words as it treats claimchecks: it is conditioned to seek varied content behind the word, to seek the right claimcheck for the right coat, and to seek beyond alien objects and alien words its own property by its own descriptive word. Furthermore, for Luther another very important outcome emerged from this quest. Nominalism directs attention to the subjective activity of comprehension and of the will by enabling the will to recognize the world and to overcome its trials and temptations. Out of these impulses evolved for Luther, the thinker, the problems whose solutions took on a significance of their own.

In October 1508, the young theologian was suddenly transferred to the University of Wittenberg. Wittenberg was a small town of barely three thousand inhabitants. Until the end of the fifteenth century Wittenberg had neither a trade of any great significance nor a commercial life of unusual note. Only at the beginning of the sixteenth century, in the wake of political events, did a noticeable change take place. In 1485 the brothers Ernst and Albrecht of the House of Wettin which since 1422 had ruled the Saxon electorate, agreed in Leipzig to divide Saxony, their common inheritance. Albrecht received the mark (border province) of Meissen with Dresden, Meissen, Pirna, and Freiberg as the main cities, the city of Leipzig, and the foothills of the Erz mountains as well as Sangerhausen south of the Harz. Ernst received the electorate as well as the Thuringian regions of the Wettins with Weimar as the center, Zwickau, Altenburg, and the city of Wittenberg with its immediate environs and hinterland. A portion of the rights to mining in the Erz region was also included. From this time on there were two Wettin lines: the Ernestine and the Albertine. Electoral Saxony was henceforth exclusively of the Ernestine line.

Meissen, Freiberg, and the university city of Leipzig, the three urban centers where the great ducal residences were found, had fallen into Albertine territory. The Ernestine line had to erect its own residence and university. Wittenberg was selected as the site of both because the Golden Bull, an imperial edict of 1356, had stipulated that the Saxon electoral title was to be associated with Wittenberg. In addition, the city had an advantageous position on the Elbe River. A new city wall, a castle, a new bridge, and a university were built. Thus Wittenberg was considered the capital of the Ernestine line and of electoral Saxony, but in fact it was not the city where the elector chose to reside. The current elector, Duke Frederick the Wise, under whom these construction plans for Wittenberg took shape, usually resided in the region of Lochau (now Annaburg) and in Torgau.

In 1508 when Luther came to Wittenberg, the city could not have made a strongly favorable impression. In that year the city extended no more than one kilometer east and west along the river. In ten minutes one could walk the length and in five minutes the breadth of the city. This long oval was bordered on the north and on the east by swamps; along the southern border flowed the Elbe; to the west lay fields, meadows, and uncultivated land. This university city always retained a pronounced agrarian atmosphere. But the new university, established in 1502, was in 1507 endowed with ecclesiastical property, and the building activity gave the city a somewhat more vibrant life.

At the "Leucorea,"* as the Wittenberg University was called among the humanists, the Augustinian order held the professorship for moral philosophy and for Biblical exegesis. The teacher for moral philosophy, Wolfgang Ostermayer, was ill, and Luther was obliged to substitute for him; thus it came about that Luther began to read lectures on the Nicomedean ethics of Aristotle as well as to supervise exercises and disputations. Since Lu-

---

* Wittenberg is derived from *Weissenberg*, which means "white hill", for which *Leucorea* is the Greek equivalent.

ther's notes and pericopes on these lectures are not extant, we are unable to say whether or not or to what degree Luther demonstrated in these dissertations any talent for original thought. It is certain only that he assumed his task without great enthusiasm: in a letter to a friend in Erfurt, Luther expressed the desire to concentrate on theology and stated that he considered the obligation to read Aristotle as a disruption of his preferred course. Despite this annoyance Luther continued his theological studies and received the *baccalaureus biblicus* on March 9, 1509. With the degree went the privilege to lecture on the Bible and to supervise student exercises in biblical studies.

In the autumn of 1509, Luther returned to Erfurt from Wittenberg. Just at that time civil disturbances racked the city; there was an uprising of the so-called Black Band against the city council and against one of the elected ward committees. During the uproar the university library was damaged. This was reason enough for the academic leaders to look askance at the mob which disrupted their circle and with whom scholars of Latin and theological-philosophical-humanistic education preferred no association.

The mob was considered vulgar, commonplace, and without understanding. Scholars thought of themselves as being refined, elite, and wise. Luther shared the opinion of the circle to which he belonged. He did not expect too much from *Herrn Omnes* (Mr. Everybody) as years later he described, not without reference to the Erfurt uproar, the unruly members of the populace. This attitude toward the common man was not peculiar to Luther; it was rather typical for the humanists to despise the masses and to speak about them in denigrating terms. Exceptions to those among the humanists who demonstrated such contempt were rare, and Luther was not one of the exceptions. "Mob," "mass," "crowd" always applied to others, never to one's own circle.

At the university noses were turned up at the Black Band because it was considered a mob. Apard from merchants and artisans, the Black Band was made up mostly of the population's poorer elements, who were permitted to pay taxes, serve their betters, slave, work, and be oppressed. These poorer elements found no relief, whether the clique of intermarried, rich dealers in the dye-yielding waid plant and their special merchant friends sat alone in the city council or shared power with representatives of other wealthy circles.

The Erfurt unrest, the so-called "mad year," belonged to an entire wave of social conflicts which, at the end of the fifteenth century and the beginning of the sixteenth, shook many German cities. These upheavals were symptoms of the tensions in the Holy Roman Empire. The causes for these tensions lay in the long-smoldering conflicts between the old ruling classes of the commercial bourgeoisie (patricians) and the wealthy guild masters. Also new conflicts which arose from the progressive stratification of the

urban population into rich and poor as well as from difficulties for the traditional urban order caused by several phenomena accompanying early
capitalism. In addition to the internal urban tensions, political friction between the cities and their feudal lords often exacerbated the general unrest. The turmoil in Erfurt in 1509 clearly demonstrated the tendencies toward social tension.

At that time Erfurt was one of the more significant urban centers of central Germany. The population then is estimated to have been between
16,000 and 19,000. With a population of that size, Erfurt ranked with the
other imperial cities.

Erfurt's economic importance was based on waid, a plant from which a
blue dye used by cloth makers was extracted. As the Saiger investors
gained a controlling interest in copper mining, so the waid merchants
gained a key position in the manufacture of cloth. The waid dealers bought
waid from the farmers, extended credit to them, and thus led the waid
farmers into economic dependence. The waid was dried and sold to dyeing
mills where the last process in preparing cloth for the market was completed. The cloth was sold to the dyeing mills by the same merchants who
supplied the waid. These merchants purchased their supply of cloth from
the spinners. By extending credit to the spinners as to the farmers, the
merchants rendered both groups dependent, thereby eroding the social position of those immediately involved in production.

Erfurt possessed an extensive hinterland. The city had acquired more
than eighty villages over which the city council ruled like a feudal lord. But
Erfurt itself, not fully independent, was under the authority of the archbishop of Mainz, whom Erfurt was obliged to recognize as suzerain. In addition, the city and its environs, surrounded by the territory of electoral
Saxony, were in a position highly advantageous to the Saxon dukedom,
which exerted political and economic pressure and engaged in a continuous quest to absorb the city into the dukedom. Thus for a time Erfurt was
forced to acknowledge subservience not only to Mainz but also to the protective lordship of Saxony. The city council was thereby obliged to pursue
a policy seesawing between Mainz and Saxony and at the same time to
erect a second city wall and defense perimeter outside the city walls in order to be prepared for an assault from either quarter.

Because the cost of the defense projects exceeded the financial capability of the city, it was necessary to raise taxes. The increase included an
indirect beer tax than was especially resented by the common people. The
affluent burghers—the "Elect"—who had not yet been admitted to the city
council used the growing unrest to coerce the council to allow a citizens'
committee sponsored by these burghers to participate in council affairs.
On July 16, 1509, the Black Band led an unsuccessful insurrection against
both the city council and the Elect but without success.

However, in August 1509, the members of the Black Band received new encouragement when they were given support from Mainz, seeking for reasons of its own to exploit the unrest in Erfurt. The Erfurt city council and the Elect sought help from electoral Saxony, but the Erfurt patricians suffered a defeat in December, and in January 1510, they were forced to resign in favor of a new city council in which the political authority was exercised by artisans, merchants, and nonpatrician dye merchants. In December 1509, a representative of the archbishop of Mainz had already been installed as lord mayor of Erfurt. Heinrich Keller, the mayor of the deposed city council, was executed.

Erfurt fell under the hegemony of Mainz for some years. But because neither the financial misery nor the social evils were alleviated, the new council in the long run was unable to stabilize its rule. Now the new opposition vented its rage much more vehemently not only against the new council but also against Mainz. The opposition turned once again for help to Electoral Saxony. In 1516, the former city council was reinstated and the conditions which had existed before the Mainz intervention were essentially restored.

From autumn 1509 to autumn 1510, Luther lived in Erfurt and experienced firsthand one of the most tumultuous phases in the city's history. This first experience with the political and social tensions and problems, which at that time troubled many German cities and all too frequently led to bloodshed, impacted on Luther in a negative and repulsive manner, although he was limited to the vantage point of spectator and not participant. The uprisings did not gain Luther's sympathy or approval or in any way enlist his willingness to assist. If there is any conclusion to be drawn from these experiences and Luther's continued subjective intellectual development, it is probably that Luther all the more decisively concentrated on what he considered the heart of the matter: theology.

He completed another degree and became sententiary; i.e., he was now permitted to lecture on and interpret Peter Lombard's *Sentences*, a textbook for dogmatic theology. At this time he also studied Greek and Hebrew and occupied himself with the works of St. Augustine, the patron of his order. In his concentration on St. Augustine, he became familiar with the patristic world of the early Church fathers. Augustine was the most important of the Latin fathers. He had experienced the assault on Rome led by Alaric the Visigoth and the conquest of North Africa by the Vandals. Thus he was an eyewitness to the beginning of the breakup of the Roman Empire. In the generally pessimistic mood of the declining empire he set the theological course for the survival of the Church. His teaching concerning the two cities, the City of God which is eternal and the City of Earth which is temporal, made in indelible impression on Luther's mind.

Luther was occupied with his studies and academic responsibilities until

October 1510. At that time he received an assignment from his order that would take the twenty-seven-year-old monk to Rome. A dispute among the Augustinian monasteries concerning their rule of discipline was the immediate cause for his journey. The dispute centered around the question of whether the severity of the Augustinian rule could be lessened and whether certain monasteries might on their own initiative introduce more relaxed conditions and be granted a greater degree of independence. The adherents of the strict position were called "observants," while those in favor of a more relaxed rule and greater independence for individual monasteries were called "conventicals." The Augustinian monasteries in Erfurt and Nuremberg were sympathetic to the observant view and strove to be excluded from the number of those monasteries under the supervision of the Augustinian vicar-general, Johann von Staupitz, who supported the conventical position. In order to represent their cause in Rome, the Augustinian houses in Erfurt and Nuremberg together sent a two-man delegation to the ecclesiastical capital. The monk in charge of representing the observant cause was a priest from Nuremberg whose name has not been transmitted. Brother Martin was selected as his travel companion. From Nuremberg their journey took the two Augustinians to Ulm, through Switzerland, and over the Septimer Pass to Milan, Bologna, and Florence. The two monks arrived in Rome in late November or early December 1510. In Rome they celebrated masses and visited the seven major churches, the catacombs, and the holy places.

Rome, once the capital of the western empire, now the seat of the popes, was all the more maliciously maligned because it was secretly admired. Luther found himself in the center of Christian culture, spirituality, and ecclesiastical authority. Here were knotted the threads and here was anchored the net with which the Church encompassed the countries to the south, to the west, and in central and northern Europe—the net which she cast over the commercial highways, the coastlines, the seas and oceans, always in quest of new peoples and new tribes. Luther was in a world different from the little mud nest on the Elbe which he only a short time earlier had come to know. Rome was also different from the Erfurt on the "mad year".

Furthermore, Luther found himself surrounded by the pollution of Rome. Garbage and waste lay several feet thick on the streets and squares where once Julius Caesar and Augustus had walked, where Peter and Paul had preached. Refuse in the arena where the gladiators had fought covered the spectators' seats, where in imperial times the patricians and plebeians, caught up in the circus atmosphere, had been entertained by the death of Christian martyrs. But from the debris that buried Rome were recovered ancient statues and sculptures whose beauty and proportion medieval Europe had not been able to reproduce.

The Annaberg Bergaltar at St. Annen Church, centre part,
completed by Hans Hesse in 1521

A peasant paying his tithe
to a monastic brother
woodcut by Hans Schäufelein
Augsburg 1517

Money-changer
painting by Marinus Claesz von Romerswaal
1541

Ancestral house of the Luther family in Möhra
Colour lithograph, 19th century

View of Eisleben
City hall and Andreas church (centre)

Luther's birth place in Eisleben, garden view

The Luther family's dwelling in Mansfeld

Luther's parents Hans (✝ 1530) and
Margarete Luther (✝ 1531)
painting by Lucas Cranach, 1527

House of the Cotta family in Eisenach

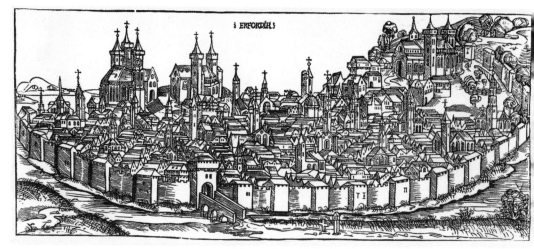

Erfurt
Woodcut from Hartmann Schedel's "World Chronicle"
Nuremberg 1493

Augustinian monastery in Erfurt. A model of the monastery site in 1890 as it appeared in 1669

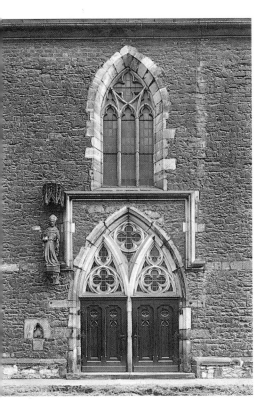

Main door of the Augustinian church
and refugium of the Augustinian monastery in
Erfurt

OBSCVRI VIRI

Epiftole Obfcurorū virorū ad Magiftrū Ortuinū
Gratiū Danentrienfem Colonie latinas litteras pro
fitentē nō illg ǧdē veteres et prius vifæ:fed et nouę er illis pilotibȝ
Elegantia argutijs lepore ac venuftate longe fuperiores.
Ad Lectorem.
Rifum Deraclitæ eft: rafti ridere parati
Arida murarūt pectora Stoicidæ
Da mihi triftem animū:ferales obȳce luctus
Difpeream nifi mor omnia Rifus erunt.
Exerce pulmonem.

Title page of "Letters of Obscure Men" part 2,

517

Causati em sumus/ Iudæos & græcos oēs sub peto esse.

Sicut scriptu est: Quia nō est iustus quisq: nō ē intelli-

gēs: nō ē requirēs deū. Oēs declinauerūt/ simul inutiles

facti sūnt: nō est qui faciat bonūm: nō est usq; ad unum.

Sepulchrū patēs est guttūr eo2: linguis suis dolose age-

bāt: venenū aspidū sub labiis eo2. Quo2 os maledictōe

& amaritūdine plenū est: veloces pedes eo2 ad effun-

dendū sanguinem. Cotritio & infœlicitas in viis eo2: &

viā pacis nō cognouerūt: non est timor dei ante oculos

eoru. Scimus aūt qm quæcūq: lex loquit: iis qui in lege

sunt loquit: Vt oē os obstruat: & subditus fiat ois mūd9

deo. quia ex opib9 legis nō iustificabit ois caro cora illo.

Per legem ēm cognitio peccati. Nūc aūt sine lege iusticia

dei manifesta ēst/ testificāta a lege & prophetis. Iusticia

Luther's interpretation of the Epistle to the Romans (3,9–21)
with his marginal and interlinear glosses

Now the ancient masters were once again followed. In Italy they were imitated with national ardor, for the ancient world was Rome's glory, her sublime and proud past, reflecting in her former ideals the contrasting impotence of medieval Italy, divided into many city states and feudal dukedoms as a plaything of the great European powers. In the south of Italy, Spain governed; in the north, France, the Hapsburgs, and Spain wrestled for control. And if the foreign powers on occasions should grant respite from intervention, the native Italian princes attacked one another.

The popes participated zealously in the internecine Italian wars. The pope was after all not only the visible head of the Church and the bishop of Rome; in Italy he was also ruler and potentate as were the many other Italian princes. The popes equipped armies, led them on compaigns, plotted intrigues, and pursued political activity of all description in order to maintain, consolidate, and expand the papal state. Pope Julius II, during whose pontificate (1503–1513) Luther visited Rome, was more field commander and diplomat than pastor. He was well acquainted with the ways of the world, as had been his two predecessors, Alexander VI (1492–1503), formerly known as Rodrigo Borgia, and Innocent VIII (1484–1492). Innocent VIII was the first pope to celebrate the weddings of his children in the Vatican.

The Renaissance papacy provoked the resentment of many contemporaries because the popes allowed themselves luxuries which others indeed enjoyed as a matter of course but which were difficult to reconcile with the papal office. The conduct of the Renaissance popes conflicted with the role expected of them, which in public opinion was closely associated with the papal office.

Measured by the traditional medieval world view, something inconceivable was occurring at that time in Rome. For one thing the deterioration of the Church and the papacy, given the condition of its head and members, made it obvious that the Church could no longer live up to its image or fulfill the function that it had for so long performed in the European feudal system. The claims by the papal Church of universal spiritual and institutional leadership stood in contradiction to the realities; they were increasingly regarded as monopolistic, patronizing, and purely political in their arrogance.

Early capitalism and feudal power, spiritual as well as secular, for a time joined forces to their mutual advantage. As the Augsburg Fugger family became the symbol of early capitalism in Germany, so the Florentine Medici family, along with other great families, became the symbol in Italy. Both the Fuggers and the Medicis had risen from modest beginnings; the Fuggers began as weavers, the Medicis as pharmacists. On the basis of great wealth both families rose to positions of prominence. Nine years after Luther's visit to Rome Fugger the Wealthy financed the victorious candidate in the imperial election in Germany, whereas in 1513 a Medici, Leo X, had already been elected pope. But that papal election was the non plus ultra of the union of money and ecclesiastical authority. Furthermore, the glory of the Renaissance papacy exposed the crisis in the Church.

Rome, as well as other Italian cities, was culturally very advanced. When we speak of sixteenth-century Rome, we must keep this fact in mind. In the Holy City most current intellectual streams of Renaissance humanism had struck root early and had found among the popes and in their immediate entourage eager patrons and learned disciples.

The appeal of humanism was not due simply to the intellectual curiosity arising from the casual interest of an individual. It reflected the effect of an economic, social, and political development which permitted Italy, already a full century in advance of the rest of Europe, to become the first flourishing center of early capitalism. By the sixteenth century the capitalistic vitality of Italy had declined markedly. In Italy, whose early capitalistic experience influenced the entire terminology of the bourgeois bank and credit system, economic and social conditions, for various reasons, characterized the genesis of capitalism. But in the cultural field this early capitalism brought forth a harvest which up to that time could be matched in no other land. The Renaissance was nourished on Italian soil, where the rebirth of antiquity—the model for style in art, literature, and enjoyment of life—motivated artists, writers, and poets to the highest achievements which, because they truly presented a higher esthetic development, were then imitated and copied in other countries.

However, the Renaissance opened a gulf between itself and the ecclesiastical preaching concerning humility, modesty, penance, and the consolation of eternity in heaven as reward for toil and work. With the advent of Renaissance humanism—in essence a bourgeois intellectual current to which several popes owed their learning—Rome itself countenanced the research of primary sources and evidence and the skepticism which arose wherever scholarship remained channeled solely in scholasticism. This humanism was in no sense unchristian or even anti-ecclesiastical, but it was unorthodox in terms of Church dogma. It tended, with its esteem of ancient literature, to reduce the sensibility for the qualitative peculiarities of a Christian life of faith and to interpret Christianity primarily as a set of moral and ethical rules for life. The function of this moral teaching was, on the one hand, to bring about in the social consciousness an assent for ecclesiastical reform within the Church and, on the other hand, to prompt a search for a new view of the world and of humanity. Thus the papacy was quite paradoxically characterized by those qualities attributed to the Renaissance.

In the year in which Luther and his brother Augustinian visited Rome, St. Peter's, the new pastoral church of the pope, was being built. The construction had not proceeded very far. It had begun in 1506, during the pontificate of Julius II, following the plans submitted by Bramante. Raphael was at his painting in the Vatican. Michelangelo stood on a scaffold to paint the creation of man on the ceiling of the Sistine Chapel. Marvelous works of world culture were being created. Luther was in Rome, but he was unaware of these marvels.

The mission which had brought the two Augustinians to Rome was a complete failure. Rome was too preoccupied to concern itself with a quarrel between German monks. Luther and his brother monk were given no access to officials of great authority. The emissaries were kept waiting: for six weeks they waited for a decision and then, with no firm answer, they departed for Germany.

As far as Bologna, Luther and his Nuremberg brother retraced the route that had brought them to Rome. From Bologna, they took another route, which passed through Verona, Trient, Bozen, Innsbruck, Augsburg, and Nuremberg. At the beginning of April 1511, Luther reentered Erfurt. The visit to Rome had not weakened Luther's trust in and loyalty to the Church; but a certain suspicion of all things Italian, in which he sensed something sly or subversive, remained with him.

Luther drew certain conclusions from the failure of his diplomatic mission to Rome. While other brothers continued to murmur against the proposed changes within the Augustinian order, Luther and his friend, Johannes Lang, decided to support Vicar-General Johann von Staupitz. This decision probably offended their Erfurt Augustinian brothers and led to the transfer of Luther and Lang to Wittenberg in the autumn of 1511.

Johann von Staupitz rewarded Luther's support with a generous promotion. In May 1512, at an Augustinian chapter convention in Cologne which tabled the disputed conventical question, von Staupitz instigated the election of Luther to the position of subprior—that is, associate administrator—of the Wittenberg monastery. Von Staupitz had still greater plans for Luther. The vicar-general was the professor of Bible at Wittenberg, a position which gradually became too taxing for him because it demanded time that he needed to invest in his administrative responsibilities for the order. He thus sought a successor for his professorship in Bible. The gifted brother Martin Luther, who furthermore had shown himself prudent in matters of monastic discipline and had entrusted himself to the vicar-general's supervision, appeared to von Staupitz to be the right selection for the chair of biblical lectures. Years later Luther described the conversation with von Staupitz which initiated Luther's elevation to the highest rung on the academic ladder.

Staupitz, my prior, sat thoughtfully under the pear tree, which still stands in the middle of my courtyard. Finally he said to me, "Master, you should study for the doctorate and that would bring you a worthwhile challenge." When he once again under the pear tree brought up the same subject I sought to beg off by giving many reasons why I could not study for the doctorate: my chief excuse was that I did not have the stamina for such a rigorous undertaking and that I did not anticipate living long in any case. Staupitz answered: "Don't you know that our Lord God still has many things to accomplish? He needs clever and intelligent people for His work—those who can assist with advice. Regardless of when you die, you must provide counsel here and in heaven." (WATR XII 2255a)

On October 19, 1512, the Wittenberg University school of theology, under the deanship of Andreas Bodenstein von Karlstadt, bestowed the title of doctor biblicus, or doctor of Holy Scriptures, on Father Martin Luther. On October 22 Luther became a member of the theological faculty. From October 22, 1512 until his death Martin Luther occupied the chair of biblical studies at Wittenberg University. On the condition that Luther remain at Wittenberg, Frederick the Wise of Saxony paid the promotion fee of seventeen gulden from his treasury. The young Dr. Luther personally went to Leipzig to receive it.

Chapter 2

Teacher of Holy Scriptures:
The Quest for the Foundations of Faith
1513–1516

Learn by teaching: this was Luther's motto during his student days and it was not abandoned when he entered the monastery. On the contrary, he followed it with greater intensity as a stimulus to intellectual maturity. After he had taken his doctoral oath, the emphasis was reversed. Now he was no longer merely a tutor: he was a teacher in the full sense of the word. In accordance with the requirement and custom of the universities, it was no longer simply his duty to disseminate to the beginning classes and to the liberal arts faculty what had been learned in the theological lectures and disputations of the higher classes.

The distinction was fundamental. Formerly he had disseminated knowledge, but now as a doctor, the responsibility was greater. Additional obligations were derived from the volume and uniqueness of material to be used and the personal responsibility incumbent on him by reason of his doctor's oath. Now he must be more than a sponge which merely exudes in its initial form what has been absorbed. Now, before his auditors, he must plumb his own depths and give of his own personality instead of merely relying on memory and logic.

In this sense, Luther's lectures are especially interesting as a witness to the development of his personality. Much—in fact most—of what is contained in his lectures was, to be sure, neither new nor original. How could it be? Luther was not the first whose responsibility it was to elucidate and disseminate theological teaching, and he did not indulge the ambition to invent something novel and to be original. He merely wanted to fulfill his responsibility to the best of his ability.

Martin Luther took his monastic and professional vows very seriously. As monk and priest he was obliged to do penance regularly and to examine his conscience. As professor he was obligated to lecture regularly, to lead disputations, and thereby to preserve and disseminate knowledge. Knowledge and conscience had to be brought into accord. Monk, priest, and professor were to belong to the same personality; otherwise, the monk-priest-professor would have neither respect nor effect. On the contrary, he would be regarded with sullen cynicism as just another person without creativity and spiritual impact. It was one and the same Martin who, in fulfilling the prescriptions, expectations, and obligations of his society, was cast in several roles, yet had to remain an integrated personality if he wanted to satisfy at least one of his obligations. The monk in him was oriented toward humility and obedience; the priest toward the dispensing of the sacraments; the teacher toward research, teaching, and example. The miner's son and farmer's grandson steeped himself in work and liberated the man still confined in monk and priest. The academic teacher dispensed with those elements of scholastic thought which he could not reconcile with conscience. This jettisoning of scholasticism did not occur at once or with one swift heave: for a long time to come monk and priest would contend with the professor.

The problems which would occupy him for the next years as an academician had two primary roots: monasticism and scholasticism. Monasticism had led Luther to a path of personal salvation, a path marked primarily by the observance of certain requirements, including prayer and meditation, enabling the monk to lead a life pleasing to God and thereby secure for himself eternal life. On the other hand, Luther had absorbed from Occamism a concept of God as absolute Will, a concept which emphasized God's role as creator and world judge and repeatedly conjured up the view of God as an unpredictable cosmic arbitor. This occamistic concept, derived from scholasticism, was on a collision course with Luther's concept of the path of personal salvation, a concept which also sprang from scholasticism and which impelled him to clear that path with those tools with which monasticism had provided him. In addition to the view that man must do something to achieve salvation was the view that the path of salvation was prepared through human and divine cooperation. God gives the law; the fulfillment of the law by man results in his salvation, his "righteousness" before God. To be sure, man is weak, but he must perform to his capacity *(facere, quod in se est)* in order to procure salvation. The rest, which man cannot of himself perform, God will grant out of His grace. In this view God's grace is the stopgap for insufficient human strength. Thus this concept according to which man contributes to his salvation or to the extension of divine righteousness is called "synergism" (the teaching that human cooperation with divine grace leads to salvation). The central idea in synergism is that man is not totally directed by the divine will, but rather that man possesses a "free will" that he can employ to choose good or evil and thereby select for himself the path of salvation or the path of damnation, or that he can by his own efforts at least influence his course.

We know from remarks which Luther made years later that these problems not only occupied his thought but to a certain extent provoked an existential disquistude: by his own introspection he came always to the conclusion that, despite his rigid observance of all regulations and the great effort of the will, he never could arrive at the feeling that he had done enough or that he could be certain of salvation. Luther scrupulously gave attention to the theological questions that had always occupied theologians, questions that in his age were associated with a fear that terrified many people at all levels of society.

Luther solved the problems for himself by revising the traditional concepts of the nature of God, the nature of man, and divine righteousness, or, in other words the means of salvation, and by creating his own interpretation of the righteousness of God, in which his view of God and his view of man were synthesized.

The Bible provided him with the ideas which enabled him to arrive at his new interpretation. His methodology was to place Christ at the center of the questions which he addressed to Holy Scriptures, to accept the apostle Paul as the authority for the significance of the person of Christ, to distinguish between law and gospel as well as between letter and spirit, and to inquire of every biblical passage not only what it had to communicate to the Church or to Christendom but also what it had to say to him personally. It was the unique aspect of Luther's biblical exegesis in continuous reference to his subjective experience as an introspective monk, and the gradually increasing objective experience in the execution of his official duties, at the university, and as curate that led him to a new theology.

On August 16, 1513, Martin Luther began his lectures on the psalter. In preparation for these lectures, copies of the psalter with broad margins and interlinear spaces had been prepared by the Wittenberg printer Grunenberg at Luther's request. Each student purchased a copy and wrote Luther's explanations of the text between the lines or in the margins. Luther called these brief explanations "glosses." If they were written between the lines, they were called interlinear glosses; if they were written in the margin, they were called marginal glosses.

Luther himself employed as his source the *Psalterium Quincuplex* of the French humanist, Johannes Faber Stapulensis (Jean Lefèvre d'Etaples), which had appeared in Paris in 1509. In the *Psalterium Quincuplex* Stapulensis had published five different Latin translations of the psalms. This procedure was designed to facilitate interpretation without reference to the Hebrew text, by which most interpreters, because of their deficient knowledge of Hebrew, were intimidated. Luther, it is true, had a copy of *Rudimenta Hebraica*, the Hebrew textbook by Johannes Reuchlin, but in 1513, Luther had hardly progressed beyond the elementary steps in mastering the Hebrew language. Not until several years later, with the help of Melanchthon, did Luther concentrate on learning Hebrew.

In his copy of the *Psalterium Quincuplex* Luther wrote with a raven's quill his interlinear and marginal glosses. In addition, he prepared short outlines, which he called *summarien*, of individual psalms, and he also wrote detailed explanations—*scholien* or *collecta*—of individual verses.

Luther's interpretation of the psalter as presented in the *scholien* and his interpretation of texts selected for later lectures were a combination of his own ideas and those related ideas that he discovered in literature. It is not possible to confirm to which authors he owed his greatest stimulation or inspiration, or to specify what models he followed; usually, insofar as he cited other works at all, Luther quoted from memory, and even then he most often provided only the author's name without reference to the work or chapter quoted. He frequently referred to Nicholas Lyra, Faber Stapulensis, and Gabriel Biel. The fact that echoes from his Erfurt teachers Trutfetter and Usingen can be recognized suggests that Luther probably used his own notes taken as a student at Erfurt as the foundation for his lectures. In principle, he worked just as any academic teacher works today: he evaluated the literature at his disposal, organized the ideas in order of importance, and permitted his own thoughts to flow into the material. Traditional and current interpretations, selected authors, and his own ideas were united in a presentation of his own stamp.

In his lectures it was necessary that Luther deal with the historical material which had come down to him and that it was in turn his obligation to interpret. In principle, Luther's task was no different from that of a professor of literature or of history: to read the sources at hand, interpret, and explain them. The teacher had to understand both the language and the meaning of the source, and to derive from it what could be learned for human conduct in general and for one's personal life in particular, or perhaps what could be learned about the future. Thus Luther faced the ancient problem of historical interpretation, which confronts every generation of researchers and must always be solved anew, especially when, in principle, it is assumed that the problem has already been solved long ago. Insofar as the researcher permits himself in his pursuit to be enticed by the assumption that something is reported in the source which not only arouses curiosity but also in some manner explains "what holds the world together in its innermost parts," he is in quest of what we today call the paradigm, the repeatable, necessary, and essential in historical occurrences, the general correlation or the meaning in historical phenomena.

What distinguished Luther's work (and, supposedly, that of the whole theological guild) from the task of the historian and the literary academician was twofold. First, Luther started with the assumption that what appears today to be obvious fantasy and legend was indeed anchored in history as it has been recorded; second, he persistently queried what the report had to say about each person with respect to his personal life. For Luther, God and the devil were no figments of the imagination but frightening, serious realities. He took his source, the Bible, most seriously, while we take it not as historical record but as poetry. For Luther, the Bible contains God's revelation, an irrevocable and eternally valid truth, which captivated him. Luther wanted to be able to discover and convey this truth. If we do not believe his assertion of purpose, we shall never be able to understand him. To believe him in order to understand him does not imply sharing his belief, but it does imply comprehending and recognizing it as the center of his personality. God's revelation of Himself in the Bible was the theme of Luther's life. To this revelation his full attention was attracted and from it all of his thoughts emanated. The fact that his probings were not restricted to the Scriptures but that he evaluated in relation to the Scriptures everything of any importance within his society makes his theological perspective historically fertile as an ideology or world view.

With this emphasis the place of theology in the intellectual life of Luther's society becomes generally visible. We can interpret what Luther did in his lectures and later in his writings as productive intellectual activity. The Bible was to a significant extent his object of investigation. Languages, logic, and all the ways and means of his approach were his intellectual tools. The peculiarities of the object and tools of his investigation determined to a great degree the intellectual and spiritual problems that confronted him. But these problems in turn fostered a relative independence in his intellectual development, thereby permitting the emergence of his own ideological edifice. In other words the social problems of Luther's age are only indirectly reflected, and the reflection is to a certain degree broken by the prism of the Bible, his object of investigation. This does not mean that whatever Luther posited or thought concerning the Bible was unimportant in relationship to the society of that time. On the contrary, Luther approached with an open Bible the basic questions of human existence and with an open Bible he answered the questions, consciously or unconsciously relating them to the general needs and problems of his age. We cannot appreciate the impact of his approach and of his themes if we do not acquire an appreciation of the historical material and the specific experiential content of the Bible.

God's word in the Bible is communicated in human language: Hebrew in the Old Testament, Greek in the New Testament. If this word is to be understood, it must be read and comprehended in the original tongues. This conviction constituted the marvelous (and for us today the obvious) lesson that the European current of humanism impressed on Luther. From the beginning Luther conceived of Bible reading and comprehension as a philological task, and thus he prepared himself for a scientific study of the Scriptures, a pursuit that was bound to embroil him in controversy because theretofore practical theological thought had not begun with the prerequisite that the original text be consulted. Insofar as medieval theology was based on the Bible, it was based on the Latin translation of St. Jerome, the so-called Vulgate, rather than on the original Hebrew and Greek texts.

At first, however, especially with respect to his early lectures on the psalms, the problem concerning original languages as it related to Bible comprehension did not stand in the forefront, although this problem had already begun to surface. In the beginning Luther was content to follow the traditional hermeneutics of the scholastics, which had been shaped by a long historical process and rested on the concept of the fourfold meaning of Scripture. According to the scholastic axiom every Bible passage has a literal and a symbolic meaning. Taken factually and without corollary or supplement by the reader, the Bible simply records what took place. This view attributes a literal meaning to the biblical text. The literal interpretation corresponds with what the biblical authors claim to have seen, heard, or experienced as recorded in language available to them. The Bible reader and exegete must give attention to these words. Only after such an attentive study should commentary be made. But commentary on the text based on conversance with it still has not addressed the question of whether or not the text is significant, and if so, what is to be learned from it.

Scholastic biblical exegesis, responding to these additional questions, proposes that the intention of the Scriptures is not only to report what happened but at the same time to transmit a message that has meaning for the Church, for the individual, and for the future. The recorded event is interpreted, in part, as a model for historical phenomena and for human destiny in general. Such expanded and symbolic meaning of the biblical word becomes apparent through the comparison and contrast of various biblical texts and accounts. This hermeneutical view is described as allegorical.

The desire to learn something from the obligation, essence, and mission of the Church stood at the center of the allegorical interpretation of the Bible. Admittedly, thereby a way was opened which enabled the interpreter more readily to read his own ideas into the text. The temptation to infuse subjective ideas and the demand to confirm the allegorical figure with as many biblical citations as possible—to support, strengthen, and enhance it—tended toward a wild course of fantasy which could not be confined efficaciously within tolerable limits. Of course, allegorizing must not be considered simply a depravation of scholastic thought, and thus evaluated merely in a negative vein. Associated with allegorizing and necessary to the content of thought is an aspect of reflection, mirroring the most varied multiplicities and preserving the elasticity of concept and idea.

A third type of scriptural interpretation is prompted by the question as to what significance the biblical message has for the personal conduct of the individual Christian. Seeking an answer to this question leads to tropological—or figurative and moral—interpretation. A fourth type is required by questions as to what the text reveals concerning the end of the world, the second advent of Christ, judgment day, and the new creation. Anagogical interpretation seems appropriately to answer these questions. The tropological and anagogical methods might be considered as independent approaches or as variations of the allegorical approach to interpretation.

This fourfold methodology for interpreting Holy Scripture is more than just a scholastic whim. Allegory approaches the Bible not with arbitrary questions but with a certain socially anchored interest that questions those things which are important for the Church and for the individual. Allegory speculates about the future by pursuing the scholastic tradition of classifying problems by type, model, and standard, through the study of ancient accounts of events in terms of what has happened, what has been reported, what has been thought.

In his interpretation of the psalter, Luther arrived at a radical simplification of this fourfold approach. Unable immediately to liberate himself from the scholastic method, he used it with a restraint imposed by his theory of "spirit and letter." In the Holy Scriptures a distinction must be made between letter and spirit, and it is precisely this distinguishing capability that identifies the theologian. The psalmist, Luther wrote, asks for spiritual understanding of the inscribed letter, for understanding is spirit. But as historical epochs were added one to another, so also was spirit, or spiritual understanding, added to letter. Of what was once sufficient to give understanding, only the letter remains to us. Because of the passage of time, the letter is of a more subtle nature today than previously. For everyone who travels life's way, what he abandons is letter while what he strives for is spirit. Letter is what is already possessed in contrast to what remains to be gained (WA IV 365).

The progress from the fourfold approach of interpretion to an approach based on the theory of spirit and letter is methodologically an advance toward the essential. Historically it is a return to that original paradox from which the scholastics had arrived at their complicated and subtle hermeneutics. The original framing of the problem is found in Paul's epistle to the Corinthians: "The letter kills, but the Spirit quickens." It is the influence of humanistic thought that reveals itself here in the methodology: "back to the sources" points toward the older books. The adage thus resurrects original paradoxes, occasionally rejects even long-accepted solutions that were not derived from primary sources, and incites the spirit to start again from the beginning.

With this methodological exegetal tool Luther approached the psalter. The psalter, a part of the Old Testament, contains a collection of 150 songs that praise and extol God, petition His help, invoke destruction and disaster on enemies, and sing about the deeds that He has performed for Israel. Many of the psalms are ascribed to David, who ruled Israel about 1000–960 B.C. The accumulation of the psalms took place over a very long period of time and was completed in all probability not in David's time but rather after the Babylonian captivity of 597–539 B.C.

The psalms are still sung today; they are employed in prayer not only because they are beautiful but also because they concern themselves with an idea considered very important by the ancient Hebrews, along with many other peoples of antiquity, and by people today—namely, that of God as creator and sustainer of the world.

With the God of the ancient Jews—whom they called "Jahweh," "Elohim," and sometimes "Zebaoth," and to whom Luther referred as "Herr Herr" (literally, Lord Lord)—there was a unique case. Jahweh claimed to be the only true God, beside whom there was no other. When God's claim was not received or believed, He became very angry and sent hail, storms, plagues, and illness in order to demonstrate His power to the extent that all would submit to Him and worship Him only. His anger then passed and He permitted the sun of His grace to shine once again. For He is a jealous God, but He also freely forgives when given the opportunity.

This is at least what the ancient Jews believed, and they must have known because the Lord God had revealed Himself to them in a burning bush, has liberated them from Egyptian bondage and parted the Reed Sea in order that they could cross over, had preceded them in a pillar of fire and smoke, had spoken to them in the thunder, had given them their laws, and when they were in dire need had sent manna from heaven in an environment where more stones than bread were at hand. It was a pitiful little company—strangers in Egypt, slaves and servants of Pharaoh, the children of Jacob whom God henceforth called Israel—that He selected in order to make a holy nation. God and his people had difficulty with each other. The Jews were troublesome, disobedient, and recalcitrant; they married foreign women, worshipped strange gods, and erected altars on high places to strange gods. Then this people melted in penitence, tore their hair in grief, and returned contrite once again to their one und true God, who graciously received them because He had waited for their return. But He welcomed them back with a sigh because He foresaw that the tranquil union would not last long and that they soon again would wrangle with Him— despite His promise which he kept to give them the land of Canaan, flowing with milk and honey. Or did this promise to the tribes of Israel first come to mind when the people of Canaan, subjected to holy war, were slaughtered by the Israelites during the conquest?

The psalter does not record these events. The conquest had already taken place long ago. The Israelites no longer trekked through the desert from oasis to oasis. They had become sedentary farmers and shepherds. They discarded the rule of judges and, finally ascending the cultural and constitutional ladder of the disdained but secretly admired Egyptians, erected for themselves a kingdom and a temple. Henceforth, the Bible constitutes part of the historical record and explanation of the world in the class-structured society of the temple state.

In the temple-state, history was written by priests and officials. Thus written history was court history, characterized by the extolling of kings, officials, and priests. It reeks of court gossip as well as the deeds of kings and generals. The priests, all from the tribe of Levi, enjoyed a unique position because this tribe had received no patrimony after the conquest. Levi was sustained by the temple tax, the predecessor of the tithe. The priests were the guardians of the state archives—declared sacred—and of the Ark which contained the tablets on which Moses, on Mount Sinae, had inscribed the law: the commandments, or fundamental rules for the tribal amphictyony of Israel, whose highest and first commandment prescribed the union of the people of Israel, including all her members, with the one God who had elected this people, had led them out of Egypt, and had commanded them to believe in Him. This commandment distinguishes the law code of the ancient Hebrews from similar legal tablets, columns, and steles of their neighbors and of other ancient Near-Eastern peoples. All other commandments of the Mosaic code are, as compared to the first commandment, of less significance and interchangeable with those of the stone codices of Israel's neighbors. This first commandment is the decisive one. As long as the first commandment is honored, the Israelites are Israelites. It is the first commandment that presents the idea of a holy people, the people of God. If Israel disregards the first commandment, she loses the idea of her origins. The first commandment forges origin, blood-tie, and cultural community into one single absolute value. The Lord God, beside whom the Israelite should have no other, represents the highest value of the ancient Hebrews, the inspiration for the visionary "we" of a people, Jahweh, who is conceived as the ideal and omnipotent father whom the individual may address as "Thou".

The peculiarity of ancient Israel's historical record is contained in the fact that all historical events are referred to this highest value, related to Him, and explained by His existence.

The history of Israel did not long remain court history. The books of Kings and Chronicles are followed by the prophetic books, whose authors were endowed with divine grace and who, in holy anger, stirred up revolt among captives dreaming of freedom and of return to the promised land. The prophets repeatedly exhorted the people to do God's will and hold fast to the faith of the fathers. From the prophets Thomas Müntzer received inspiration and discovered arguments for his cause.

Statecraft and revolutionary rage are separated by only a few pages and both are declared expedient for the same people. Historical recordkeeping reflecting the view from above and historical record-keeping reflecting the view from belowe are both necessary. Both assist in formulating correct conduct in new situations and also in preserving the essence of changing form.

The psalter contains the poetry of the responsible individual in this history of the ancient Hebrews. The verses cry for help and plead for God's righteousness, and they praise the Lord who is righteous regardless of what He does; they appeal to His grace and mercy with confession of the psalmist's unworthiness and with an oath of fidelity. The Roman Church included the psalter in its liturgical prayers. Thus with the discipline of the poetry of righteousness in laved the souls of its worshippers. When Luther took up the psalter for his course of lectures, he critically probed the stereotype of priestly mentality. He dissected the daily liturgy of the priest in the solitude of his recitation of the penetential psalms, where the priest was alalone and with his conscience even though others, intoning the same psalms, surrounded him in the monastery chapel.

What for a historian may appear not at all obvious and very questionable was for Luther not only beyond doubt but indeed the starting point of his investigation: the discovery of Christ in the psalms, which had been composed many centuries before Christ. With respect to the psalms, Luther asked, How do they preach Christ? The entire Old Testament, but especially the Psalms, was for him signs pointing to the coming redeemer. Just as the Old Testament led to Christ, the New Testament emanated from Him. Jesus thus became the center of history, which was conceived as the course of salvation that God initiated with and for man. Luther, therefore, embraced the idea that the early Christian community in Jerusalem and with it the entire world of early Christendom cherished. In order to demonstrate the unique religious quality of Jesus the Nazarene carpenter, and to prove to opponents and doubters the validity of the Church's claim, Old Testament passages were zealously sought that could serve as confirmation that such a religious teacher was foreseen. Early Christianity felt an urgent need to legitimize itself before the political and religious authorities of Israel and could not have neglected to do so. Thus from the beginning, the gospel narratives were interpreted to satisfy this need to justify faith in Jesus by appeal to the Old Testament.

His view of Jesus helped the young Wittenberg professor to solve the question concerning God's righteousness and thereby to find an escape from the fear provoked by the theory that God had predestinated some for damnation and some for salvation. This theory no longer greatly troubled Luther. Several years later, Luther described the problem and its solution:

> The words "righteous" and "the righteousness of God" worked upon my conscience like a lightening bolt; whenever I heard them I was terrified. Is God righteous? Then he must punish. But once while in this tower, reflecting on the words (Romans 1:17) "The just shall live by faith" and on the "righteousness of God," I suddenly thought that if we because of faith become righteous and if the righteousness of God is extended to everyone who believes, righteousness then is not our achievement, but

rather it is a result of God's mercy. My spirit was comforted because the righteousness of God consists in our being justified and redeemed through Christ. Now these words, "God's righteousness," became for me beloved words. In this tower, the Holy Spirit revealed the Scripture to me. (WATR II 3232c)

We cannot be certain when Luther's "tower experience" took place, but according to his own account this discovery stood in close association with the placement of his Christology at the center of his theology. In any case the foundation for his Christocentric theology is already laid in his first lectures on the psalms.

Luther did not find a sudden solution to the problems that beset him; even when the solution seemed at hand in certain contexts, the same or similar problems arose in others, because a complex overlapping and interfacing system of thought confronted him. Moreover, even when he seemed to have reconciled the contradictions, new thorns growing out of his thinking, experience, and daily activities bored once again into the old questions. However, inasmuch as his thinking is stayed on Christ, his first lecture on the psalms reveals the foundation of his thought and therewith the path along which the solution has been found.

Whereas in his first lecture series he occupied himself with Old Testament themes, in his second series, which began on April 8, 1515, and concluded on September 7, 1516, he devoted himself to the New Testament, to Paul's epistle to the Romans.

The lecture series on Paul's epistle to the Romans focused Luther's thought more sharply on Christ and strengthened the Christocentrism in his theology. At the same time the signs multiply which reveal that he was beginning to place greater distance between himself and scholasticism and to take offense at philosophy, with which Aristotle, for Luther, is synonymous. Luther emphasized the distinction between the Bible and the scholastic compendia with their categorical analyses which, with respect to biblical content, destroyed and dissected more than they explained.

Luther struggled to understand the Bible, and he did this with the conceptual tools which Occamism offered him and which he had learned to employ. But the results did not satisfy him. On the contrary, the conclusions disquieted him because he was not a cold, rational thinker who was contented with formulas, even if they were well polished and neatly packaged.

Luther was a master of philosophical tools. In his student days his classmates had presumptuously nicknamed him "the philosopher." In fact, he thought himself not only through but also away from philosophy. This liberation from philosophy made his ear free for the voice proceeding from the Bible, the ancient book of books in which the Jews had assembled the literary witnesses of their historical self-awareness.

The Bible deals with the history of the people of Israel under the command of God: a history of brutal deeds in the conquest for Canaan; of rebellion and mutiny against the heavenly commander; of deception and of wrangling with God; of rebellion, blasphemy, and apostasy; but also of collective penance and of contrite return to the faith of the fathers. This is the heart of the Old Testament.

The New Testament does not merely continue the story of the Old Testament; it transforms this story and gives it a new dimension in the account concerning Jesus. To be sure, the books of the New Testament also deal with the return of the penitent to God. But in the New Testament the return is not seen as a collective political act like the struggle for independence against foreign domination and the smashing of foreign idols or, as depicted in the Old Testament, the gleeful butchering of an idolatrous priesthood. In the New Testament return to God is something quite different: a childlike faith in Jesus, the man from Nazareth, as the Son of God, the savior of the world who redeems humankind from sin by His crucifixion at Golgotha and His resurrection from the dead.

This belief of the Christians was an "offense to the Jews and folly to the Greeks." Although the decision of the Sanhedrin, the supreme religious court among the Jews, to deliver Jesus to the Romans for execution because of His blasphemy in presenting himself as the Son of God must be regarded with abhorrence and regret, the judicial consequence of the Sanhedrin's decision cannot be gainsaid, because in the conviction of the Sanhedrin Jesus had violated the faith of their fathers in the most flagrant fashion.

The apostle Paul, the former Saul who had once persecuted the Christians under a mandate from the high priest, undertook, after his conversion on the Damascus road, to preach this "foolish" and "offensive" gospel, and especially to disseminate it not only among the Jews living in the cities on the east coast of the Mediterranean, but soon thereafter among educated Greeks.

Paul, therefore, had to defend the folly of the gospel against the hypercriticism of hellenistic philosophy and to protect it against specific arguments. Within the Jewish diaspora Paul had to make the gospel immune to the demand of the ceremonial laws, a demand that exerted itself with the force of sanctified tradition and unquestioning assumption, a demand which stemmed from the faith of the fathers in whose time this faith had become traditional national law.

What distinguished the Jewish Christians from the traditional Jews was not traditional customs nor the ethnic distinction among peoples; the two groups had much in common in these areas. And what distinguished the Greek Christians from the Greek pagans was neither the platitudes of hellenistic philosophy that seasoned their common language nor the hair-splitting that was a common practice of both groups. What really distinguished the Christian groups and marked them as unique was faith. It was faith alone that distinguished Christians from other Jews or unconverted Greeks and that incorporated believers into a new community totally apart from national, ethnic, and philosophical considerations.

Through the centuries since apostolic times this seed from which Christian communal growth germinated was repeatedly surrounded by problems and buried under layers of thought. The necessary result was a historical evolutionary process in which experience was gained, assimilated, and intellectually categorized in the form of dogma, offices, rites, rules, codes, summaries, and compendia.

As he concentrated on the Pauline epistles in his lectures, Luther penetrated through these layers of tradition to the historical essence of Christianity. His penetration through the layers of theological speculation at first resulted in a sharper distinction between Old and New Testaments. This distinction between the testaments would be at least as determinative for his future thought as would be the already confirmed Christological emphasis. In later years Luther evaluated the breakthrough to the distinction between Old and New Testaments as exceptionally important. "What I had failed to see was the distinction between law and gospel. I had assumed that they were the same and had concluded that between Christ and Moses, apart from chronology and the degree of perfection in their respective persons, there was no difference. But when I discovered the right distinction, namely that law and gospel are two different things, I achieved a breakthrough" (WATR V, 5518).

If Luther's own evaluation is taken literally at every point, an astounding conclusion is drawn. His statement suggests that there must have been a time when Luther recognized only the human nature of Christ but not his deity. Such a phase in his thought may be implied in his lectures on the epistle to the Romans, but only as a didactical approach to a fuller understanding of Christ's dual nature. Thus, in order to capture the full significance of Christ, Luther recommends that we first concentrate on the concept of Jesus as truly human, and only when this concept has been mastered with all its consequences should we go on to the concept that Jesus also is true God. When we remember that in his lectures on the psalms Luther had sought Christ in the Old Testament, it is not surprising that Luther, in principle, had regarded Christ as not essentially unlike Moses, albeit on a higher plain of perfection. In this context, then, he had seen Christ as human, as the one who had been made the instrument of God, but not as God who for a period had become man. Thus this view is in keeping with Luther's perception of the astounding exile of the man on the cross and with Luther's preoccupation with the crucifixion event of Good Friday. Only with the greatest difficult could Luther divert his attention from the exile and crucifixion of the man on the cross to the resurrection event of Easter. This attitude corresponds with Luther's predestination fears as well as with the fact that he made so much of what had long been recognized: salvation depends on faith.

To see in Christ only a Moses of a higher order was to philosophize or to explain history rather than to believe. If faith is to be faith and nothing else, it must be liberated from philosophy and from sober historical explanation. Luther was in the process of freeing himself in this manner in 1515 and 1516. By 1509 Luther had moved away from philosophy and toward theology and had complained that philosophy was a waste of time; these complaints became louder as he sought faith through theological channels and thus resisted the influence of philosophy on theology. Luther did not simply desire to separate theology from philosophy in order to recognize them as two distinct academic disciplines. He sought rather a faith theology as opposed to a philosophical theology. He writes in the *scholia* for Romans 8:19,

> When will we ever see, that we waste valuable time with such foolish studies and that we place the best at the end? We conduct ourselves in such a manner that Seneca's words apply always to us: "We don't know what is needful because we learn the superfluous; indeed the salutary we do not know because we have learned the damnable." I feel constrained before the Lord to raise my voice loud against philosophy and to admonish us to turn to the Scriptures ... Thus I advise you as well as I can, abandon philosophy because it is high time that we make place for other studies and learn Jesus Christ and Him crucified. (WA LVI 371)

The distinction between law and gospel had led him at the time of the lectures on the epistle to the Romans to assessments of a principle criticism of the Church. Luther wrote in the *scholia* for Romans 14:1,

> To select certain days for fasts and not others has no place in the new covenant; just as little place has the practice of selecting certain foods and rejecting others, or selecting certain days as feast days and excluding others, or building or not building this or that church, or adorning the church in this or that manner, or singing or not singing. Finally it is not commanded that priests and monks trim their hair in a certain fashion or that they wear a special habit. All these prescriptions are shadows and signs of things and they are childish. No, every day is a feast day, every food is permitted, everything is acceptable, with the stipulation that in all things moderation and love must be exercised. Teaching the people to regard certain vanities as necessary to salvation, many false apostles preach and seduce the people away from the liberty confirmed by the apostle. (WA LVI 493)

The distinction between law and gospel intensifies the inclination to ascribe to faith all good which a person is or does, and the inclination to seek salvation in faith. Luther's ability to distinguish was accompanied by a keen psychological talent for observation, especially as expressed in the *scholia* for Romans 3:27, in Luther's complaint concerning the effects of the law on people.

The law of works puffs up; whoever is righteous and has fulfilled the law no doubt has reason to glorify himself. Such people do not humble themselves ..., do not seek to be justified ... . Thus it is to be noted that the law of works says, "Do what I command"; but the law of faith says, "Grant what Thou commandest" (St. Augustine). And therewith the people of the law answer the law and God who speaks in the law, "I have done what Thou hast commanded." The people of faith say: "I cannot do what Thou commandest; I have not done it, but I yearn to do it ..., and I petition Thee for the strength to be able to do it." Thus the former people who appeal to law are proud and seek their own glory; the latter people who appeal to faith are humble and weak in their own eyes. Thus the entire life of the new people consists only with heartful sighs in word and deed to plead and to seek and to pray until death that they might be justified; they will not remain quiescent, never claim that they have arrived, they will always wait on righteousness as though it existed outside of them, they will always confess that they are yet in sin." (WA LVI 263) Of no small significance to Luther's future spiritual development is his interpretation of the call to the teaching office in the Church, as presented in his lecture on the epistle to the Romans. The Catholic Church derives its authority for its clergy from the commission which was supposedly received directly from Jesus and which the apostles then transmitted personally, but the laying on of hands. In this commission the apostle Peter was preferred by Christ himself, and this then became a decisive argument for the primacy of the pope as the successor of Peter. Paul, however, was not one of the first apostles, nor was he a member of the original church in Jerusalem. He claimed to have received his commission directly from Christ on the Damascus road. Luther accepted and subscribed to Paul's claim, prescribed before the original apostles and also before Paul's audiences and congregations, that the holder of any office validates his claim to that office by words and deeds. The idea of a call to office directly by God and the validation of this office by word and deed contradicts the Church's practice of hierarchical appointment and makes the authorization for preaching God's word independent of ecclesiastical authority. Translated into practice such an interpretation must erode Church discipline and pave the way for anyone who believes that he possesses the Spirit to have a voice in matters of Church doctrine and preaching.

The Christocentrality of biblical exegesis, the distinction between law and gospel, and the suppression of philosophy for the benefit of a pure biblical theology were important methodological starting points to help Luther overcome the nagging fear provoked by predestination and to solve the question of the righteousness of God in a satisfying manner. These starting points helped him to clarify the problem of theodicy (the question of the righteousness of God), which the idea of the historical evolution of deity had provoked.

From a jealous tribal god to the gods of a polytheistic world environment to the Prime Mover in a monocausal epistemology—this was the course of the idea of deity from Moses to the books which Luther read and the school of thought from which he must liberate himself. In this course God forbids His elected people to have association with His rivals, disparages the heavenly colleagues as demons and devils, until finally, with the help of logic and enveloped in the Eleatic concept of being, He has them declared nonexistent and nonpersons.

But the victory to which philosophy assists the God of Abraham, Isaac, and Jacob is a Pyrric one. The colleagues of Jahweh, robbed of their own conceptual existence, avenge themselves in a most frightful manner. Together they ooze, with their works and practices, into the marrow of their conqueror, and they ascribe to the solitary victor their own evil works that continue to be performed in the world. As an amicable tribal God Jahweh created the world as an emanation from His spirit; His spirit, philosophically elevated to absolute Being, absorbs creation back into the concept of Himself so that He must now be answerable for all that takes place in the world. Deity as absolute Being suffers from the contrariety of its own insatiability. The illness is called theodicy; the fever which caused it, a predestination fear; the cure, faith; the therapy, prayer and works.

Jahweh's arrogance costs Him dearly. He tolerates no other gods; thus He has no colleagues to whom He can ascribe cosmic errors. For those people who firmly believe and insist that Jahweh is entirely alone, enthroned in heaven, and that there is no other god who shares that heaven, there is no choice other than to consider Jahweh as the originator of evil and the creator of the devil. In his lectures on the epistle to the Romans Luther came to this conclusion.

Theodicy—consisting of the intellectual knots in the concept of God's sovereignty, with His goodness on the one side and the existence of evil on the other—cannot rationally be unraveled without tangles because the composite that is always offered is a split being, a gaping monster, a being in contradiction with himself, a god who has a devil in him. Such a god can be worshipped and placated with incense but can hardly be loved and revered. Luther himself could not love and revere such a god. Luther was afflicted by this supernatural monster erected by scholasticism. This image of God horrified him and granted no peace of soul. But Luther needed God. How could he in good conscience explain to his students the Holy Scriptures and the nature of God revealed in the Scriptures while he himself, antagonistic and perverse, and perhaps erupting in an agitated and blasphemous spiritual hypochondria, stood in secret quarrel with that Being?

The concept of God's sovereignty, the concept of His grace and righteousness, and last but not least the painful idea that God had from the beginning elected some for salvation and had appointed others irrevocably to eternal damnation, occupied Luther again and again in his lectures. One of the most memorable and incisive reflections on this theme is found in his lectures on the epistle to the Romans. Driven by the disquieting question as to whether or not he belonged to the elect or to those assigned to damnation, Luther seized the initiative and rationalized that whoever really places himself in the will of God must be willing to accept even God's will to damn him. The resignation *ad infernum*, the acceptance of hell, the willingness to permit oneself to abandoned by God, becomes the irrational sign of those who are completely saturated with the spirit of God. No one can really wish to be damned or believe that anyone would assent to such judgment. Such resignation is neither true humility nor faith. Such resignation is convoluted thought in the delirium of predestination fear, a noose for faith which strangles rather than tests. In later years Luther would consider this concept as a work of the devil, but in 1515 and 1516, by continuing seriously to present the view, he indicated the scholastic maze he would still have to grope through before discovering the security he sought.

Here lay in wait one last self-deception. Luther overcame it by focusing on Christ on the cross: "Why hast Thou forsaken me?" The destitution of this cry Luther could not dismiss. He must not be more Christlike than Christ and thereby deceive himself. Self-esteem and love for God quake in horror at this cry: profound hatred is kindled against that monster which sacrifices man and plunges him into hell. Here at the cross the faith which acquiesces in such an act becomes the sadistic laughter of Satan; the false trust in God becomes the triumph of the adversary. The straw hat of humility is consumed in the fire of hell. Only naked faith (confirmed by nothing other than the biblical word) can lead the believer away from such horror that Good Friday is followed by the Easter resurrection. At this point no number of rational and philosophical crutches help. The story of crucifixion and resurrection must be believed without ifs or buts; otherwise, the account is reduced to an interesting tragedy from antiquity. Understanding the story as an ancient tragedy is not without merit, and for an increasing number of people in the modern world this is the only possible interpretation. Such an interpretation, however, was for Luther impossible. As a theologian with a broad philosophical education, he remained a believing Christian. Whenever philosophy disturbed faith, Luther exiled philosophy. And where theology did not satisfy faith, there he reshaped and recreated theology to conform to faith.

Luther turned away from the resignation *ad infernum*, from the believer's assent to be damned if God wills, to the man on the cross who had lived the simplest life of faith imaginable. Whatever the Father says is true. Truth is not found in rational categories, but rather in what comes from the mouth of God. This is the leap from the religion of prescriptions and anxieties to one of trust and faith; from law to gospel; from Old Testament to New Testament; from the constraint of tradition to the revelatory word. The passage in the lecture on the epistle to the Romans where Luther ponders assenting to be damned if it be God's will probably indeed depicts the low point to which the spinning out of predestination teaching had led.

The thought that it is God alone and no other power apart from Him who is able to work in history had a soothing effect on Luther after he saw in God not primarily the judge but rather the redeemer of the world. Good works belong to God alone; evil works, though alien to Him, are worked in contrast to the good in order to demonstrate good in all its power and strength. Salvation thus comes from God and indeed as an unearned gift of grace. No human free will and no human merit cooperate in achieving salvation, which is, on the contrary, singularly the work of God.

Thus Luther permits mercy, wrath, goodness, austerity to exist unreconciled in his view of God. Furthermore, he does not seek to avoid the paradox that God created the devil, that He enlists the devil for His purposes and thereby is the author of evil. Luther's reflections on God reach their extreme dimensions at this point. His reflection on God projects the contradiction in the world into the creator himself. In this most extreme dimension Luther's thought becomes blasphemous; the view of God is transformed into a taunting portrait out of which God smiles on us as an indulgent father and then immediately grins at us through a devil's mask.

Where thinking must end because it destroys the object of its attention and transforms it into its opposite, there the realm of faith begins. Faith possesses no reason. What thinking threatens faith sustains. Faith possesses only trust. Faith must renounce understanding and reason, for otherwise it goes awry and cannot function. The purpose of faith is to provide support where reason has reached its limits and knowledge has nothing more to offer. Seen philosophically, faith is the stopgap of knowledge, the refuge of ignorance; psychologically, faith may be regarded as something similar to a continuation in uncertainty with the hope for a good conclusion. In accordance with its origin, faith can be prejudice. According to its function in daily life it is a trust, the necessary precondition for everyone to be able to some degree to live tolerably in human society. Theologically faith may be all these things, but above all else it is the precondition, content, and result of thinking that is concerned with and based on the material which the Bible offers—the half-defiant, half-wily wisdom of the adage *credo quia absurdum est* (I believe it because it is absurd).

Luther's belief is faith belief, trust belief. He has confidence that Jesus Christ is not a deceiver. He builds on the assumption that Jesus spoke the truth and that he will fulfill his promises. "Certainty" of Christ's integrity is provided by one source only—the biblical word. Luther believes the word about the Word. This attitude could to a certain extent be considered childish and naïve. Touching simplicity? Not at all; just the opposite. The Word Jesus Christ is the only witness whom the monk and professor believes at all any more; even with this witness faith is not extended without investigation, for Luther examines his faith from every angle. Luther's faith is for him the fixed point, found at last, from which he can critically scrutinize the entire conceptual and intellectual world of his time. Much of what for others was plausible and obvious, Luther discarded.

Luther discovered the seed of the primitive gospel, the belief that Jesus Christ was God's Son and that by His death on the cross he reconciled man with God. Whoever believes this gospel, Luther insisted, is forgiven of his sin for the sake of Christ. This is the righteousness of God. God gave us His righteousness; we could not have earned it by any deeds of our own, by observing the regulations, by performing exceptional deeds, or by effort of the will. We receive God's righteousness ascribed to us by grace. The single deed which God requires of us is to excercise faith, and even this faith is not totally ours, for it comes directly from God out of His word.

If this faith be genuine rather than merely simulated, it transforms the entire person from within. Christ is then in us and we are spiritually born again in Him as new creatures. The person born again in Christian faith is so "naturally disposed" *(genaturet)*, as Luther said, that he, on the basis of his new being, can do no other than that which pleases God.

If we framed Luther's fundamental thougths in a secular form, we would say, "Grant man a new consciousness of himself and of his position in the world, and he will, liberated from inner anguish, so act that humankind will find itself once again." Sin, the alienation of man from God, is simply the theological version of what we, with Karl Marx, call the alienation of man from his fellow man. To be sure, this concept is surrounded by a mythological lattice work which should not merely be dismissed but which can be understood on the basis of its historical roots and then appreciated in its poetic grandeur. Christian theology is systematized poetry concerning the being and pilgrimage of humanity. Martin Luther is one of Christian theology's meistersingers.

Luther's basic thought embraces not only his concept of the significance of faith for man but also his concept of the nature of God. God does not permit man to bargain, speculate, or haggle with Him about salvation. He does not sell His righteousness as so much goods might be sold. Rather He bestows His righteousness out of grace and mercy upon him who believes. God does not forgive the sins of him who would pay for forgiveness with hard cash or deeds, but He forgives only him who believes Him without any rational argument and without if, and, or but. Whoever does believe will work industriously and do good to others, not in order to play the hypocrite before the public and not to call God's attention to himself in hope of reward, but because his new Christian nature permits no other course. The true believer does not boast about his works nor about his faith. He is not concerned with himself because he is totally captive to the will of God, and it is just this submission to the divine will liberates him and enables him happily to take up his daily chores and without hypocrisy to love his neighbor.

What we find in Luther's early lectures from 1513 to 1516 or 1517, and what appears in the light of later personal testimony as seeds of his intellectual originality and future doctrine, are not only speculations or systemized thoughts. We find also the attempt to correlate his own experience and those concepts which his lectures indicate are to be discussed. This effort to correlate his experience to his convictions becomes clear when we learn what duties, apart from his academic responsibilities, Luther had to fulfill.

In 1515 Luther was selected vicar of the Augustinian order for Saxony. In this capacity he had to inspect eleven monasteries and to see to it that discipline was maintained. His duties as vicar were clearly distinguished from his many duties as professor. As professor, his interpretive, rhetorical talents as well as his use of logic were demanded. As vicar, he had to represent disciplined authority and exercise that authority; he had to lead men and to judge their conduct, or, as it was expressed at that time, to execute ecclesiastical discipline and to exercise pastoral care. To promote obedience meant to maintain order, coerce, command, and admonish; to exercise pastoral care meant to comfort, encourage, advise, and help.

Luther was able to fulfill both his academic and his administrative duties. He necessarily encountered resistance, but he also demonstrated himself to be a sympathetic helper. In his former Erfurt monastery he insisted on appointing his old friend, Lang, as prior. We have no report as to what led him to insist on this. We do know that Johannes Lang and Martin Luther in 1509 and 1510 experienced some unexplained mutual difficulties with their brother monks in Erfurt. Now, as vicar, Luther turned the tables. The appointment of Lang indicates that Luther was beginning to discover how an office and specific circumstances were to be employed in order to achieve success and to consolidate power. No timid monk behaves with such boldness; only the skillful and willful act so tenaciously.

Wherever Luther could not achieve his goal by the exclusive exercise of official authority, he resorted to his pastoral talents. An example is provided by the letter to the prior of the Mainz monastery, who had given refuge to a monk who had fled from one of the monasteries under Luther's supervision. Luther wrote:

The evil news has reached me that one of my brothers from our Dresden monastery is staying with you. This brother has unfortunately come to you for reasons and in a manner which are disgraceful. I am indebted to your loyalty and to your friendly cooperation that you have received this brother so that the disgrace of his leaving the monastery might be ended. He is my lost sheep. He belongs to me. It is my obligation to look for him and to lead him out of his error, if it pleases our Lord Jesus Christ. I beseech you, therefore, honorable Father Prior, for the sake of our common faith in Christ and for the sake of our common vow to Saint Augustine, if it is at all possible for you in your zealous love, please send the brother to me, either to Dresden or to Wittenberg, or better still convince him to come here on his own, and inform him in a friendly manner that he should come voluntarily. I will receive him with open arms. All he need do is to come. From me he need fear no vexation. I know that offenses must come; it is not unusual that an individual falls. The miracle is that he gets up again. Even in heaven, an angel fell, and in paradise, Adam. Peter fell also and daily the heaven aspiring cedars of Lebanon fall. No wonder then when a reed is whipped about by the storm. (WA BR I 39)

One of the deepest themes rooted in Luther's conviction concerning the sinful nature of man—a lifelong conviction which seems to reflect a contempt for human nature—is here revealed: the responsibility to be a helper to those in need, to dispel fears, and to restore the erring to the community.

Because of this conviction regarding human frailty, Luther had a firm aversion to all things associated with perfectionism in the quest for salvation. He opposed the teaching of Pelagius, so vehemently attacked by St. Augustine, which posited a spotless, pure, and harmonious human nature empowered by an individual will to achieve the highest perfection. Luther had learned by his own experience that this teaching deceived, that it dangled before man an unattainable goal, that it permitted man to become arrogant and in the end plunged him into ever deeper despair because it unrealistically demanded of man what he could not fulfill. Pelagious' teaching did not comfort; it evoked fearful apprehension. In a letter to George Spenlein, his Augustinian brother in Memmingen, Luther expressed this fundamental motif of his theology even more clearly than in his lectures.

Therefore, my dear brother, learn Christ and Him crucified, learn to praise Him, and out of the depths of your own soul-despair learn to say to Him: "Thou, Lord Jesus, art my righteousness, but I am Thy sin. Thou hast taken on my condition and granted me Thine. Thou hast assumed what Thou wast not and given me what I was not." Avoid seeking any spotless perfection which might seduce you to believe that you are no longer a sinner or to believe that you no longer desire to sin. Christ lives only among sinners. It was for sinners after all that he left heaven, where he had dwelt only among the righteous, in order to make his home among the unrighteous. Think untiringly of Christ's love; then you will perceive His sweetest consolation. If we must gain our own peace of conscience by our own efforts and pains, why then did Christ die ...? That righteousness is barren that measures others by its own standards, will not tolerate those who are weaker, and yearns only for flight and the desert when by patience, prayer and example is should immediately seek to help the weak. Such conduct buries the entrusted talent and does not grant to one's fellow servant what is owed. (WA BR I 35)

Thus up to the end of 1516 or the beginning of 1517 certain ideas in Luther's theological concepts were taking shape which we, with an eye to future events, can immediately recognize as a potential for conflict. Luther discards Aristotle; Luther mistrusts the free will; he thinks that an entire series of ecclesiastical regulations have nothing in common with the New Testament; he does not believe that he is obligated to earn righteousness, but, on the contrary, that he must permit righteousness to be bestowed upon him. Luther's contempt for Aristotle promises problems with scholastic sages; his displeasure with the concept of free will may draw upon him the enmity of humanistic circles. Luther's subjective reflections concerning which practices correspond to the New Testament and which do not point to potential conflict because matters concerning ecclesiastical prescriptions are thereby subjected to an evaluation of their practicality and disciplinary value. Luther's ecclesiastical superiors may critically note his position and doctors of canon law may feel challenged to rebuke him.

Does Luther really acknowledge any authority outside his own thought? Does he really believe that he could ignore all the great names in his circle and of his time and that he might consider himself more clever that all of his contemporaries? Is not he, who always warns his students and his friends of arrogance, himself possessed by the sin of arrogance? Must not his attitude eventually lead him into a hopeless isolation in which, at best, he will be condemned as a laughable oddball? Is there any authority that he will acknowledge? Yes, there is. And this authority, to which he subjugates everything else, takes precedence over everything else: the word of God in the Bible. This word has become his second self; it has become a superego which subjects everything in his soul to itself. This word has enslaved Luther and captured his will, but it has not dulled him to the world around him. On the contrary, it has quickened all his senses, and his whole personality is sensitized in the highest measure imaginable to everything around him and in him which rings false, hollow, or spurious.

Chapter 3
—
Faith versus Scholasticism
1516–1517

The personal tone of Luther's lectures did not go unnoticed by his Wittenberg colleagues. Challenges came from Professors Karlstadt, Lopinus, and Amsdorf. The skepticism concerning Luther's thought was not incited by his occasional criticism of this or that undesirable condition in church practice, nor was their criticism based on their general desire to defend scholasticism. It was based rather on Luther's anthropology, his view of man; because here Luther contradicted not only the scholastic teaching, but, much more significantly, the humanistic assumptions, which could not praise "abstract" man highly enough. As fifteen hundred years earlier Paul had been obliged to steer a course between Jewish law and Greek philosophy, so Luther was obliged to contend with ecclesiastical tradition and humanism, the most modern intellectual strain; it was necessary to liberate himself from both while remaining stimulated by both.

When in this context it is mentioned that Luther occupied himself with humanism, a possible misunderstanding may come about because the meaning of the word has changed since Luther's day. Today "humanism" is simply a synonym for "humaneness," or, perhaps most precisely, it means "that which pertains to humanity." In the sixteenth century, when a humanitarian or humane act was described, it was not described as an example of humanism, but rather as an act of mercy *(misericordia)*. The present concept of humanism first appears in the nineteenth century, about 1820. In earlier usage, humanism related to a complex of philosophical theories, literary reflections, and those *humaniora* of the scholars and writers of the end of the fifteenth and first decades of the sixteenth centuries who devoted themselves to the nontheological disciplines of rhetoric, poetry, history, ethnology, ancient languages, and other similar subjects. Pursuit of these subjects precluded theocentric mediation and a preoccupation with theology. The humanities directed attention to man and his mundane affairs. Humanism facilitated the dissemination of new ideas since the humanistic disciplines did not stand immediately under ecclesiastical control as did theology. Those who were interested in the humanities and sought to promote them came from a heterogeneous educational background with a strong middle-class strain.

Luther did not reject these subjects. He himself liked to read ancient authors, and he considered them indispensible to education. He himself was
stimulated in many ways by the humanities, especially the study of languages. Not the least attractive attribute of the humanities was the methodological axiom by which ancient authors answered the questions
raised in the volumes of antiquity. This methodology early appealed to Luther. By engaging in such exercises, Luther identified himself with the
German humanists. He made common cause with the German humanists
who, stimulated by Italian humanism, buttressed the German national consciousness and attacked the Roman curia and the papacy. But of one characteristic Luther was suspicious: all these poets and writers extolled man
too much to suit Luther; they spoke only infrequently of God, and they
tended, not infrequently, with a smile or with an all too quick consent to
any proposed solution, to disengage themselves from the uncomfortable
questions of the Christian faith. Here Luther sensed unbelief; he opposed
the skepticism of humanism, but not to the extent of rejecting humanism
completely, nor would he have rejected humanism in the current humanitarian sense of the word.

Luther's debate—and dispute—happy colleagues had listened with
sharp ears, had identified the peculiarity of his thought, had segregated it
from the traditional consensus, and had branded it as alien, perhaps initially as a new and interesting topic of collegiate discussion until a public
disputation should be held. On September 25, 1516, this debate took place at
the university in the school of theology.

The promotion of Bartholomew Bernhardi from Feldkirch in Swabia to
theological sententiar presented the occasion for the forum. Bernhardi had
studied in Erfurt in 1503 and in 1504 had gone to Wittenberg, where in 1508
he had taken his master of arts examination in the school of liberal arts. In
1512 he received the *baccalaureus biblicus*, and in the winter semester of 1512–
1513 he served as the dean of the school of liberal arts. Thus in 1516, after
thirteen years of study, Bernhardi was no novice or beginner in theology
when he selected as the theme of his disputation basic ideas from Luther's
lectures on the epistle to the Romans. His theses were concerned with the
inability of man to fulfill God's commands and to do good by the exercise
of his own strength and will. In his disputation, Bernhardi's position was
that man's natural potential is geared only to self satisfaction and carnal
goals; without grace man cannot keep God's laws, and the reception of
grace cannot be summoned or earned by one's own power.

Bernhardi had formulated the theses himself, but in content they corresponded so closely to the opinion of Luther, who chaired the disputation,
that Luther soon spoke of Bernhardi as his first disciple. Luther had already taught many students, and his lectures were well attended, but now
someone had for the first time independently represented in an academic

disputation one of the key ideas of Lutheran theology. With this disputation Luther's academic activity began to show an impact. Within the academic community, Luther had become a personality who, by the originality
of his thought, forced his colleagues to assume a position.

The professors Nicholaus von Amsdorf and Andreas Bodenstein von
Karlstadt, representatives of the traditional *via antiqua* at Wittenberg, expressed reservation and doubt that Luther's interpretations were defensi-
ble. Amsdorf, who came from a noble family in Meissen, was a few weeks
younger than Luther. He had gone to school in Leipzig; immediately after
the founding of Wittenberg University in 1502, he began to study there and
to pursue with great diligence his academic career. In 1511 he had been promoted to doctor of theology, and in 1513 he had served as rector of the university. In late autumn of 1516, Luther won in this man, to whom was
ascribed a gruff and passionate character, a reliable and true friend who, in
all future storms, gave his unwavering support. Amdorf's loyalty was
sparked by debates which the Bernhardi disputation provoked, and the Lu-
ther-Amsdorf relationship became consolidated. It was a study of the
works of St. Augustine to which Luther had urged Amsdorf that dispelled
Amsdorf's earlier reservations.

Karlstadt's objections were stronger than those raised by Amsdorf. In defense of his own interpretations, Luther needed to appeal consistently to
the Scriptures and to St. Augustine. These two sources were for him the authorities by which he challenged the doctors, the guardians of scholasticism. Karlstadt must have felt threatened by Luther's theology because
Karlstadt was a Thomist; that is, he was a proponent of the theology of
St. Thomas Aquinas not necessarily because he did not know other views
or because he rejected them but rather because his teaching position prescribed Thomism.

Under these conditions, the difference of opinion between Luther and
Karlstadt, which came to the fore at the end of 1516 and the beginning of
1517, was vented in the manner of academic jousting. Luther's position at
the university called on him to teach the Bible. He gave this obligation
highest preeminence and placed the Scriptures first among all authorities.
On the other hand, Karlstadt had another duty to perform as teacher: to
make the students aware of scholastic authority. Thus in the rivalry between Luther and Karlstadt a tug of war between two curricula is suggested. The vanity of the two professors played a role in their dispute. Andreas Bodenstein von Karlstadt was a few years older than Luther. He
could point to his publications; Luther had none, and, in October 1512, it
was Karlstadt who, as dean of the theological school, had placed the doctor's beret on the head of the newly promoted candidate Luther. Karlstadt's educational path covered a broader geographical range than Luther's,
and the older scholar had inhaled more academic winds than had Luther,

the disseminator of novel ideas. Luther, though not a novice, was nevertheless the younger of the two in the field of academics. In 1502 Karlstadt had received his *baccalaureus artium* in Erfurt where he had become familiar with the basic ideas of nominalism. In 1503 he had gone from Erfurt to the University of Cologne, the citadel of Thomism and of the *via antiqua*, but he had remained in Cologne only for one year. He had then gone to Wittenberg where he had quickly climbed the academic ladder in the school of liberal arts, and as early as the winter semester of 1507–1508 had served as liberal arts dean. At the same time he had begun, with the same determination and success, his theological curriculum which, in 1510, he had concluded with acquisition of the doctor of theology degree. In 1511 Karlstadt had become rector of the University of Wittenberg.

In 1515, just as Luther was occupied with his lectures on the epistle to the Romans and had become the district vicar for the Augustinian order in Saxony, Karlstadt left Wittenberg for Italy. His Italian trip caused some fallout because he left without naming a substitute to assume his duties in Wittenberg. The clergy of the chapter house of All Saints at the Castle Church in Wittenberg, to which Karlstadt belonged, were angry because the chair which Karlstadt occupied at the university was one of the responsibilities which the elector of Saxony had assigned to the chapter house. Not the least of the reasons for their anger was his arbitrary decision to travel to Italy for the purpose of procuring the doctorate for both imperial and canon law, thereby qualifying himself for the position of provost at the chapter house. Karlstadt's announced intentions awakened rivalries, and jealous mutterings followed. In March 1516 Karlstadt actually received the doctorate in imperial and canon law in Siena. Basking in this new honor, he returned to Wittenberg. A doctorate from an Italian university carried high prestige, and Wittenberg, not daily honored by the recipient of such a prestigious degree, sought to retain him.

Karlstadt could not let Luther's attack against the scholastic authorities go unanswered. He was obligated by his name and position to take up Luther's challenge even though it was not directed at him personally. Karlstadt was not impressed with Luther's appeal to Augustine and the Scriptures. After all—and this was his chief argument against Luther—the scholastic doctors had also read them. Karlstadt was no doubt correct in this claim, but his argument did not shed much light, at least not on what Bible reading entailed, because the Bible is a mirror. The spirit that looks out of the biblical text is the same spirit which is read into the text. More risky for Karlstadt was his admission of Augustine as an authority, because Augustine is much clearer than the Scriptures even though, of course, one can also interpret his writings. But the Bible deals with the history of a people over a period of more than a thousand years. Augustine presents only the sum of one life, a life of rich subjective and objective experience in association with people and in the application of faith and dogma in the administration of the Church, but in the last analysis only a modest span of fifty to sixty years in contrast to the many centuries reflected in the Scriptures.

Augustine offers direct answers to questions raised in the Bible and in fact to precisely those very simple questions, which for centuries have been considered and reconsidered, concerning grace and whether or not man is able to act according to God's commands. Thus Augustine answers those questions addressed in Berhardi's disputation, which Luther had chaired.

This question of grace plays a great role in Christian pastoral care and ecclesiastical guidance. The word "grace" is the final answer to the question of what makes a person a Christian; since Golgotha, it has been synonymous with what gives man the power to do what God expects of him. The answer "grace" comes out of the experience of early Christian witness as well as from the logic of that concept of God by which this experience is interpreted.

Augustine lived approximately 350 to 400 years after the apostle Paul. The period of martyrdom marked by the early persecution of Christians was past; nevertheless, it was Augustine who, in the post-Pauline period, became the great Pauline theologian as the teacher of grace among the Church Fathers. Augustine is the first great introspective writer and autobiographer in Europe. He described and analyzed his spiritual development and also his travail for acceptance of Christian dogma. To be sure, he did not experience a conversion like Paul's. Augustine's mother Monica was a Christian; he had absorbed Christianity with his mother's milk.

Nevertheless, his Christian path was not without pitfalls and obstacles. That he would one day become bishop of Hippo Regius near Carthage in North Africa was not at all evident from his youth, but on his way to that spiritual office Augustine's inner experiences were analogous to those of Paul. If they were less striking than Paul's, at least they were of the kind which could provide insight into the central concept of Pauline theology; that is, Augustine himself was indeed a Christian, but not without error or blame. In his youth Augustine was merely a snobbish disciple of Mani, who, with his dualistic kingdom of light and kingdom of darkness, provided a theology which seriously rivaled Christianity. The teacher of rhetoric, Augustine, hated the Catholic Church until he overcame his Manichaeism and was ordained a priest although he had not done anything to deserve ordination. Conversion did not overtake him like a lightning bolt; through philosophical systems and by the renunciation of intellectual pride he drifted toward conversion. Augustine's conversion was thereby no less solid than Paul's.

Conversion to Christianity was for many the decisive experience of their lives. What was the impact of conversion and baptism? They were certainly not embraced for material gain because earthly goods could not be won by baptism. On the contrary, conversion and baptism entailed incalculable physical and material danger. Conversion for material benefit would have been incomprehensible to the early Christians; it would have contradicted all their experiences and would also have been difficult to reconcile with their true self-image. Early Christians were simple people: fishers, carpenters, custom officials, tentmakers, day laborers were the first to be converted. They knew little of doctrine and whom they should follow. The decision to convert came not out of knowledge but rather out of hope and faith. First a person believed and then he would acquire wisdom in order to sustain himself in the polemic battles. But why did some believe while others did not? If a shrug of the shoulders does not satisfactorily answer this question, the only other answer is that the Lord granted faith to some and not to others. The Lord must have granted faith by His grace without regard to outward appearance because not everyone who believed and was baptized distinguished himself from the unbaptized by demonstrating spiritual gifts or by leading a pious life.

At this juncture, one disconcerning question remains; Why does God give it to some to believe and not to others? This is a question critical to faith because here lurks the quarrel with God. The answer is that there is no answer. Thus faith is thrown back on itself: that God acts thus and not otherwise is the prerogative of His secret council and man does not need to know why. God has so decreed and the matter is settled. Precisely at this point the concept of God's majesty takes preeminence. Majesties cannot be queried; they can only be served and believed; they are to be revered. This ancient oriental view of God in all of its bluntness is conveyed by the Latin word *praedestination*.

A classic example that conversion to Christianity is not to be explained as one's personal achievement nor as a reward for past services, but that, on the contrary, conversion may indeed be imposed against the will, is that of the apostle Paul. Paul's persecution of Christians could hardly be considered a good work for which God was bound to reward him. Paul's will was contrary to that of Christ; he was thus a sinner. Conversion came to Paul by way of an external force which hurled him to the earth. That the sinner and persecutor of Christians was accepted as an ambassador of the gospel was a grace and a miracle. This fundamental experience determined Paul's theology, which revolved around sin, faith, and grace. It ascribed nothing to the natural strength and merit of man; it attributed to God all the effective work of salvation, and finally it embraced faith not as that which can be achieved by man but rather as that which is granted by the grace of God.

This theology has an advantage difficult to surpass: it lends itself very well to systematic thought. It is as simple and paradoxical as the event which initially inspired it: the work of salvation originates with God; before God man is only the object rather than the subject of salvation. Whoever permits himself to be convinced of this doctrine can breathe more easily insofar as the question of salvation causes him unrest: the responsibility for salvation lies with God. Martyrs are carved from this wood, because whoever does not depend on himself but trusts in God alone need not fear even before the gates of hell. That man of himself tends to evil and pride before God and the Church, and that being enlightened by the gospel is an undeserved manifestation of grace which finally leads out of the maze of pagan philosophy and heretical opinions, constitute the most important content of St. Augustine's inner experience. Weapons against Luther's theses could no more readily be found no less strongly in Augustine than in Paul. On the contrary, what Luther had summarized as theses within a few years through his intellectual reflection, his scholarly zeal, and his introspection was in accordance with Paul's experience on the Damascus road and with Augustine's long personal struggles that extended into his administration of a bishopric. The concept of grace as a gift was authenticated in the struggle against heresy and rival schools of thought.

Nevertheless, after Bernhardi's disputation, Karlstadt used Augustine to resist and contradict Luther. For this purpose Karlstadt procured the works of Augustine from Leipzig in January 1517 and began to study them intensively. He became so fascinated with them that he slipped into the very channel of thought which he had proposed to refute. It speaks for both Karlstadt's intellectual honesty and his ardor that he not only candidly declared himself defeated but that now he also composed 151 theses, presented in April 1517, in which he embarked on a course similar to Luther's.

Following Augustine, Karlstadt listed in his theses a series of fundamental, controversial theological subjects: "concerning the authority and credibility of the Church fathers," "concerning the outward and inner man," "concerning the efficacy of baptism," and most significantly, "concerning law and grace, letter and spirit" and "concerning predestination."

Karlstadt's theses evoked Luther's highest enthusiasm. Luther found them clearly, beautifully, and nobly expressed, surpassing the *Paradoxa* of Cicero in the same way that Augustine, or, more precisely, Christ, had surpassed Cicero.

Karlstadt employed Augustine against the scholastics. Because of his own persuasion Karlstadt was united with Luther in a common cause which for the moment overshadowed all else. Karlstadt attacked free will and praised justifying grace. This approach had determined the course of argument that Luther had pursued in chairing Bernhardi's disputation.

But Karlstadt had been persuaded by St. Augustine, not by Luther. Thus Karlstadt became Luther's independent partner, not his disciple. Karlstadt's theses were Augustinian, not Lutheran. Grace did not appear to Karlstadt as justifying faith, but as spirit which enabled man to fulfill the law. For Karlstadt Christ is the means for fulfilling the law, not, as for Luther, the end and the fulfillment of the law. In Karlstadt's view, man, infused by the spirit, remains somewhat the subject of salvation. For Luther, salvation can be only the act of God. With the small degree of responsibility ascribed by Karlstadt to the individual, we are once again on a detour. The newly capped jurist, the doctor of imperial and canon law, here reveals himself: he cannot liberate himself from the view that man must fulfill the law. Confronted with the concept of law, the theologian becomes ensnared by the jurist. As theologian, Karlstadt seeks salvation from God; as jurist, he seeks good deeds from man. In 1517 Luther took no offense at Karlstadt's view. Luther even sent Karlstadt's theses to Nuremberg and hoped for their dissemination.

In December 1516, before Karlstadt had consulted Augustine, Luther's name appeared for the first time on a publication. A preface of only thirteen lines was signed by "F. Martinus Luder." This short introduction was to a fourteen-page quarto entitled *A Spiritual Noble Little Book of Right Distinction and Understanding: what the old man is and what the new man is; what a child of Adam is and what a child of God is; how Adam should die and how Christ should grow in us.*

This spiritual pamphlet, a fragment of the writing of an unknown Frankfurt priest of the Teutonic order, probably fell into the hands of Luther coincidentally during one of his visitations. The pamphlet fascinated Luther. He discovered in it his own thoughts and his own views of human nature. Luther wrote to Spalatin, the librarian and secretary for the Elector, that a pure, solid theology, similar to ancient theology, could be read in German in this booklet. Neither in Latin nor in German had he found a theology healthier or more harmonious with the gospel than was found in this little book.

The joy of discovery did not blind Luther to the fact that the booklet did not correspond in all places to his views. To be sure, it stated that the virtuous deeds of man did not make him good, but it went on to state that goodness must exist within. The latter point expresses almost exactly the view that Luther criticized in Aristotelian ethics. Luther would agree that the exercise of the arbitrary will make one restless, but that Christ instilled peace in the heart; moreover, that disobedience was sin and existed in man's self-esteem, self-emulation, and self-serving pursuits in the belief that of himself man could accomplish something. By the end of 1516, all these ideas could have come from Luther himself. Nevertheless, one cannot assume, despite the high praise which Luther gives to the booklet, that he completely identified with it. Total endorsement was probably not his intention. It was enough that the most important passages corresponded to what Luther thought at that time about the scholastic view of man. This struggle so captivated him that he accepted every argument which could be employed for his cause. The struggle consumed him to such a degree that in his praise of the booklet to Spalatin, he asserted that not even Erasmus or Jerome, so highly regarded by Erasmus, could have written these pages. Here we have a clue of an irritability toward Erasmus, who in that same year began to publish the works of Jerome in order to create deliberately a rival to the authority of St. Augustine.

As Luther noted in the foreword, the Fankfurter, as the author of the booklet can be called, had written in the fashion of the illustrious Johannes Tauler, a mystic. The fundamental idea of mysticism—achieving union with God through meditation and the imitation of Christ—must have been uncomfortable for Luther, for in that idea there lurks something of human hubris (likeness to God), which transformed the angel of light, Lucifer, into the devil and brought Adam to the fall in paradise. It was probably not simply by coincidence that Luther omitted a passage of the booklet which dealt with man's union with God, for this did not appeal to Luther as the ideal of true piety. Nor did the idea of the imitation of Christ, which very easily could be misunderstood as an outward imitation, as pure mimickry in word and action. Rather, obedience to God's word in all things and permitting oneself to be completely captivated by it, while leaving Him his majesty, transcendence, and mystery, provided for the life of piety which gave direction to Luther's thought and quest. The ideal of such piety he found in the psalter, especially in Psalms 6, 32, 38, 51, 102, 130, and 143, which are known as the penitential psalms. The psalms captivated Luther and were the subject of his first lectures. Thereafter, he never put them aside, because here he found the relationship of man to God as clearly and amply described as he himself conceived of it. As a petitioning and praying sinner man stands alone before his God and addresses Him. Man's entire righteousness consists in the fact that he relies only on God and on no one else and that his reliance on God is without mediator second person, or other support. Standing naked before God, man cannot call attention to his good works, nor can he demand compensation for them. He may only hope that God will look kindly upon him and bestow His grace on him.

In his lectures, Luther always thought through new variations on this idea, illuminating it, explaining it to his students, and finally, with Bernhardi's disputation, bringing it before the faculty. But Luther did not wish this theme confined to disputation. This was more than a question of an interesting formulation in which the art of disputing could be cultivated. In this theme Luther had seized upon the meat of the nut, which he had sought to discover seven or eight years earlier.

If this idea really constituted the meat of the nut, then it concerned not only theologians; all must hear, read, and be acquainted with the matter. But that meant speaking and writing German, the language of the people, and not confining the message to the scholarly language, Latin.

Luther was not concerned about personal fame or approval, although it was important at the university to make a name for oneself and to be able to defend one's position and to vindicate one's theses with good argument. But the revocation of a thesis presented in a debate was not considered a disgrace, even though a professor owed it to his professional standing that such revocations did not occur too frequently. Luther's concern, however, was that he be understood and that he communicate his idea to all, and in order to be vindicated he was obligated to take seriously what he had to say and to regard it as truth.

To be understood meant to write German, and to be vindicated meant to secure for oneself the highest unimpeachable authority; to unite both understandig and vindication meant the translation of the word of God into German. Vulnerability, of course, still remained, but it was shifted from theology to philology.

To present the word of God in the German language was the logical and inevitable consequence of that conviction in Luther which cried for expression. In his lectures he occasionally resorted to German. From the pulpit in the Wittenberg city church he, of course, was obliged to preach in German, and now he must permit his pen, not just his lips, to do likewise. With the "spiritual, noble little book" he had made a beginning. However, the booklet was not God's word but only a theological opinion, albeit an attractive one for Luther. In the spring of 1517, just before Karlstadt composed his theses, Luther's German translation of the seven penitential psalms came off the press. This was his first successful publication. The first copies were sold out immediately and a new printing was needed to satisfy the enthusiastic demand.

The translation was a gamble that paid off, as the sale of the book testified. Luther had translated not from the Hebrew original but from the Latin Vulgate of St. Jerome. In order to be on firm ground Luther consulted one of Reuchlin's Hebrew editions of the penitential psalms, compared the Hebrew with the Latin text to establish the meaning as accurately as possible, and then translated into German. He had to accept that experts would find fault. It was, after all, the first time that he had attempted to translate passages of the Bible into German. Luther was confident with his Latin, which was his daily vehicle of communication. In this language he solved problems and communicated his ideas. But he did not speak Hebrew; he could only read it. Nevertheless, he was proficient enough in the language to interpret the nuance of thought and precision of expression of each Hebrew word. With respect to Hebrew, Luther had more confidence in the knowledge of his friend Johannes Lang than in his own. Therefore, in order that Lang could correct the manuscript for the printer Grunenberg, Luther sent his translation to Lang by a young Augustinian monk, Gabriel Zwilling, who was studying Greek with Lang in Erfurt. "The psalms are here translated and interpreted by me in our mother tongue, German, and even if they do not please anyone else, they please me very much," he wrote with unabated joy to Lang (WA BR I 93). But to translate and interpret the psalms and thereby to discover an attractive market among the public, set mocking tongues wagging. Luther countered by commenting that there was no need to distribute this little portion of Scripture among scholars. To underestimate what one had done, to diminish the accomplishment as though it were not worth mentioning—that was the custom of the day. Not for sophisticated Nurembergers but for raw Saxons, for whom Christian teaching could not be sufficiently digested in Latin, had he translated the psalms into German, as he wrote to Christoph Scheurl in Nuremberg.

Luther possessed a rich vocabulary enabling him to render the teaching readily digestible. Each psalm was printed in its entirety. Then he added the glosses verse by verse and line by line. From the biblical text he took whatever words and pictures he could discover. Thus he interpreted the Bible, immersed himself in the text, and made biblical authority his spokesman.

What he derived from the biblical text, interpreted, and enunciated was his view of God and man. This view was centered in his thought concerning the righteousness of God. His manuscript was an initial summary and brief synopsis of the fundamental idea of his theological investigation, presented not as a scholastic concept and categorial structure but rather as consolation to the reader and as pastoral guide for man's attitude before God.

The penitential psalms deal with penance, that is, what man should do when he is punished by God. From the very first verses of these psalms Luther is able to expand this theme to the question concerning the total situation of man before God, for he starts with a paradoxical postulate: in all suffering and temptation man should first of all flee to God and accept the suffering as having been sent by God, "whether the suffering come from the devil or people." The most consequential of all imaginable concepts lies at the root of this advice to the penitent: to regard God as the final cause of all events, even if such a view seems absurd; to posit a God who directs the devil and employs Satan as His tool. This God punishes in two ways: first, in grace as a good father, and temporally; second, in anger as a severe judge, and eternally. But since man does not know in which way the punishment will be applied to him, despair arises and he cries out: "O God, do not punish me in anger, let Thy chastisement be gracious and the punishment temporal; be father and not judge, as also Saint Augustine pleads" (WA I 159).

Luther's view of penance is as consequential and paradoxical as is his concept of God. The penitent should not pray for liberation from punishment, because that would not be favorable; on the contrary, he should plead to be chastised, but as a child is chastised by his father. An appropriate love for God is revealed in such a plea, because God should be loved not out of fear of hell or hope of heaven but for His own sake. Otherwise, piety is only self-love or even *amor dei concupiscentiae*, a love of God based on self-interest. As in Luther's lectures German words occasionally make their way into the Latin discourse now that he is writing in German (a German for "crude Saxons"); Latin terms name concepts for which German has not yet found a word, or Latin expressions organize ideas, thereby lending direction and clarifying purpose.

The direction which Luther's thought takes moves from teaching into life, out of theory into deed. God is such a being that He makes something out of nothing. Where something already exists, as in the case of one who sees himself as a saint, beware, for God can do nothing; but where nothing is, as in the case of a sinner, God can make of the sinner a saint. Therefore, get to know yourself and learn to hate yourself: do not seek righteousness in yourself, but in God, because

> all outward righteousness—works and actions—is not able to comfort the conscience and to take away sin. Despite all works and good deeds the impotent and terrified conscience remains until Thou shower me with Thy grace and lave me and thus create in me a good conscience so that I listen to Thy still, small voice, saying: "Thy sins are forgiven thee." This is afforded to no one except to him who hears; no one sees it, no one comprehends it. It is good to hear and the hearing of it makes for a comforted, happy conscience and trust in God. (WA I 189)

The forgiving of sins communicated by a still, small voice from God? And no one else hears it, sees it, or comprehends it? In his academic preoccupation, had Luther completely forgotten what it was his duty as ordained priest to pronounce and affect in the confessional? In the confessional there was no still, small voice from God; it was the clear word of the priest that was to be spoken: *Ego te absolvo ab omnibus peccatis tuis* (I absolve you from all your sins). Pronouncement of forgiveness was the duty of the priest, the obligation of his office, to which he, Luther, had been ordained ten years ago in Erfurt. The idea of the forgiveness of sins by still, small voice does not merely arise spontaneously. Rooted in Luther's view of man and God, this concept of forgiveness surfaces in the gloss of the fourth penitential psalm as a fully developed idea. The psalmist's apt and precise choice of words betrays that he is thinking in terms of the still, small voice, or in terms of the inner dialogue that accompanies thought. But voices here, voices there—while a priest must bind and loose! That is the reason that the priest through ordination participates in Peter's power of the keys; let him whisper who will! The priest must walk and act in the Petrine tradition. But doctrine, which every village priest could have communicated to him and which he himself knew so well, did not satisfy the teacher Luther. He was on his way to thinking himself beyond the priesthood in that ever more profoundly the thought of himself as being in the relationship of man standing alone before God, as man experiencing the relationship between the solitary penitent and God, which he found in the penitential psalmist.

"Hear my prayer, O Lord, give ear to my supplication: in Thy faithfulness answer me and in Thy righteousness," the psalmist prays in the first verse of the seventh penitential psalm (Ps. 143:1). Luther employs the glosses for this verse to define that concept by which his theology sounds an unchanging note: the righteousness of God. He writes: "Here it is to be noticed that the little expression 'Thy faithfulness and Thy righteousness' does not refer to God's inherent faithfulness and righteousness but rather to the faithfulness and righteousness imparted by grace through faith in Jesus Christ, as explained in Paul's epistle to the Romans, chapters 1, 2, 3" (WA I 212). Almost three decades later, in the last year of his life, Luther will describe this concept as the *justitia dei passiva* (passive righteousness of God) and will regard it as his greatest discovery: the suffering righteousness of God, as a righteousness which God suffers on behalf of man and which man does nothing to achieve; he may but submit and surrender to it. Suffering righteousness? This is only explicable in that Luther cannot conceive of God apart from Christ, that he sees God only through and in Christ. God's righteousness is the grace with which God through Christ makes us truly righteous, and, pursuing Luther's thought, we can confidently add here that there is no other righteousness.

This understanding of grace and righteousness—resulting from the tower experience, which cannot be exactly dated and which was probably arrived at after an evolution of thought—actually stands in the center of Luther's theology. This theology bears the thorns which increasingly prick the theological community and the ecclesiastical hierarchy.

At the foundation of Luther's theology lies a very specific theological question. The question is not concerned with divine attributes, which are concealed and are permitted to remain so. God interests Luther much more in His acts on behalf of man and in His word in which He reveals Himself. Thus Luther can write that God's faithfulness does not correspond to that faithfulness and righteousness with which God is faithful and righteous. A scholastic theologian would label such reflection presumtuous and immediately know how to lecture on the *aseitas* of God, the Being of God in Himself, so that every deed proceeds from an attribute or essence of the Acting One, and is made possible by the attribute or essence; thus the deed is simply the outflowing and the consequence of the attribute. These are fine points which were familiar to Luther, but they were not pertinent to what he was seeking. He was seeking neither God in Himself nor man

in himself but rather God before man and man before God. This relationship is determined, on the part of the Deity, by grace and mercy; on the
part of man, however, it is determined by sin which resides in man's nature
and by faith which Christ places in the human heart. Faith is the grace
which comes from God. Grace, faith, and righteousness are one and the
same thing. They cancel sin, but they cannot abolish sin. Sin remains; however, grace, faith, and righteousness are the signs that God does not hold
the redeemed accountable for sin.

These ideas came to Luther out of the Bible. In his lectures on the
psalms and on the epistle to the Romans he examined these ideas from
every angle. Luther also presented these ideas in his glosses on the penitential psalms. The kindred ideas which he had found in the "spiritual, noble little book" had fascinated him. Whatever he spoke about, whatever biblical theme he studied, he related to grace and to Christ. For him nothing
else seemed to exist or to be worth discussing.

Thus his critics, perhaps derisively, noted his monotony. Therefore, Luther, entirely lost in his subject and oblivious to all about him, finally in
the glosses answered his mockers:

> If someone says to me, "Can't you do anything but talk about human
> righteousness, wisdom, and strength, always interpreting the Scriptures
> by God's righteousness and grace and thus always plucking the same
> string on the lyre and constantly singing but one song?" I answer: "Let
> each one look out for himself. This is my testimony: the more I found
> only Christ in the Scripture, the more insatiable became my appetite; the
> more I found other than Christ, the poorer I became, so that it seems to
> me that God the Holy Spirit desires no more nor to know more than Je-
> sus Christ .... Christ is God's grace, mercy, righteousness, truth, wis-
> dom, strength, comfort and salvation, given to us by God, without any
> merit on our part." (WA I 219)

Luther answered with a confession of faith the criticism that he sang only
one song. Instead of seeking to evade criticism, Luther snapped it up.
From now on this would be his typical polemic. In fact, Luther sought confrontation. Who could have coerced him to become polemical, especially
in a little inspirational book, against unnamed opponents, if the conversations and discussions had not been a clear echo from his immediate environment? Thus the concluding gloss suggests what opinions and arguments
were circulating in the winter and spring of 1517 after Bernhardi's disputation, and also indicates that Luther desired to disseminate his ideas in a
wider audience beyond the university.

The fact that Luther continuously emphasized the same theme provided
his critics their first argument in favor of ignoring him. A second argument
against him was more weighty: his monotonic message was self-evident.
Luther echoed their mockery: "Who does not know," he recited, "that

without grace there is no good thing in us? And they believe that they understand it very well. Indeed, furthermore, if asked if they hold in low esteem their own righteousness, they are quick to reply, 'Of course. We know our own unrighteousness'" (WA I 219).

No one reacted. No one challenged Luther. What more did he want? Thus he was forced to bore more deeply. "It is a miserable, terrible blindness," he added, "that they who regard themselves in the high grade of perfection have never yet understood or tasted degradation. For how can a person be proud? Who is permitted to say that he is free from all pride and all evil inclination? For spiritual pride is the ultimate and deepest of all blasphemies because it has not yet escaped from human tendency." This is an argument from the "spiritual, noble little book." With this argument Luther drives the opponent into the corner and locks him into his sin. Luther accepts his opponent's concurrence and allows him to reason himself into a snare. Human tendency—as to concupiscence, the fleshly appetites, or even the spiritual tendency toward arrogance—is not a mortal sin; one is indeed not so blind as not to be able to distinguish venial sin from mortal sin.

This distinction between venial sin and mortal sin, with which Luther permits his imaginary opponent to argue, was common. Such a distinction facilitated confession because not every molehill could be made into a mountain. But Luther considered just such distinction as arrogance with which the proud in his blindness assailed Christ on his judgment seat. If the nature of man before God consisted entirely of sin, as Luther insisted, what sense did it make to categorize sin and to distinguish neatly between the severity or triviality, the pardonability or unpardonability, the temporal or the eternal nature of sin? Such distinctions led to acknowledging our debt before God for the sole purpose of haggling about the price to be paid rather than for the purpose of building on grace. "Therefore it is dangerous," Luther concluded, "to speak of venial sins in order that one might derive a security and false comfort which resists the fear of the Lord and secretly despises God's judgment" (WA I 220).

The Bernhardi disputation, the approval of Amsdorf, and Karlstadt's participation assured the victory of Luther's theology at the University of Wittenberg. Amsdorf had been at the university since its beginning in 1502, while Bernhardi and Karlstadt had been there since 1504, several years before Luther's arrival. These three respected men, all of whom had begun their careers at Wittenberg, placed themselves on Luther's side. With great satisfaction Luther could write to Johannes Lang on May 18, 1517: "Our theology and St. Augustine are making significant progress and, thanks to divine guidance, dominate our university. The study of Aristotle gradually declines. It stands before a complete nadir. The lectures concerning the *Sentences* for the most part evaded and no teacher can count on auditors who does not identify himself with this theology, i.e., with the Bible, St. Augustine, or some other teacher of ecclesiastical authority" (WA I 99). To be sure, such an euphoric evaluation made in the optimistic joy of his first victory was somewhat exaggerated, because the entire university had not yet been won over to Luther. In the following years there would remain much resistance to be overcome, and the study of Aristotle was not yet abandoned. But the trend toward Luther's theology was undeniable, and this success encouraged him. Up to this point Luther's emphasis had been on gaining knowledge from the Scriptures, but henceforth another emphasis was to become evident: he wanted to gain recognition for what he had learned from the Scriptures. Luther promptly assigned six or seven students to research themes of the new theology.

For one of these students, Franz Günther from Nordhausen, Luther prepared ninety-seven theses which, in a disputation on September 4, 1517, Günther defended against scholastic theology. The Bernhardi theses which had been disputed just one year earlier and which had not been prepared by Luther personally had surely become for the theological faculty an important sounding board, on which the echo had signaled the formation of a pro-Luther group at the university. But Bernhardi's theses sounded no reverberation outside Wittenberg. However, to these new theses Luther seemed to attach greater significance and to intend wider distribution from the very beginning. In any case he sent the Günther theses not only to Johannes Lang in Erfurt but also immediately to Christoph Scheurl in Nuremberg; he asked him to forward them to Johann Eck in Ingolstadt. In content the Günther theses go beyond Bernhardi's theses. At that time the theme of the disputation was whether or not man of his own power and without grace could will or do good. Luther, within his intellectual framework, now built on these thoughts and directed his thought against the recognized platitudes of scholastic theology as articulated by Duns Scotus, William of Occam, and Gabriel Biel—the intellectual authorities for nominalism, the *via moderna*. The human will was highly regarded by the nominalists. Their esteem for the will made them suspect to Luther. He wanted to dethrone them.

Luther did not attack Thomism. He did not need to liberate himself from Thomism; he was familiar with that school of thought but had never been captivated by it. However, his teachers in Erfurt had taught nominalism. Now he cut his ties with his former teachers. Luther was no longer a pupil; he was himself a teacher and had gained a profile of his own. Since his transfer to Wittenberg, Luther had won intellectual independence from his Erfurt teachers. His independence was buttressed by the quarrel concerning the recognition of his academic promotion at the University of Wittenberg and by the geographical distance between Erfurt and Wittenberg.

Martin Luther had achieved maturity and had found himself. This maturation was a step-by-step process of reaching forward while relinquishing the intellectual mentors who had commanded his respect until they became superfluous and were replaced by new authority. The entrance into the monastery had led him away from his father on the young man's own independent path. For one year a "fine old gentleman," his novice master, took him under his wing. With his profession he had become independent of his novice master and had become a monk among monks. But he did not long remain at that station. The rapid successive ordinations soon elevated him above the lay brothers in the monastery. Thus he became a priest of his order among other priests of his order. The study of theology elevated him still higher, above his fellow priests. Now responsibility for Luther's studies was assumed by his theology professors, under whose tutelage his respect for Aristotle—whom he had studied thoroughly in the school of liberal arts—waned. He received a short teaching tenure at Wittenberg, arranged by his Augustinian order. Now, for five or six years, the guidance of Johann Staupitz, his Augustinian superior, was clearly manifested in Luther's life.

The influence of his theology professors faded. Staupitz prepared the way for Luther's advancement at the University of Wittenberg and in the Augustinian order. Staupitz' visits to Wittenberg, however, became increasingly infrequent, and in 1516 he moved permanently to Nuremberg. For a few years, Jodocus Trutfetter, under whom Luther had studied in Erfurt, continued to teach in Wittenberg; he then returned to Erfurt. By the autumn of 1517, no one under whose authority Luther had previously found himself was any longer in his immediate environment. Martin Luther was now thirty-four years old; he accepted guidance no longer. He had become his own guide. Authority no longer surrounded him. Authority—the Bible—lay before him on his desk. Luther interpreted the Bible, and in his studies of Scriptures he permitted no one to be his guide.

Thus in the autumn of 1517 he was prepared for action. Bernhardi's disputation had been a reconnoitering and a preliminary skirmish. It had demonstrated an important fact: Luther was not alone; others also became persuaded by the authorities which Luther had introduced. From May 1517, his letters reveal the certainty of victory; Luther was confident and euphoric. What he now formulated and his student Franz Günther had to defend rang a much more aggressive tone than did Bernhardi's theses or Luther's own glosses on the penitential psalms. Luther had once heard from the bishop who had ordained him that without Aristotle no one could become a theologian. Now Luther contradicted that statement: "On the contrary, no one can become a theologian who does not become one without Aristotle" (WA I 226). According to Luther, it was heresy to believe that a theologian without logic was a monstrosity, and vainly did one imagine a logic of faith, because no syllogisms led to divine concepts. In brief, Aristotle agreed with theology as darkness agreed with light.

Luther insisted that we are not from the beginning to the end masters of our deeds, but rather slaves. We never became righteous because we practiced righteousness, but we practiced righteousness because we had been made righteous. Aristotelian ethics were the worst imaginable and the enemy of grace. It was a great error to believe that Aristotle's concept of happiness could be reconciled with Catholic teaching.

But what Luther said about Aristotle in the Günther theses did not open new fronts. On the contrary, Luther's conclusion pronounced the final verdict against a mode of thinking and a name which for years had filled him with increasing provocation. More significantly, in the Günther theses were indeed the paradoxical extremes of thought concerning sin and penance with which Luther in the concluding glosses of the penitential psalms had sought a dispute.

In these glosses Luther had his opponents consent to the teaching of grace with a shrug of the shoulder, and he sought to entrap them by accusing them of pride, the worst blasphemy. This approach was not long pursued because it was too obvious a play, and the monks were thoroughly familiar with the course of argumentation. Spiritual pride in those who considered themselves righteous was a great danger, and wherever possible it was implanted by the most clever trick of the devil. But now Luther seized upon the true doctrine of grace knotted together with the concept of predestination. Neither anti-Aristotelian invectives nor prideful humility gained further ground. Luther's doctrine of grace, however, was explosive. This doctrine now revealed its clear authority, the *sola* (only): only grace and nothing else. The Catholic Church had always recoiled before this doctrine; even St. Augustine's victory over Pelagius had proven only temporary. The Catholic Church could not and did not wish to renounce the cooperation of the human will in receiving grace. There were good reasons for the Church's reluctance, for if human nature was entirely corrupted and the free will of man could in no manner on its own with good intention turn toward the divinely offered grace, how could man be held responsible for what he did or did not do? If there was no free will, man continually stood before God only to be commanded—not even that, because he was unable to recognize his state of distress.

At the Council of Arausio in 540 the Church had drawn its conclusions from this dilemma and had attributed to free will the ability to cooperate in the preparation for the reception of grace. The Catholic Church steadfastly continues to affirm this position today, and this position has not proven to be a bad one for the Church of Rome. This dogma of human cooperation with divine grace corresponds beautifully with the doctrine of penance. If the penitent possesses free will, then he is ethically and morally capable of offering satisfaction and of being responsible before God and the Church.

With this interpretation a practice of penance could be established, in which regulated penalty for sin was imposed on the penitent. The penance would remove the guilt of sin and lead penitent, rehabilitated, back into the sacramental community. In this practice the Church merely followed the customs of Roman law. Furthermore, the Church no longer renounced society as in the first two or three centuries of early Christianity; society was now in fact represented by the Church. The formation of the practice of penance, in analogy to the Roman juridical process, favored that hardly avoidable integration of secular legal concepts and the concepts of the righteousness of God. Under these conditions Church and theology operated in ever stronger measure as elements of the established culture; in contrast, the Church and theology, in the days of the apostle Paul and, with diminished success, in the time of St. Augustine, established the leading ideas of a counter-culture.

But Luther oriented himself toward Augustine and, to an even greater degree, toward Paul, adopting their leading ideas. Thus, as Paul and Augustine had disavowed Roman society, Luther now rebelled against any element of theological thought which, on the basis of its ideological function, was favored in the prevailing society. Luther's teaching of grace and sin led to the outright denial of man's ability to stand legally before God. Thus Luther arrives at his rejection of the dogma of the confession and penance.

In the September theses, Luther articulated the *sola gratia*, the principle of grace alone, with irrevocable firmness. "The best and infallible preparation for grace and the only disposition for grace is the eternal election and predestination by God. From man comes only indisposition and even increased rebellion against grace, rebellion preceding the gift of grace .... It is not true that invincible ignorance entirely pardons, for ignorance of God and His good work in nature is always invincible" (WA I 225).

In a letter to Spalatin Luther elaborated on this last idea: "Each entire ignorance is innocence for us and there is no invincible ignorance aside from God's grace because we of ourselves can do nothing, but by the grace of God we can do all things; the more we seek wisdom the more we discover ignorance" (WA BR I 124).

This is formulated paradoxically, but the meaning is quite simple. Grace and sin have nothing at all to do with knowledge and ignorance—neither with complete wisdom or half wisdom, nor with guilty or innoecent (invincible) ignorance. This becomes clear in the following thesis: "There is no moral virtue which is not linked to pride or self-denigration, i.e., not linked with sin" (WA I 226). That means sin has nothing to do with virtue or morality. Sin is not immoral or unethical. Therefore, because sin is not a moral category but a theological one, it cannot be defeated by moral preaching.

Here is the heart of the matter. According to Luther, sin is never the object for ethical or moral teaching. That is why Aristotle cannot advise on these matters. Aristotle may serve philosophy but not theology. Theology deals with God, and, on that question, only the Bible speaks authoritatively.

Sin has nothing to do with what transpires between people; it is not a type of infraction which can be rectified. Sin pertains only to God. This concept of sin indicates once and for all the unique basic relationship between man and God; apart from this human-divine context, the concept of sin is meaningless. Sin is not virtue or nonvirtue; it is the human condition—thus the nature of man under the governance of God in the plan of salvation. If this statement were read from a moral point of view and not from a theological one it would lead to indignation, as it did for Luther before his tower experience.

But if the statement is read theologically, that is, if God is permitted to remain God and God is not thought of as a man, then the indignation disappears and even gives place perhaps to relief. At least this is apparently what happened to Luther, if we evaluate all those things which happened to him and what we know of his inner development up to 1516 or 1517.

Luther encouraged the theologians and everyone who was interested to recognize God as God and not to confuse God with morality. Luther sharply rejected the presumptions of the accepted morality of God. God does not bow before human morality. God needs no justification by human standards. Luther freed the concept of God from all the moralizing that integrated social concern. Thereby he completed a revolution in theology, which enabled him to play a role for revolution in society.

Chapter 4

"From a Pure Love for Truth":
With Faith, Against the Deceivers of the People
October 1517–March 1518

In his lectures and sermons, in his studies and meditations, there is no indication that Martin Luther ever conceived of transforming society. Occasionally critical remarks concerning this or that undesirable social condition were included in his lectures. But these criticisms did not exceed generalities; in fact, Luther's criticisms were never as cutting as were those enunciated by others. In the years 1516 and 1517, Luther was concerned not with social reform but rather with correct Christian doctrine. He was not prepared to compromise on this, and what appeared to him to be true he wanted to express, disseminate, and confirm. Luther did not view the social order to be necessarily unchangeable, but in comparison to questions of salvation, social questions seemed to him secondary and insignificant. Nevertheless, it is essential to review sixteenth century society if the impact of Luther's theology is to be understood.

At the beginning of the sixteenth century, society still bore the clearly delineated stamp of feudalism, but it also contained the sprouting seeds of an early capitalism which, within the existing structure, hastened social differentiations and inconsistencies. This early capitalism caused confrontations and led to frequent bloody conflicts and to louder and more frequent cries for reform. From about the middle of the 1470s until the beginning of the 1490s a wave of unrest, tumult, riot, and bloody confrontation swept over the cities: Augsburg, 1475–1478; Cologne, 1481; Hamburg, 1483; Regensburg, 1485; Zittau, 1487; Braunschweig, 1488; Osnabrück, 1489–1490; Rostock, 1489–1491. In the Tauber valley in 1476 there arose in association with pilgrimages a socio-religious movement led by the shepherd Hans Boheim of Niklashausen, in which for the first time under the invocation of "The Righteousness of God" the feudal social order was seriously called into question. In 1493, 1502, 1513, and 1517 the authorities in Alsace, in the Breisgau, in the Black Forest, and in the Rhine-Main region were discomfited by the Bundschuh, a peasant secret organization which prepared itself for violent revolt. Each time before the assault could be carried out, however, the planned uprising was discovered in the confessional and exposed.

Since 1509, the aforementioned "mad year" in Erfurt, a second wave of urban riots had crested over Schwäbisch Hall in 1511, Nordhausen, Speyer,

and Ulm in 1512, Aachen, Braunschweig, Göttingen, Cologne, Neuss, Nordlingen, Regensburg, Schweinfurt, and Worms in 1513, and Höxter in 1514.
The greatest urban unrest corresponded exactly with Luther's immersion
in the psalms and his search for Christ in the psalter. In 1514 in Württemberg the "Poor Conrad" movement arose as a result of increased taxation
and financial mismanagement.

If the uprisings signaled increased activity from below, the authorities
from above were not completely inactive: they attempted with imperial reforms to stabilize their position of power and to put in order the court system and the defense system, to establish domestic tranquillity, and to balance the imperial budget. These attempts at reform were not completely
successful. Failure was due not only to the conflicting interests of the emperor and the princes but mainly to the confusion concerning the financing of the Reichsregiment, the proposed executive organ of the empire
that was to embrace the imperial government, courts, and armed forces.
Since there was no operational imperial executive organ, the proposed imperial taxes—the so-called common penny—could not legally be collected;
since taxes were not collected, the imperial executive organ could not be
established. A *circulus vitiosus,* or devil's circle, was thus drawn.

If the ruling class demonstrated that it was unable to reform the empire,
it also failed in its relationship vis-à-vis the most noticeable phenomenon
of early capitalism, the great commercial houses or monopolies. It was not
without justification that popular opinion held the monopolies responsible
for the rising prices which everywhere were noticeable. Owners of small
and medium-size businesses, artisans, and entrepreneurs felt oppressed by
the monopolies. Princes and nobles reacted with displeasure to the increasing political weight of these financial powers, especially as the princes and
nobles often found themselves in debt to the monopolies. Thus in the first
half of the sixteenth century an antimonopolistic movement formed which
increasingly determined public discussion. Anticapitalistic tendencies
were, to be sure, articulated in the movement, but it was not all purely conservative or profeudal. The movement gave expression also to the interests
of the smaller or more modest early capitalist entrepreneurs who were
threatened by the power of the monopolistic association. Under the influence of this antimonopolistic movement, the Reichstag, convened at Trier
and Cologne in 1512, issued a prohibition against monopoly. The prohibition, however, proved ineffective because neither the emperor nor the
princely authorities desired, by severe strictures, to trifle with the good
will of those whom they needed as lenders. Thus although the antimonopolistic movement was confirmed by Reichstag authority, it was disappointed in its expectations, which inevitably would lead to the radicalizing
of demands and actions.

Urban and peasant unrest, the Reichstag reform efforts, and the antimonopolistic movement were promoted by very different class interests. These classes pursued opposite and contrary goals; nevertheless, their singleness of purpose bound them together: they all wanted to change the existing conditions in order to be able better to represent and protect their respective interests. Because they espoused the same cause, the same fate was decreed for all: they failed. Temporary successes soon dissipated. Again and again the same scenarios, the same impulses, the same demands—all were in vain, with no relief, no solution to the prevailing questions. This condition prevailed for two or three decades. The situation may truly be described as a crisis.

The reaction of social forces to the new objective conditions took two principle directions. The one thrust attempted to change the objective conditions; the other thrust, however, was aimed at the alteration by their own will of the mentality of individuals and social groups as they created a new picture of themselves and of their society and determined their own position in this new world. The paths of the two thrusts frequently intersected. In pursuing these paths, the populace was undergoing a social education. Despite defeats and setbacks, a new dynamic was finally born which overcame the frustrations associated with the learning process, sparked a revolutionary movement, and led to permanent transformation.

The first thrust found expression as the social and political conflicts exploded in increasingly violent confrontations between the opposing forces, whose unrest provoked repressive reaction by the ruling powers. This development is demonstrated by the chronology of the uprisings, conspiracies, and riots. The second thrust was more complicated and paradoxical. In the first, dissidents challenging the social order placed moral blame on the existing conditions and thereby achieved for themselves a new self-awareness and justification for their demands and actions. The second thrust was characterized by greater willingness to do penance, by religious subjectivity, and by increased and intensified pious deeds. Pilgrimages, religious hysteria, increased religious commerce, processions, recitation of the rosary, rumors of miracles, increased interest in astrology, prophesying and interpretation of signs as well as pronouncements concerning the end of the world, the last judgment, and the dance of death in contemporary instructive art characterize this movement.

People caught in the dynamics of this thrust tended to blame themselves for the woeful conditions, to accuse themselves or a supernatural power which could be placated by penance to ameliorate the conditions. Of course, such practices had always existed. They belonged to the normal systematic oscillation of society, but in the early sixteenth century they were multiplied. The second thrust toward solving existing problems was also expressed in the basic quest for a realistic view of the world and of man as mirrored by many German humanists in the art of the time, espe-

cially by Albrecht Dürer, Lucas Cranach, Hans Holbein, Matthias Grünewald, and other great artists. The ruling classes and the established powers
could no longer control the situation with reprisals alone. These rulers be-
stirred themselves with religious excitement, indulged the preachers of
penance, and patronized the artists. Furthermore, a group of princes articulated demands for change: for example, in the *Gravamina* (complaints
against Rome), in attempts at imperial reform, and with the prohibition of
monopolies. Their inability to implement the desired reforms aggravated
their frustration. Thus there developed within the opposing forces as well
as within a great part of the ruling class the need for new ideas and concepts, the willingness to test them, and, if they proved valid, to adopt
them.

In this second trend, a central role may be ascribed to Luther. He offered
something new which led out of the crisis, affected permanent change, and
thereby created a new point of departure for further historical development. Luther seized upon a specific sector: theological justification for the
prevailing order. More exactly he reformulated the concept of God—the
highest possible value conception, the highest and ultimate tenant of all
theology. His effort was of exceptional intellectual brilliance and—should
this idea seize the masses—of unforeseeable impact. Because of the crisis
situation in early sixteenth century society, the probability that such an
idea would seize the masses was stronger than ever before.

Luther's subjective views and attitudes with respect to the condition of
the Church interfaced well with the subjective needs of the society. In Luther's deepest conviction, what happened or did not happen in the
Church, what was to be done or left undone, should be determined by
Christ's reason for coming into the world. The Church was to preach
Christ's gospel, and wherever a servant of the Church failed to carry out
this mission in the correct manner, he was to be opposed.

Luther's opinion consistently corresponded to the Church's obvious assumption regarding itself and the manner in which it was to interact with
society. That the Church understood itself to be the dispenser of salvation
was simply the somewhat mystical expression of its real and, for society,
very important function of offering man a substitute for what, under existing conditions, could not be offered by the society: comfort. This role of
the Church rightfully belonged to society, unable to fulfill its obligation because it was riddled by an irreconcilable class order.

But the Church's social function was not limited to the dispensing of salvation. It was also a significant patron of architecture and art. In addition,
it operated as a career institute which stood open to the masses whose ta-
lented children the Church promoted, educated, and bound to itself by the
granting of social prestige. The Church's buildings were centers for public
communication, the pulpit a form of media for influencing public opinion.

But the Church was also an exploiter. On its huge estates it held the peasants in feudal dependence and fleeced them not infrequently with the same indifference with which the secular feudal lords exploited their workers. Moreover, in many areas of Germany, especially in the Rhine region (described as "Priest Alley"), the Church exercised secular authority. Three prelates—the archbishops of Cologne, Trier, and Mainz—were electors of the Holy Roman Empire, which meant that, together with the duke of Saxony, the margrave of Brandenburg, the count of the Rhine Palatinate, and the king of Bohemia, they possessed the privilege of electing the emperor. The lower clergy—various types of priests—and their acolytes often remained closely associated with the common people from whom they came, while the higher ecclesiastical ranks—abbots, bishops, and archbishops—usually but not always sprang from the ranks of the nobility. This latter group employed the Church to preserve the interest of the ruling feudal class and enlisted it as an instrument of feudal authority. In this role the Church also stood watch against revolutionary activity which, for example, broke out in the Bundschuh movement and was betrayed by means of the confessional. Thus any social movement was bound to collide continuously with the Church while, on the other hand, changes in the Church could not occur without corresponding social impact. Despite all characteristics attributed to the Church as peculiar to it, society in toto was reflected in the Church.

In that Luther wrestled to discover what the Church was or should be, he dealt with a central realm of the society of that day, and he saw through the prism of the Church what the world around him was. This insight into society as reflected by the Church brought about the broader influence of his theologizing, incited a response to his ideas, and led to an acceptance of them, whether or not he had anticipated that they should be so well received. Metaphorically speaking, he read the Bible with a view colored by social problems, and he measured his society with a view colored by his reading of the Bible.

Until September 1517, Luther had fully expended his energies at the University of Wittenberg to disseminate what he understood as correct teaching. This was accomplished through lectures and disputations. A few weeks after the disputation of Franz Günther's theses Luther instigated an academic disputation of theses that he now made public concerning the misuse of indulgences. He is said to have posted his public announcement on the door of the Castle Church in Wittenberg on October 31, 1517. There is a question as to whether or not the posting of these theses occurred in the manner usually described, but the probability is in favor of the traditional account because the door of the Castle Church was the university's bulletin board, and it was customary to post information there concerning such academic matters as lectures and disputations. Whether or not the theses actually hung on the door is insignificant academic triviality in view of the fact that Martin Luther from this point on was drawn into a strife which expanded to ever increasing dimensions and which within a few years had shaken not only the Church but also the entire social order.

With these theses Luther desired at first only to attack the abuse of indulgences and to accuse the indulgence hawkers. His attack was not at first leveled against the entire Church. A servant of the Church who was an indulgence hawker, the Dominican Johann Tetzel from Pirna, antagonized Luther because Tetzel did not conduct himself in accordance with the gospel. He was a salvation salesman. He had holy merchandise to sell— indulgences. An indulgences was a printed letter stating that the bearer or the person named in it was released from so many years of the temporal penalty imposed by the Church for sin. Luther considered the practice of selling indulgences to be a swindle, but the Church needed money.

Because everyone had some minor or major sins on the talley and was thus obligated to do penance, indulgences were very practical and not at all unpopular. The degree of penance was revealed to the sinner in the confessional. It was the sinner's obligation to examine his conscience and to determine when, where, how often, whether alone or with others he had committed an offense against divine and ecclesiastical commands. Confession handbooks assisted the sinner in searching his consience. The ten commandments given by God to Moses on Mount Sinai, along with detailed explanations that classified each command under a simple heading and demonstrated what personal action violated each command, were contained in the handbooks. Thus the sinner in examining his conscience had to ask himself, among other things, how often he had blasphemed, how often he had failed to attend Sunday Mass, and how often he had violated feast days by working. He had to ask himself if he had been insubordinate toward his parents or the authorities; if he had physically injured or perhaps even killed someone; if he had remained continent or had submitted to fleshly lusts; if he had lied, stolen from his neighbor, or defamed him; if he had coveted his neighbor's wealth or his goods; if he had regarded his neighbor's wife with sexual lust. The confessional handbook also required the sinner to answer whether these sins had been confined to thought, had been verbally expressed, or in fact had been translated into act.

After the sinner had thus examined his conscience, he was obligated to confess contritely to the priest in the confessional the sins of which the sinner was aware. Having heard the confession, the priest granted the penitent absolution; that is, the priest absolved the penitent of his sins and assigned to him a penance, which consisted of prayers, fasts, and almsgiving. For daily little sins the matter was not so complicated: a few Our Fathers and Hail Marys, an additional day of fasting, and a few pennies, heller, or groschen in the collection plate, and the penitent could breathe a sigh of relief; he could attend Mass, receive Communion, and go about his daily chores with a good conscience. Though new assaults and temptations waited for him, they need not trouble him further because, after all, the confessional continuously remained available to him. One could live with that arrangement. This Catholic penitential custom was practical and humane.

However, it had its pitfalls, especially for those who took the word of the Church seriously and for whom Church and faith were more than hereditary custom. The belief that each sin had to be purged by penitential satisfaction before the penitent could enter heaven was insidious. If one should die in sin, that is, without having confessed or without having received absolution, heaven remained closed to him. And since death could overtake one at any time, there always remained a factor of uncertainty. The disquietude and insecurity were caused not so much by the fate which awaited the sinner mired in mortal sin; on the contrary, such a case was clear. The fate of such a sinner was eternal damnation in hell.

That is why mortal sins were called mortal: they resulted in the spiritual death of the believer because they completely diverted and hindered divine grace. The seven major sins—pride, greed, lust, envy, gluttony, anger, slothfulness—were mortal sins. In these sins all others had their origin, especially the sins against the Holy Spirit—unbelief, dispondency, despair, and blasphemy as well as the four sins that cried out to heaven: murder; sodomy; exploitation of the poor, widows, and orphans; and the deprivation of a just wage.

Whoever committed these sins was spiritually dead, so that not even the thought of hell was especially disturbing because he did not believe any longer. Hell is no terror to unbelievers. The Church, however, could assist the believer because it possessed the means of grace. According to medieval teaching, Jesus, the martyrs, and the saints laid up a treasury of merit in heaven. This treasury was administered by the Church, and from it merit could be ascribed in necessary cases to the contrite sinner. These means of grace were infallible in their effect solely because the Church (that is, the ordained priest) dispensed them. Their effect did not depend on the faith or the worthiness of the recipient or whether or not the dispensing priest led an exemplary life or possessed true faith. This teaching transmitted a certain security because it freed the conscience of the recipient from doubt and scruples.

More dangerous than the mortal sins, however—as paradoxical as it may sound—were the venial sins: the little careless miscues of the soul in daily life. These venial sins did not completely exhaust grace but only weakened and diminished it. They did not burden the conscience as heavily or clamor for grace as forcefully as did mortal sin and, therefore, could easily be overlooked in the examination of the conscience before confession. Furthermore, the probability that one would die with venial sin on the soul was much greater than the probability that death would surprise one with unconfessed mortal sins. Venial sins were of the same nature as the seven major sins except that they were milder in form and, so to speak, of more limited import: laughing in church, malicious gossip, gleeful pleasure in the obscene, a little carelessness in the weighing of goods, one beer too many, gluttony at the table, and other indulgences that make life pleasant.

For such sins one was not sent to hell, but neither was one admitted immediately to heaven, because the soul first had to be purged from these impurities. The purging took place in purgatory. Purgatory was a certainty for almost everyone, and hardly anyone realized the possibility of completely avoiding it. Purgatory was thought to be under the earth or on the other side of the earth. In it the soul had to simmer and to undergo physical pangs for a prescribed time until it was purified; then the perfected soul could ascend to heaven and there be permitted to behold the eternal glory of God. No one could know how long the purification would take, but, since heaven reckons with eternities, periods of centuries or perhaps even millennia were possible. It is, therefore, understandable why purgatory was more terrifying than hell.

It was fortunate that the Church had a solution for the fear of purgatory, but that, after all, was the purpose of the Church: to assist tormented souls. The prayer of the Church reached into the other life, ascending into heaven and bringing down grace. Prayer for the souls of the dead belonged, since earliest Christian times, to the assumptions of the life of faith. It is thus not at all surprising that one day the idea was born that the ecclesiastically administered heavenly treasury of grace was meant not only for the living but also for the dead, to shorten their period in purgatory. This idea was an essential precondition for masses for the dead and for making available to the Church testimonial bequests supporting priests and altars that, after the death of the benefactor, were to provide continually for his spiritual benefit. Thus belief in purgatory came to be, one might say, institutionalized. Purgatory had a threefold social function: it promoted the growth of mortmain, that is, the secular possessions of the Church; it justified the existence of an ever increasing number of a specific group in the priesthood who were occupied with the offices for the dead; and it provided the ideal motivation for believers to acquire firm guarantees and security for the period after death. Purgatory was an ideal means to bind the individual closer to the Church.

Fundamental to the functioning of this system—essentially a social system—was the idea of representation. The individual does not stand alone before God; the Church represents him in eternity. In dialectical fermentation purgatory became not only a terrifying threat to fearful souls but also the leaven enabling the Church to serve as mediator for man.

The concept of representation suggested the possibility of satisfying the penance requirement by other means or in fact of having penance vicariously performed by others. This custom developed first after the fall of the Roman Empire. It reflected aspects of Roman Law to which the Church had adapted as it now adapted to social circumstances and the legal concepts governing the gradual feudalization of the Germanic kingdoms in which old Germanic laws prevailed. For example, that the wergeld could compensate for bodily harm (including homicide), thereby morally rectifying the abridgment of law, was one of the fundamental stipulations under the old Germanic laws. Moreover, this was one of the measures that for its time was very rational and progressive because it showed how to avoid the urge for blood vengeance and dispensed with the concept of revenge: merciless "eye for an eye, tooth for a tooth." Christ had announced the forgiveness of sins; He died on the cross to procure this forgiveness. Roman legal concepts, apart from the teaching of the forgiveness of sin, had imposed a demand for satisfaction. *Satisfactio*, the compensation for the sin, had become the condition for the forgiveness of sin. Germanic legal concepts diminished the demand for satisfaction by introducing the possibility of substituting service. Roman and Germanic legal traditions along with the concepts of late antiquity and early feudalism added to the Christian gospel: satisfaction in the prescribed form or in acceptable substitutionary service were now prerequisite for the forgiveness of sins.

This conclusion was the exact opposite of what Christ had bequeathed in His gospel because it was just for that reason—the forgiveness of sins— that He as God had become man and had had to die on the cross: man by his own effort was not adequate to achieve satisfaction before God or justification before the divine presence. At least, this is what Lutheran theology teaches.

The more European society became feudalized, the more the Church distanced itself from its early Christian origins and its formative period during late antiquity; and the more firmly the practice of confession and penance became established in the Church, the more the Church was penetrated by feudalistic concepts concerning substitutionary service. To be sure, the Christian concept of forgiveness and the Roman idea of satisfaction were not completely suppressed. The indulgence system challenged by Luther had its roots in the feudalization of the forgiveness of sin.

As early as the sixth century, imposed penance could occasionally be satisfied by substitutionary service, and after this custom had been established the popes of the late Middle Ages seized on it during the period of the crusades. At first the custom was employed to enlist troops. Pope Urban II in 1095 promised the crusaders pardon from all imposed penance. This became especially attractive when land was promised in Palestine. But a crusade to the Holy Land was difficult and full of danger. The nobles were prone not to embark personally on a crusade but rather to equip one of their servants and send him. The popes, happy to be able to mobilize troops at all in the face of bitter Islamic opposition, promised indulgences to the nobles for this vicarious service.

Soon the popes permitted indulgences for money contributions for a crusade. The popes followed a general trend in feudalism; just when the crusades were taking place, the most progressive regions of Europe were demonstrating a transition from payment by work and production to money payment. The feudal lords now demanded from the peasants not only the cultivation of the demesne or the presentation of agricultural products like grain, milk, eggs, poultry, or cattle; money was primarily what they now wanted.

This gradual development of a money economy was the economic prerequisite for the fact that indulgences could—having been granted for money—be developed into a profitable source of income for the Church. It was necessary that indulgences become an object of sale which had a useful value and for which the price could be escalated to the ceiling.

The useful value of indulgences was established by the Church itself: it created a need on the part of its communicants and then satisfied that need with indulgence letters. Because of the yearning for security and eternal salvation and the dread of purgatory, prices could easily be lowered because indulgences were no longer sold to cover all sins for all time. Instead, they addressed the nature of the sin committed, and the effectiveness of the indulgence was limited. The kinds of indulgences were increased, the life span of the product was diminished, and the profit was thereby escalated.

The greatest increase in the distribution of indulgences was realized through the penance letters and the fast letters. The penance letters permitted the possessor to procure complete indulgence at confession; that meant that he could confess without thereafter having to perform such works of penance as praying, fasting, almsgiving. Such penance letters could be issued for long term use throughout one's life or for one or more applications within a certain period. The fast letters, like the penance letters, canceled a religious requirement: they permitted the possessor to eat egg and dairy products during fasts.

The indulgence for the poor souls in purgatory, which Pope Sixtus IV promulgated in 1476, was a striking novelty. With this bull the souls of the deceased could be completely freed from purgatory, or, in the case of limited funds, their period of anguish could at least be significantly reduced. Because almsgiving in the Middle Ages was a matter of social prestige, the procuring of purgatory indulgences was a mark of piety appropriate to a "respectable" reputation.

The indulgences that Tetzel sold remind one, in a certain way, of a construction lottery. One half of the indulgence income was earmarked for the costs of building St. Peter's Church in Rome; the other half was earmarked to cover the debt to the papal curia incurred by the archbishop of Mainz, Albrecht of Brandenburg. This debt amounted to 21,000 gulden, the fee for the acknowledgment by the curia of his election to the archbishopric of Mainz after he had in 1513 already become the administrator of Halberstadt and Archbishop of Magdeburg. The Fuggers had lent Albrecht the 21,000 gulden plus an additional 9,000 gulden.

The Augsburg Fuggers were the most famous banking house in Europe. They financed the political adventures of the Hapsburgs, and by this connection the Fuggers acquired rights to silver mining in the Tirol and in Slovakia. Naturally the Fuggers also enjoyed a close business connection with the papal curia. Thus they found a pleasant way to make money. By lending to Albrecht of Brandenburg they enabled him to participate in the St. Peter's indulgence. Pope Julius II had proclaimed Peter's indulgence in 1506. In 1515, Julius' successor, Leo X, promulgated a bull concerning Peter's indulgence in the provinces of Mainz and Magdeburg, as well as the areas subject to Albrecht of Brandenburg as the archbishop of Mainz and Magdeburg and bishop of Halberstadt, and the margravate of Brandenburg.

From the indulgence revenue the archbishop of Mainz was permitted to employ half of the profit to satisfy his debt. For permission to pay his debt to the Fugger banking house out of indulgence revenues, Albrecht was required to pay an additional 10,000 gulden to the papal curia. The other half of the monies collected went directly to the pope. The financial account of the entire indulgence sales was taken over by the Fuggers while the necessary preaching and sale of the indulgences in the several ecclesiastical provinces were conducted by specially commissioned clergy named by the archbishop. For the Magdeburg province, to which Wittenberg belonged, the provost Johann Gerthink and the Leipzig Dominican Johann Tetzel were named.

Martin Luther was completely unaware of all these background details. But it soon leaked out that the Fuggers had their hand in the game and that the entire enterprise was an arrangement of great intrigue to assist the Hohenzollerns out of their financial trouble, as migth have been suspected in view of the fact that the indulgences were promulgated in Hohenzollern territory. At least Hohenzollern envolvement seemed obvious to Frederick the Wise, Luther's prince, and to Frederick's cousin, Duke George the Bearded, from Albertine Saxony. Duke Frederick and Duke George did not permit themselves to be impressed in any way with the papal bull, and they forbade the sale of the indulgence in their respective territories. Since Duke Frederick and Duke George had sought but failed to place a member of the House of Wettin in the bishopric of Magdeburg and in the archbishopric of Mainz, they had no intention of permitting salt to be rubbed into their wounds by financing the success of the Hohenzollern rival with money from their Saxon subjects.

Therefore Luther did not have to reckon with difficulty from Duke Frederick when he penned his Ninety-Five Theses against the abuse of indulgences. Thus were the Ninety-Five Theses introduced:

> Out of love for truth and the striving to establish truth, under the sponsorship of the honorable Father Martin Luther, Master of Arts and of Sacred Theology and Professor of Theology at Wittenberg, the following theses will be disputed. Thus he requests all who cannot be present to present their arguments in writing. In the name of our Lord Jesus Christ, Amen. (WA I 233)

The posting of the theses was only a formality rather than an actual call for academic debate. In any case the call was not for one of the regular disputations which the university, according to its charter, was required to conduct from time to time. Such disputations were arranged by the faculty with a definite date set on which the disputation would take place. Luther's indulgence disputation, however, was neither called for nor scheduled by the faculty, nor did it ever take place. Luther acted on his own initiative without preliminary discussion with the university community. His action can be reconciled, however, with his authority as professor. His approach provided the possibility for a long view of the subject, a stimulus to discussion of a theme for which a formal disputation might be convoked if disputants should emerge. Karlstadt had followed the same course with his theses in April.

Luther's procedure is a sign that he knew he was taking up a much more difficult matter than a mere academic disputation about still-undefined teaching. Up to that time he had disputed about grace, about man who was a sinner and whose good works were invalid before God, against Aristotle and scholastic theology. But this time the dispute concerned the Church—what it practiced but ought not to. The questions Luther now took up did not reside exclusively within the province of university professors and some intellectuals in the Church. It was rather the honor of the pope as well as the interests of an archbishop that these questions touched upon. Caution as well as diplomacy would be required in the formulations. But, caution notwithstanding, what in Luther's opinion had to be said—that the sale of indulgences was a religious swindle, an exploitation of the people—indeed had to be said.

The foundation of what Luther wanted to proclaim was a bold statement, formulated in the first thesis: "Since our Lord and Master Jesus Christ says do penance, etc. (Matt. 4:17), He intended that the entire life of the believer should be penance." This was a bold interpretation because, while such an interpretation of the words ascribed to Jesus was indeed possible, it cannot be demonstrated that such an interpretation is incontrovertible. However, it is derived from all the ideas which Luther had worked out concerning the position of man before God in the procuring of salvation, and it enabled Luther to avoid a discussion concerning the accepted pronouncements for the sacrament of penance. Luther concluded in a second thesis that Jesus' words concerning penance cannot be applied to the sacrament of penance, which is administered by the priestly office. With this claim Luther raised the question to the level of biblical interpretation, for which he knew himself well prepared and which was associated with his teaching duties and talent; he created for himself a space for discussion without reference to dogmatic pronouncements. This posture also enabled Luther to sweep from the table in one gesture all theories concerning the various kinds of penance and with them that attempt to achieve satisfaction before God and the Church: the penalty remains "as long as the hate for oneself remains—that is, the true heartfelt contrition—thus until heaven is achieved" (thesis 4). For Luther's third thesis stated that Jesus' word was not applied only to an inner penance, which would be no penance at all if it did not lead to many outward works that affect the mortification of the flesh. But the mortification of the flesh, as understood from Luther's earlier concept of the nature of man, was ineffective because human nature with its unchanging drives tended toward sin.

The Ninety-Five Theses were a logical culmination of the fundamental concepts gained through the disputations of Bernhardi and Franz Günther and the lectures in wich these concepts were developed. But if the penalty remained as Luther maintained in the fourth thesis, of what purpose was the power of the keys, bequeathed by Jesus to Peter and thus to the pope and the Church? Without here mentioning all consequences, suffice it to say that Luther with this thesis shook the foundation of the entire concept of the Church. In contrast to the trend of thought of the fourth thesis, the following theses seem worded with what are generally recognized as conciliatory statements and concessions to common platitudes: for example, God did not forgive the guilt of anyone without "at the same time humbling him in all things to subject him to His deputy, the priest" (thesis 7).

Luther permitted this caution to govern in all his theses relating to the power and authority of the pope. He approached the pope with the greatest imaginable flattery. The Holy Spirit spoke through the pope. This sounds unquestionably orthodox and devout, but it was a defensive shield in order to permit the following outrageous insolence to be unleashed. For example, each priest had, in reference to purgatory, the same authority as the pope. The pope, moreover, did not desire that indulgences should be equated with works of mercy. He needed prayer more than money and would have preferred to see St. Peter's Church in ashes rather than erected from the hide of his sheep; besides, indulgences granted no salvation even if the pope himself were guarantor. The pope could cancel only the penalties that he himself had imposed. Every Christian who was truly contrite had a right to forgiveness and did not need an indulgence (thesis 36).

Thesis 36 stands in juxtaposition to thesis 4, in which Luther had postulated that the penalty remained until entrance into heaven. If thesis 4 is taken seriously, then thesis 36 has meaning only under the condition that Luther, for the purpose of the disputation, placed it facetiously on the floor of valid dogmatics, either to scrutinize it more thoroughly or, perhaps, to escape the accusation that he negated everything associated with the sacrament of penance. This thesis gives a clear indication of how carefully Luther had to tack in the slippery currents of the indulgence question.

The pope himself is good but he has bad advisors; this thought runs through the entire Ninety-Five Theses. It corresponds with a general intellectual attitude that, analogously, is always observed in the early phases of the bourgeois movements against the feudal monarchies. The monarch, as far as possible, was excused from criticism, which consequently was directed all the more sharply against the ministers, officials, or other advisors. The ideology of the Middle Ages and of early modern times also gives expression to this monarchism. It serves as a precautionary tactic.

Luther was not free of this thought pattern; his conduct was channeled in the traditional modes. "Let him who speaks against the truth concerning papal indulgences be anathema and accursed." "Let him who guards against the lust and license of the indulgence preachers be blessed" (theses 71 and 72).

The theme of the difference between a good pope and the evil indulgence preacher served Luther's purpose for formulating unpleasant questions addressed to the pope. "These insolent indulgence sermons," as they are called in thesis 81, "make it difficult even for learned men to rescue the honor of the pope from slander or from the sly questions of the laity." For example, "Why does the pope, who is richer than Crassus, not build this one basilica of St. Peter's with his own money rather than with the money of poor believers?" (thesis 86). Or, "To what degree does the pope seek the salvation of the soul more than money in the indulgence …?" (thesis 89). Or, "Why are Masses for the dead as well as annual Masses for the dead continued, or why does he not return or permit the return of the benefices, if it is forbidden to pray for those already redeemed?" (thesis 83).

One of the strongest arguments for the practice of papal indulgences was, as previously mentioned, the concept of the treasury of merit to be administered by the Church. Luther speared this argument with the observation that the treasury of the Church does not consist of temporal goods. In that case, the preachers would not distribute this wealth so generously; instead, they would hoard it. "Nor are they (the merits laid up in the treasury) the merits of Christ and the saints, for, even without the pope, the latter always work grace for the inner man, and the cross, death, and hell for the outer man" (thesis 58). The answer provided by Luther concerning the treasury of the Church in its way sums up his concept of the nature of the Church: "The true treasure of the Church is the most holy gospel of the glory and grace of God" (thesis 62).

With these statements Luther introduced a view of the Church which, if it were made the foundation of the building and activity of the Church, would pave the way for the Church to divest itself of all material possessions and to make the preaching of the gospel the major thrust of each activity. Luther did not yet express these conclusions in the Ninety-Five Theses, but they could be read between the lines.

The matter was delicate and dangerous. From outward appearances, Luther's act was merely a call for academic debate, but from the content of the theses arose the question of what the Church was permitted to do and what it was not permitted to do and who was to decide; therefore, the question concerned the very nature of the Church and of ecclesiastical authority. Theologians and university scholars could indeed dispute, but they were limited to disputation. Others—surely primarily those whose social power was firmly established in the Church—had to decide the question. The problem had to be placed before the powers that controlled ecclesiastical leadership. That is why Luther, if he were interested in having any impact, had to address himself and his theses to his ecclesiastical superiors. Luther's superiors were Jerome Schulz, bishop of Brandenburg (because Wittenberg was within Brandenburg's diocese), and Albrecht of Brandenburg, the archbishop of Mainz and Magdeburg, to whom the bishop of Brandenburg was subject. Thus the path of ecclesiastical jurisdiction led directly back to Albrecht, archbishop of Mainz, whose financial interests stood behind the indulgence trade and who in any case would certainly be injured if Luther's theses should find a hearing among the people. This was a fatal situation, not exactly propitious for a free exchange of ideas concerning theological problems.

In consideration of his ecclesiastical subjection to Archbishop Albrecht, Luther was very cautious in his formulations when he sent his theses with an accompanying letter on October 31, 1517, to the archbishop. Luther wrote that he had no intention of attacking the indulgence preachers; after all, he had never heard them preach. But there was a popular misunderstanding concerning indulgences that must be corrected, he wrote, and therefore it would be necessary to revoke the commission for the indulgence preachers and to compose a new one lest someone appear and take issue with the indulgence preachers to the embarrassment of the archbishop. Luther wrote a similar letter to the bishop of Brandenburg. He wanted to retain an escape route, and his intention was to urge his ecclesiastical superiors to intervene before it was too late.

But it was already too late. Luther had so eroded the stage on which the balancing act had been taking place that the act could no longer continue. But how could an archbishop—merely because a university professor who was a subject of a rival dynasty had composed a few theses—act against his own interest and revoke a commission which he had personally issued? And how did Luther plan to obvert embarrassment for his archbishop should someone challenge the indulgence commission after Luther himself, by the publication of his theses, had taken the most decisive step to disgrace the archbishop? The revocation of the indulgence commission and the successful protection of the archbishop's reputation were both improbable. The notes in this ditty would be sung too high for Luther to hear them, he was warned. No one registered for the disputation. Albrecht did not respond to Luther's letter; neither did Jerome of Brandenburg. Luther could not know that Albrecht placed the matter before his advisors, ordered an evaluation of the question from the University of Mainz, and referred the entire matter to Rome. For Luther there remained only anxious apprehension.

It was rumored that Luther, with his indulgence theses, carried on a preconcocted game and that he undertook the whole matter at the instigation of his prince in order to strike a blow at the Hohenzollerns. What is of concern in the delicate nature of this matter is that this rumor can neither be definitively affirmed nor denied. If Luther really had received a gesture from Frederick the Wise that, given the rivalry between Wettin and Hohenzollern, cannot with complete confidence be dismissed, then such encouragement probably was communicated only orally and constituted mere intimation. But the rumor was dangerous, whether it was empty gossip or really had foundation. The rumor defamed Luther's intellectual honesty in that it imputed to him the role of mercenary, and beyond that the rumor was designed to disturb his relationship with the electoral court, because, if the rumor were true, he would be under suspicion at court for not having preserved the secret. If the rumor were based on a lie, the suspicion could mount that Luther himself started it in order to hide behind his prince.

At the beginning of September he wrote to Spalatin: "I do not desire that our views should come into the hands of our most illustrious prince or of his court before those people receive them for whom they are intended, so that no one will be able to conclude falsely that I published these views against the Bishop of Magdeburg at the command of our prince or in order to please him, as I now hear many fantasizing. Now the time is ripe for me to avow that my views were proclaimed without encouragement from our prince" (WA BR I 118).

Although Luther referred in this letter to "our views," there is no reason to assume that he had discussed the matter earlier with Spalatin, but the letter does point to the fact that Luther did not feel that he was alone and that his relationship with Spalatin already had assumed a confidential character. "Our views" referred to the views of the Wittenberg theology which Luther had developed and for which he had won recognition from his colleagues.

Contrary to his usual custom, Luther did not sign this letter with a simple "Lutherus" but rather with an elated "F. Martinus Eleutherius, the liberated Brother Martin," following a humanist custom, with a flourish of self-confidence, giving a slight indication that he would be compensated for his uncertainties and insecurities. But he soon returned to his former self.

More significant in this letter is a short postscript that comes after his signature: "You wrote to me that the Prince is sending me a gown. I would like to know whom he has selected for the mission." Just at that time Luther could have used a gown or material for a new one, not only because the old gown was perhaps torn and already a bit shabby but also as a gesture of favoritism from his prince. The liberated man needed the princely favor of a garment. Therefore, Luther did what he had never done before: he personally wrote to his prince in German so that a translator would not be required. Luther reminded Frederick that one year ago the prince promised him a gown. The court chamberlain should really present him with a gown and not just promises. The chamberlain "spins good words, but no gown is thereby produced." Luther included in the letter a request for the provincial of his order, Johann von Staupitz. Luther had heard that "Your Princely Grace had formed an unfavorable opinion of Doctor Staupitz." Luther wrote that he himself knew that Staupitz loved the elector of Saxony very much, and Luther did not believe that Staupitz ever could have given Frederick cause for anger. Therefore he, Luther, petitioned Frederick in Staupitz' behalf, asking that the prince "provide Staupitz with all favor and loyalty." And, enlarging his petition to the fullest measure, Luther even dared to plead that the prince should not impose new or heavy taxes. Already the current taxes have robbed the elector in recent days of so much "good reputation, name, and favor." "God has endowed Your Princely Grace with great intelligence so that the Prince is able to discern these matters better than I or perhaps better than all the subjects of Your Princely Grace. But it may also be that God wills that great intelligence occasionally be advised by weaker reason, in order that no one rely entirely upon himself, but upon God our Lord" (WA BR I 119–120).

About one week later Luther was able to thank Frederick through Spalatin for the gown. Thus within one week Luther with varied success had appealed to two electors of the Holy Roman Empire. These appeals opened for him new dimensions in social contacts.

Up to this point Luther had dealt with monks, students and professors, occasionally with educated court scribes, advisors, and Frederick's private secretary. Monastery and university continued to shape his daily life for the next years. But from this point on Luther became known to great lords: bishops, archbishops, princes, and finally the pope and the emperor, who had to concern themselves with him and with the questions that he raised. Thus he entered high politics, not with one blow of course, but step by step; nevertheless, he penetrated so deeply that never again was he able to free himself from the clutches of politics, a field in which he still had to prove himself.

However, neither were the politicians ever freed from the questions raised by Luther, since his advance had exposed an entire assortment of social problems simultaneously. Luther had asked about the nature of the Church and the authority of the pope in the questions concerning the Church and faith. But the Church was at the same time the most encompassing of all social organizations. As far as the papal Church extended its geographical and political boundaries, everyone naturally belonged to it from birth, de facto by baptism, because baptism took place as a rule just a few days after birth. But that meant that in the Church all stations, ranks, classes, and groups were represented. Regardless of the differences among people and regardless of their respective social positions, in one respect all people were the same: as baptized Christians, they all belonged to the Church. This led unavoidably to the fact that ecclesiastical questions in one way or another concerned everyone; whether one belonged to a higher or lower station made no difference. Church and society were so closely joined together that major changes in the Church could not but have an impact on the society; also, no social movement could develop without immediately touching on ecclesiastical problems and producing to a greater or lesser degree an impact on the Church. Much as the question of how a social order really was created and what had to be done to change it was debated when revolutionary movements developed, the question of what the Church was and what had to be done to reform it was disputed in the last decade of the fifteenth century and at the beginning of the sixteenth century. Thus the Church was a holy institution and at the same time the most representative cross section of society, or the ideal common denominator of society. Whoever was to any degree intellectually alert could not remain indifferent whenever the Church was discussed. Agreement and support, rejection and decisive opposition were the inevitable response to Luther's undertaking.

Under these circumstances, Luther's indulgence theses took on a life of their own. They found quick dissemination without much effort on his part, and in the long run he was unable to hinder their distribution. In addition to Albrecht and Jerome and his Wittenberg colleagues, Luther had sent a copy of the theses only to his Erfurt friend, Johann Lang, but others

had copied and circulated them. The Wittenberg canon, Ulrich von Din-
stedt, sent them to Christoph Scheurl in Nuremberg. The Nuremberg patrician circle around Scheurl, Willibald Pirckheimer, and Anton Tucher
were very enthusiastic about the theses and had them reprinted by Jerome
Hölzel. Casper Nützel translated them into German. Scheurl sent them to
Johann Eck in Ingolstadt and to the Augsburg humanist, Konrad Peutinger. Pirckheimer sent them to the cathedral canon Bernhard Adelmann
from Adelsmannsfelden in Augsburg. Reprints appeared in Basel and in
Leipzig. In a scant fourteen days the theses had spread like wildfire
throughout Germany as though, Luther later remarked, angels were fanning
the flames.

Albrecht Dürer, Germany's greatest artist, sent wood carvings and etch-
ings to Luther in gratitude for the theses. The bishop of Merseburg wanted
to see the theses posted everywhere in order that the people could be
warned of the indulgence swindle. Others accused Luther of impudence
and pride, as Luther wrote to Lang on November 11, 1517. In his own monastery the monks were thunderstruck by the imprudence of Brother Martin.

Theologians, monks, and priests reacted energetically, torn between secret satisfaction and uneasiness. Luther ought not to bring his order into
disrepute, the prior and subprior of the Wittenberg Augustinian house
whined. The Dominicans would now rejoice that an Augustinian was ripe
for burning, a reference to the burning of four Dominicans, accused of
blasphemy, that had taken place just a few years earlier.

Full of hate, the Dominicans rallied to battle. Tetzel, after all, was one of
their own. Those theses in which Luther had leveled the charge of heresy
were doubtlessly directed at him. The Dominicans regarded Luther's
theses as an attack on them, and they had to expect only the worst if they
did not succeed in parrying the charge of heresy directed at their Brother
Tetzel and in turning that same charge against Luther.

Thus Luther's attack suddenly revealed the latent contradictions that lay
in the very structure of the Church itself and that with more or less pot-
ency were transmitted into the secular society. The rivalry for prestige between monastic orders, the competition between the secular clergy and the
monastic orders, the balancing act of promoting one's own career and
obeying authority, all tested moral leadership within the ecclesiastical hierarchy. In addition, there was the rivalry between the universities, a typical
group conflict among the intellectuals, which was heightened by the fact
that the universities were a part of the territorial political superstructure
and were obliged to represent the interest of their princes.

Luther's action affected not only the ecclesiastical supervisory duty of
the bishop of Brandenburg and the archbishop of Mainz but also the financial duty of Luther's prince in support of the Church. From these connections the threads wove through the ecclesiastical sphere to the curia in

Rome and through the secular sphere to the emperor and the Reichstag. In the maze of dependencies, lines of communication, responsibilities, opposition, and interests, the conflict was thickened from instance to instance. It became even more complicated by the addition of every new concern until the problems of historical social development were brought to a focal point.

Thus one might say that society received Luther's personal ideas through the channels of social control. Luther's act gyrated the social system in swelling amplitudes of agreement, rejection, and critical evaluation. Personal views were amalgamated into the societal construct, and the impact was reciprocated. Theology became revolutionary and revolution became theological.

In hindsight, with the experience and picture of the proletariat and bourgeois revolutions in mind, we can regard what came into being in the following years as an early form of the bourgeois—that is, the middle-class—revolution. Indeed, society had already experienced in the years before the posting of the theses a whole series of urban upheavals and riots, and one could be tempted, in discussing bourgeois revolution, to see its beginning in the urban uprisings more readily than in comparatively harmless attempts at theological disputation. Nevertheless, the posting of the theses proved to be the decisive moment for a movement of greater influence than riot or unrest in that it introduced powerful, continuous changes in the class struggle and created bourgeois energies for a greater area of activity in the society. This point is the most essential to the Marxist concept of bourgeois revolution.

In the preceding two or three decades, clearly defined opposing forces had arisen that consisted primarily of groups formed by princes striving for imperial reform. The complaints against the papacy were summed up in the *Gravamina.* The revolts of urban bourgeois, guilds, and plebeian circles against the oligarchical councils and their financial misadministration in the cities erupted in several waves of urban rebellion and upheaval. The antifeudal struggle of the peasants as well as the disenchantment of the knights and minor nobility, the deep-rooted discontent among the lower clergy who expressed their views in biting sermons to the populace, the resistance of humanistic circles to scholasticism, the clerical tutelage concerning what people should think, and, not the least in significance, the riots of the small businessmen and early capitalist entrepreneurs against the monopolistic privileges of the Fuggers and other large commercial houses—all of these endeavors and upheavals called attention to conflicts and inconsistencies in the social order. The solution of the moment demanded transformations of varying degrees for the continued existence and functioning of the feudal system. A look at the contemporary conditions in other European countries shows that many of these inconsistencies, demands, and endeavors could have been solved or satisfied within the context of the feudal system. This was especially true with respect to rendering the ecclesiastical system more independent of the papacy and to centralizing the political system. The ruling classes in France, Spain, and England were in the process of solving these problems by strengthening the central royal authority, which was supported by an urban bourgeois base. On this matter, the social movement in Germany had to overcome a backwardness in comparison with other western European monarchies while overcoming a backup of problems within the feudal system.

Sections of the ruling feudal class were able to join the movement against the papal Church and indeed to become the spearhead of the movement without threatening their own position in society. Foremost among these groups that offered opposition were the imperial princes who opportunistically appealed to Luther for help and favor. However, in additional groups ready for revolution and opposition surfaced as early as the crisis year of 1517 in the urban and agrarian populace. These groups, whose demands were difficult to meet under the dictates of the traditional feudal hierarchy, shook the foundation of the feudal order.

Internal feudal reform and antifeudal strife were closely related. Both were manifestations of the call for reformation. As a social heterogeneous movement for the transformation of the Church, state, and society, the Reformation was very much broader and more complex than that encompassed by Luther's immediate protest. But Luther was integrated into the total social movement. He became the leading exponent of the general desire for change. Without consciously either promoting or excluding any of the far reaching aims, Luther provided arguments for the ideological justification of demands of all opposing forces.

The sixteenth century was not yet familiar with the word "revolution" as a name for profound social transformation. What later centuries described as revolution had not yet been experienced in the society of Luther's day. Only individual elements of revolution were known: unrest, riots, conspiracies, tumult, and reforms. Under the classification of "reformation" and in the rather innocuous written regulations for the monastery, university, and civic order, there could be concealed very volatile concepts linking achievable goals with utopian or futuristic fantasies.

From the time of the great councils of Basel and Constance in the fifteenth century, reformation had been associated with the idea of return to the supposedly better and more just conditions of the primitive apostolic Church and early Christianity, and suggested at the same time relatively clear views about the corruption of Christianity and the Church— especially with respect to the papacy, the curia, the clergy—which in the intervening centuries had taken place. The hallmarks of reform were a return to the Bible, idealization of primitive Christianity, and criticism of the contemporary Church. These hallmarks the Reformation shared with heretical movements of the Middle Ages.

The sixteenth-century Reformation, however, was much more than the continuation, reproduction, or resurrection of medieval heretical ideas. The Reformation distinguished itself from medieval heresies principally in that it broke down the barriers of sects and did not confine itself to theological or religious questions, reflecting instead the total complexity of social inconsistencies in all their breadth and variety. The broad basis of the Reformation was demonstrated at first not only in the rapid dissemination of the theses (a development that astounded Luther) and the enthusiastic response they provoked, but also in the strong opposition they encountered.

In January 1518, in Frankfurt-on-the-Oder, the provincial chapter of the Dominicans convened. The chapter protocol called for a disputation in which theses were presented by Johann Tetzel as a challenge to the Wittenberg theses. The Frankfurt professor Koch (also called Wimpina) had composed them. Tetzel and Wimpina boldly asserted that with His command to repent, Jesus was referring to the act of repentance practiced by the Church and not just to a penitent attitude on the part of individual Christians. The three hundred assembled Dominicans declared Luther a suspected heretic and denounced him to Rome. In accordance with canon law, such an accusation would necessitate an immediate heresy trial. The routine mechanism to protect the unity of the Church was put in gear; the mills began to grind. Joyfully the Dominicans published the Tetzel-Wimpina theses and railed against Luther from the pulpit.

The mood at the University of Wittenberg was not very encouraging for Luther. Everyone admonished him to be cautious. In this situation, Luther did the only thing that he could do: he continued lectures. Mondays and Fridays he lectured from twelve to one o'clock on the epistle to the Hebrews. He had begun this series at Easter 1517, and from October 1517 to Easter 1518 he concluded the lecture series. In the summer semester of 1517 he had dealt with the first five chapters of this epistle; on October 26, 1517 he had arrived at chapter 6, and he introduced the theme of penance, the fundamental theme of his indulgence theses. Thus what Luther dealt with in his lectures corresponded not only in content but also chronologically with the problems that in the formation and consolidation of his own theology he had been required to solve. This correspondence is of great significance for understanding his personality: it permits one to sense how in Luther's academic work theological thinking and the onset of political struggle merged.

Luther's lectures played a special role in this regard. With them he created for himself an intellectual head start. In his lectures on the psalms and the epistle to the Romans, he had worked out the fundamental elements of his theology, the Christocentrism and the concept of the passive righteousness of God, the suffering righteousness of God, according to which everything in the plan of salvation depends on God's grace and not on human merit. These concepts were so basic and concealed so many consequences and contingencies that only in the course of a long process of discussion with reference to other concepts and in the working out of new experiences did they emerge with full validity and with a clarity. With respect to the doctrine of penance the lectures on the epistle to the Hebrews were not nearly as significant as were those on the psalter and on the epistle to the Romans, for in these earlier lectures the decisive intellectual breakthrough had already been achieved. However, now a new factor surfaced that could not have been present in the earlier lectures but that could gain recognition only by occasional references to contemporary events. Luther was beset by the confrontation of lecture themes and problems with *Anfechtungen* (assaults, as by the devil), temptations, and outward and inner pressures that vented by criticism over the indulgence controversy. The intellectual thrust now apparent in Luther's lectures was less poignant but also more solid and more clearly oriented to the next stage of battle than it had been earlier. In his previous lectures Luther had been obliged to deal with the Bible, God, and his own *Anfechtungen*, but now he was obliged to deal with his opponents.

From autumn 1516 until Easter 1517, Luther lectured on Paul's epistle to the Galations. In this epistle, Paul sought to impress the congregations in Galatia that they were not obligated to observe the ceremonial law of the Jews, that they need not submit to circumcision in order to belong to God's people, and that they need only exercise faith in Jesus Christ. The study of the epistle to the Galations decisively accentuated the application of the Christocentrism and the doctrine of grace that Luther had already used in lectures on the psalter and on the epistle to the Romans at exactly the time when debates about Berhardi's disputation had won the first supporters at the university. And now with the study of the epistle to the Hebrews, the question concerning the priesthood of Christ took on enhanced significance.

The epistle to the Hebrews was probably not written by Paul; nevertheless, medieval theologians ascribed the book to that apostle occasional dissension notwithstanding. Luther himself raised doubts concerning the epistle's Pauline authorship, but he provided no final answer and he permitted the question to go unresolved. The question concerning the authorship of the epistle to the Hebrews is significant in Luther's theology insofar as the doctrine concerning justification is presented with a certain shift in emphasis. In Paul's writing the theological thought focuses on the antithesis, "justification of the sinner by faith, not by works"; but in the epistle to the Hebrews, the focus is on the antithesis, "forgiveness of sins by

Christ's sacrifice, not by the sacrificial ceremonies performed by human priests in an earthly temple" (Wilckens 776).

With this focus the attention of the believer is transferred to the priest, from the place of congregational worship to the altar. In this connection Luther explains the difference between Christ's priesthood and the Levitical priesthood of the Old Testament, for "in the new law the priest was distinguished from the people not by different clothes and dress but by exceptional sanctity and righteousness. For the ceremonies and dress which we see are prescribed by the Church and have only in the course of time become so prevalent" (Vogelsang 104).

In the epistle to the Hebrews, Christ the redeemer, perceived by faith, is presented as the high priest of the New Testament and as the pattern for the priesthood of the Church. As in the preceding years Luther had employed Christ and faith against scholasticism and theological thickets grown on Aristotelian soil, so now a new thrust appeared that, in the coming years, was to take on increased significance as Christ was recognized as the measure of the priesthood, against whom the prevailing priestly hierarchy was found to be corrupt and was rejected.

This theme concerning the priesthood began to occupy Luther in those very weeks and months during which Rome was alerted by zealous, fanatical, and hateful defenders of priestly prerogative who denounced the self-willed theologian, monk, and priest. Rome was moved by their complaints to intervene. In the *scholia* and glosses with which he interpreted the epistle to the Hebrews, Luther with perceptive instinct felt his way to the vulnerable spot of his opponents: the mystery of the priesthood. Thereby he claimed for himself from the outset that position which in the next round of the fight gained him an advantage of the highest imaginable authority as a priest of Jesus Christ.

However, at first he had to be careful to justify and expand the claims quickly marshalled in the indulgence theses, and to make them as impregnable as possible, because even though no one had accepted the invitation to debate the theses, it was clear that looming intellectual confrontation would transcend all routine disputations. In order to equip himself for the coming fray, to better express himself, and to prevent all eventual misunderstanding or distortions, Luther composed explanations of the theses much more comprehensive than the theses themselves. In these explanations Luther formulated the acknowledgement: "The Church needs reformation. However, this reformation is not a matter for the papacy alone or for the cardinals alone but rather for the whole world, or, more significantly, for God. The advent of this reformation is known only to God. In the meantime, it is our task to expose the obvious corrupt conditions ..." (WA I 627).

The explanations, entitled *Resolutiones disputationum de indulgentiarum vir-*

tute, were written in a Latin as well as a German version. The Latin version was meant only for scholars. On February 13, 1518, Luther sent a copy of the explanations to Bishop Jerome Schulze of Brandenburg. In an accompanying letter Luther asserted that with his theses he had not intended to make any pronouncements but simply wanted to debate. Moreover, since it was the bishop's prerogative to evaluate religious teaching, it was only right that Luther submit his ideas to the bishop and thus cast himself at his superior's feet. The bishop should promptly strike from the explanations whatever he believed should be deleted. Luther would accept his bishop's judgment, and he realized that Christ could do without him, a mere monk.

Bishop Jerome informed Luther through the abbot of Lehnin that he found nothing offensive in the explanations, but, in order to prevent dissension, he requested Luther not to publish them for the time being. Luther without hesitation agreed. His compliance so convinced the bishop of Luther's loyalty to the Church that he granted permission for the explanations to be published in April, although the actual publication was delayed until August. Furthermore, the bishop had no objection to additional publications by Luther.

Luther had thus cleared the first hurdle in his battle with his superiors. At least he could assert that he had not acted behind the backs of his ecclesiastical superiors; on the contrary, he had presented his views to them in the most comprehensive writing he had penned until then, and he had submitted himself to the judgment of his superiors. Luther seems to have believed that this modest cover was necessary because he was concerned about the uncertainty of the future course of the matter, and this uncertainty filled him with apprehension. Traces of this apprehension are to be found in his correspondence as well as in his lectures and sermons. Thus on March 5, 1518, he wrote to Christoph Scheurl that he had not sent the theses to him because he had had no intention of publishing them. But now they were "so frequently mulled over and translated that their stench disgusts me ... I myself am not without great doubt ..." (WA BR I 151ff). Therefore, Luther related, he had decided to write the explanations for the theses, but had deferred their publication at the request of the bishop of Brandenburg. In order to bring the widely circulating, vagrant theses under control, he wanted to publish a little book in German concerning the power of indulgences when he could find the necessary leisure.

The little book that Luther apparently had in mind, which was to supercede the indulgence theses, was the *Sermon on Indulgence and Grace*, published in Wittenberg at the end of March 1518. Its goal was brilliantly achieved. The *Sermon on Indulgence and Grace* appeared in so many editions and reprints that the Ninety-Five Theses faded into the background. But the controversy itself was not in the least defused. On the contrary, everybody now talked more than ever about Luther and his struggle against indulgences. By his work on the explanations, Luther achieved, meanwhile, a definitive clarity on the indulgence question, and he now presented his opinion more succinctly and more clearly than he had been able to do in the theses. The explanations, however, refrained from concealed attacks against the pope. Instead, Luther directed his assault against the concept of God which lay at the foundation of the indulgence system—the concept according to which God demanded satisfaction from the sinner. Luther argued that nothing in the Holy Scriptures supported that teaching. God demanded no satisfaction, for He was gracious. God demanded from the sinner only contrition and the desire to improve.

In the *Sermon on Indulgence and Grace*, Luther for the first time publicly addressed the accusation of heresy made against him: "Although some, for whom the truth is very damaging to their purses, accuse me of heresy, I, nevertheless, do not consider such monotonous screeching very seriously, since those who make the accusation are dimwits who have never even smelled the Bible, have never read Christian teaching, and have never understood their own teaching" (WA I 246). Thereafter this theme was continuously emphasized in Luther's writings and was a technique of rebuttal. He boldly presented his opponents as lacking understanding and with clouded intellects; he ignored their monotonous songs. This indicates that Luther was now interested in saving his own skin rather than disputing or discussing. In the face of the accusations that he was a heretic, Luther's deportment could hardly have been otherwise. The accusation of heresy, once pronounced, demanded a hearing and a judgment, not a disputation or an argument.

This accusation was for Luther an immense burden. He was very familiar with Church history and he knew what awaited him if he failed to defuse and repudiate this charge. He was seized by fear which accompanied him for years. Repeatedly, by prayer and intellectual concentration, he had to suppress his apprehensions. Whether or not he ever completely overcame such fear is doubtful. Thus it is the more noteworthy that in the spring of 1518, at the time when the heresy accusation confronted him, he developed a specific theology for combating and overcoming fear: *theologia crucis*, the theology of the cross.

Luther had to learn to bear mockery and suspicion while holding firmly to his teaching. Thus on March 17, 1518, he made the bearing of suffering and ridicule the subject of a Lenten sermon. This sermon is about what one should do "in order to repulse satanic power and to achieve a tranquil heart." Luther discovered his answer by fixing his eyes on Jesus on the cross: the most noble aspect in Jesus' life was the manner in which he bore sorrow and ridicule. When you bear sorrow and ridicule, you are fashioned like Jesus in the depths of your soul, and when you take up the cross, then the devil has no power over you. We prefer to see what is beautiful, pure as gold and silver; we prefer a young Gretchen or a young Hans to an old woman or an old man. And this is the trap that ensnares our mind. But for this cause Christ came: that we make no distinction between young and old, beautiful and ugly, but rather consider all equal—wise or unwise, clever or foolish, man or woman; and it is sufficient that the neighbor be a human being of the same flesh and blood, of a common human makeup.

But ridicule not only depressed Luther; it also came to his rescue. The very next day after his Lenten sermon, the ridicule directed against him provoked sympathy for him. On that day a printer transported by cart 800 copies of Tetzel's and Wimpina's theses against Luther from Halle to Wittenberg. In the market square, students ripped the these from the book merchant, turned his cart over, and burned the books. This action, however, was too much for Luther. He did not want to be identified with such excesses, and he immediately and publicly disavowed such action. But as much as he protested that he desired to fight only with spiritual weapons, there was little he could do to contain the indulgence controversy within the channels of academic dispute, ecclesiastical jurisdiction, and the warfare of opposing pens. The first symptom of a growing popular movement of reform had appeared.

Chapter 5

"I Will Be Branded a Heretic":
Faith Versus Hierarchical Authority
April 1518–January 1519

In the second half of March 1518, Luther learned that the curia had commissioned the Augustinian order to warn him and that he was expected to renounce and repudiate his errors. This was a delicate situation for Luther's provincial vicar, Johann von Staupitz, for Luther until that time had been his protégé. Even though some of Luther's formulations seemed to von Staupitz bold, he was not at all convinced that Luther's opinions were totally invalid. On the other hand, von Staupitz could safely assume that the Augustinian order was not interested in permitting one of its monks to be suspected of heresy.

A convocation of the Augustinian chapter was planned for April 1518 in Heidelberg. This was a propitious opportunity to clarify the situation as much as possible and to afford Brother Martin the occasion to appear and rebuff the accusations made against him. Thus Luther received a summons to Heidelberg. At the electoral court there were reservations about permitting him to travel to Heidelberg because of apprehension about his safety. In any case, letters of recommendation to the counts of the Palatinate were provided him. Furthermore, Luther was informed that the elector would not allow his professor to be sent to Rome.

On April 9, 1518, Luther left Wittenberg accompanied by his brother monk and student, Leonhard Beyer, and by a herald, Urban. In Weissenfels, the local pastor recognized him and offered him hospitality. In an inn in Judenbach, the travelers encountered the electoral chamberlain, Pfeffinger. Luther arranged for Pfeffinger to pay the ten groschen cost of the midday meal for Luther and his companions. The road then took the travelers to the Coburg, the fortress in the southernmost part of Saxony, and then to Würzburg. In Würzburg, Luther presented a letter of recommendation, received a letter of safe conduct from the bishop, and met his Augustinian brothers from Erfurt, chief among them his friend Johann Lang. With his Erfurt brothers he continued his trip to Heidelberg, where on April 21 or 22 he arrived and, after presenting the elector's recommendation letter, was hospitably received by the Palatinate count, Wolfgang.

On the 25th or the 26th of April, a disputation took place in the lecture hall of the Augustinian eremite monastery in Heidelberg. In preparation for this disputation, Luther had composed forty theses, twenty-eight on theology and twelve on philosophy. Luther himself chaired the disputation while his student, Leonhard Beyer, defended the theses.

These forty Heidelberg theses are a direct continuation, reenforcement, and further development of the Ninety-Five Theses against scholastic theology that had been posted in the fall of 1517. In these Heidelberg theses the indulgence question was avoided as much as possible. In its place Luther returned to his previous notion concerning the corruption and sinfulness of human nature, underscored his idea by juxtaposing human and divine works, and stressed the contrast between law and gospel, which he had studied intensively for the first time in the lectures on the epistle to the Hebrews and which now gave his whole train of thought a new turning point by the introduction of the contrasts in the "theology of glory" and the "theology of the cross." Ideas that just a short time earlier had electrified his Lenten sermon in the native tongue of his congregation were now contracted in the jolting terms of his precise theses, described by Luther himself as paradoxes. "The theology of glory calls evil good and good evil; the theology of the cross calls the thing what it is ... it is not everyone who works much that is justified, but rather the one who without works believes in Christ .... The law demands, Do this, and nothing comes of it; grace says believe in this One, and all is accomplished" (WA I 364).

Naturally, lusty blows were also struck against free will. Free will, after Adam's fall, was only a pretext, an empty ascription in that even when doing one's best one remained a mortal sinner. Free will had become for Luther a provocation: to resist free will, to expose it in all its emptiness, and to ascribe all imaginable evil to it was Luther's firm purpose. Lashing out against free will seems to provide him release.

It can no longer be conclusively determined whether it was his invective against free will, the paradoxes concerning the theology of the cross, or, as seems likely, the entire construct of his thought, that simultaneously aroused the enthusiasm of his auditors and shocked them. In any case, Luther later informed Spalatin that one of the Heidelberg professors present at the disputation had derided him amid the laughter of the entire auditorium: "When the peasants hear this, they will stone you to death." Seven years later this same audience would not have laughed at such a possibility. Luther's contemporaries must have sensed intellectual and ideological associations, to which we today can relate only with great difficulty; they realized at least that in this kind of theology lay a danger for the society.

But the contagion that some shunned attracted others at first by its inner and biblically buttressed logic, and the fact that the author of the paradoxical theses had aroused the displeasure of the highest authorities added spice to his ideas. Thus the resentment felt by many against the highest authorities could be expressed by applause for Luther.

Apart from Augustinians, citizens of Heidelberg, highly respected persons from the Palatinate court, and students and faculty of the university attended the disputation, which thereby became a convivial event that drew attention from a circle much wider than a mere monastic convocation. By his patient listening and his factual presentation, Luther won the sympathetic ear of the audience. Among the young auditors he found enthusiastic supporters who a few years later became the initiators of the Reformation in southern Germany. Among them was Martin Butzer from Schlettstadt, a humanistically educated Dominican who became the reformer of Strasbourg and who later was to have a significant impact on the English Reformation; Master Johannes Brenz, the reformer of Schwäbisch-Hall; and Theobald Billicanus, who established the Reformation in Nordlingen.

At the beginning of May, Luther departed from Heidelberg. As far as Würzburg he traveled in the same wagon as his colleagues from Nuremberg. From Würzburg his colleagues from Erfurt took him with them as far as Erfurt, where his colleagues from Eisleben supplied Luther with their wagon and accompanied him to Wittenberg. On this return journey from Heidelberg to Wittenberg, Luther bared his convictions to his former Erfurt philosophy teacher, Bartholemew Arnoldi von Usinger; however, Luther sought not to convert Arnoldi to his views but only to provoke him to reflect on the issues. The four days that Luther spent in Erfurt before resuming his journey to Wittenberg finally convinced him that the Erfurt Occamists could not be converted. Jodokus Trutfetter, whom Luther wished to visit on the evening of May 8, refused to open his door to him. A conversation that was later arranged failed to reconcile differences. Both men remained firm in their positions. Luther maintained that Trutfetter could not prove his own position nor refute Luther's. The two made different primary assumptions on which to base their arguments. While Trutfetter appealed to natural reason, which impacted on Luther like "chaos of darkness," Luther insisted that one must preach Jesus Christ as the true and solitary light. The "Sentences" of the Erfurt Occamists appeared to him as a beast that devoured itself. Luther became convinced that the Erfurters were defending their propositions through "pure vanity" and wanted to be right at any cost. They therefore sentenced all of Luther's writings to extinction, and his theology was for them detestable. These old gray heads, as Luther wrote to Spalatin, were deeply rooted in their concepts. The spirit of the young and of all youth was totally contrary to these old monitors, and a deep ravine separated the old from the young. As Christ turned to the heathen after having been rejected by the Jews, now Luther hoped that true theology, which had been rejected by the proud sages, would be received by the youth (WA BR I 178–79).

On May 15, 1518, Luther was again in Wittenberg. On the very next day he stood in the pulpit of the city church and preached a sermon against the power of the papal ban, describing it as of no validity and unjustified, more damaging to the pope than to those against whom it was directed. Dominican informers attended the sermon, wrote it down, published it, and immediately informed Rome.

While the Dominican charge against him was on its way to Rome, Luther completed the *Resolutiones* (explanations of his Ninety-Five Theses), whose major section he had already sent in February to Jerome, the bishop of Brandenburg. Luther dedicated the *Resolutiones* to no less a personage than Pope Leo X, following the advice of Staupitz, to whom he also had drafted a dedication of the *Resolutiones*. This was a tactical maneuver, designed as a demonstration of dependency on the pope, to counter the charge of heresy. Luther admitted that possibly he had erred, but he insisted that he could not be a heretic. The elector of Saxony would not tolerate such a corrupt boil at his university. "Therefore, most Holy Father, with all that I am and have, I throw myself at your feet: quicken, kill, call, revoke, approve, condemn, as it pleases you. I recognize your voice as the voice of Christ which rules and speaks in you. If I have deserved death, I will not refuse to die ..." (WA I 529)—impressive words that we can conclude almost with certainty Luther never for a moment entertained any thought of honoring. If he had really been prepared to listen to the voice of the pope as to the voice of Christ (a view absolutely contradictory to the fundamental line of his thought), he hardly could have prepared, just a short time earlier, the sermon that made the papal ban laughable. That Luther could abandon himself to such explanations reveals that he had at this time begun to practice political tactics and to learn not only to attack directly but also to maneuver, shift, dissemble, retreat, and evaluate the situation while holding firmly to his fundamental concepts and refusing to surrender.

Even before he left for Heidelberg Luther had written a brief essay in reply to Johann Eck in Ingolstadt. Eck had attacked Luther's Ninety-Five Theses in his pamphlet *Obelisks*. During Luther's absence from Wittenberg, Karlstadt had composed a series of theses opposing Eck that he wished to use as a basis for a debate. Luther entitled his answer to Eck, *Asterisks*. To refute Luther's first thesis that the entire life of the Christian, according to Jesus, was to be one of penance, Eck appealed to universal Christian belief that individual acts of penance remove the guilt of sin. Luther rejected the basis for Eck's argument. Generally accepted opinion means nothing. An error shared by many does not make for truth. Christ is the king of the soul by faith, but the will is a slave. The will is always a whore. In a letter accompanying the *Asterisks* Luther requested Eck not to be too severe on Karlstadt. Luther obviously had no interest in accentuating the intellectual strife with Eck because the association with Eck had been established through Luther's Nuremberg friends, and he had not really reckoned with unfriendly confrontation from that quarter.

Luther was much more aggressive toward Tetzel, whose theses jointly issued with Wimpina's against Luther were followed by a second publication in early summer in which Tetzel did not hesitate to threaten the Saxon elector with a heresy proceeding. Luther wrote in his treatise on _Freedom of the Sermon Touching Papal Indulgence and Grace_ that Tetzel strummed the Scriptures as a pig plays the lute. With more caustic ridicule and sarcasm than he had ever before used, Luther addressed Tetzel: "Here I am at Wittenberg, Dr. Martin Luther, Augustinian. Is there a heretic hunter who dares devour iron and scale cliffs, let him know that in Wittenberg he will have safe conduct, open gates, free lodging according to the gracious consent of the elector of Saxony" (WA I 392).

But the heretic hunters did not accept this invitation. Instead, just at the time when Luther was having the invitation printed, the heretic hunters persuaded the pope to approve an investigation of Luther based on a suspicion of heresy. Within three days the Dominican Sylvester Mazzolini Prieras composed a dogmatic evaluation of Luther's writings in which the Ninety-Five Theses were in all points declared to be refuted and heretical. The entire Church in its essence was united in the pope, out of which union the infallibility of the pope was deduced. Prierias had his critique published under the title _Dialogue Concerning the Presumptive Theses of Martin Luther on the Power of the Pope_. The highest judge of the curia, Girolamo Ghinucci, issued, on the basis of Prierias' critique, a notice that within sixty days of receiving the summons Luther was to present himself in Rome to answer the charges made against him.

The summons was transmitted first to Cardinal Cajetan, general of the Dominican order, who, as papal legate, was attending the Reichstag in Augsburg and was a guest of the Fuggers. Cajetan forwarded the summons along with a copy of Prierias' critique of the Ninety-Five Theses to Luther by way of the Fugger branch office in Leipzig.

Luther received the summons on August 7, 1518. The rumor and apprehension that had oppressed him for months now became a real threat. In order to parry this threat Luther would have to mobilize all available sympathizers; above all the support of the elector would be most important. The power and support of the elector would determine whether or not curial juridical authority would be permitted to penetrate into the heart of Saxony. Advised and urged by his friends, Luther by a special emissary immediately appealed to Frederick the Wise, who was at that time attending the Reichstag in Augsburg. Luther petitioned Frederick to assure, through his influence, that Luther should be heard in Germany before impartial judges and not be delivered to Rome. The University of Wittenberg also appealed to Rome with the same plea. In this appeal, the Wittenbergers could build on an early feeling of nationalism which was quickened by every attempt at curial intervention in German affairs.

Whether such an appeal from Wittenberg would be successful was doubtful, all the more so because Cajetan in the meantime had received new incriminating material concerning Luther's sermon against the papal ban. Under these circumstances, Cajetan was successful in persuading Emperor Maximilian to write a letter to the pope requesting condemnation of Luther as a heretic without delay lest Luther contaminate not only the simple folk but also the princes with his heresy.

The position was now clear for the curia. When Luther declared the papal ban as unchristian and invalid, he undoubtedly became guilty of heresy. Consequently the canonical proceedings initiated on the basis of mere suspicion of heresy now were founded on the charge against notorious heretics. Therefore Leo X, in *Postquam aures*, published on August 23, 1518, ordered the immediate arrest of Luther. The Saxon elector should hand over the "son of evil." The general of the Augustinian order received instructions to bring Luther, bound hand and foot, to Rome. Before the Saxon monk loomed the stake. Luther's fate appeared sealed. It could be evaded only if his prince placed him under his protection. To provide such protection was not a simple matter for the elector, but political circumstances aided Saxon diplomacy. Saxon diplomacy was able to exploit the papal political interest in the intrigue involving the successor to the Emperor Maximilian.

Maximilian, born in Vienna-Neustadt in 1459, had been successor of Frederick III since 1493 as king and since 1508 as emperor. In 1518, at fifty-nine years of age, he attempted at the Augsburg Reichstag to procure from the imperial electors binding assent that they would select his grandson, Charles I of Spain, to be his successor. Such a promise would ensure that the imperial crown would remain in the house of Hapsburg. But for the papacy, such a prospect was less attractive because Charles already held the kingdom of Naples in addition to the Spanish Netherlands and other overseas possessions. If he now also received the imperial crown, the papal states ruled by the pope, which extended from Rome through the middle of the Apennine Peninsula, would be placed in an intimidating Hapsburg vice. That the papacy, under these conditions, provided diplomatic resistance to the emperor's plans for regulating the imperial succession was, of course, known to Maximilian. In order to appease the curia despite its opposition to the election of Charles, Maximilian was prepared to accommodate the papacy as far as possible in all other matters. One of his moves in this direction was the above mentioned letter to the pope condemning Luther.

Maximilian wanted most of all to accommodate the curia in its demand for imperial support in war against the Turks, approved in the fifth Lateran

Council in 1517. The legate, Cajetan, had come to Augsburg primarily with the commission to solicit an imperial tax for the war against the Turks. Cajetan's request was sympathetically received by the emperor but not by the imperial estates. The estates of the diet declared that the war against the Turks had never actually been waged and that the campaign plans against the Turks had been used only to wring money from the estates. The indulgence for providing money for the building of St. Peter's was a similar exploitation. The money realized from the sale of the indulgence flowed into various obscure channels and was in no case exclusively used for the building of St. Peter's. Already there had been far too much money sent to Rome.

The imperial estates appealed to the aforementioned Gravamina of the German Nation against the Holy See in Rome, a collection of complaints and demands that had been compiled at previous Reichstags and now were discussed repeatedly by an increasingly heterogeneous populace.

With the *Gravamina* the ruling class announced its discontent with the papacy, which exercised one of the more important functions in the German feudal system: the allocation of status in the organization and the territories of the Church. In the investiture controversy of the late Middle Ages, Rome had secured for itself the right to confirm persons nominated to bishoprics, archbishoprics, and large abbacies, and had reenforced this right by the Concordat of Worms in 1122. But these offices also served as very important functions of the ruling class of Germany. The ecclesiastical offices constituted a considerable part of the power apparatus and establishment for the maintenance of the upper nobility and the imperial aristocracy. With these supreme rights the papacy secured for itself the privilege of participation in the surplus of the German economy. The papacy, in claiming its rights to fees for confirmation to ecclesiastical office, reduced in a parasitical fashion the income of the German feudal class. It is understandable that there was no end to the complaints about the invalid extension and collection of dues, fees, and taxes from bishoprics, abbacies, and ecclesiastical jurisdictions.

In the face of the process initiated against Luther and the excitement concerning the role of indulgences caused by the dissemination of the theses, the resolve of the imperial estates in appealing to the *Gravamina* must have led the curia to fear the worst, especially since the estates candidly pointed to the mood of the common man and to the Bundschuh.

The Bundschuh, originally a description of the simple peasant's shoe in contrast to the feudal noble's boot, was the code name for a series of secret conspiracies directed against the nobles that, as has been mentioned, were betrayed through the confessional in 1492, 1502, 1513, and 1517. The major area for the activity of the Bundschuh was the upper Rhine (southern Germany), Alsace, the Black Forest, and the Rhine-Main region. Reference to the Bundschuh under the circumstances prevailing in 1518 served the estates well in stemming the demands of the papal curia.

The request for taxes for fighting the Turks collapsed under the Gravamina complaints. The Reichstag, to be sure, passed a resolution that each person attending communion should, within the next three years, make a contribution for the war, but the princes insisted of first discussing the matter with their subjects, whereby the topic became, de facto, a dead letter.

Since Cardinal Cajetan had to accept a rebuff in the matter of the tax, it became very important to him not to suffer a second defeat in the question of the imperial succession. But success in this realm meant not to antagonize those electors who had not yet promised to support a Hapsburg candidacy. After the electors of Brandenburg, Mainz, Cologne, and the Palatinate had promised Maximilian on August 27, 1518 to vote for Charles, the only electors still not committed to Charles were Richard Greiffenklau of Trier und Frederick the Wise of Saxony.

Under these circumstances, Cajetan could not easily decline Frederick's request for the cardinal to grant Luther a "paternal" hearing in Augsburg, because now Cajetan's diplomatic mission depended very much on an agreement with the elector of Saxony. In response to Cajetan's dispatch to Rome, Leo X immediately sanctioned a hearing for Luther before the cardinal in Augsburg and empowered Cajetan either to sustain or dismiss the charges against Luther.

Thus at the end of September 1518, Martin Luther started on the most difficult journey of his life. With the fate of Jan Hus, burned at the stake in 1415, ever on his mind, Luther was dispirited as he considered the shame that he would bring upon his parents if he now also were condemned to the stake. His deep anxiety affected his stomach. During the last miles of the journey, Luther suffered such severe stomach cramps that he could not walk, and had to be transported by wagon. He entered Augsburg on October 7, but the electoral advisors, Rühel and Feilitzsch whom the elector had left in Augsburg to care for Luther (since the elector himself had departed Augsburg at the conclusion of the Reichstag), prevailed on him not to present himself immediately to the cardinal. First the advisors procured for him an imperial safe-conduct before they permitted him to be seen publicly on the streets of Augsburg.

Between October 12 and 14, Luther appeared three times before Cajetan. The cardinal had prepared himself well for the meeting. He had studied Luther's writings and had composed brief tractates on which to base detailed questions. Cajetan wanted nothing less than for Luther to recant. Luther refused and applied himself to disputation concerning the power of the papacy.

Luther's revocation would have meant the intellectual and moral defeat of all who had joined his cause. In addition, it would have damaged the reputation of all who had promoted his theses, recommended his solutions, and worked hard on his behalf. By his refusal to recant, insisting in the discussion that he be proven wrong by the Scriptures, he forced the papacy into a position of moral embarassment. He left the papacy no option but to appeal to naked power, to plain coercion. This was, however, the beginning of the end of that power, and here it was exposed as nothing more than arbitrary compulsion.

With the demand for correction by the Bible, Luther introduced a new principle of legitimation over the prevailing principle of established authority. For the papacy to have yielded to Luther's demand would have meant the self-abdication of its power, for the papacy claimed the right to be the authorized interpreter of the Scriptures. This exegetical monopoly was the necessary result of a long historical development. Since the Bible is a collection of various writings which in a period of over 1,000 years were integrated into the collection known as the Holy Scriptures, the Bible, to be understood by the contemporary generation, must be interpreted. But the Bible can be interpreted from the most varied perceptions and points of view. Dogmatic teaching derived from interpretation presents no scientific statements, but rather precepts, the acceptance of which tests devotion more than intellect. Dogma is neither true nor false; the question is to a great extent of validity or invalidity. But what is valid and what is invalid can be decided, and the final decision can rest only upon the power vested in the Church.

At Augsburg Luther could not be faulted for lacking the necessary devotion to protocol. At the first meeting on October 12, Luther prostrated himself at the cardinal's feet. At Cajetan's first gesture, Luther rose only to his knees and finally stood only after a second gesture from the cardinal. But then he did indeed take his stand. If someone would demonstrate his errors to him, then he would gladly recant and submit.

The cardinal sought in vain to persuade Luther to acknowledge his error. On two points the cardinal believed that he could persuade the doctor of Holy Scriptures that he had erred. The fifty-eighth thesis concerning the treasury of the Church contradicted Pope Clement VI's bull *Unigenitus*, promulgated in 1346, and in his *Resolutiones* Luther falsely had made the effectiveness of the sacraments dependent upon the faith of the recipients. On the first point, the cardinal was forced to submit to a very painful correction. Luther showed him that the bull *Unigenitus* expressed something entirely different from what the cardinal had claimed. On the other point also Luther refused to be moved. By the word of the Bible he was bound in conscience and could never elevate the sacrament over faith.

In this manner, in the face of the highest authority of the curia, the fundamental theme of the new Wittenberg theology came up for discussion—that conviction on which the entire Lutheran theology is based: *justificatio sola fide*, justification by faith alone. If Luther had retreated on this point, he would have sacrificed his personality, because it was just this recognition that had led him to a new view of the Church; this recognition provided him the inner security to challenge the established ecclesiastical authorities and spiritually equipped him to become Luther the Reformer.

This recognition of the role of faith was the starting point for a new ethic based on obedience not to human authority but to the dictates of one's own conscience. From this standpoint the resistance of the individual to clerical tutelage could be justified. The decision as to what was to be considered the norm and what was to be considered flexible in the Church and finally in society became, with Luther's new ethic, bound to the conscience of the individual. In the socially critical situation in which Germany found herself at that time, this conscience ethic exercised an important function and opened the way for an intellectual questioning and negation of all existing norms.

The Church had long been criticized on the basis of practical reason and of wholesome humanistic, rational arguments. This criticism emanating from the humanists and their acknowledged leader, Erasmus of Rotterdam, was especially effective. The curia was accustomed to such criticism. In pragmatic decisions, the curia, without compunction, could permit criticisms of this nature to go uncondemned for, after all, cooperation and compromise in responding to questions that arose from day to day were part of the curia's technique of power. A companion of Cajetan shamelessly had said to Luther before the hearing that it should not be too hard for Luther to pronounce the little word *revoco* (I revoke). To such a suggestion Luther had responded only with a contemptuous smile. His ethic went deeper, depriving the existing order of its façade of holiness and, instead of measuring the individual by his agreement with the established authorities, subjecting the Church and the circumstances sanctioned by it to the judgment of the individual.

Here it becomes clear that in a specific but central sector of the social consciousness, a revolution was being prepared. A new ideology was arising, the Reformation ideology of the early bourgeois revolution. The theoretical part of the new Reformation ideology was to be found in Luther's theology, which had its ethical center in the teaching concerning justification by faith alone. The personal contribution of Martin Luther to the development of the early bourgeois revolution was the tenacious and unerring defense of this fundamental concept at the risk of his life, a defense wrung from him at Augsburg and repeatedly reaffirmed by him in the following years.

Luther did not really stand alone at Augsburg. His provincial vicar, Staupitz, hurried to his aid; his Nuremberger brother monk, Wenzel Link, had accompanied him from Nuremberg to Augsburg; the electoral advisors protected him; the Augsburg city scribe, Dr. Konrad Peutinger, helped him; and an entire network of supporting connections were woven into the Augsburg hearing and upheld his cause.

From Peutinger Staupitz received the warning that the cardinal was empowered to arrest Luther and that furthermore Staupitz himself was not free from danger. The Augustinian vicar then fled Augsburg. Staupitz had already released Luther from his monastic obedience. On the night of October 20, Luther also secretly left Augsburg through a small gate in the city wall. A groom with a horse waited for him outside the gate. At a fast pace for one not used to riding, with every bone in his body aching, Luther galloped away from Augsburg and at the first inn along the way sank exhausted into the straw. The monk rider racing for his Saxon sanctuary must not have presented a very edifying appearance. In the vicinity of Saalfeld, he met Count Albrecht of Mansfeld who laughed loud and long over this strange rider without spurs, but, as befitted a noble personage, the count reached generously into his pocket and invited the monk to dinner. The monk on his nag was anxious to return home. On the way, in Nuremberg, the news from Spalatin reached him that the pope had ordered his arrest. On October 31, Luther once again was in Wittenberg.

Until now, Luther had felt secure in Wittenberg, but what would ensue if the pope insisted on his arrest? Earlier in Augsburg Luther had weighed with friends a plan to abandon Germany completely and to go to France because he believed that he could find better protection from the papacy there than in Germany. Staupitz had attempted to raise money for Luther's French exile, but he was not successful and the plan was necessarily abandoned. In Augsburg Luther had confronted the cardinal. Cajetan was a high ecclesiastical authority but not the highest. In this situation Luther was able to cling to the fantasy that all might still turn out all right if only the pope were clearly informed about the questions on which the problem was hinged. In order to preserve his integrity before the world, Luther, therefore, while still in Augsburg, had a notary record his explanation in which he appealed to "the poorly informed pope or to a pope who was about to be better informed." But now Luther knew that the pope even before the Augsburg hearing had definitively condemned him. This was an unnerving piece of news that was reconfirmed in mid-November when the elector, Frederick, received a letter from Cajetan ordering him to deliver up Luther or expel him from Saxony.

Thus the weeks after his return from Augsburg became the most critical and dangerous period of his life. The curia persistently demanded that Luther be turned over to Rome. The elector vacillated and would gladly have been rid of this man who caused him such discomfort. Luther had to reckon with the possibility that his stay in Saxony would not last very much longer. Flight to France was possible but also fraught with danger. Earlier, in the summer, he had received warning from the count of Mansfeld that he should be cautious about trips outside Saxony and that he should remain in Wittenberg as much as possible because the count possessed reliable information that a price had been set on Luther's head. Luther did not want to believe that his prince would deliver him to Rome. He had received reassuring guarantees of protection as early as the end of March 1518. On one hand, he dared not delay his departure from Saxony until the elector should officially expel him, because such an expulsion would announce to the whole world that the elector was no longer willing to protect him; such a public announcement of expulsion not only would have been a great blow to Luther's prestige but also would have greatly encouraged his opponents. On the other hand, to wait for a negative decision from the elector also meant placing his prince protector under pressure, forcing him into the role of culprit, the role of expelling a defenseless subject; and thereby Luther might incur the prince's antagonism. Incurring the prince's wrath was entirely possible, because as recently as the middle of November Luther had received very clear indications that the elector's limits of toleration had been reached. The elector forbade him to publish his descriptions of the Augsburg hearing. The prohibition to publish arrived too late, however. Two sheets of the description had already left the press; only the third sheet was still in preparation. In order to placate the elector, Luther had one passage on the third sheet covered with printer's ink to render that passage illegible. This remedy only aggravated the situation, because it aroused rather than subdued the curiosity of the reader.

Fortunately for Luther, however, he could maintain that at the intervention of the elector he himself had deleted the insidious passage, in which he had maintained that the papal breve which called for his arrest was forged by Bishop Jerome of Ascoli and that Cajetan had been involved in its composition. This claim was an obvious error which, if it had been circulated, would have made it easy for Luther's enemies to accuse him of deception and thereby to deal a serious blow to his reputation.

Under these circumstances, it seemed best to seize the initiative and voluntarily leave Saxony before the elector would expel him. Thus Luther addressed this problem in a letter to the elector responding to Cajetan's desire to have him turned over to Rome. Luther offered to leave the territory of Frederick and go wherever a merciful God would lead him.

In a ceremonial act in the Wittenberg Holy Spirit Chapel on November 28, 1518, Luther appealed for a general council, and on December 1, 1518, he hosted a farewell dinner in the Black Cloister. Some advised him to turn himself over to the elector and to permit himself to be placed by the elector in some secure place. These counselors suggested that the elector might then inform Cajetan of the elector's decision. On the next day Luther wrote to Spalatin, "How valid this advice, I leave to your judgment." He also informed Spalatin in the same letter that he had already prepared his departure but that he was still open to both possibilities, that is, to remain in Wittenberg or to depart. He suggested that he would have departed "if your letter had not arrived yesterday ..." (WA BR I 260). Luther stood on the razor's edge, but he was permitted to remain in Wittenberg after all, this "Eleutherius"—the liberated one, as he had signed his letters in the midst of his elation in the autumn of 1517. In a letter to Staupitz in November 1518, Luther signed himself *pauperculus* (friar). On December 9, 1518, the worst had been endured and "Eleutherius" appeared once again as the signature in new letters with new plans. Luther reached an agreement with Bartholomew Bernhardi—his former student, who, in the meantime, had become rector of the University of Wittenberg—to drop the lectures on Thomist physics and logic. The money saved by dropping these courses was to be used for improving the salary of Philip Melanchthon. Luther was very anxious to achieve this goal because he wanted Melanchthon, with whose intellectual gifts he was greatly impressed, to remain at Wittenberg.

Philipp Schwarzerd, who was born in 1497 in Bretten in the Pfalz and who, in the humanistic custom, had adopted the Greek name Melanthon or Melanchthon, had arrived in Wittenberg as teacher of Greek only a few months earlier and had presented in the Castle Church in August 1518 his highly proclaimed initiation lecture concerning the education of youth. The twenty-one-year-old Melanchthon, of small stature and with a slight lisp, was a grandnephew of Reuchlin, the scholar of Hebrew. The young man outlined in his initiation lecture a reform of the curriculum. Melanchthon's suggestions corresponded well with Luther's convictions; in the weeks after the Heidelberg disputation Luther came to the conclusion that the youth must be won over to the new ideas, because from the old fossilized sages there was no hope of support in any case. Above all, Melanchthon demanded a decisively improved language curriculum. Greek and Hebrew, as the original biblical languages, mathematics, history, and the classical authors of antiquity should be placed at the center of the curriculum. In solicitude and recognition as well as in the spirit of collegial fun, Luther addressed Melanchthon with *Tua Graecitas* (Your Greekness) on the occasion of commencement festivities. These promotion festivities took place in the second half of November, when Luther's position in Wittenberg was most tenuous and he was forced to confront the fact that at any moment he might be required to pack his bag and leave. On the same day of the initiation lecture, Luther invited Melanchthon to dinner. The invitation, of course, was in Latin. Luther could not yet venture using the Greek language. He campaigned for a higher salary for the new young and unassuming professor and continued this campaign until he finally achieved his goal at the court.

To help his friends, to consider their material needs, to laud them publicly and to praise their intellectual gifts in the highest tones, to help them find a position and to secure benefices for them—these matters were part of Luther's general conduct towards others with whom he, with sure instinct, built and maintained a friendly circle and gradually expanded his own influence. This circle was bound primarily by the ties of common beliefs complemented by common social interests. Through these associations Luther earned the gratitude of those whom he benefitted. Among them was Bartholomew Bernhardi from Feldkirch, whose disputation in the autumn of 1516 had initiated the recognition of Luther's theology at the University of Wittenberg. Bernhardi acquired at the end of 1518 the newly available benefice of provost of Kemberg. In addition, Franz Günther, who in September 1517 had defended the theses against scholastic theology, received a preaching office in Jüterbog and soon thereafter ascended to the positions of court preacher in Lochau and confessor to the elector. Supported by Spalatin but also by other connections made in the course of time, Luther found positions for his people. In this manner the Wittenberg theology was disseminated, and its theologians began to operate as an influential group far beyond the boundaries of Wittenberg.

Luther gained influence; nevertheless, he increasingly entered into associations that required him to give due consideration to Saxon diplomacy. Saxon diplomacy protected him, but it also exploited and somewhat restricted him. His prince's diplomacy had done this in Augsburg and now was acting upon him in the same manner.

For some time the rumor had circulated that the pope would bestow the Golden Rose on the elector Frederick. The Golden Rose was an award bestowed by the papacy in recognition of Christian virtue, a mark of favor, and, in this case, certainly a clear recognition of the fact that in Saxon diplomacy as it concerned the Church there was a rather large area of elasticity which could be manipulated in the Luther affair. Thus on December 18, 1518, the elector reached a final decision neither to turn Luther over to Rome nor to exile him. Before this decision became known, Frederick had sent his chamberlain, Degenhardt Pfeffinger, with a message to the emperor that it was difficult to exile Luther without a hearing inasmuch as Luther was prepared to be instructed. Perhaps the emperor could put in a word on Luther's behalf to the pope.

In this matter, the Saxon advisors assumed a great deal from their court and from the curia. They convinced the elector that Saxony just at that moment could afford to delay and must do so, that Saxony must resist the curia and must drive the price for cooperation as high as possible. Pfeffinger even aspired to the prospect that Luther easily could acquire from the pope a bishopric or other honors if he would only recant. Christoph Scheurl of the convivial Nuremberg circle passed on the interesting bit of information that a knight also associated with this group, Karl von Miltitz from Meissen, was prepared for all eventualities.

Miltitz turned up in Nuremberg on December 17 or 18 together with Pfeffinger and delighted Luther's Nuremberg friends with the statement that he wished to reconcile Luther with the pope. The happy-go-lucky young man, born about 1490 in Rabenau near Dresden, had been in Rome since 1514, and through an influential uncle had been appointed papal notary. The papal curia had selected Miltitz to deliver the coveted Golden Rose to the elector Frederick of Saxony. In his diplomatic pouch, Miltitz carried a bundle of commissions: ten nominations to doctorates of theology and ten to the coronation of poets laureate, nominations for five Lateran counts, nominations for papal prelates and notaries, and, as a special attraction, two dispensations legitimizing illegitimate births. The dispensations should not fail to impress Frederick the Wise, for they now provided the possibility of elevating his two sons Fritz and Bastel—borne to him by his mistress, Anna Weller von Molsdorf—to high office and honor. To be sure, Miltitz's pouch also contained decrees against Luther and his followers, and Miltitz had been instructed to discuss carefully in advance with Cardinal Cajetan all steps in his mission.

The deal which the curia had in mind was clear: the Golden Rose of Christian virtue and the dispensation legitimizing Frederick's two illegitimate sons in exchange for delivering Luther to Rome or at least "persuading" him to recant. Compliance with Rome's request to deliver up the heretic was the Christian virtue for which Frederick was to be honored. With this delicate task assigned to him, Miltitz hurried to Augsburg, but he did not arrive in time to meet with Cajetan. Miltitz quickly deposited his diplomatic pouch and the Golden Rose with the Fugger bank and went to visit his acquaintance, Degenhardt Pfeffinger, on the latter's Bavarian estate. There Miltitz learned that Luther's following was much larger than he had assumed and that Luther's exile from Saxony should not be expected. This information aroused Miltitz's diplomatic ambitions. Since his primary mission was to achieve an agreement between the curia and the Saxon elector, he knew that he should pursue that end. The ways and means by which the end was to be achieved Miltitz believed himself commissioned to determine. Thus together with Pfeffinger, he took up the journey to Saxony. In Nuremberg he discussed the Luther affair for two days with Scheurl. Leo X, Miltitz reported, was not at all pleased with Tetzel nor with Prierias, who had written the dogmatic condemnation of Luther's Ninety-Five Theses. Leo had called Tetzel a robber and a swine when he was informed of Tetzel's remark concerning the power of jingling money. (As soon as corn in coffer rings/The soul from purgatory springs.) There was talk, the zealous Miltitz went on, that the pope would reward with a cardinal's hat the settlement of the whole affair that was alarming him. Everything could be reconciled, but the pope must not be gainsaid.

On December 28 Karl von Miltitz arrived in Altenburg where Frederick the Wise was holding court. The Saxon advisors were happy to take up Miltitz's plans and requested Luther to come to Altenburg for discussions, which took place on January 5 and 6, 1519. Luther declared himself prepared publicly to admit that he had been too zealous and abrasive and that he had revealed truth at an inconvenient season. Luther also promised to publish a notice to admonish everyone to obey and revere the Roman Church. The matter was left to die a natural death; from now on he would let the matter stand, but nothing came of the call for revocation. In this frame of mind, Luther drafted a letter to Pope Leo X.

The counselor Fabian von Feilitzsch, who attended the meeting at Altenburg, suggested at the advice of Spalatin that the archbishop of Salzburg, Matthew Lang, should be named as arbitor. Spalatin, remembering that Lang had defended Reuchlin, saw hope in the archbishop's assistance for Luther. Luther agreed to Lang's arbitration, but added that if the pope would not accept an arbitor, neither would he (Luther) accept papal judgment.

Luther's declarations did not help Miltitz very much. Thus the parties met again and agreed that both sides would refrain from preaching, writing, and negotiating on the controversial points. Miltitz also intended to write to the pope and request him to name an arbitor who would demonstrate which of Luther's articles were erroneous and would have to be revoked. Luther agreed to this arrangement provided that preconditions be stipulated: "And as soon as I shall be instructed of my error I should and gladly will revoke and will not detract from the honor and authority of the Holy Roman Church" (WA BR I 294).

That the revocation would not be forthcoming Luther had already announced definitively a day earlier; that he would accept correction from just anyone was highly unlikely. His thinking had already been so fully developed and had found culmination in such a self-contained system that no opposing argument could unnerve him. The disputations and debates already had demonstrated that fact. The *theologia crucis*, the theology of the cross, presented in Heidelberg, had immunized him against all other alien-sounding theological arguments, because the theology of the cross permitted him to interpret every contradiction and threat from the very outset as the necessary confirmation of his own position and indeed to defame as the instruments of the devil the contradictory elements. Luther, in a letter to Wenzel Link just three weeks before the negotiations with Miltitz, had confided the extremities of his intellectual posture: the suspicion that the Roman curia was ruled by the antichrist and that Luther believed himself able to prove that Rome was more evil than the Sublime Porte (WA BR I 270). This was Luther's reaction to the proceedings of heresy directed against him: As you treat me, so I treat you. Here was a sign of his spiritual health and his peasant cunning. With such talents, Luther had finally dealt his enemies such an intellectual defeat that he could regard them with the deepest contempt and feel no scruple or pang of conscience in implementing his own tricks.

Miltitz had negotiated with Luther a compact of silence, but without any legally binding authority, because Miltitz was not empowered to speak for all those who were moved to speak against Luther nor to force their silence. But if Luther's opponents would not be silent, then Luther need not be bound by the agreement with Miltitz. Whether the curia would approve of the Miltitz-Luther agreement remained to be seen. Finally, after a dinner which Miltitz hosted, the disputants peacefully adjourned. At departure, Karl von Miltitz was moved to tears, and Luther was obliged to accept a Judas kiss.

At the same time that Miltitz was striving for his cease-fire agreement, an event occurred around the anticipation of which high diplomacy had revolved for quite some time. In January 1519, Emperor Maximilian died without having achieved a solution to the question of succession. This open question of imperial succession (which had for some time occupied political minds) already had caused Cajetan in August 1518 to exercise caution in his dealing with the Saxon elector and to comply with the wish of Frederick the Wise to grant Luther a "paternal" audience. The imperial succession question also moved the curia to be considerate of Saxony and, for the time being, not to drive the Luther affair to extremes and to permit the heresy proceedings against Luther to remain dormant, or at least to refrain from vigorously prosecuting the case.

Besides Charles I of Spain, who was the grandson of Emperor Maximilian, the French king, Francis I, announced his candidacy for the imperial title. Henry VIII of England also showed interest but withdrew when the matter became too expensive for him. The interests of the French king in this matter demonstrated a certain affinity with the interests of the curia. Francis I wished to prevent an enclosure of France by Hapsburg power as much as the pope desired the papal states to be saved from the Hapsburg vice. Thus the papacy was prone to support the French candidacy. But since France was a firmly established state with strong royal power which, under certain conditions, could also prove to be a threat to the papacy, as it was suspected the House of Hapsburg would prove to be, the candidacy of a German prince would not at all displease the papacy. For a while the plan was considered to persuade the electors Joachim of Brandenburg or Frederick of Saxony to put themselves forward as candidates for the imperial crown. Both, however, declined. Electoral Saxony, to be sure, had a good reputation in the empire, but after the partition in 1485 into Ernestine and Albertine lines, it was too weak to compete against the Hapsburgs. Two factors provided the final reason why, after months of haggling, in the summer of 1519 the electors voted unanimously for the Hapsburg candidate. First, the Fuggers made available to the Hapsburgs 544,000 gulden, and other lenders provided an additional 300,000 gulden toward the Hapsburg candidacy—money which, plainly stated, bribed the electors and bought their votes. (Frederick the Wise pocketed 70,000 gulden for his vote.) Second, the German princes were suspicious of France. They wanted to retain the imperial title in the German nation and not grant it to a foreign power. Thus, finally, the Hapsburg candidate seemed more acceptable than the French one.

While the Luther affair already played a role in high politics, the agreement at Altenburg really did not alter matters in any objective way. The Altenburg agreement remained a secret, and except for the immediate participants present, no one knew about it. To be sure, Luther remained silent a while, and for some weeks he published nothing that was directed against the pope or the curia, but otherwise the polemics continued through sermons, speeches, maledictions, words, pronouncements, and crude rhymes with which Luther's opponents and his supporters attacked one another. The conflict followed an independent course even without Luther's participation, and the provocation became vitriolic.

Challenging the exegetical supremacy and jurisdiction of the pope, Luther, in Wittenberg, had called for a general Church council. This was not a novel idea. Here Luther touched on a fundamental problem in the ecclesiastical constitution, a problem that from the beginning and throughout the entire Middle Ages had predetermined the debates over the constituting of a supreme ecclesiastical authority. Born of the necessity to arrive at a synthesis of opinions and to create an executive will from among the many honorary prelates and representatives of the episcopal and ecclesiastical provinces, the councils had proven themselves not only the preservers of ecclesiastical unity in critical periods but also, from time to time, the rivals of the pope. They had even deposed popes. To a certain degree in the late Middle Ages the councils paralleled the secular estates of the empire.

By the interweaving of family ties in the ecclesiastical hierarchy—a practice of the noble dynasties—the secular feudal order exercised, in the councils no less than elsewhere, its influence on the major decisions of the Church, and feudalism made the Church a useful tool for the aggrandizement of political power. To be sure, the papacy in the long run always overcame the conciliar power, because the pope held the bureaucratic executive authority in his hand, but this papal authority was continually threatened by the latent conciliarism concealed in the Church's own hierarchy. In critical situations, appeals to a council could therefore bring to a head festering inconsistencies between various factions in the higher clergy and especially between secular and ecclesiastical feudal lords. Tensions were produced by these inconsistencies within the feudal system and were heightened by the outbreak of bourgeois revolutionary activity from 1517 to 1524. This activity constituted a struggle to determine which power structure would exercise ultimate control over persons, finances, property, and ecclesiastical organization.

As long as and insofar as the viable authorities demanded a council and at least verbally agreed to respect that council, the reform movement developed through disputation provided for within the feudal system. Within this channel the ruling class attempted to guide the conflict and to resolve it in its own interests. However, the rising popular movement—at first somewhat spontaneously, later with deliberation—used the social elasticity for action which feudalism offered, soon going beyond the parameters of traditional conciliarism and increasingly tending to make the peasant and urban communities the decisive authority for the regulation of social relations. With this development decisions concerning social norms, values, rules of conduct, and laws, hitherto primarily derived from the feudal classes, were transferred directly to the common man and projected into the sphere of influence of the citizen and farmer in cities and villages. A transformation and renewal of society in accordance with the interests, needs, and views of citizens and peasants began to emerge. The originally vague contours of this social transformation became increasingly clear in the conciliar movement and the confrontations of the year 1519.

Chapter 6

"Each City Should Have Its Own Bishop"
The Leipzig Debate and the New Concept of the Nature of the Church
1519

From the beginning of 1519, Franz Günther, whose disputation in September 1517 had played a major role in the victory of Luther's theology at the University of Wittenberg, held a preaching position in Jüterbog and soon became involved in strife with the Franciscans in that city. Franz Günther had experienced the development of Lutheran theology from very close proximity, knew the internal debates, and was completely captivated by the new ideas. What he had heard presented in Latin in the Wittenberg University lecture halls he now preached in German in a popular and barbed idiom, adding some of his own ideas that, of course, had been included in the Wittenberg disputations but had never before been expressed in such a coarse fashion.

The Bible alone is the only standard for the Christian. He should hold to the Scriptures alone; he needs nothing more. The Franciscans who listened to his sermons and who suspiciously lay in wait heard something far more extreme than the claim that the Bible was the sole source of salvation. Günther stormed against penance, fasts, and relics, called the Bohemian Brethren the better Christians, and accused the pope, bishops, and councils of greed. He maintained that a simple person, equipped with the Bible, was much more credible than the pope.

The proposition that the average person might interpret Holy Scripture became symptomatic of the attempt of the Wittenberg theologians to seek liaison with the common folk. Furthermore, it was not coincidental that this idea was preached from the pulpit and circulated outside the university in precisely those places where the audience did not consist of scholars, masters, and doctors, but rather of peasant farmers, artisans, apprentices, tradesmen, maids, and the inquisitive, attentive populace.

This appeal to the common man corresponded well with the intentions of Luther's theology. At the existing stage of development of his theology, this appeal was inevitably deduced from the teaching of justification by faith alone. When bishops, doctors, and cardinals attacked Luther, then the average person representing the general populace would prove who was correct according to the Bible. We will see that some years later a new situation arose in which Luther was no longer willing to allow such conclusions unreservedly. In 1519, however, Luther had nothing against such a popular appeal; in fact, such an argument appeared at the moment attractive to him, and he took no offense in the fact that Franz Günther attacked the councils, thereby rendering superfluous Luther's recent call for a council and preempting its effect.

The appeal to the common man was directed against the established authorities. To be sure, the common man at first was granted only the right to decide whether and to what extent an opinion corresponded to the Bible. But having been granted this much in questions concerning the Bible, it was no great step also to assign him the right to decide social and political questions. Thus this appeal to the common man strengthened the self-consciousness of a reformed popular movement which, in its first stirrings, was gaining visibility.

The Franciscan appeal to the Brandenburg court of Bishop Jerome Schulze resulted in the censoring of Franz Günther. While the Franciscans believed that they had nipped the dangerous Jüterbog development in the bud, Luther sent another preacher to Jüterbog, Thomas Müntzer. In Luther's life story we encounter for the first time the name of that man whose revolutionary energy brought into clear focus the social and epochal limitations of Luther's impact. In 1519, to be sure, nothing of Thomas Müntzer's future role was revealed. On the contrary, Müntzer steps into the light of history as that associate of Luther who is at first characterized by the Jüterbog Franciscans in their polemical pamphlets by the contemptuous description, "Lutheran."

There are only meager accounts concerning what Thomas Müntzer experienced and thought before coming into contact with Luther. Born in 1489 or shortly before in Stolberg in the Harz mountain region into an artisan's family, Müntzer matriculated in 1506 at the University of Leipzig. In 1512, he studied theology at the University of Frankfurt on the Oder. In 1513, he was employed as tutor in Halle on the Saale, in 1514–1515 in Aschersleben, and in 1516–1517 as prior in the monastery of Frohse near Aschersleben. As these few dates suggest, Müntzer had difficulty after he had completed his theological curriculum in finding a satisfactory position. In the light of later development, we can with some justification venture to guess that the search for a new position also was an expression of a struggle for self-realization and personal growth. That one day Müntzer's attention was drawn to Martin Luther, and that as a result his path would turn toward Wittenberg, is not surprising given the geographical proximity to Wittenberg of the places where Müntzer was employed.

Luther made a good choice in assigning Müntzer to Jüterbog. Müntzer pursued the same goal in Jüterbog as that of his predecessor, Günther. He launched a frontal assault against the papacy and supported his position with the argument of the conciliarists, who held that only in partnership with the bishops was the pope the head of the Church. The pope was obligated to convoke a council every five years, but in reality the papacy had permitted only three councils in four centuries. The bishops were empowered to convene a council even against the will of the pope, but they thought only of themselves and were not holy fathers but vain tyrants. They were able only to "fart and stink"; they deceived the people, and they understood neither Greek nor Hebrew. The scholastics, Thomas Aquinas and Bonaventure, were unjustifiably canonized. Their teachings were founded on natural reason, but natural reason was of the devil. As whores and pimps invaded the cities, the teachings of Aquinas and Bonaventure invaded the Church. The gospel had been obliterated *(unter der Bank gelegen)* for the last three or four hundred years, and many heads would have to roll before the gospel could be rescued from neglect.

Müntzer's preaching was too much for the Franciscans. Quickly they appealed again to the bishop of Brandenburg. The bishop had already warned Luther in February that he should cease criticizing the papacy and not disseminate the thesis that the papacy had obscured the gospel for three or four hundred years. But this was the very thesis that Müntzer preached in Jüterbog. What could be more obvious? Müntzer was a "Lutheran." Thus at the end of April, the Franciscans, convoked with the representative of the bishop, decided not merely to polemicize against Müntzer and Günther personally but to attack in them the whole Lutheran movement. Hence, the Franciscan Bernhard Dappan composed a tract, *Articuli per fratres Minores ... contra Luteranos* (Articles of the Franciscans Against the Lutherans). The name of Luther had become the name of a movement. This fact describes in a certain way a new phase in the public consciousness: a new name for a new movement was a sign that the previous identifications were no longer sufficient to convey the understanding of the movement which now ominously began to swell.

Luther, who received a copy of the articles of Bernhard Dappan in their handwritten form in mid-May before the articles were printed, identified himself with his followers Günther and Müntzer. Günther and Müntzer had acted in total agreement with Luther and had disseminated those ideas among the people which Luther himself in the past months had promoted. Since his work on the *Acta Augustana*, his description of the Augsburg meeting with Cajetan, the thought persisted that the papacy was the antichrist, that opponent of Christ whose rule would presage the imminent end of the world. In December 1518, Luther for the first time mentioned this dreadful suspicion in a letter to a friend. Luther's suspicion corresponded with that mood of an all embracing crisis which, for example, found its artistic expression in *The Four Horsemen of the Apocalypse* of Albrecht Dürer, in pictures of the reaper, and in pictures of the dance of death. Luther's suspicion testifies above all to the fact that he from now on would be driven by the logic of the intellectual and political confrontation into eschatology, or the theological teaching concerning the "last things," and was thereby to sever spiritually the last inner ties to the Roman ecclesiastical system. With this break, Luther suffered through almost all those stages of intellectual liberation from traditional authority that we can repeatedly observe with astonishing regularity among the leading men of the first German revolution. These pangs were apparently the necessary prerequisite for giving birth to the new ideas for a new social order. Luther's idea which presented the picture of a new life and enabled him to unite all forces opposed to Rome was his new concept of the Church.

Originating and assuming form from Luther's fundamental interpretation of justification by faith alone—the interpretation that made it possible—this new concept of the Church first came to light in all its brilliance in the debates of the year 1519. The immediate occasion for such a breakthrough was offered in the Leipzig debate with the Ingolstadt theology professor, Dr. Johannes Eck.

Luther had first met Eck in October 1518 in Augsburg and had agreed with him that the argument which had erupted between Eck and Karlstadt in the spring of 1518 should be settled in a disputation. Leipzig was selected as the place where the debate could be conducted. But for Eck, the skirmishing with Karlstadt was only a preliminary maneuver to draw out Luther. At the end of December 1518, Eck published his theses for the disputation. The questions that had caused the strife with Karlstadt Eck dealt with only cursorily. But some propositions from Luther's Ninety-Five Theses and the explanations of the Ninety-Five Theses Eck examined more carefully. In his *Resolutiones,* Luther had made the incidental observation that the Roman Catholic Church in the time of Pope Gregory the Great (590–604) exercised no sovereignty over the Greek Church. There hardly could be an argument against this observation because it corresponded with the facts. But Eck instinctively sensed that behind Luther's observation dangerous ideas lurked: doubt about the primacy of the papacy and therewith doubt about the primacy of the Roman Church, doubt which already could be suspected from some insidious statements in Luther's theses. Eck wanted to expose Luther's hidden heresy and therefore he baited Luther with the thesis that it was false to maintain that the Roman Church had not achieved sovereignty over the other churches before the pontificate of Pope Sylvester (314–335).

Luther easily could have escaped Eck's stratagem. He needed only to respond that he had never made such a claim and that Eck's thesis therefore did not address itself to him. But Eck had not miscalculated. Luther took the bait. In reply to Eck's thesis, Luther wrote in thesis 12 (in the later edition, thesis 13), "That the Roman Church is sovereign over all other churches is proven from the very feeble papal decretals that have appeared

Pope Leo X (1513–1521)
painting by
Raffaelo Santi 1519

Dispensing of papal blessing on St. Peter's Square in Rome
copperplate, 2nd half of 16th century

Johann Tetzel riding a donkey. Caricature of Tetzel's selling of indulgences; one-side woodcut, about 1517

View of Wittenberg
copperplate, 1546

Market square in Wittenberg with city hall,
Melanchthon and Luther memorials,
and city church

Castle Church in Wittenberg about 1509
woodcut by Lucas Cranach

Castle Church. Bronze door with the 95 theses

Emperor Charles V
painting by Barent van Orley, around 1521

Elector Frederick the Wise of Saxony
copperplate by Albrecht Dürer, 1523

Archbishop Albrecht of Brandenburg
copperplate by Albrecht Dürer, 1523

Duke George the Bearded of Saxony
painting by Lucas Cranach, workshop, 1534

Martin Luther's Meeting with Cardinal Cajetan after the Augsburg Reichstag in 1518
coloured woodcut, Strasburg 1557

Georg Spalatin
contemporary woodcut

Martin Luther with doctor's cap
copperplate by Lucas Cranach, 1521

M. GEORGIVS SPALATINVS,
Misnensium ac Nariscorum Evangelista,
Primus Superintendens Altenburgensis,
Trium Electorum Consiliarius Ecclesiasticus,
Primusq; Historicus Saxonicus,
Natus Spalati MCCCCLXXXII.
Denatus Altenburgi MDXLV.

IN SILENTIO ET SPE. ERIT FORTITVDO VESTRA

MARTINVS   LVTHERVS

ASSERVIT CHRISTVM DIVINA VOCE LVTHERVS·
CVLTIBVS OPPRESSAM RESTITVITQVE FIDEM·
ILLIVS ABSENTIS VVLTVM HAC DEPINGIT IMAGO
PRÆSENTEM MELIVS CERNERE NEMO POTEST·
M · D · XXI·

The Pleissenburg in Leipzig
watercolour by Gottfried Bachmann, 1782

Disputation between Luther and Eck at Leipzig's Pleissenburg in 1519
after a painting by C. F. Lessing

Violation of the Ten Commandments
painting by Lucas Cranach, 1516
left to right — top: Thou shalt have no other gods
before me; Thou shalt not take the name of the Lord
thy God in vain; Remember the sabbath day to keep it holy;
Honour thy father and thy mother; Thou shalt not kill
below: Thou shalt not steal; Thou shalt not
commit adultery; Thou shalt not bear false witness
against thy neighbour; Thou shalt not covet thy neighbour's
wife; Thou shalt not covet any thing that is thy
neighbour's.

only in the last four hundred years. Against these decretals speak credible history of the first eleven centuries, the text of Holy Scripture, and the decree of the Council of Nicaea, the most sacred of all councils" (WA II 161).

For this master stroke, Luther received no praise from his colleagues and his supporters in high places. What for Luther was the knowledge derived from history and inner necessity, they considered to be improvident. Spalatin implored him to avoid this theme. The elector called attention to the agreement of silence worked out with such difficulty with Miltitz, and the elector desired the agreement to be respected. The bishop of Brandenburg sent an earnest warning to Luther. Thomas Müntzer, on the other hand, seized upon the thesis, as we have seen in the Jüterbog events, and used it for agitating the populace.

This thesis introduced a new stage in Luther's intellectual development. If up to this point he had come to a clear understanding with respect to the basic questions of faith, of the place of man before God, and of the nature of the gospel of Jesus Christ, now he set for himself the goal of examining the basic question of the Church's constitution. Previously he had broached this question in his appeals, first "to a pope better informed" and then to the general council. Luther's motivation in pursuing this theme was provided by his ultimate, most decisive idea—that for the Christian no higher authority may exist than Jesus Christ exclusively. Luther's questioning of papal authority was propelled from the necessity to defend himself against the authorities mobilized against him, and that questioning received its caustic sharpness from the suspicion aroused in him concerning the papacy as antichrist.

Luther himself sensed that in his argument with Eck something new was being introduced. "The matter tends toward the holy canons (Church law), as you may see," Luther wrote to Willibald Pirckheimer on February 20, 1519. "I will preserve and acknowledge the power of the high priest, but I will not permit the Holy Scriptures to be corrupted" (WA BR I 348). In the light of his suspicions about the papacy that in these weeks oppressed him, which he publicly revealed a little later in the first printing of the psalter lectures and which in a letter to Spalatin he reaffirmed, the first part of this statement of Pirckheimer indeed suggests that preserving the office of the high priest was not an insoluble task or merely lip service to the office. How was Luther able to recognize the power of the pope when he considered him to be the antichrist? And how did Luther expect to hold fast the Scriptures and not permit them to be corrupted? Without sophistry this balancing act between Bible and Church law could not be mastered. Because, in case of doubt, Luther consistently decided in favor of the Bible, a conflict with Church law was unavoidable.

Luther prepared for the Leipzig disputation by studying the papal decretals and Church history. This approach was necessary since Eck with his theses had pressed Luther into an area of historical argumentation. From Eck's theses it was clear that the disputation would concern itself with the question of how long the Roman Church had exercised authority over other churches, a question of fixing a date.

For months it was uncertain whether Luther would ever be admitted to Leipzig in Albertine Saxony for the debate. Leipzig University was not at all pleased at the prospect of offering a forum to a person suspected of being a notorious heretic in order that he might disseminate his condemnable teaching. It took the command of Duke George to persuade the Leipzig faculty. Duke George was interested in having the debate take place because he wanted once and for all to silence Luther. In the meantime an invitation arrived in Wittenberg from Karl von Miltitz, inviting Luther to Coblenz where Luther was to place himself under the arbitration of the bishop of Trier and to conduct still another conversation with Cardinal Cajetan. Luther declined the invitation. He had had enough of Cajetan and wanted to concentrate on his preparation for the Leipzig debate with Eck.

In Wittenberg and Leipzig the students became greatly excited about the upcoming disputation, and an ever-increasing public interest anticipated the big event. From Görlitz, Dresden, Annaberg, Regensburg, and many other cities many people made their way to the city on the Pleisse River; among the throng was Thomas Müntzer. Accompanied by 200 armed students, Karlstadt, Luther, and Melanchthon entered Leipzig on June 24, 1519, through the Grimma Gate. On entering the city an accident occurred, a bad omen as the popular mind would immediately interpret such things. A wheel came off the wagon in which Karlstadt was riding, causing the wagon to tip over. Karlstadt fell from the wagon so violently that he hemorrhaged and suffered severe sprains which the physicians treated with bloodletting, causing him to be weak for days and significantly hampering his ability to concentrate. Luther took accommodations with the printer, Melchior Lotter, on Hain Street. Eck had arrived in Leipzig two days earlier on June 22, welcomed and flattered by the venerable of the city who provided him with a horse for his daily riding exercise.

After a solemn worship service in St. Thomas' Church and a ceremonial procession, the Leipzig professor of poetry, Peter Mosellanus, opened the disputation on June 27 in the festively decorated court chamber of the Pleissenburg. With a mind for symbolism, the sponsors indicated in pictures with which they decorated the places of the disputants what was expected of the debates and what results were anticipated. A likeness of St. George the Dragon-Slayer was placed on Eck's lectern and a likeness of St. Martin at Luther's podium. Mosellanus described the dragon-slayer:

> Eck is tall with a solid, burly build. The resonant, genuinely German voice that reverberates from his deep chest sounds like that of a town-

crier or a tragedian actor, but it is more harsh than distinct. The euphony of Latin, so highly praised by Fabius and Cicero, is not to be detected in Eck's speech. His mouth and eyes, or rather his whole physiognomy, suggest a butcher or a raw soldier rather than a theologian. Concerning his intellect, he has a phenominal memory. If his understanding matched his memory, we would have a picture of the ideal man before us. But he lacks quickness of comprehension and discernment in judgment, qualities without which all other gifts are useless .... His gestures are almost theatrical, his appearance imperious. In brief, he gives no hint of being a theologian. He is no more than an unusual, cheeky, indeed, brazen, sophist. (Walsh XV 391)

To be sure, Mosellanus in his introductory speech did not possess Eck's harshness; Mosellanus' voice was sputtering and unsure rather than distinct. Confusion, croaking, and stuttering did not exactly give the impression that one might expect from a professor of poetry. It is not wonder that Eck—the stocky, self-assured Swabian—displeased Mosellanus. With respect to critical judgment and ready comprehension, the whole debate proved Mosellanus' evaluation of Eck inaccurate. In any case, Karlstadt paled before Eck, and Luther had no easy time with his Ingolstadt rival. While Karlstadt awkwardly sought for citations and references in the books that he had piled before him on the lectern, thereby bringing the tempo of the debate to a standstill, Eck quoted freely and unhesitatingly from memory and poured forth references so fast that no one could check them. Eck was displeased that the debate followed the German custom, according to which each debater was required to speak slowly enough for four protocol notaries to write down each word. Eck would have preferred the Italian style of debate in which each debater could develop his own technique freely without regard to the note takers. In Louvain, Bologna, and Vienna, Eck had met with glorious success in this debating style; he was such a lion in the grandiose style and continental format of debate that the Wittenbergers appeared somewhat provincial. The people who previously in Augsburg and now again in Leipzig defended the interest of the Roman Church were not mediocre, not mere butchers or mercenary hucksters; they were part of the intellectual elite of Europe. The questions raised in these debates were of a nature that justified the participation of Europe's intellectual elite.

Martin Luther formulated the questions in a general but cautious manner in a sermon given at Leipzig Castle on June 29, 1519, the first Sunday after the beginning of the debate and before Luther himself had begun to debate, while Karlstadt alone for several days tiresomely dragged on with Eck. Duke Barnim of Pomerania had requested Luther to preach. Originally Luther was to have preached in the Castle Church, but the crowds were so large that the service had to be transfered to the court debating hall because the populace was anxious to hear explained in German what was being discussed in the interminably long Latin speeches. Luther explained that they were discussing grace, free will, and papal authority. The first themes, that is, grace and free will, had been explored by the great sages and saints of the past who believed that by their own device and their own works they could order everything. But the Lord taught that all things of flesh and blood were in vain because no one born of flesh and blood could recognize Christ (let alone follow Him) unless God in heaven revealed Him. With such words, Luther summarized in simple and clear language the conclusions of the disputations of 1516-1517. He placed all Christianity on the foundation of revelation alone and thereby severed all imput of philosophizing and natural science from the matter of Christian teaching. Luther employed simple German without if, and, or but. His clarity signified that, for him, this stage of his intellectual development had been completed and that it had led him to unshakable certainty that left room for little further reflection and that he at all times could confess.

Luther spoke less clearly concerning papal authority, the other theme. For Luther there were still many unanswered aspects of this question. The disputation on this question had not yet taken place and hence it did not seem advisable to commit oneself to firm affirmations. "It is not necessary for the common man to dispute extensively about St. Peter's authority or papal power; how to use it for salvation is more important" (WA II 248). Luther formulated his thought in thus preparing the sermon for publication. It may have been presented differently in the actual oral delivery: in the disputation Eck tried to pin him on the despicable utterance concerning the papacy that Luther was alleged to have made in the sermon, though one searches in vain for the offense in the printed text. Instead of a despicable utterance, one finds a very clear expression concerning the power of the Petrine keys. Luther from the very beginning insists that this does not mean a papal supremacy over souls, even if there is an inclination to regard the popes as the legitimate successors of Peter. "It is true, the keys are given to St. Peter, though not to Peter personally but rather as to the person of the Christian Church, and thus they are given to you and to me in order to comfort our conscience" (WA II 248).

The keys are given to you and me—this is a bold assertion which cannot necessarily be justified from the words that Jesus spoke to Peter, at least not in the sense that you and I possess power freely to apply the keys. But this does not exclude consideration of Luther's more democratic interpretation, which shows the direction in which Luther sougth a solution to the question of Church organization.

After a week of parrying with difficulty Eck's rhetorical assaults, Karlstadt gave place to Luther. On July 4, Luther entered the lists. Mosellanus described his appearance:

Martin is of medium height with a gaunt body that has been so emaciated by worry and study that one can almost count the bones under the skin. He is of a virile, fresh age and has a high, clear voice. He is so learned and knows the Scriptures so well that his biblical references are at his finger tips. He knows enough Greek and Hebrew to be able to form judgments concerning interpretations. He is not lacking in command of his subject matter, in his great store of words, and in illustrations. In his deportment he is very courteous and friendly, and he is not austere or morose; he is a man for all seasons. In society he is jovial, witty, vivacious, and always appears happy, no matter how threatening his adversaries. One can see in his countenance that God is with him in his difficult task. The only flaw of which everyone accuses him is that he is sharp and caustic in reprimanding, in fact more than is seemly for one who would blaze new trails in theology, and certainly more than is seemly for a divine. (Walch XV 391)

The major theme of the debate between Luther and Eck was the authority and primacy of the pope. The discussion concerning this theme lends to the Leipzig debate its principal significance. What was said concerning purgatory, indulgences, penance, and other subjects was of less significance and was certainly less effective in arousing the interest of the listeners. Eck sought to lead Luther onto thin ice. Thus his first pronouncement was that monarchy and primacy in the Church are divine rights. Luther agreed without ado but added that this was not relevant. Eck had reckoned with such a response and was able to notch his first plus. Eck now had only to illustrate the principle of monarchy, already acknowledged by Luther. This principle was applied in the Roman papacy. If Luther should resist Eck on this point, then it would be easy to accuse him of heresy because the Council of Constance had concluded that the papacy was necessary for salvation and was divinely ordained. Therefore, Eck asked the ensnaring question concerning the supreme head of the Church: "If the Church militant cannot be without a monarch, I would like to know who this monarch could be or ever could have been other than the Roman Pontifex, or whose chair was the first if not that of St. Peter and his successors" (WA II 256). Luther answered: "As the monarch of the Church militant and as her head, I recognize no man but Christ Himself, and His headship rests on divine authority … . There are many chairs upon which the one Christ sits; we see the chairs but not the one who sits upon them and is king" (WA II 257). With this answer Luther's tactic is clear: Christ is juxtaposed to papal authority!

However, Eck was not so easily deterred. On the contrary, Luther's answer opened more widely than ever before the possibility of concentrating the question on the primacy of Peter and thereby on the primacy of the pope, because the fact that Christ was the head of the Church would be challenged by no one but the antichrist. Nevertheless, Christ was the mystical head of the invisible, triumphant Church and not of the visible, militant Church, which needed a visible, natural head. Eck was absolutely certain of his opinion on the matter and in agreement with the doctors of canon law. Eck was prepared to grant Luther's point that Christ was the head of the Church, but Eck also possessed many sources from which he derived that, apart from Christ, there was another head in the Church and that Peter had been appointed head of the apostles and of the Church.

Luther also knew Eck's references; they did not intimidate him in the least. Luther picked them apart one by one and indicated that these references dealt only partially or not at all with the question at hand; in other instances they supported Eck, though often they opposed him and what he was seeking to prove. What was finally decisive for Luther, however, was that the references were subordinate to God's Word, which for him was the single, absolute authority.

In order to repudiate Luther's answer, Eck elevated the argumentation to a new plane and drove Luther onto the heresy stage. Among the condemned statements of Wycliffe was the proposition that it was not necessary to salvation to believe that the Roman Church occupied a preference over other churches. Moreover, one of Hus's pestilential errors was that Peter is not and was not the head of the Holy Catholic Roman Church.

This charge that Luther's thought resembled Wycliffite and Hussite heresy stuck. Now matters became serious. Luther bristled. Curtly and bitterly he rejected such association. Already in his theses Eck had suggested that Luther's ideas were similar to those of the Hussites. Now Eck hammered home the similarity of the thinking of Hus and Luther. Eck could not have wished for a better place than Leipzig to charge Luther with Hussitism. The devastating Hussite wars were still a terrifying memory for the Saxon nobility and especially for Duke George, who happened on the day of the charge to attend the debate. As Eck cleverly turned the debate toward the Hussite question, Duke George became sensitive. The Hussite king, George Podiebrad, was his maternal grandfather, and Duke George, ashamed of this stain on the family history, bitterly resented any allusion to his grandfather's Hussite beliefs.

Luther sought to evade the point. He was not a Bohemian and had no interest in defending Bohemian errors. Luther could have pointed out at that juncture in the debate that he himself as early as 1518, in his exegesis of Psalm 109, had written against the Bohemians. At that time Luther was displeased with the withdrawal of the Bohemians from the Roman Church, and he had ridiculed their opinion, "We are not like the Germans; we, out of a fear of God, do not wish to remain in the Roman Church." Luther had commented, "That is the same as saying, in the name of God we want to go to hell and let the Germans in the name of the devil go to heaven" (WA I

697). However, now at Leipzig, Luther did not speak about this earlier reference, but perhaps he thought about it when he replied to the question with which Eck goaded him: "If the Bohemians are so displeasing to the famous doctor, why does he not tax his memory and talent and write against them?" (WA II 278). Luther marveled that the Bohemians met only with accusers and with no one who would fraternally instruct them.

But all of Luther's evasive tactics did not help. Eck bored more deeply and called Luther a patron of the Hussites. Luther protested and forbade that such a suggestion be made concerning him. Finally on July 5, after the midday meal, the statement erupted from Luther, "Among the articles of Johannes Hus or the Bohemians there are many that are genuinely Christian and evangelical which the general Church cannot condemn: for example, the statement that there is only one universal Church" (WA II 279). Eck had waited for this moment. Now Luther was trapped. He had defended the opinion of a legally condemned heretic as Christian and evangelical! To be sure, he had not defended Hus and the Bohemians in general; in fact, he had expressly distanced himself from their errors, but that he had praised some of their statements was enough to raise the charge against him that he despised conciliar judgments.

Luther once again protested, but the rationale of Luther's previous statements tended to confirm Eck's suspicion. Thus to move Luther to revoke his contention that some Hussite ideas were Christian and evangelical (revocation would have been equivalent to defeat in the debate) or to elicit from him additional heretical statements, Eck had only to emphasize repeatedly that conciliar judgments must be respected because they were inspired by the Holy Spirit and were the consequence of divine law. On the next day Luther wriggled and squirmed in seeking to present an explanation, but his explanation led only to new contradictions. "I agree with the doctor that conciliar judgments are to be respected in all cases in which they concern faith, but one thing must be said: that councils have erred and sometimes do err in matters which do not concern faith and also that the council has no authority to enact new articles of faith; otherwise, we would end up with as many articles as we have opinions among people" (WA II 303).

Such a position was untenable for, if the conciliar judgments were binding in matters of faith, then it was necessary that the council have the authority to state such valid decisions as articles of faith. In fact, the councils had always done just that. Luther knew this, but he considered it an intolerable presumption that men make claims of infallibility for themselves; such claims, in his opinion, could be made only by God's Word. Luther was prepared to recognize and respect conciliar decisions as man's word, but not as the Word of the Holy Spirit. Thus Luther firmly rejected the experience and the wisdom of more than a millennium of Church history when he challenged the venerable Dr. Eck the next day to prove that a council could not err and had not erred; Luther declared that a council could not decree divine law because in its nature the council was not divine, and only that which was against divine law was heretical (WA II 308).

The gap between the two positions was unbridgeable. Eck's response was motivated not only by his inquisitional intention regarding Luther. "I say to you honorable Father, if you believe that a legitimately convoked council errs and has erred, then you are to me as a pagan and tax collector. I do not need to definde for the audience what a heretic is" (WA II 311). Eck could not have responded otherwise because his thought and feelings were based on a view of the Church entirely different from the view that molded Luther's thought. For Eck the Church as ruled and represented by the pope was hierarchical in structure, a strictly organized body for the preservation of the sacraments by which the priest mediated salvation to man. Luther had once held the same view. But through his study of the Scriptures a new picture of the Church had emerged. Even before the disputation Luther had expressed his new view of the Church: "Wherever the Word of God is preached and believed, there is true faith, an unshakeable rock. Where faith is, there is the Church. Wherever the Church is, there is the bride of Christ; where the bride of Christ is, there is everything that belongs to the bridegroom. Thus faith contains everything which follows from faith: keys, sacraments, authority, and everything else" (WA II 208).

By "Church" Eck meant an institution to which one must submit; Luther, on the other hand, defined "Church" as a movement that lived by faith. Eck's definition was buttressed by the rationality of the existing institution developed over a 1,500-year period. Luther canceled the 1,500 years and returned to apostolic times so that the institution which now existed in contrast to the primitive model appeared irrational and corrupt. Primitive Christianity knew neither a pope nor a primacy of the Roman Church. The Jerusalem congregation was at least twenty years older than the Roman one. The apostles who founded churches on many sites were not commissioned by Peter but were called by Jesus. To this apostolic band the Lord called the apostle Paul to a mission entirely outside the precincts of Jerusalem, and Paul shepherded more sheep and founded more congregations that did Peter. When Luther spoke about the beginnings of the Church, a flood of arguments poured forth from him, critical of the primacy of the pope and the supremacy of the Roman Church. From Luther's interpretation it is plain that he regarded the Church as a body of congregations, especially urban congregations, fitly joined together. "Each city should have its own bishop," Luther wrote later in summarizing the Leipzig debate (WA II 433). He based this conviction on the words of St. Paul (Titus 1:5) and concluded from this text that all bishops in principle were equal because all had been ordained by the Church. According to divine law, the Roman bishop was just like any other bishop; insofar as he possessed a primary position, however, it was to be attributed to human covenant. In this sense, Luther was prepared gladly to recognize the supremacy of the Roman Pontiff as it did, does, or would exist: "But one thing I know, that it is a new dogma to confirm the Roman primacy by divine law because none of the ancient fathers mention such an article of faith" (WA II 434). This form of recognition of papal primacy was no admission or concession at all. On the contrary, the primacy of the pope was abandoned unprotected to the will of legislative bodies that exercised authority over everything not protected by divine law. With the pronouncement: "Each city should have its own bishop" and with the restructuring of papal primacy to human convention, theoretically the course was set to solve the constitutional questions of the Church independently of Rome and under the special consideration of urban interests.

For four days the debate concerning the authority and primacy of the pope continued under the riveted attention of the auditors who sought to write down the most important statements. Attention waned as the less interesting themes were introduced. On July 14, Eck and Luther met at 7:00 A.M. for one more hour of debate, and finally it was again Karlstadt's turn to debate for two days. On July 16, the debate which had lasted for three weeks was declared ended. The themes had been exhausted and the most important points had been made; besides, Duke George was expecting other company, a visit from the elector of Brandenburg.

In a certain sense such a debate is to be compared with a tournament. That, at least, is the way the contemporaries regarded it. It was necessary to observe the established rules: prescribed, polite addresses; an exchange of theses in advance; note taking of the whole debate; assigned seats for the speakers; an honor guard; and silence on the part of the audience. At the conclusion of a tournament, however, a winner is declared. The spectators see who lies vanquished in the dust. No such scene is visible at the conclusion of a debate. Of course the auditors have their own opinion concerning victor and vanquished, but appearance deceives and, therefore, competent juries were enlisted to evaluate such debates. Eck and Karlstadt had agreed to recognize the University of Erfurt as jury. Eck and Luther, in addition to recognizing the University of Erfurt as jury, submitted their arguments to the Sorbonne in Paris. In order to ensure impartiality, it was agreed that no Dominican or Augustinian from the University of Erfurt be permitted to serve on the jury.

Luther accepted all the conditions. One thing, however, made him uneasy: that scholastic theologians, all of whom he had offended, should serve as judges of the Leipzig debate. The response to his "theses against scholastic theology" had confirmed in the autumn of 1517 and had reconfirmed in the Heidelberg disputation of April 1518 that the old, gray-bearded theologians shook their heads skeptically and braced themselves against the new ideas while the youth joyfully assented. Therefore Luther demanded that not only should theologians participate in judging the theses of the Leipzig disputation but that in Erfurt and Paris the entire faculty should take part. In a memorandum to Duke George, Luther justified his demand with the claim that the younger members of the faculty were more discerning than the older ones, who knew only what was written in their own books. Material presented by him, Luther claimed, was regarded as new and was repugnant to those who until the present time had been the theologians. The time had come "that according to divine order all things which dissemble and deceive are suspect by all and it has almost come to the point that they are not theologians whom one believed to be theologians, for the learned are ignorant" (WA BR I 431). According to Luther, Dr. Eck had spent himself in ridiculing Luther and his theses while presenting his own theses with the greatest favor, currying approval from the old theologians, who made Luther look like a fool.

However, Duke George rejected Luther's suggestion. The disputation protocol was to be sent to the theologians and canon lawyers in Erfurt and Paris because people who were not experts in these matters could not serve as judges. Thus the protocol was duly sent to Erfurt and Paris, but no decision regarding the Leipzig debate was ever rendered. Erfurt declined to give an opinion, and Paris' exorbitant fee for services was too high for Duke George.

Luther was very dissatisfied with the Leipzig disputation. He was outraged at the treatment that he had received. Eck had been condescending to Luther and Karlstadt and had feigned the role of their instructor in scholastic thought. Eck's treatment of Karlstadt was especially contemptible. In reality Eck's pronouncements concerning free will were no different from Karlstadt's. Eck admitted that free will was nothing without grace, that without grace free will could only sin, and that even in good works sin was present. But Eck acted as if his own statements regarding free will were completely different from those of Karlstadt. Eck had no strong convictions concerning indulgences, and he even admitted that he could easily have agreed with Luther on all points if only the question concerning the papal primacy had not been raised. Eck's manner of speech in the debating forum was quite different from that used in the pulpit. When Karlstadt reminded him of the discrepancy, Eck bluntly responded that it was not fitting to teach the common people that which was debated. "And thus, it does not seem wrong to him at one time to say this and at another time to say that, but the Leipzigers do not catch on to his tricks: they are too dull," Luther angrily informed Spalatin (WA BR I 423). A righteous indignation had forced Luther to pen this verdict. Luther's anger was not reserved for the Leipzigers and for Eck, in whom he could see only an example of outrageous conduct. That not everything which was said in the lecture halls and in the debate forum would be proclaimed to the people from the pulpit was the practice of the scholars. The reason for such a custom was partly intellectual arrogance, partly the inability to speak clearly in good German about theology and philosophy, but also partly because difficult questions first had to be clarified in one's own exclusive circle. Finally, the practice of speaking to the common people in a manner different from that in which one spoke to one's colleagues sprang from the position of priests and scholars in the social structure of feudalism. It was possible to reach agreement with colleagues on sublime questions of the formation of ideology, and that was of no concern to the people. The common people should confine their interests to what had long been accepted as certain knowledge.

Luther himself was not free of this practice of that class to which he belonged. He also knew how to distinguish between what should be discussed with friends and what could be said on the street. But what had bothered Luther for a long time was a theme which could no longer be treated as of no concern to the people. The sparrows sang from the rooftops that matters in the Church were not always conducted according to the Word of God. Thus it was not only from inner compulsion that Luther spoke to the people, concerning himself with what was being said on the street and how the people judged his cause; but the street, the market, the city well, the inn, the tavern, the artisan's atelier, and the apprentice's bench spoke to him. They did not direct his pen; Luther was the master of that. Neither did they peer over his shoulder; they would only have annoyed him by so doing. They were simply present and demonstrated to Luther a healthy common sense. As early as the fall of 1517, in the theses against the abuse of indulgences, Luther had incorporated barbed questions from the laity. Now after the Leipzig debate he took up these threads once again; the deeper he penetrated into the „pure" theological questions on the nature of the Church, the more practical became the conclusions that imposed themselves on him; the closer the affairs of daily life pressed in on him and determined the problems that occupied his attention and to which he turned, the more fully developed became his line of thought.

This practical approach helped him overcome the dissatisfied mood which plagued him after Leipzig. Eck unintentionally contributed to the restoration of Luther's confidence. In order to place the Wittenbergers in a bad light and to expose them as liars, Eck wrote letters to Elector Frederick, presenting his interpretation of the course of the Leipzig disputation. Luther and Karlstadt were obliged to respond to Eck's account. They did so thoroughly and completely and with increasing conviction, depicting themselves in their version of the debate as the victors. Luther especially praised Karlstadt. Presentation and counter-presentation continued until

November 1519. Eck's primary purpose was to rob Luther of his strongest support, the favor of the elector. But Eck received no more than a polite acknowledgement from the elector. Luther, however, in the meantime, could remind the elector of the cloth promised him and, after a brief period, upon reception of the gift, could write a thank you letter to the elector, his prince. Luther stood in uninterrupted favor at the electoral court. Knowing among other things how to consolidate that position, Luther composed a consoling letter to the ill elector. The unusual title is derived from the *Tessaradeka*, the fourteen helpers to whom the Christian in need and despair should turn. But this appeal to the saints no longer had any significance for Luther. Instead of the saints, Luther presented to the elector seven evils and seven virtues on which the elector was to fix his gaze and from which he was to seek solace.

Luther wrote *A Sermon on Preparing to Die*, a small pamphlet of similar content, for Markus Schart, an advisor of Frederick the Wise. Luther demonstrated his masterful pastoral talent in this work. Man should think of death and dying as long as things went well with him and he had time to do so. When the hour of death approached, it was too late to begin to think about death and dying. Man should not torment himself with the thought of sins committed because sin increased when one thought about it too much. One should make use of the sacraments, for they combatted the terrible image of death, sin, and hell. One should not think about whether he was elected or condemned. Behold Christ! When one found solace in Him, then one was of the elect; then one had faith, and then the sacraments also would prove beneficial to him (WA II 685-97).

Luther advised turning to the sacraments when death approached. In the fall of 1519, the sacraments more than any other subjekt occupied his thought. Uninterruptedly his thoughts revolved around the sacraments, and he repeatedly returned to this theme. The sacraments stood in an inner connection with the realization that the traditional concept of the Church which had been handed down to him now had become problematic for him. In the discussions concerning the primacy of the pope Luther was compelled to occupy himself with the constitutional questions of the Church. One of the more important conclusions to which he came was that the bishops were in principle all equal. At the same time the distinction between the visible and invisible Church had become a point of contention in the Leipzig disputation, and Luther had revealed that he tended to make the nature of the visible Church as well as that of the invisible Church entirely dependent on faith. But that which was visible in the Church was demonstrated above all in the office of the priest, and this visibility existed primarily in the administration of the sacraments. It was thus logical and unavoidable that the sacraments should become a problem for Luther.

In three pamphlets which he dedicated to Margarete, the dowager duchess of Braunschweig-Lüneburg, Luther presented his interpretation of the sacraments. The sermons were entitled *A Sermon on the Sacrament of Penance. A Sermon on the Revered Sacrament of Baptism,* and *A Sermon on the Revered Sacrament of the Holy True Body of Christ and of the Brotherhoods.*

There was much which displeased Luther about the administration of the sacraments, above all that the routine in the administration had led people into a false sense of security. Luther believed that the priests were to blame for this because they had spread false teachings and opinions. Luther's fundamental idea was that faith made the sacraments sacraments, that is, signs of salvation which are able to help man. Without faith baptism remained a bath which affected nothing; without faith neither the words of the priest as absolution from sin nor the confession of sin and penance at confession affected anything. Without faith the eating of bread and drinking of wine at the Mass were merely that, eating bread and drinking wine.

With these observations Luther resurrected an ancient problem that the Church, like other religious communions, has found necessary to address throughout the ages. Concerning the profession of the priest, the question may be formulated generally as follows: Does the effectiveness of a religious practice depend on the specific quality of the religious personnel or is it simply dependent on the perfect performance of the prescribed practice? Can the magician learn his trade by training or must he be born to it, that is, equipped with a special power? The Church answered this question by tying the effectiveness of the religious practice to the privileged order of the clergy stemming from priestly ordination. The unique order of priestly ordination was considered indelible. Therefore the validity and effect of that which the priest performed in religious practice did not depend on the existing characteristics of the priest but lay now in the execution of the religious act. Thus the individual priest always remained somewhat of a medicine man, and an aura of magic hovered over the religious act. Luther made the efficacy of the sacraments dependent neither on the privileged position of the recipient or priest, nor on the completed act. Instead, Luther entirely divorced the efficacy of the sacrament from the human act and bound the effectiveness exclusively to the saving will of God. In 1519 Luther rejected the magical effect of the sacraments and demoted the medicine man in priestly garb; he could not entirely, however, restrain him; a residue of priestly power remained as long as religious functions were reserved for the priest, and only in dire necessity might the laity represent the priest.

Luther taught that three characteristics pertain to the sacraments: sign, significance, and faith. Sign and significance varied; faith was always the same. The sign of baptism was water; the sign of the Eucharist was bread and wine; the sign of the sacrament of penance was the word of forgiveness. The significance of baptism lay in the spiritual rebirth of Christians; the significance of the sacrament of penance lay in the forgiveness of sins; and the significance of the sacrament of the Eucharist lay in the common fellowship in the body of Christ. The priest could indeed dispense the signs, but faith could be given only by God. And because this most decisive element in the sacrament could come only from God, Luther rejected every idea that the simple performance of a sacramental act could be a work well pleasing to God. God did not regard the work, but rather he esteemed the person who performed the work. The sacraments were instituted not in order that they should please God but rather that they should benefit man. Sacraments as performed acts *(opus operatum)* dit not please God; they pleased God as the works of him who performed them *(opus operantis)*.

Luther carried the idea that everything depends on whether the person pleases God to its ultimate conclusion and expanded it to include the divine word; the divine word is of no benefit to me if it does not please God "in me." Furthermore, with this statement, God's Word is segregated from salvation magic. Luther removed God completely from the grasp of man. I may embrace God as firmly as possible in my heart; yet if I do not please Him, my embrace counts for nothing. In the background of this thought stood the distinction between God and idol. Man arbitrarily elevates an idol to a position of highest good and value. This definition can apply even to God's word, which can become an idol of the heart when it has nothing to do with the God of Abraham, Isaac, and Jacob. Idols can be manipulated; God cannot. For Luther, it is important to insist on the majesty of God. But majesty is possible on condition that God exists not merely as an object of thought or as a spiritual excitement in us but rather that He exists outside of us and independently of us and that consequently we know of Him only what He Himself chooses to reveal. This prerequisite was naturally the fixed starting point of Luther's thought. Luther was obligated to gain validity for his thought by expressing it with utmost clarity; he makes the validity of the sacraments dependent on faiht, for faith is doubtless something that arises within us, a spiritual awakening. If this faith is not expressly bound to the „Christ outside of us" and expressly to what is revealed to us in the Bible concerning Christ, then a teaching that makes the sacrament dependent on faith throws open the gates to any subjectivism. God does not permit Himself to be enclosed in the heart. He enters Himself if He chooses; since He is merciful, He will indeed enter. It is no wonder that a few years later during the Reformation a bitter argument ensued concerning the nature of the sacraments. The Roman Catholic view that the dispensed sacrament by an ordained priest in the completed act is efficacious and that this efficacy does not depend on faith alone provides the primary force for avoiding subjectivism, dispelling doubt, and providing assurance. A long experience was stored in this practice. Luther pushed this view aside. Assurance is not gained by the act of the priest; one can only trust Christ: "Believe, you are saved; doubt, you are damned" (WA II 733). This is the most synoptic formulation of Luther's views on the sacraments.

With this interpretation of the sacraments Luther was on a course that led inevitably to his estrangement from the priesthood. The uniqueness of the priestly order began to wane for him. This unique order increasingly appeared as superfluous in the administration of the sacraments in the Church. Nevertheless, Luther could not yet free himself from the thought that the priest was exceptional. In the *Sermon on Baptism*, Luther considered the question of the Christian estate. The question was inherent in the subject because baptism, after all, was the initiation ritual into the Christian community. Luther emphasized that baptism was more important than all vows of continence and of the priesthood, but then, he continued, baptism, or the drowning of sin, could be realized in many ways and at various stations in life. One could be married or remain continent in holy orders. In addition, there was still a higher estate—the ruling estate in the spiritual realm. But baptism *opus operatum*, ways, and stations were all forgotten. They became irreconcilable with the conclusions in his teaching concerning the sacraments. A year later, in the light of his new position, Luther once and for all abandoned his earlier view concerning the unique order of the priesthood.

Sacraments had a special significance; they were signs and acts that symbolically revealed the essence of Christianity in the Church. This symbolism had to be taken seriously, especially by those who invoked it. This responsibility pertained to the priest but also to the laity because the sacraments made the Church visible and capable of being experienced as community. Therefore, the question concerning the meaning of the sacraments and the correct administration of them was always linked to the question of how a Christian congregation should appear and how it should function. This meant that the teaching concerning the sacraments was linked to the ideas about society and community in vogue under the prevailing conditions of the sixteenth century. This was especially true of the sacrament of the altar, the Eucharist. In all cultures and under all social or socioeconomic conditions the manner and way in which people come together to dine, who sits with whom and on what occasion, reveals something of the relationship of those people. Table companionship symbolizes community. For religious reasons, the Jews in the Old Testament limited participation in this community to members of their own people. Distinguishing Christianity from Judaism was therefore linked, not insignificantly, to the liberation from the Old Testament prescriptions concerning

Jewish dietary laws. In this matter the apostle Paul found it necessary to oppose Peter and James, the brother of the Lord. Jesus Himself had been accused of eating with the heathen and with tax collectors. But the new religious community established by Christ found its own common memorial meal, instituted by Him in remembrance of His sacrificial death. This memorial meal was one of the most important means to promote fellowship and to segregate believers in Eucharistic fellowship from those who did not belong to the community. The ancient concept concerning the Last Supper, according to which only persons who had demonstrated religious purity and were not burdened by sin were permitted to participate in the eucharistic meal, led to the practice that not every baptized Christian could be admitted to the sacrament. First, confession and penance were demanded of the believer. Ultimately, as a result of this practice, the Church as the community of believers was no longer necessarily identical with the eucharistic community. Distinguishing gradations in the Christian faith, measured by the rule of worthiness to participate in the Holy Eucharist, were established. There was a reason for this practice. It was utilized by the priest as a tool to discipline the congregation; insistence on worthiness incited and maintained a keener reverence for the altar. But this practice also had a fatal side effect. Participation in the Eucharist became a status symbol for the position of the believer in the community. The religious quality of a Christian was judged by his standing in the congregation; spiritual and secular were intertwined. Moreover, the possibilities afforded by the tool of discipline were immediately seized upon by the various social groups and authorities and used to establish their own eucharistic parties or circles. Membership in these fraternities was only minimally dependent on the quality of the Christian life. Much more important for membership was the nonecclesiastical rule of belonging to a certain social category, to a certain profession or merely to the right clique, or to possessing a certain social reputation. By this circumstance the structure of feudal society became immediately visible in the Church.

Luther considered the fraternities incompatible with the nature of the Church. With a violent wrath Luther thundered against the fraternities as though against a pagan and obscene institution. The fraternities were, however, from a practical standpoint, really rather harmless: the sixteenth century equivalent of a club. There were social reunions for celebrating common holidays, preserving traditions, and spending holidays in a convivial circle. The members were enrolled in a registry and paid dues to the fraternity treasury, from which the cost of the celebrations were paid. In order to conform to custom, the fraternity first attended church before adjourning to the tavern.

What angered Luther was not the "gluttony and swilling," although he joined in the chorus of criticism directed against these excesses. But the gluttony and swilling was only a superficial problem that constituted a favorite theme for preachers who enunciated moral criticism independent of their theological positions. Luther, on the contrary, criticized the fraternities on the basis of their misuse of the Christian name. He accused the fraternities of self-indulgence. They sought only their own advantage; Christian love dissipated within them. The money that was used for excessive drinking should have been lent to a needy artisan and used to feed the poor; such acts of charity would characterize a genuine fraternity.

There are three kinds of fraternities, Luther taught. First, there is a heavenly fraternity, the communion of saints in which we are all members as brothers and sisters. It is our faith in the one Christ that binds us in this fraternity. Scond, there is a natural brotherhood of one flesh and blood, of one inheritance and of one house. That is a natural arrangement that cannot be criticized. But then there is a third fraternity, a partisan fraternity constituted of membership lists, the hallmarks being special Masses, charitable works, regular meetings, dues, beer, gluttony, and swilling. This third brotherhood possesses not faith. "If a pig should be made the patron of such a group, soon the pig would be revolted by the conduct" (WA I 209).

Only the Christian fraternity possesses the right spirit. The Christian brotherhood is the genuine one, and from it no one is excluded. The Christian fraternity serves the entire community of Christendom. Improvement lies in the increase of faith in the sacrament, not in the multiplying of Masses. This genuine brotherhood appealed to Luther as the ideal pattern for the Church. Luther measured the ecclesiastical conditions of his time by this ideal fraternity, and from this model he also developed the first concrete suggestions for reform. These suggestions appeared in the fall of 1519 in his writings concerning the sacraments; they included suggestions for the dissolution of the fraternities, limitation of the number of Masses, and the dispensing of the Eucharist in both kinds, that is, both bread and wine. The last point is only a suggestion, not a definite requirement.

Led by the sacramental question to the problem of ecclesiastical communal life, Luther frequently expressed his displeasure that people were more attracted to material wealth than to the gospel. Luther considered interest-taking or usury one of the worst and most corruptible abuses emanating from the emphasis on material wealth. In this respect there was no distinction between Luther and his most vitriolic critics among the Franciscans and the Dominicans. On the contrary, sermons against usury and complaints about avarice and greed belonged to the standig repertoire not only of pulpit preachers but also of the humanists as well as of their opponents of high and low rank. No world religion misses the opportunity to speak contemptuously about money and to direct its devotees to "higher values."

Christianity inherited its aversion to despicable mammon in general and its aversion to interest and usury in particular from the Old Testament.

Historically, money lending appeared at first as neighborly assistance for a short period, for which loan naturally no interest was demanded. This simple circumstance was elevated in the Old Testament to the moral norm and confirmend by Jesus in the Sermon on the Mount. The Church held firmly to his norm and anchored the prohibition of interest-taking in canon law.

In the business life of a developing goods-money economy the canonical prohibition against interest-taking could not be strictly enforced. Thus a casuistry was developed that permitted the practice of the forbidden. As with so many other complicated questions, Thomas Aquinas found in this case also saving solution in that he invented an innocent name for a morally proscribed but practically unavoidable practice. Interest-taking and the making of money on loans were considered as revenue purchases, and now the practice gained moral and legal acceptance. It was no longer assumend that the borrower provided the lender with interest for the sum of money lent, but rather that the lender bought from the debtor a fixed return guaranteed by collateral. With this arrangement the problem was solved, the conscience troubled by the restrictions of canon law on interest was soothed because buying and selling were not forbidden.

Thus the Church invented this artful device to accommodate itself to the goods-money economy, even to engage in lending activities itself and nevertheless repeatedly to renew the prohibition against usury, the last time at the fifth Lateran Council in 1517. But even the boldest semantic acrobatics could not delude the simplest simpleton as to what really took place in the lending-borrowing practice. The creditor loaned money and, without having done any work, received more than the original sum while the borrower had to work himself to death to repay the debt, interest as well as principle. This practice did not seem fair to the common man.

This very volatile problem, which was an irritant to the entire population, was addressed by Martin Luther at the end of 1519 and at the beginning of 1520 in his *Sermons on Interest-Takers.* In keeping with the traditional criticism of interest and usury, Luther criticized interest-taking primarily from the standpoint that it was in violation of the biblical commands, especially the Sermon on the Mount. But Luther did not stop at the biblical argument. He picked apart the scholastic casuistry concerning „repurchase" and delved deeply into the nature of interest-taking. For the first time in the history of economic thought Luther exposed the fact that the creditor purchased the work of the borrower and that the interest on the money lent did not come out of some magic power of money or from the natural fertility of a mortgaged farm: it came from the work of the borrower. "Thus where I collect a return on a given piece of ground, I do not purchase the land but rather the borrower's toil and effort on that land, by which he is to bring me my return" (WA XV 57).

Such a view assumed that the lending of money was regarded not from the standpoint of the creditor but rather from that of the borrower, and primarily from the standpoint of the common man. Furthermore, Luther recognized that it was impossible to abolish all return on the loan in the economic life, especially in commerce where a modest interest imposed on delayed payment for goods delivered would be justified in that the supplier might be inconvenienced by the tardiness. In this aspect of interest-taking, Luther followed the traditional views.

The usury-taker had become a problem for Luther as well as for many of his contemporaries. Luther was introducing a concern which at that time oppressed many levels of society. In the Mansfeld mine enterprises Luther's own family was personally and repeatedly subjected to the oppression of the interest-takers. Furthermore, Luther exposed the inconsistencies related to usury as it was practiced in early capitalistic society.

In this period in his life Luther was very conservative in his demands for action. He was, to be sure, convinced that a reformation must and would come. However, he mistrusted those quick interventions which would, legally or arbitrarily, alter matters. Luther was convinced that improvement comes rather by the increase of faith. Preach, explain, convince, disseminate correct doctrine, and strengthen weak faith so that it grows and becomes strong: that was Luther's recipe for reformation. Later he held himself in principle to this course even when, against his will, he was obliged to admit that it was impossible to proceed without firm structure and coercion, but that the introduction and use of those elements had to be left to the authorities and were valid only on those matters that did not concern faith. Nothing should be attempted without previous conviction.

Luther's concern was correct faith, not correct life. If faith was really genuine and correct, then it would, according to him, express itself in life. Thus Luther's idea of reformation contained from the very beginning an irreducible tension. In principle, Luther ascribed no good to human nature but expected at the same time that people would be seized by the preaching of God's word, come to correct faith, and then do good. Finally, Luther hoped for a miracle, for God's intervention. But he did not condemn man to inactivity and to passive anticipation of the course of events that were to come. On the contrary, with the call to preach and to disseminate true doctrine, Luther hit precisely upon the task that must be accomplished in the preparation and initiation of every revolutionary movement: equipping the revolutionary forces with a new consciousness.

Chapter 7

With the Nobility Against Rome:
The Reformation Program of 1520

The more Martin Luther linked his theological goals with daily concrete problems, the more he became the foreman of the new reformed consciousness. Such a union was not difficult for Luther, and he did not need to force it. His profession (or his concept of it) had already provided for such a union. His major occupation was to lecture at the university, but the lectures did not occupy the whole day. No less important was his preaching to his fellow Wittenbergers, his preoccupation as curate, and the necessity, as author, to defend himself against all the new attacks continuously mounted against him from every quarter. The attacks against him served an important function for his intellectual development as his opponents called attention with delight and satisfaction to those passages in his writings where he, in their opinion, rendered himself vulnerable. His opponents called attention to his parenthetical remarks and marginal notes, which he was thereby forced to clarify. His society drew out of Luther what he had to offer, but in so doing it also imparted to him something of itself. He opened himself in communicating with his contemporaries. Thus his ideology was increasingly enriched with practical concepts concerning a new form of Church and society. The stimuli for such ideas came to him from all quarters. The resistance, hate, and threats of his enemies were balanced by expressions of support and encouragement. Luther had launched a movement; now the movement began to carry him in its flow. In his fashion, he gave expression to this interplay:

> Others carry my burden; their strength is my strength. The faith of the Church comes to the help of my timidity; the chastity of others withstands the assault of my impure lust; the fasting of others profits me; the prayers of others benefit me; in brief, the members care so well for one another that the honor of the one protects and saves the honor of the other, as Paul in I Corinthians 12:22 so beautifully states. Consequently, I can glory in the blessings of others as if they were my very own for they are indeed my own when I rejoice in them and give thanks for them. I may be base and ugly while those whom I love and admire are fair and beautiful. By love I claim their blessings and become one with them. (WA VI 130)

If we look more closely at the circles that supported Luther and at the problems that confronted him, it will become clear how varied, contradictory, and differentiated the reform movement was. Educated burghers took up the pen in order to defend him. The Nuremburg Council secretary, Lazarus Spengler, composed a *Defense and Christian Response of a Sincere Advocate of Christian Truth*. Luther's opponent, Eck (the name means „corner"), was presented in a satire as *The Planed Eck*, which probably the Nuremburg humanist, Willibald Pirckheimer, had written. Also, a work entitled *The Response of the Ignorant Cathedral Canons* by the Augsburg Cathedral preacher Johann Oecolampadius, was directed against Eck. Albrecht Dürer, who had already enthusiastically greeted the news of Luther's indulgence theses, requested Elector Frederick to protect Luther for the sake of Christian truth on which more depended than on all the wealth of the world, and added that when Dürer should come to Wittenberg, he would carefully "copy the likeness of Luther and etch it in copper for a lasting memorial to a Christian who rescued me from great fears." He further stipulated that when Luther should write a new work, a copy of it would be forwarded and billed to Dürer (Ullmann 140).

After the Leipzig disputation, keen interest prevailed, especially in Bohemia, where it was regarded as marvelous that a German university professor had elevated the name of Jan Hus and had not shunned defending Hus' teaching as Christian. Previously, during the Leipzig disputation, the Bohemian organ builder, Jakubek, had visited Luther to converse with him. A little later, the Prague clergyman Jan Poduška and Vaclav Roždalovsky honored Luther with a gift: a few knives and a copy Jan Hus' *De Ecclesia* (Concerning the Church). The gifts were first presented to Luther in October 1519, by way of the electoral court. The court was cautious and saw no advantage in establishing closer ties with Bohemia, especially since the Dresden court chaplain, Jerome Emser, had published a pamphlet in August 1519 about Luther and the Hussites. In a public letter to Johann Zack, the provost of Leitmeritz, Emser had defended Luther from the accusation of supporting the Hussites. In vain the Hussites would pray for Luther, because nothing in Leipzig had infuriated him more than the Hussite charge, and he had distanced himself from nothing more promptly than Eck's taunts charging him as a teacher of Hussite errors. Furthermore, even when Luther admitted that some articles of faith among the Hussites were indeed valid and true, he discerned very correctly the essence of heresy which mingles truth with falsehood but elicits punishment not of truth but of falsehood.

Emser's pamphlet was a unique masterpiece. In feigned friendship for Luther, Emser appeared to take Luther's side in order to free him from the most damaging suspicion that was uttered against him in Leipzig. But precisely in that feigned attempt to exonerate Luther lay Emser's knavery.

Emser's pamphlet made the public aware that the Bohemians set their hope in Luther, and now Luther was drawn out; either he must agree with Emser and write against the Hussites, thereby contradicting his Leipzig statements concerning valid and true Hussite doctrine, or he must assume a position that would indicate friendliness toward the Hussites. Both alternatives were unattractive. Was Emser building for him a golden bridge or leading him onto thin ice?

Luther saw no golden bridge in Emser's knavery. He sensed only deception, subtlety, and the kiss of Judas. With this perception of Emser's pamphlet, Luther prepared his answer *To the Mountain Goat Emser.* The title was a play on the coat of arms that Emser had chosen for himself; the coat of arms featured a goat. This response to Emser was Luther's first insolent work, but it would not be his last. In Luther's response there is a hail of obscene goats. The tone is violent, forceful, and bitter. Nevertheless, the major argument retained its principal importance: Luther could not abandon his view simply because it pleased the Bohemians, and if the Bohemians found any worth in his thought, that did not signify that what pleased them was necessarily unworthy and heretical. With a complete reversal in his argument, Luther came within a hair's breadth of acknowledging the Hussite doctrine: "I desire, wish, pray, am grateful and happy that my teaching pleases the Bohemians; may it also please the Jews and the Turks, yes, even you and Eck, that you abandon your godless errors!" (WA II 663). It was not the Bohemians he defended, but himself.

Luther's action was determined not only by caution. In Leipzig he had reached the limits of what he could say in a positive way regarding Hussitism because the teachings of Jan Hus were known to him only from the decrees of the Council of Constance; he had not yet read any of the writings of Hus. From what he had heard of the "Bohemian heresy," he found it suspicious and blameworthy. Luther was most offended that the Hussites segregated themselves from the communal Church. Luther sensed in this act the spiritual arrogance of sects. He could not yet have been fully aware that the Hussite movement was supported by the heroic, reformed, social, and national struggle of the Bohemian people, and that the segregation of Bohemia from the Catholic Church was a teeth-gnashing concession granted by the Roman hierarchy in consultation with the emperor and empire, in order to form a cordon sanitaire that would quarantine the Bohemian heresy and prevent is spread. The decade-old propaganda against the Hussites was not without effect. "Hussite" was so pejorative that the accusation of being a Hussite was shunned and the very mention of the name instinctively provoked defensiveness. Luther did not immediately overcome the effects of this propaganda, nor did he ever completely overcome it.

Luther left it to Melanchthon to reply to the Bohemians. Melanchthon accepted the charge and composed a response marked by discretion, diplomacy, and amicable reserve. Luther did not immediately begin to read Hus' book *De Ecclesia.* Only months later did he begin to read the work, and then with growing amazement. He was speechless; he was forced to admit that he already had walked for a long time in Hus's tracks. Luther conceived of a real spiritual and historical relationship which the Church itself through its historical development had established and transmitted. It had drifted so far from its morrings that the attempt to anchor it once more to its origins, as Hus had sought to do, appeared as heresy. Its problems since the days of Hus had changed so little that inevitably Luther had to some degree unwittingly followed Hus's line of thinking, though never by conscious intention. Hus, therefore, became a mirror for Luther in his own situation in Germany in his struggle with the established ecclesiastical authorities.

Circumstances in Hus' Bohemia and in Luther's Germany were parallel. The Hussite revolutionary movement in Bohemia and the Reformation in Germany demonstrate in their causes, course, and ideology a whole series of similarities in that both movements to some degree were directed against the same opponent, namely, the universal papal Church. Of course, there were differences between the Hussite and the German reformation movements. One significant difference was that, in the environment of the German Reformation, elements of an early capitalism were more clearly and intensively at work—elements which had not existed during the Hussite period in Bohemia. Thus there is an historical demarcation between the two movements. Both the Hussite and the Lutheran movements were reformations. Their similarity consisted primarily in their common criticism of ecclesiastical conditions.

Like other accusations, the one associating him with the Hussites could not prevent Luther's name from becoming the symbol of hope for a growing circle of leaders. The canon of the cathedral of Constance, Johann von Botzheim, rejoiced to live in such a time as that in which Luther cured sick theology, and Botzheim sought Luther's friendship. The prior of the Franciscan convent in Basel, Konrad Pellicanus, enthusiastically reported to Luther concerning the printing of Luther's most recent works in Basel. Another strong supporter of Luther in Basel was Johann Lüthard. The theologian and mathematician, Sebastian Münster, proficient in three languages and known to Melanchthon, had translated Luther's study on the ten commandments; the preacher Wolfgang Fabricius Capito also was captivated by Luther's erudition.

At Easter of 1520 Wolfgang Capito went from Basel to the court Archbishop Albrecht in Mainz. Albrecht certainly should not be numbered among Luther's unyielding opponents although he would have had good reason for intransigence vis-a-vis Luther. As an elector and chancellor of the empire his interests were not necessarily completely identical with those of the ecclesiastical hierarchy. As patron of the arts and of humanistic learning, he had little interest in monks' quarrels. Above all he wished to avoid tumult and unrest. Discussions concerning difficult theological questions should not be conducted in public, he wrote to Luther at the end of February 1520. He knew that it was appropriate for a prince of the Church to adhere to the counsel of Gamaliel. However, Luther should not incite disobedience; he should not teach anything that would challenge the authority of the Church; he should hold fast to the truth of Scripture; then his work would prove itself to be a work of God, firm and indestructible. To be sure, this communiqué from Albrecht was merely a mild and patient gesture on the part of an elevated lord, and yet the letter suggested that Luther and his ideas were out of the ordinary and of a distinctive nature—a persuasion shared by an ever-increasing number of Luther's contemporaries.

Casper Hedio, the preacher from Basel, gave exuberant expression to this feeling: "You are the commander; we want to be the soldiers under your command in order that our deeds might prove to be beneficial to others ... ." Hedio wrote to Luther on June 23, 1520. According to Hedio, Luther's doctrine was from God. The Basel preacher found nothing in Luther that was not firmly declared and explained by the Scripture, nothing that was not confirmed by the Word of God and sturdy as steel; in fact, Hedio was carried away into an apotheosis: "If the ancients once equated deity with assisting mortals, then you have every right to speak as God because you have caused all Christendom to rejoice with the greatest benefit ..." (WA BR II 128–29). This sounds blasphemous, but it is merely a humanistic technique which employs models from ancient rhetoric.

The knight, Ulrich von Hutten, sought to win Luther not as the commander in the battle but as a comrade in the struggle for the freedom of Germany. Von Hutten's humanism was of a different kind from the humanism of Erasmus or Melanchthon: it was not a contemplative, formal learning; not keen, finely balanced judgments with concealed sarcasm between the lines characterized it; no weary skepticism and no patronizing smiles at the folly of the world were in it, even though von Hutten was thoroughly familiar with the sources and knew all the stylistic techniques. Humanism for von Hutten was not erudition, attitude, philosophy, or a method for discovering truth, and in no case was it an end unto itself; rather, it was leaven for an ardent German patriotism.

Von Hutten was born in 1488 at the Castle Stekelberg near Fulda. In 1505, the same year in which Luther entered the monastery, von Hutten escaped from a monastery and then studied in Cologne, Erfurt, Frankfurt on the Oder, and Leipzig. Next he embarked on a itinerant life, traveling through Germany and Italy and, for a time in 1513, served as a mercenary. In 1517, he was crowned poet laureate by Emperor Maximilian, and he then entered the service of the patron of humanism, Archbishop Albrecht of Mainz, becoming one of the internationally known German poetic and literary figures. Not the least of his claims to fame was his support of intellectual freedom in the struggle against the Cologne "Obscure Men" in the so-called Reuchlin affair.

Since 1510 this affair had captured the attention of the German intellectual world. The strife broke out because a baptized Jew, Pfefferkorn by name, succeeded in persuading Emperor Maximilian to issue a mandate to prohibit and to destroy all nonbiblical Jewish writings. It is sufficient to note that this barbaric idea sprang from the narrow-minded zeal of a convert who had become alienated from his own tradition, a tradition that was struggling for survival. Most significant of all, however, is that the best minds of progressive German cultural life immediately rallied to the defense of the Jewish writings. Johannes Reuchlin, the father of the study of Hebrew in Germany and the granduncle of Melanchthon, energetically opposed Pfefferkorn and his followers in his apologia, and defended the Talmud and the Kabbala. The philologists accepted the fact that Hebrew was a necessary prerequisite for understanding the Old Testament. Reuchlin went beyond this argument: he not only defended Hebrew as a holy language but also defended Hebrew writings as possessing independent cultural value. Such a view was of major importance in the struggle against the latent anti-Semitism of medieval thought that was significantly nourished by the bigoted concept that the Jewish people, by crucifying Jesus Christ, had brought upon themselves guilt for which they must be punished.

Under the influence of the Dominicans, especially that of the infamous inquisitor of heresy, Jakob von Hoogstraeten, the theological faculty of the University of Cologne unleashed a smear campaign against Reuchlin and achieved the convocation of a heresy investigation which went on for several years. Humanists, jurists, patricians, and nobles took Reuchlin's part. In 1514, under the title of *Letters of Famous Men*, Reuchlin published their letters and supportive affirmations with a foreword by Philipp Melanchthon. Then in 1515, the Erfurt humanistic circle around Crotus Rubeanus, Mutianus Rufus, and Eobanus Hessus achieved a tour de force. The Erfurt humanists published fictitious *Letters of Unfamous Men*, which became known as *Letters of Obscure Men*, in which the Erfurt humanist circle parodied the Cologne monastic theologians and exposed their bigotry to public ridicule. In 1517, a second part of *Letters of Obscure Men* appeared, composed by Ulrich von Hutten, far more aggressive than the first part, sharply anticlerical, and directed against monasticism and the Roman Church. Under these circumstances, Luther's protest appeared to many humanists as a continuation of the Reuchlin strife, and the humanists demonstrated spontaneous sympathy for Luther without informing themselves

about the distinctive origins of the two arguments. Von Hutten personified several significant thrusts of protest: that of the German knights, the
aggressive humanists, the German patriots, and the radical opponents of
Rome.

Thus Hutten, because of his support of Reuchlin, was considered by the
curia even before the opening of the Luther heresy investigation as a dangerous opponent and agitator. Almost simultaneously with the second part
of the publication of *Letters of Obscure Men*, Hutten had, in 1517, published a
treatise of the Italian Lorenzo Valla concerning the "Donation of Constantine." According to this donation, the Emperor Constantine had presented
to Pope Sylvester the city of Rome and large sections of Italy. On this donation the papacy based its claim to secular lordship in the papal states,
which extended through the Apennine Peninsula. Valla had demonstrated
that the Donation of Constantine was a forgery stemming from the eighth
century. Luther read Hutten's publication of the Valla treatise at the beginning of 1520 and found his own views confirmed by Valla's scholarship.

In the beginning, Hutten did not pay much attention to Luther's activity. He regarded the Lutheran affair as the usual monkish petulance. The
fact that Hutten was in the service of the archbishop of Mainz, the man attacked by Luther, may also have played a role in Hutten's attitude. Hutten
expressed his scorn for monkish querulousness in the same 1518 letter to
Willibald Pirckheimer in which he formulated his motto for humanism: "O
century, O knowledge! It is a joy to be alive! But to fold one's hands in the
lap, that does not bring joy, my Willibald. Studies blossom and the spirits
rouse themselves; barbarism, your day is over; reconcile yourself to exile"
(Mettke I 40).

After the Leipzig disputation, Hutten changed his mind about the "monkish quarrel." He pictured himself with Luther in a common cause against
Rome and, following Luther's example, he overcame, in the manner described in his verse, the barrier that separated the common people from
the humanists:

> Though Latin was at my command,
> My words one could not understand.
> I summon now the fatherland:
> Enable me in language strong,
> In German, to avenge this wrong.
>
> (Mettke III 44)

Hutten remained no longer at the archiepiscopal court in Mainz. He joined
the knight and mercenary leader, Franz von Sickingen, who welcomed him
to the Ebernburg in the Nah Valley. In these months, swiftly, boldly, and
with an insolent air, he turned out pamphlet after pamphlet: *Trias Romana,
Vadiscus. Die Anschauenden,* and other pamphlets bound together in a *Con-*

versational Booklet. In these writings, inspired by his hatred for Rome, Hutten's description identified Rome as the enemy for the anti-Roman movement and presented in political dimension what Luther in the religious realm and with theological arguments had raised to consciousness. In stark black-and-white contrast Hutten ascribed to Rome and the papacy all imaginable filth, dirt, and rubbish, but to Germany and the Germans he ascribed all things noble, true, beautiful, great, and good. Complaints about the political disunity of the fatherland, about the simplicity and stupidity of the Germans, their gullibility and naiveté, their addiction to drink, and their pugnacity were molded as nothing more than the contemporary form of national self-criticism into the mood of Hutten's writings. On June 4, 1520, Hutten began a letter to Luther with *Viva libertas* (Long live liberty). Hutten had been in contact with Luther; he had represented Luther's cause to von Sickingen, and the latter had several times requested Hutten to write to Luther to inform him that he should come to the Ebernburg in the event that he no longer felt secure in Wittenberg. Now the rumors multiplied concerning the anticipated condemnation of Luther. It was known that Eck had been summoned to Rome in the spring of 1520, and there could be little doubt that Eck's journey was related to the reopening of the heresy investigation against Luther. In April Luther was warned of a conspiracy to assassinate him. At the beginning of June when Hutten wrote his letter to Luther, Eck's return from Rome was expected daily. Luther's condemnation was anticipated at any moment. Hutten encouraged Luther:

> You will be excommunicated; how great, O Luther, you are, if this expectation is fulfilled! ... Rome also has designs against me. In any case, I am alert. If Rome employs might, there will be men at hand, not, I hope, only from among the German knights but also from among higher authorities. Let them condemn me. Eck denounces me, claiming that I support you. In that he is correct; for so far as I can understand, I feel myself united with you. Strengthen yourself, be firm, don't falter! I am your helper in every contingency. You can trust me with all your plans. Let us together save freedom; let us liberate our long suppressed fatherland. May God be with us! If God be with us, who can be against us? (WA BR II 115–118).

That Hutten and the noble and knightly circles to which he appealed and whose ideology he expressed were completely captivated by the theological views of Luther may not be assumed simply on the basis of the fact that these groups supported Luther and rallied to his side with strong words. The common interest that Luther and the nobility shared revolved around their common front against Rome, but their motivations were not the same. It was not a particular political calculation that directed Luther's view to the nobility (at least such a calculation cannot be demonstrated).

Luther's orientation toward the nobility developed rather from his idea of the duty of secular authority, a view that he at first apparently only superficially discussed in response to deliberate misrepresentations of his fundamental positions. The distinction in rank and the quarrels among the nobles themselves hardly interested Luther. His attention was at that time directed to secular authority from still another quarter.

It was Luther's major idea that faith alone justified man before God that was most often subjected to misunderstanding and calumny. For the average person the idea was not easy to grasp. For the learned and unlearned, among the priests and the laity, even among those who seldom bothered with theological problems, the question was immediately raised, with a degree of anxiety and restlessness, as to whether man need still concern himself with the ten commandments and whether simple belief were enough. All morality appeared threatened by the axiom of justification by faith alone, especially since the new idea circulated as a slogan and no one took the trouble actually to read Luther's writings. The assiduous preaching of Luther's opponents contributed to the distortion of his idea.

The major problem in establishing the practical application of this idea was not the reservation of the intellectuals and the resistance of the theological guild, although such reservation and resistance were serious enough. A more serious concern in adapting the new teaching to Luther's society was the cunning of bourgeois self-satisfaction, which gladly accepted the teaching of justification by faith alone and interpreted it to its own advantage as a reprieve from all possible annoying obligations. Such a distortion seemed to confirm the accusation that Luther's teaching destroyed morality. In the bourgeois simplistic interpretation of his ideas Luther sensed dangers. Thus for months he preached repeatedly in the Wittenberg *Stadtkirche* (city church) on the ten commandments. He rebuffed the misinterpretation of his teaching that he desired to abolish the ten commandments, and in conjunction with these sermons he developed a series of ideas, concepts, and suggestions which in fact resulted in alleviating the burden upon the middle class. Thus his opponents had not really misunderstood him entirely: his ideas did not jeopardize morality in general, but they did in fact jeopardize the interests of those who made their living from the Church.

The conclusions of his preaching and of his entire thought up to that point Luther summarized in *On Good Works.* It was Spalatin once again who moved Luther to prepare such a pamphlet. The work appeared in May 1520 and was dedicated to Duke John, the brother of Frederick the Wise. Its basic idea is that faith is the foreman of good works. Everything that comes from faith is good; whatever occurs apart from faith is useless for salvation even though it may outwardly correspond to what God has commanded. We need not pursue these ideas any further here or explain them in all their details, since Luther was simply repeating in different words what had been his fundamental theme since 1516: Believe, you are saved; doubt, you are damned. However, *On Good Works* has a broader context of daily activities in Church and society. Reverberations from the writings on the sacraments and on the fraternities, and from the sermons on usury now found extension and were enriched by new tones. The purely theological developed into a framework embracing secular content. Theology increasingly took on social relevance.

This social relevance is especially clear in Luther's presentation of the fourth commandment, "Honor thy father and thy mother ... ." He presents here a short selection of his view on authority. Luther's view of authority is clearly patriarchal. Father and mother constitute the apex of the original pattern of all authority. Parents are to be honored and obeyed. God has willed such an order. The obedience that we owe to parents is extended to civil authority because God wills that each person should have a governor. Disobedience is a greater sin than homocide, immorality, theft, or deception. The obedience owed to authority is unconditional with one exception: authority may not command faith.

Luther enjoins both obedience and the recognition of its limitation. Parents and civil authority are to be obeyed. The fear of offending parents and civil authority should be stronger than the fear of punishment. If the parents, however, are so unwise as to rear their children only by secular standards and not to teach them God's commandments, children should not render obedience to such parents. The same rule applies to the Church, the "spiritual mother." We should obey her. However, she treats those submissive to her like the mother who deserts her children. The Church should really prohibit and condemn adultry, inconstancy, gluttony, worldly display, and the wearing of excessive jewelry. Instead, the Church employs excommunication in order to collect debts and continuously ordains new holidays, which were better not introduced. The Church should preserve discipline and order in the convents, monasteries, and schools, but these institutions have become "schools for knaves." The Church illegally imposes excommunication and illegally collects and dispenses money. She teaches what indeed she should condemn and she siphons off to Rome funds that had been pledged to support worship and children. The Roman whores and knaves are the real Turks whom the kings, princes, and nobles should attack first.

Thus Luther names kings, princes, and nobles as the proper public officers, embodying in their persons that power which, in his opinion, should be exerted against Rome. Luther's remedy for social ills is thus based on his patriarchal understanding of authority. Kings, princes, and nobles are the authorities instituted by God to care for their subjects as father and mother care for their children. If the spiritual authority fails, then the secular authority must take up the slack in order to provide harmony in the Church. This view of the secular authority as helper in necessity remained determinative for Luther. Luther was not consciously concerned with the transformation of social and political conditions but rather with the freedom for preaching the gospel. The social and political conditions interested him only insofar as they preserved this freedom or seemed to curtail it. In his eyes the major enemy of evangelical freedom was the papacy, which he now suspected of being the antichrist. Therefore, the papacy must be resisted. Because in the struggle against the papacy preaching was not an adequate weapon, force was necessary to correct abuses. The use of force, in Luther's opinion, was the prerogative of those authorities to whom the office of employing force had been given: the secular authorities. These authorities were not necessarily restricted to kings, princes, and nobles; under certain circumstances they might be city councilors, but in every case they were obliged to represent legitimate and duly instituted authority. Herein something of that class position is revealed which in later decisions will become even more evident.

Intellectually, Luther's point of departure with respect to the question of authority is, as clearly indicated in his reflections on the fourth commandment, completely relative to his actual situation in Wittenberg and electoral Saxony. In the late fall of 1518, Luther's realization of the extent to which he was dependent on the favor of the elector was driven home, but he also learned from this experience that his elector did indeed effectively protect him. Luther was happy to know that he was popular among the masses, but it was not within his purview to perceive in the masses a protective or transforming force. Luther preached to the people in order to educate them in faith. The masses were for Luther a raw material to be shaped rather than a base on which to build politically. In this view of civil authority the Wittenberg professor appears as the representative of a social category whose function was to educate leaders for society and personnel for civil authority. Those belonging to this category expected that kings, princes, and nobles would make the political decisions, and that the civic counselors would eagerly, to the best of their ability, cooperate in the implementation of decisions. It is thus no wonder that Luther naturally first thought of kings, princes, and nobles as those who should first exercise authority.

The nobility should intervene! Since the beginning of 1520, this idea had recurrently come to mind and had found expression in Luther's writings. The notion provided him with both hope and temptation. He turned the thought this way and that; he permitted himself to be attracted by it, appeared, in bursts of anger, to be completely committed to forceful intervention by the nobles, recoiled, however, before the consequences, and sought orderly channels for mediation. "It is said that the antichrist will find and utilize the treasures of the earth. I believe that the Romanists have discovered them and that their discovery harms us body and soul. If the German princes and nobles do not soon bravely and earnestly take action against this exploitation, Germany will become a wilderness or be forced to devour herself" (WA VI 289). In the same pamphlet, *Concerning the Papacy at Rome and the Very Famous Romanist in Leipzig*, which Luther was writing in May–June 1520, he challenged the Franciscan, Augustin von Alfeld, who had attacked him in the same fashion in which Eck had attacked him and who had defended the primacy of the pope. "Romanists" were for Luther all those supporters of Rome. And a little later, Luther erupted:

"It appears to me that if the madness of the Romanists continues, no remedy remains except that the emperor, kings, and princes must violently assault this global pest and settle the matter not with words but with iron ... . If we punish thieves with the gallows, robbers with the sword, heretics at the stake, why do we not employ every type of weapon against such teachers of corruption, against these cardinals, popes, and the entire cesspool of the Roman Sodom and wash our hands in their blood." (WA VI 347)

This outpouring of hate says something not only about the fears that tormented Luther but also about his confidence that there were enough battle-ready men in Germany to make a strike. About the time that he was writing this pamphlet against the "very famous Romanist at Leipzig," an offer of a covenant of alliance and protection had come to him from the circle of German knights.

The knight Sylvester von Schaumburg had written to Luther on June 11, 1520: "For I and, I believe, a hundred knights whom I can bring together, will protect you until your opinions have been heard and examined by a common Christian council or by impartial, learned judges, and you yourself become better instructed; for you yourself have agreed to submit in such a case" (WA BR II 122). But Luther did not primarily have knights in mind when he appealed for help against Rome. He thought first of the higher nobility, the princes as well as the counts and the barons, but not knights. As executives of secular power the nobility attracted Luther. There was no hope left on earth except with them, he concluded in a writing directed against Augustin von Alfeld.

Placing his hope in the nobility, Luther appealed with a program for a German national council to the Christian nobility of the German nation: *To the Christian Nobility of the German Nation Concerning the Reform of the Christian Estate*, Luther entitled this pamphlet that appeared in August 1520. The work enjoyed a brisk sale; the first 4,000 copies were sold in no time. The news that Luther was preparing such a pamphlet had already circulated, and thus voices of alarm were also heard. Lang and Staupitz wrote to Luther from Erfurt and requested him to delay publication. However, it was already too late, and Luther was unwilling to wait any longer. His concepts and suggestions concerning change and improvement were scattered throughout his various writings, and it was time to synthesize them. For Luther the picture was now complete. Rome was corrupt, help could come only from secular authority, and the orderly way to introduce reform was by the convoking of a national council. It was the responsibility of the nobility to execute this design.

In order to achieve this goal, it was necessary first to establish the right to convene a council without papal approval or even against the papal will. Thus it would be necessary to topple the three paper walls with which the papacy sought to protect its primacy.

> In the first place, when secular authority had confronted papal authority, the papacy had always decreed and declared that secular authority had no jurisdiction over spiritual authority but that, on the contrary, spiritual authority supersceded secular authority. In the second place, if appeal was made to the Holy Scriptures to correct the papacy, the papacy had responded that only the pope was permitted to interpret Scripture. In the third place, if the papacy was threatened with the convoking of a council, it responded that only the pope was authorized to convoke a council. (WA IV 406)

But these walls could no longer resist reformation. The presumptive primacy of spiritual authority over secular authority Luther rebutted with the teaching on the priesthood of all believers:

> Since the secular authority also is baptized with us, espouses the same faith, and holds to the same gospel, we must admit it to be priest and bishop and to consider its office as one which pertains to and is profitable for the Christian community. For whatever emerges from the waters of baptism may pride itself on being already priest, bishop, and pope .... Since we are all priests, no one should elevate himself without our approval and election since spiritual authority is shared by all the baptized. For that which is committed to all no one can appropriate to himself without the approval and endorsement of the general will. (WA VI 408)

Luther confronted the exegetical authority of the papacy with the authority of the community, and he confronted the exclusive papal right to convoke a council with the right of the Christian community to convoke a council. From the equality of the children of God, Luther posited within the Church the equality of all ranks. For the realm of the Church Luther proclaimed equality for all the stratifications. In the Church there is no distinction because of social position but only on the basis of activity, of profession, of office! Luther did not apply this concept of equality to the secular realm or to the entire community. From the very beginning he limited the validity of this idea to the eccclesiastical realm. But, once proclaimed, this idea of equality would develop its own life. In a society in which everyone belonged to the Church, it would be difficult in the long run to adhere to the limits which Luther defined. Thus, with his fundamental principle of the priesthood of all believers, Luther also provided a frame of reference for those social forces that were not at all willing to be satisfied by ecclesiastical reform alone. The more the reform movement advanced from academic dispute and literary argumentation toward concrete political action, the more the principle of spiritual equality was spontaneously extended to the secular realm. The degree of application of this principle to the secular environment became in the following years a measure for the radicalization of the reform movement.

According to Luther's presentation of the priesthood of all believers, he developed a detailed reform program of twenty-six points. In the first eight points he considered the complaints and demands that had already been discussed frequently at the imperial diets and that were known as the *Gravamina of the German Nation Against the Holy See at Rome.* What had been formulated as complaints in the *Gravamina,* Luther raised as demands: no annates from German bishoprics to be paid to Rome; no German benefices bestowed on Rome's favorites; no confirmation of German episcopal elections by Rome, and no Roman legal jurisdiction over German matters; no episcopal oath taken to the pope; no papal authority over the emperor, and no recognition of papal claims to Naples and Sicily; abolition of the curial offices at the imperial court; no kissing of the pope's foot.

The papacy and the curia were to be deprived of every rigth and possibility to exist at the expense of Germany, to co-rule in Germany, and to intervene in German affairs. This was the meaning of Luther's demands, which corresponded to the interests of the German nobility and of all the imperial estates, and aimed at the strengthening of national sovereignty. Luther's demands represented something of an effort to catch up with what France, Spain, and England had for the most part already achieved: the full administrative authority of a national monarchy over the Church within the jurisdiction of the monarchy. Germany, of course, was not a national monarchy; therefore, the estates represented in the Reichstag were called upon, in regard to the Church and its independence from Rome, to assume the role which in the western monarchies was assumed by the king. Luther did not exclude the emperor from playing a role. On the contrary, he made a point of reminding the emperor, in a foreword, of his responsibilities. But, reckoning with the political realities, Luther naturally addressed himself not only to Charles V but also to the entire German nobility.

It was indeed because these estates to no insignificant degree lived off the Church as "spiritual feudality" that Luther's demands touched primarily the interests of the princely houses and the noble dynasties. Princes and nobles, after all, possessed the majority of the bishoprics and thus found it burdensome when it was necessary for them to seek papal confirmation and approval and to pay handsome sums for this. It was the nobility above all who made up the majority of members in the cathedral chapters, who elected bishops, and who felt their prestige injured when their choice had first to be approved in Rome.

The dependency on Rome was burdensome not only to the dynasties; it was a financial burden on the entire country. At first the lower clergy felt the blow because the bishops passed on their burdens by imposing the fees demanded by Rome on the dioceses, parishes, and chaplaincies. The imposed sums reduced the income of the clergy. Finally it fell to the common people in the parishes to raise the money that poured into Roman coffers from the German bishoprics. What at first glance may appear as a matter for the ruling class is revealed on closer inspection to penetrate deeply into the entire population and to be interwoven into the entire social system. Consequently, Luther, with his suggestions for reform in his address to the nobility, was bringing into discussion a matter of national concern, for it was indeed the imperial estates, the ruling, still primarily feudal noble class, which represented at that stage of development and juridical maturity the "German nation." What we here encounter as "nation" was not yet a middle class German nation as it was later constituted in the nineteenth century. The nation was still primarily the ruling class of Germans who lived within the boundaries of the Holy Roman Empire; it was feudalistic and made up of estates. The German nation was distinguished from the non-German regions of the empire in that the nation recognized only German-speaking feudal lords or imperial estates as legitimate authorities of a binding legal order under which the popular law emphasized German sovereignty and respulsed every exterior attempt at intervention. In fact, the Germans were not aware of the degree to which these objectives had already been realized as they developed economically as well as intellectually and culturally toward an unmistakable and independent greatness. If the nobility at that time represented what was popularly understood as "nation," the bourgeois element, on the other hand, was so strong in this omunity that its demands exceeded what the old ruling classes had striven for. In the anti-Rome movement, it was especially the German humanists who articulated these bourgeois demands.

Luther contributed to the development of German nationalism, not least significantly by his demand, made even before he published *An Address to the Christian Nobility of the German Nation*, that the German language be used in the celebration of the Mass. This demand originated from the consideration that the sacrament of the altar was effective only under the words of institution spoken by Jesus Christ, which were received and absorbed by faith. However, it was necessary to hear and understand the words of institution if they were to be absorbed by faith. Therefore, they must not be spoken softly or in Latin but rather loudly and in German, because spoken aloud and in German the words of institution were "no less holy words and no less a promise," as Luther wrote in *The Sermon on the New Testament, i.e., of the Holy Mass*, with which he had occupied himself since April 1520, and wich he sent to his friends at the beginning of August. "Why should not we Germans read the Mass in our language as the Latins, Greeks, and many other people read the Mass in their respective languages?" (WA VI 362). Thus Luther rejected attributes of any magical power to Latin and granted the German language its rightful place in ceremonies at the altar. The German language would now take possession of the holy symbols. Employing the German language would no longer be punished by the switch as in his school days; on the contrary, it would be rewarded by the bread and wine.

Furthermore, in *The Sermon on the New Testament* Luther expanded upon those ideas on the sacraments occasionally mentioned in the writings of 1519 and in sermons, and he especially expanded upon those ideas introduced in the writing on good works. Luther examined all those seemingly minor points that in the light of his theological persuasions had become suspect, because in considering them he sniffed out religious deception, selfishness, and the completely distorted image of the "Christian." Luther's suspicions corresponded partially with those that gave the lower clergy occasion to complain and partially with what the public opinion of the urban bourgeoisie perceived as abuses. But Luther did not offer a compendium of the occasional complaints and expressions of annoyance that criticized only superficial matters. Instead of criticizing the abuse of a practice perceived as offensive, Luther abolished any practice that, from his perspective of the nature of the Church, he considered to be false and corrupting.

Not as the burgher for whom the prevailling ecclesiastical conditions had become a burden did Luther criticize the Church. On the contrary, he thought as a theologian and churchman. Luther struggled not against the merely annoying aspects of ecclesiastical conditions but rather against what in his opinion was truly reprehensible. Luther did not flatter the burgher; he demanded that the burgher radically alter his thinking. Luther was motivated by his Christian theology. His motives were in accord with the social interests in view of which, even without his efforts, the Church would have been found lacking. In this sense Luther's theology worked as a leaven or catalyst in the ideological processes of the middle class without itself ever having been completely absorbed by or reduced to middle-class ideology.

Luther demanded the dissolution of the begging cloisters, sects, and orders, and the prohibition of establishing new orders; in addition, he wanted to abolish the annual Masses for the dead, other petition and thanksgiving Masses, private Masses, interdicts, excommunications, and all spiritual penalties. He also opposed chapels and hermitages, all ecclesiastical immunities, and special privileges. Furthermore, he regarded as superfluous all the prescribed celebrations for the saints and the ritualism associated with their feasts; only Sunday should be retained as a holiday, he insisted. Celibacy of the clergy was to be suspended; the religious fraternities were to be dissolved.

With these proscriptions, much that was a burden to the artisan and trader, to the priest and the city councilor was abolished. The Church would become simpler and cheaper. Engels occasionally spoke in this connection of a "bargain church" as one of the results of the Reformation. The Church was to limit itself to preaching, baptizing, and administering the Eucharist, and it was to integrate itself without special privilege into the life of the city and country communities. Such a Church would subject itself to the good of the community. It would provide the city dweller and the farmer at the festive occasions of life with a liturgical order, and would provide city and farm with edificatory discourses. It would not rob precious work time, would not exploit the table for the benefit of freeloading monks, and would be entirely capable of adjusting to the taste of the property-owning and acquisition-addicted burgher.

This program assisted the emancipation of the Church from feudal ties and promoted the "burgherization" of the clergy, who ceased to be a special estate and became integrated as a vocation among other vocations into the burgher society. The priest was liberated from the abnormal chains of celibacy and established a family.

One of the most pronounced disruptions of the socal tradition was brought about by the prohibition of begging. Such a prohibition seemed to be a direct blow against the traditional concepts of mercy, Christian duty, and neighborly love, for almsgiving was considered a worthy work, and begging was not necessarily shameful since the Franciscans and other monastic orders, including Luther's own order, the Augustinians, had raised begging to a standard for sustaining life. In addition to the family obligation to provide for family members who could not work, the requirement of almsgiving presented the most important regulation of medieval feudal society as well as of all precapitalistic societies in that it made provision for the handicapped, ill, and others who had fallen into dire straits. The more the goods-money exchanges became widespread and rose to become the stimulus for the early accumulation of capital, the more quickly the social differentiation in society grew, and with it the number of beggars. Many cities could hardly resist the influx beggars, which added to their other problems. The cities found it necessary to create their own regulations for begging. Such programs were introduced not just on the eve of the Reformation but, in some cases, decades earlier.

But spontaneous almsgiving and the soup kitchens provided by the monasteries could only partially meet the needs of society in the absence of organization and official communal institutions. Thus Luther's point twenty-one of his writing to the German nobility brought about a significant advance in social stability by the demand that each city provide for its own poor and abolish begging completely, above all begging by the monks. At the same time Luther was obliged to defend himself against attacks that such a rigorous demand immediately provoked:

Since some think that in this manner the poor will not be well cared for and fewer great stone houses or monasteries will be built, I almost believe it. Anyway, they are not necessary. He who has chosen poverty ought not to be rich. If he wants to become rich, let him lay his hand to the plough and gain his wealth from the earth. It is sufficient that the poor be cared for well enough that they do not die of hunger or cold. It is not appropriate that one should live at the expense of another's labor or should be rich or live comfortably at the expense of another's hardship ... because St. Paul says, whoever does not work also should not eat. (WA VI 451)

Luther's demand sounds cruel, but Luther has the beggar monks in mind. Against them he marshals the instinct of the working man. The work ethic explains the keen sharpness of his train of thought. His demand applied to beggar monks, not to the poor who, through no fault of their own, had fallen on hard times.

A theme of burgher and middle-class discipline reflected in thrift and work is recurrent in these reform concepts, a theme of moderation emphasizing the practical and the useful. All luxury in dress was to be avoided. Dress style should discourage the use of expensive imported textiles. Pilgrimages, totally useless, were to be abolished because they served only to increase "swilling and whoring, waste money and work time, and lead poor simple people around by the nose." Gluttony and drunkenness were finally to be halted, brothels were to be closed, and fasting periods abolished. The universities were to be reformed and schools established.

Thus *An Address to the Christian Nobility of the German Nation Concerning the Reform of the Christian Estate* contained a reform program to be supported by the imperial estates; the program would benefit the nobles and the cities. In addition, the city councilors and those who, in one way or another, felt themselves constrained by hierarchical pressure from Rome would benefit. Even though the reform addressed questions of immediate ecclesiastical concern, further demands were not excluded. Indeed the scope of the demands was wide enough to affect in varying degrees all estates, ranks, classes, and groups.

Even without the impetus provided by Lutheran theology, many—in fact most—of the ills that Luther discussed in his *Address to the Christian No-*

bility had already been recognized, scoffed at, ridiculed, condemned, and complained about by his contemporaries, because Luther's criticisms focused on the sensitive areas of conflict in society. In the construction and arrangement of this work it is possible to follow the logical link between Lutheran theology and the interests of society, that is, the way and manner in which Lutheran theology began to function as ideology.

This linkage was affected on two levels. Luther's appeal corresponded to the structural, hierarchical composition of the late feudal social order "from top to bottom," and politically served best those who were most directly influenced by the papacy as a political force, namely, the ruling class and its institutions—primarily the spiritual and secular princes, but also the other imperial estates and all the nobles as well as the urban authorities. They were all summoned to act, not just in response to Luther's subjective consciousness but on the basis of their own objective authority and leadership function in society—a function that had come to them in the course of centuries of development and that they must protect and confirm if they did not wish to lose their prerogatives.

In this sense Luther's address to the German nobility is counsel for the ruling class. This counsel was quite extensive and insistent as it applied to the responsibilities of the nobility, but it was also applicable to areas of conflict in the lower strata. Thus Luther's purview extended from a national council to the nomination of bishops to the reform of the universities to begging and brothels.

On the other hand, the ideological function of Lutheran theology was developed on the plane of the relationship of the individual to society. Justification by faith alone, which placed man immediately before God and freed him from all the suggested institutional securities of the pre-Reformation Church, linking the conscience exclusively to the biblical Word of God, strengthened individualism and permitted the individual objectively to evaluate social norms as well as his own role as defined by feudal society with its traditional expectations based on the status of the individual. In general, in an abstract manner, this rule was valid for all members of the society. The rule, however, was distinctly defined in its variation for each class, group, or rank and was interpreted with varying intensity. For instance, the theologian's interpretation differed from the peasant's.

The Lutheran solution to the basic theological question concerning the God-man relationship ignited reaction in the Church among the intelligentsia, counselors, and jurists sooner than among artisans and farmers. This solution as it touched upon ecclesiastical and secular control mechanisms impacted upon the highest authorities and thus became a problem for the ruling class. As a result, Luther was drawn more quickly and more intensely into the problems of the ruling class than into those of the masses. Of course, the problems of the people were not alien to him, but, on the plane of development which his inquest reached in the *Address to the Christian Nobility*, those problems which preoccupied the imperial estates took priority. The reason for this priority is not merely to be ascribed to Luther's personal interest or to his predisposition to ready recognition of those problems. In the last analysis, it is associated with the fact that the popular movement was not yet developed as an independent component of the Reformation, although it is unmistakable that the economic and social problems of the common man already had emerged. However, it would be necessary for the reform movement to grow beyond the stage achieved in 1520 before it would be ready for the challenge of these problems.

Now that Luther had summarized his demands for a reform program, the time seemed ripe to present in detail his conclusions concerning the sacraments. These conclusions had been mentioned in his works on the sacraments in 1519. As early as January 1520, the *Sermon on the Body of Christ* had provoked a vigorous rebuttal by Bishop Johann from Meissen. In the Stolpen mandate Bishop Johann had banned the sermon and had taken special offense at Luther's opinion that the sacrament of the altar should be administered in both kinds, so that the cup as well as the bread would be given to the communicants. Bishop Johann saw confirmed in Luther's suggestion the suspicion, awakened at the Leipzig debate, that Luther tended toward Hussitism and that he was another Bohemian heretic.

Luther dispensed with this "more boorish than blundering scrap of paper" in a brief response marked by biting satire, which unleashed salvos of laughter in the Meissen diocese, since Luther did not attribute the boorish scrap to the bishop but pretended that he believed that one of the episcopal officials was the author. Luther then was obliged to accept reproaches from Spalatin that once again he had acted very indiscreetly and had caused difficulties for the elector with Duke George of Albertine Saxony and other high ranking personalities.

In June 1520 the zealous Leipzig Romanist, Augustin von Alfeld, took on this theme and composed *Treatise on the Communion in Both Kinds*, Alfeld, the "Leipzig Jackass" whom Luther had previously provoked in raising the question of papal primacy, hoped now to earn his spurs in the dispute concerning the sacrament. For Luther this was occasion enough not only to attack Alfeld in rebuttal but also to root up the entire "viper brood." Luther called the composition penned for this purpose *Prologue to the Babylonian Captivity of the Church*. It became the first summary of his new theology.

In 1519, in addition to baptism and the Eucharist, Luther had still counted penance among the sacraments and had refused to express himself more definitively concerning the other sacraments. Now, however, he went one step further and recognized only baptism and the Eucharist as sacraments. To penance, marriage, confirmation, ordination, and extreme unction Luther denied the characteristic of "sacrament" because they were originated by man and were accompanied by no divine promise, or, as in the case of marriage, belonged to the creative order, which was not sacramental.

Sacraments should be administerend not by priests but by all believers, by the entire congregation, for the promise is given to all who in faith receive the gospel, and not merely to priests. Furthermore, the priest has no authority to transform on the altar the bread and wine into the body and blood of Christ; this transformation depends rather on the power of the biblical words of institution—again, without any priestly contribution—by the mere presence of the Eucharist associated with Christ's words. With this view "transubstantiation," that mystical transformation of the bread into the flesh and of the wine into the blood of Christ, became obsolete. But this priestly magical act had been the heart of the Mass. Luther's view of the Eucharist made irrevocably vulnerable the view of the Church as an institution providing prestly administration of the sacraments, and simultaneously called into question the entire canon law which over centuries had developed structural norms and regulations of priestly hierarchy. Out of this dilemma arose one of the most pressing questions of the reform movement and social order for the immediate subsequent years: If each believer, because of the power of baptism, is a priest, who then should administer the Church and make the necessary decisions?

Luther had composed and published the *Babylonian Captivity of the Church* in Latin. This work was meant not for the masses but for clergy and scholars. The object of the work was to reform the priestly Church from within and to cause the priesthood to break away from hierachical discipline. In clerical and scholarly circles this work was considered Luther's most dangerous; it was more biting, more deeply penetrating, and more subversive than the *Address to the Christian Nobility*. Because the *Babylonian Captivity of the Church* was written in the scholarly language of that day, its impact was quickly felt beyond the German borders. Because of this work, King Henry VIII of England saw himself obliged to reply personally with counter arguments. The pope awarded the pious zeal of the king with the honorary title *Defensor Fidei* (Defender of the Faith), which Henry retained when he himself later withdrew the English Church from papal suzerainty because the pope would not assent to the king's divorce from Catherine of Aragon.

At the European universities scholars who up to that time had followed Luther's cause with sympathy were frightened off. Thus Erasmus declared in December 1520: "I would prefer that conditions remain as they are, though there is much in need of remedy, than that there should be new agitations, which frequently end in a result completely different from that which one had at first anticipated" (Thulin 40).

But the *Babylonian Captivity of the Church* not only repulsed; it also attracted. The Premonstratensian monk, Johann Bugenhagen, in Belbuck, felt as if he were being lashed by a whip at his first reading of the work, and he cast the book aside. But then Luther's booklet wrought in him a liberation from blindness and finally gave impetus to his decision to go to Wittenberg. Bugenhagen became one of Luther's most intimate associates. The shocking impact of *The Babylonian Captivity of the Church* was increased by the fact that it reached its readers just at the time that the bull *Exsurge Domine* (Arise O Lord) appeared, threatening Luther with excommunication. If any additional evidence were needed to justify the papal threat of excommunication, Luther himself abundantly supplied it in his *Babylonian Captivity*, the title of which alone suggested a heresy of the worst possible kind.

"Arise, O Lord, and judge thy cause …. Foxes have risen up who dare to desolate thy vineyard … a wild boar, most ravenous, also dares to desolate thy vineyard" (Thulin 39). With these words begins the bull threatening Luther with excommunication, promulgated by Leo X on June 15, 1520, two years after the heresy investigation of Luther had been set in motion. In 1519, because of the impending imperial elections, the curia, in consideration for Elector Frederick of Saxony, permitted the canonical procedure against Luther to remain dormant. On June 28, 1519, contrary to curial hopes, Charles I of Spain was elected Emperor Charles V of the Holy Roman Empire. With the imperial election settled, a strong motive for delaying the heretical proceedings against Luther had disappeared; nevertheless, the proceedings were not reopened until January 1520. The promulgation of *Exsurge Domine* marked the temporary conclusion of this heresy investigation. Luther was judged a heretic. The bull condemned forty-one of his propositions as being especially heretical. The bull granted Luther a grace period of sixty days after its publication to recant. Eck was to publish the bul in Germany; the responsiblity for publication in the Netherlands fell to the papal librarian and legate, Jerome Aleander.

At the beginning of October 1520, Luther finally received the bull. The tension that had been sustained for a whole year, and had rendered him phobic while stimulating him to produce the great Reformation pamphlets, now abated. More than once he had sighed impatiently, "If only the bull would arrive!" (WA BR II 137).

That he would not recant was for him as certain as was the knowledge that the bull must one day come. The condemnation of this writings at the end of February 1520 by the University of Cologne and the University of Louvain had strengthened his conviction. In the condemnation by the University of Cologne, the people who had their hand in the game were those who had already hung a heresy inquest around Reuchlin's neck. Luther did not hesitate to publish the two university verdicts with his rebuttal. With the publication of these verdicts and Luther's rebuttal the front between the two camps hardened. This was demonstrated not only by the fact that his friends grew more vocal and active in their support for him, but also by the fact that the matter now had become for many too hot to handle.

Symptomatic of this drawing of the battle lines was the attitude of Erasmus of Rotterdam. Some passages in Luther's rebuttal of the Cologne and Louvain verdicts had thoroughly pleased Erasmus, but he felt uneasy about the fact that Luther, in justifying his own position, had publicly cited the teaching of Erasmus. It is not surprising that Erasmus called "friend" the papal librarian Aleander, who traveled through the Netherlands with the bull. But this personal circumstance, which throws light on Erasmus' associations, was not the only or the most important reason why Erasmus distanced himself from the Lutheran affair. The alienation was inevitable from the beginning, and it was more or less clearly recognized by both men. Erasmus now merely permitted this inevitable alienation to be acknowledged.

Erasmus' view of Christendom was entirely different from Luther's. Erasmus' ideal was what he called the "philosophy of Christ": Christ is the model for morality, contributing to the moral, ethical improvement and training of humanity. At an early date, Luther had discovered this position to be in opposition with his own theological discovery that the categories of morality collapse completely before the event of the cross and are unable to establish reconciliation between man and God. To eliminate philosophy from meditations about God was, since 1516, Luther's basic concern, while Erasmus desired to place Christ within philosophy and to understand Him from a philosophical point of view. The contradiction was fundamental. The position of Erasmus was more compatible with the sentiment of educated cardinals than with Luther's theology.

"If you condemn without exception all philosophy, then you must deal not only with all academies but also with all sages and with your Augustine on whom you are so dependent," Erasmus admonished Luther in a letter from Louvain on August 1, 1520 (WA BR II 155–59). Erasmus recounted a conversation with the English king, who asked his opinion of Luther. Erasmus reported that his response was evasive: Luther was too well educated for Erasmus to judge him. The king wished that Luther would write with more reservation and wisdom. "This is just what people wish, my Luther, who wish you well," Erasmus admonished. It was dangerous to arouse those who could not be easily subdued again. Furthermore, Erasmus greatly feared unrest because it often took an unexpected turn. When the ocean was stirred up, the waves could not soon be calmed. If unrest should come, no one other than Erasmus would be held responsible; therefore, Erasmus requested that his name and the names of his friends not be misused in Luther's writings, as had occurred in Luther's rebuttal of the Cologne and Louvain verdicts, because animosity might then be directed toward those who should vouchsafe support for reform and who would be of greater service when their integrity was preserved. Erasmus then gave Luther genuine Erasmian advice: take a passage from the Holy Scriptures and consider it without admixture with anything else. "Maybe, in the meantime, the whirlwind will pass by" (WA BR II 155-59).

The whirlwind did not subside. Even Karl von Miltitz who, despite all that had occurred since January 1519, wanted once more to try to mediate, met with no more success than at his first attempt. Miltitz turned up in Saxony once again. On October 12, 1520, he met with Luther in Lichtenberg on the Elbe. Luther was very alert. The danger he faced had sharpened his faculties. He was completely given to maneuvering and temporizing. By now Luther had mastered the art of attacking and retreating, of seeming to concede while remaining firm, and of deferring to his opponent while rejecting the opposing views. These tactics caused the position of the opponent to appear much more impious. In the mood given expression by these techniques, Luther wrote *On the Freedom of a Christian*, and in this title struck the most effective slogan of the Reformation.

The conversations of Lichtenberg had provided the occasion for Luther's latest pamphlet. It was agreed that Luther should write a personal, friendly letter to Pope Leo X and include a special essay with his letter. Miltitz already had suggested this idea in August 1520 at an Augustinian chapter convocation in Eisleben, but Luther had not been present. Staupitz resigned his office as general vicar of the Augustinian order at the Eisleben convocation, and his successor, Wenzel Link, therefore visited Luther at the beginning of September in Wittenberg. Luther accepted Miltitz' suggestion, but he revoked his agreement when he discovered that Eck had posted *Exsurge Domine* in Leipzig. Luther considered petitioning the elector to request that the emperor issued a mandate prohibiting his condemnation as long as his arguments were not refuted by the Scriptures. At the suggestion of the elector, Luther had already composed a public offer to the emperor. Luther offered to listen to and accept the best suggestions from everyone, because he did not want to teach, speak, or write anything against God and the salvation of the soul. "But inasmuch as no peace or tranquility is left for me, I request that no one attempt to weary me, because my spirit, given to me by God, is sustained, so that I am bold to say that before I tire, the whole world will become weary." Christian truth frequently had depended on one person. Therefore, no one should promote hatred or disfavor against him, "because my mood is too happy and too charitable for me to want to be someone's sworn enemy" (WA IV 477-78).

This was what the handwritten draft of the "offer" said. In the printed version, however, these passages which testify to his indomitable determination were deleted. In this conciliatory frame of mind Luther at last came around to Miltitz's suggestion, for a command from the elector had ordered him to meet with Miltitz. But how could he reconcile to himself a friendly, personal letter to the pope when he had long since concluded that the antichrist resided in Rome?

He could demonstrate friendship for the pope by distinguishing between the person and the office. It was not Leo X as an individual but rather the papacy as institution that was the antichrist. This distinction may seem to suggest sophistry, but it is not. The distinction between office and person belongs rather to the fundamental and indispensable values of the ancient classical heritage. Without such distinction neither an orderly legal system nor rational politics would be possible. Thus Luther with good conscience could assure Leo X that he had never desired to attack or insult him personally, and if he had in any way done so, then there was nothing he "desired more than ... to sing the opposite and to revoke my culpable word .... I have always regretted, most pious Leo, that you have become a pope in this age; you, who would be worthy to be pope in a better era. The Roman Chair is not worthy of you or your like, but Satan should be pope, for he, rather than you, actually rules in that Babylon" (WA VII 6). Here Luther equates the papacy with the "Babylonian whore" of Revelation 17:5. Luther claimed he had never attacked his opponents because of their evil lives, but had attacked them because of their unchristian doctrine. In order not to approach Leo empty handed, he enclosed with his letter a little book. "It is a little book as one can see, but the entire sum of the Christian life is compressed in it, provided the meaning is understood" (WA VII 11). This entire sum of the Christian life was nothing other than Luther's teaching on Christian liberty. "A Christian is free, lord of all, subject to none; a Christian is servant to all, subject to all."

The distinction between an inwardly spiritual man and an outwardly fleshly man is the foundation on which this paradox rested. Only the inner, spiritual man was free and then only by faith. But the outward, fleshly man was by love obligated to serve all and obey the authorities. "What does it profit the soul that the flesh is free, fresh, and healthy, that it eats, drinks, and lives as it pleases? Again, what does it injure the soul when the flesh is imprisoned, ill, feeble, hungry, thirsty, and suffering the deprivation of all its desires? None of these things touch the soul to liberate it or to enslave it, to make it rigtheous or to make it evil" (WA VI 21). What was indicated, of course, was the freedom of the inner man, not freedom to choose a belief or confession according to one's taste; not a freedom of choice vis-à-vis faith, but freedom born only of the true faith—thus not a lordship of man over faith but, on the contrary, a submission to faith.

Contrary to Luther's intention, the writers of the German Enlightenment and of the classical period saw in his statement regarding Christian liberty a precursor to the bourgeois ideal of religious freedom. Nevertheless, theyr interpretations indicate Luther's farreaching impact.

Luther did not conceive of liberty as a prerequisite to but rather as a result of faith. But whose liberty, from what, and for what? It was the Christian's liberty whereby he was freed from prescriptive observances for achieving salvation. This was nothing more than a paraphrase of the teaching of justification by faith alone. Freedom imparted by faith, in contrast to authoritative prescriptions and society's expectations, is so great that the Christian can satisfy these prescriptions and expectations because they do not touch upon the soul's salvation. "And even though tyrants unjustly demand the fulfillment of such prescriptions and expectations, it does not injure me to comply as long as nothing in such prescriptions and expectations is directed against God" (WA VII 37). This was the freedom of mental reservation, of the "inner immigration" (introversion), of evasion. Luther had learned this lesson from Paul, to whom he specifically appealed. With this attitude, early Christians had survived persecution. This attitude lent constancy and at the same time elasticity, permitting comprise in exterior matters. It was well-suited to Luther's personal circumstances and the purpose of his letter offering Leo X a conceding gesture without surrendering anything. But would he be able to hold to this position and would his supporters be willing, in the long run, to settle for inner freedom?

Chapter 8

"Here I Stand":
Luther Before the Emperor and Empire
Worms 1521

Luther's letter to Leo X could not alter the fact that, with the promulgation and publication of the bull *Exsurge Domine*, Luther could no longer evade confrontation with the alternatives of revocation or excommunication. Since Luther had always resisted any idea of revocation, it would be necessary for him to continue on his chosen path by seeking to influence public opinion in such a way that the anticipated final ban and excommunication would appear to have been unjustified from the very outset. The foundation for such action had already been established in all his previous writings and public debates. Now Luther strengthened this foundation with a pamphlet, *Against the Bull of the Antichrist*, in which he reconfirmed twelve of his propositions condemned by the bull, and with a Latin summary for scholars, *Against the Execrable Bull of Antichrist*, in which he reconfirmed six of his propositions condemned by the bull.

In the meantime, Eck and Aleander saw to the public posting and distribution of the bull. Only in Meissen, Merseburg, and Brandenburg was it relatively easy for Eck to post the bull; on the other hand, he was so violently threatened by students in Leipzig that he was forced to flee into the Paulist monastery. Aleander had more success in the Hapsburg Netherlands. There, in October, in Louvain and Lüttich, Aleander incited at the hands of the executioner a public burning of Luther's books. Soon also in Cologne and Mainz, the pyre devoured Luther's writing.

On December 10, 1520, at the Elster Gate in Wittenberg, in an act of symbolic reaction, Luther burned a copy of canon law, the writings of his opponents, and a copy of *Exsurge Domine*. Melanchthon had summoned the students to the event.

Whoever is committed to the study of evangelical truth, let him appear shortly before 9:00 A.M. near the Holy Cross Church outside the city wall where, in keeping with ancient apostolic custom, the godless books of papal decrees and scholastic theology are to be burned because the insolence of the enemies of the gospel has reached such a degree that they have burned Luther's writings. Come on then, pious university youth, assemble to this genuine religious service, because perhaps the time has arrived when the antichrist should be revealed. (Thulin 41)

The sixthy-day period of grace had expired. Instead of recanting, Luther had burned the bull threatening him with excommunication. Thus on January 3, 1521, in the bull *Decet Romanum Pontificem* (It Is Appropriate for the Roman Bishop), Leo X finally uttered the ban against Luther and his followers. In accordance with prevailing imperial law, the imperial ban was to follow the ecclesiastical one. The legal order was clear, but this in no way automatically guaranteed the success of papal politics; on the contrary, the papacy now suffered the consequences of its deep involvement in secular affairs and its powerful intrigues against the election of the new emperor. Charles V lent his ear to those counselors who cautioned him not to move too quickly in the Luther affair.

The emperor had many concerns, and the Luther affair was not for him the most important. Charles I of Spain, who was also Charles V of the empire, united in his person Spain with its overseas possessions, the Low Countries, the kingdoms of Naples and Sicily, and the Hapsburg possessions in Austria and southern Germany. Charles was born in Ghent in 1500 and educated in a Burgundian culture; French was his native tongue. His upbringing from earliest childhood had inspired in him the desire to reestablish the Burgundian realm, which, in 1477, under the blows of France, had been demolished. This meant war with France. Nevertheless, Charles never lost sight of his goal. All other programs were subjected to this major quest. From childhood and youth he had been growing into his role of universal ruler. In 1507, at age seven, he was declared duke of Burgundy and king of Castile; in 1515 he reached his majority as duke of Burgundy; in 1516 he was declared king of Naples, Sicily, and Aragon; in 1519 he was elected emperor of the Holy Roman Empire of the German Nation. Thus in all of his territories, with the exception of the southern Netherlands, he was a foreigner. His dynastic universal rule contradicted the fundamental tendencies toward the foundation of national monarchies. Furthermore, the emperor's claims of sovereignty were as anachronistic as were those of the Roman papacy in Europe's ecclesiastical constellation. The pope and emperor, in their universal aspirations, were dependent on each other whenever, of course, rivalry and conflict did not preclude this mutual dependency.

When the new emperor, in the fall of 1520, stepped onto German soil for the first time, he hardly understood a word of German. Despite that fact, Charles was considered to be of "noble German blood" because he was a grandson of Maximilian, although German blue blood in the Hapsburg veins had long since been mixed with that of other European royalty into an amalgam unregognizable with respect to nationality. The political situation in which Charles V found himself was complicated enough. In Spain, which he had left in May 1520, an uprising had provoked instability; he was on the threshold of war with France; there were differences with the papacy; and the German princes, on the occasion of his election as emperor, had wrung from him an "election capitulation," which greatly curtailed his imperial power. He had to agree that during his absence from the empire an imperial executive would be empowered to rule, that he would not introduce foreign troops into the empire, and—which for the Luther affair became a point of great significance—that no German would be placed before a foreign tribunal without first having had a hearing in Germany.

The emperor thus agreed, as the elector Frederick the Wise requested, first to give Luther a hearing at the imperial diet before an imperial decision in this matter would be forthcoming. With all means at its disposal papal diplomacy resisted this course of action. It must have appeared to the papacy as a shocking humiliation for Rome when the imperial diet granted a hearing to a legally condemned heretic and insisted on evaluating a papal decision in ecclesiastical affairs. For weeks the diplomatic tug of war prevailed concerning whether or not Luther would be permitted to appear before the diet. Since the emperor was negotiating with the curia a united front against France, he wanted to grant concessions to the curia in the Luther affair without at the same time antagonizing the Saxon elector. Luther would be permitted to come to the diet, but first he must recant. Frederick the Wise firmly rejected this proposal; neither would he agree to a hearing for Luther in Wittenberg. The elector saw through all of these intrigues, which had only one goal: to prevent Luther from appearing before the imperial diet and to spare papal diplomacy an embarrassment.

On January 27, 1521, Charles V opened his first imperial diet in Worms. The emperor sought solutions to various problems. Above all he wanted money and troops from the Germans. There were discussions concerning the imperial court, the imperial executive, and about many other things, but the Luther affair did not even come up. It was not even listed in the diet protocol; yet it was this question which was to become the test of strength between the imperial estates and the emperor. On February 13, 1520, Aleander, the papal nuncio, in a speech lasting several hours, proposed a law against Luther and at the same time submitted a draft of such a law. On February 19, the imperial estates rejected Aleander's draft. The estates appealed to the election capitulation granted by the emperor, pointed to the ugly mood among the common people, and demanded that Luther should be granted a letter of safe conduct and summoned to a hearing before the diet.

The estates used Luther's name in order to put pressure on the emperor. They wanted to test whether the emperor was willing to honor the promises made and the obligations assumed in the election capitulation. This was of dual significance for the estates; on the one hand, the test was designed to promote respect for the German princes among the emperor's Spanish and Italian advisors and to make clear to them that in Germany they could not do as they pleased; and, on the other hand, the estates wanted to indicate clerly to the emperor early in his reign the limits of his authority. Furthermore, the appeal to the common man was more than merely a tested argument for the support of the German princes. Luther had become a public force. It was known everywhere and discussed everywhere that he had offered to permit himself to be instructed and corrected by Holy Scriptures. But this had not yet happened. If he should be condemned unheard and uninstructed, such a course could only be interpreted as completely arbitrary.

The nuncio Aleander heard these arguments at every turn. "All Germany is in open revolt," he reported to Rome. "For nine-tenths of the people the battle cry is 'Luther'; for the others it is 'death to the Roman curia.'" Aleander, the highly educated papal librarian—a scholar of Greek and Hebrew, friend of Erasmus, and once rector of the Sorbonne in Paris—was very fearful.

> A legion of poor German nobles under Hutten's command who have sworn themselves to Luther's cause is set against us and they thirst for the blood of the clergy and desire to assault us immediately …. All of the many and great dangers to which I am hourly subjected, I cannot and will not list; I will not be believed until, God forbid, I am stoned, hacked to pieces by these people who when they encounter me on the street invariably reach for the sword with gnashing teeth, and they scream a German curse at me together with a death threat. (Kalkoff 44, 81)

Whoever spoke against Luther had no audience; whoever wrote against him found no printer. Only the emperor still supported the pope,

> if he does not leave us in the lurch, intimidated by the popular uproar or by the wicked advice of his German counselors; apart from the emperor the whole world here is our enemy and these mad dogs, the Germans, are equipped with intellectual and martial weapons and price themselves that they are no longer brute beasts as were their forefathers and that they have turned the Tiber into the Rhine and that Italy has lost the treasury of knowledge to them. (Kalkoff 131)

Aleander wholeheartedly hated the Germans. Pope Julius II (1503–1513), who once as papal nuncio had traveled through Germany and had been captivated by the wealth of the German cities and the number of warlike people, had already pronounced as a maxim of papal policy that it was in the interest of the Holy See *quia la Germania sia discorde* (that Germany be disunited). Aleander formulated this pious wish even more poignantly. If the Germans, who, in his opinion, paid less than any other people to the papal treasury, would throw off the Roman yoke, then, he threatened, "we will see to it that you mutually destroy one another and drown in your own blood" (WA BR II 258). The German pamphleteers vented their wrath on Aleander, the pope's representative, and judged him capable of every despicable deed, and depicted him as the protector of the Roman whore and as a child molester. Hutten had declared war against Aleander in every form. Thus Aleander's fear of violence to his person or in general was not unfounded.

But these concerns were not his alone. They were shared by many. The new general vicar of the Augustinians, Wenzel Link in Nuremberg, thought the time had come to request Luther to write something from which it would be clear that he had never challenged the civil authority. But Luther did not respond. He could not imagine how anyone could expect anything of the kind from him, for he frequently enough had supported civil authority.

Luther now advised against the use of force. Six months earlier he had still dreamed of washing his hands in the blood of the Romanists. To utter such words now would be inadvisable; even at the time of the utterance his words were not very wise. When his opponents had resorted to the outrage of burning his books, they could be condemned by their own peace rhetoric. Calls for violence would only have placed Luther in a bad light with the imperial estates. Thus Luther did not permit himself to be provoked to carelessness by Hutten, who was chafing with impatience. Luther contended, "We do not want to fight for the gospel with violence and slaughter; I have written this to Hutten. The world has been overcome and the Church established by the Word; with the Word will she also be reestablished. The antichrist also assaults without hands and he will be destroyed without hands by the Word" (WA BR II 249). Luther had cause enough to appeal to the sword for aid. He was informed that in Meissen and Merseburg whole wagonloads of his books were burned. He sensed the growing unrest among the people, but he did not ascribe the responsibility of unrest to the people; on the contrary, he made the Romanists responsible for everything. Luther continuously returned to the Word. "The Lord himself is author and tutor of his Word" (WA BR II 271). In the meantime it would be necessary that the madness be controlled by divine counsel, for such madness, should it break out in Germany, would provoke "Bohemian-like" uprisings against the clergy. Luther refused to accept blame for such a result. He had not desired that the German nobility curb the Romanists with iron but rather with counsel and edicts. To wage war against the general clerical cowardice would be like waging war against women and children. But Luther seriously doubted that the rage of the Romanists could be assuaged with counsel and edicts alone. He anticipated that much grief would come to them because of their intractable stubbornness.

During these weeks since contradictory reports had reached him as to whether he would be summoned to Worms, Luther plunged into his work. He had always worked continously and untiringly, but now he even exceeded himself in a delirium of work. For Luther work was not only solace and sanctuary; it was also the means to create as much as possible lest the fate of Jan Hus eventually overtake him. Martyrdom loomed before his eyes. More than once he gave notice that he was prepared for any eventuality. Luther preached twice daily: in the morning, to the burghers in the city church; in the afternoon, to his Augustinians in the monastery. Twice a week he lectured. Simultaneously he was writing several works. For the crown prince, Johann Frederick, he interpreted the Magnificat. This was the hymn of praise sung be the Virgin Mary when the archangel Gabriel announced that the power of the Most High would overshadow her and that she would conceive the Savior in her womb; a hymn of praise full of historic dynamic which praises God for putting down the mighty from their seats and exalting the lowly, for filling the hungry with good things and sending the rich away empty. Many months earlier the request had come from the elector for Luther to write *Postille* (homilies): a collection of sermons which could be given at the conclusion of the reading of a passage in the Bible during the worship service. *Postille* indicates that after the reading of the Bible the words *Post illa verba* be spoken as a transition to the sermon. Luther had postponed this task for a long time, but now he took it up. With less than his original vitality, he was still occupied with the psalter, with which he had begun his lecturing activities eight years earlier.

He no longer kept the liturgical hours of the Roman Church. Matins, Lauds, Prime, Terce, Sext, None, Vespers, Compline: every three hours there was an interruption of work for prayers with psalms, hymns, and canticles, with Bible readings followed by responses to stimulate meditation. The liturgical hours may be appropriate for the monastic orders for which they were created and for priests who have only to administer the sacraments and have no other responsibilities, but not for a university professor who studies, teaches, writes, wants to instruct and debate, and constantly must guard against new attacks from all sides. Even apart from the assaults on him, merely because of his work load, Luther could not have kept the liturgical hours regularly. From time to time he thought to catch up, to make up the prayers that he had missed, and thus to satisfy his duty. Now he completely abandoned any such attempt. The ban had excommunicated him; the regulations imposed by the pope, from whom he already had long been alienated, bound him no longer. He was free of them.

Luther abandoned the liturgical prayer hours not primarily because they were a burden but because he doubted their effectiveness. They led to a mechanical recitation without a worshipful attitude, to a simple "lip worship" that could induce a false security. But above all they were commanded by the pope; that in itself was sufficient to place them in a bad light and cause Luther to reject them. The rejection of the liturgical offices was one more step away from the traditional priesthood, a victory of the teacher Luther over the priest and monk Martin. Of course, Luther did not altogether cease to pray. He merely liberated his prayers from Roman rules; he stood at the window in the Wittenberg Augustinian monastery, looked out across the Elbe River, and communed with his God.

That this work on the psalter no longer brought him the joy and satisfaction it once had after he abandoned the offices was not a coincidence, for the psalter constitutes the main content of the hours. What he had written about the psalms now seemed to Luther too long and encumbered by rigmarole. Now he saw things more clearly, and he seized matters with much greater conviction than formerly when he had begun his work on the psalter.

In the meantime, the pamphlet war against the enemies went on uninteruptedly. Eck and Emser did not rest, and others joined them in order to make a reputation for themselves out of the Luther affair. Luther could not and did not desire to take notice of every opponent. Why should he dignify these petty scribes by answering them? Luther did not stand alone; he could leave it to his friends to rebuke the less significant opponents, and he did not need to respond personally to every new outpouring even from the more important rivals. Thus Oecolampadius relieved him in the contest with Eck, and Melanchthon took responsibility to answer a pamphlet appearing under the name of the Roman Dominican, Thomas Rhadinus, which Luther suspected had for its true author the "goat Emser." Under the pseudonym of Didymous Faventinus, Melanchthon published his work against Rhadinus-Emser. But Melanchthon's work missed the mark because Emser was not, in fact, the author; suspicion had lured the Wittenbergers onto the wrong track. But the damage was not great. Emser himself was once again immediately heard from. Under the slogan "Watch out, the goat is about to gore you," Emser wrote *Against the Unchristian Book Which Appeared, Written by the Augustinian Martin Luther, to the German Nobility, a Lecture by Jerome Emser to the Entire Highly Praised German Nation.* Hardly had Luther seen the first sheets of Emser's still uncompleted work when he responded to it with *To the Goat in Leipzig,* which evoked additional invectives from the Dresden court chaplain, who also was the secretary for Duke George the Bearded. The polemics flew back and forth. *To the Bull in Wittenberg,* Emser wrote. *To the Goat in Leipzig,* Luther responded. Each one paid the other in like coin for every insult. Both were in their element.

"Dear Goat, don't gore me," Luther mockingly pleads with victorious confidence in concluding *In Response to the Super Christian, Super Spiritual, and Super Artificial Book of th Goat Emser in Leipzig.* In a subtitle Luther added, *In which also Emser's friend Murnarr (a stammering fool) is mentioned*: a jab at the Strasbourg Franciscan, Thomas Murner, who had written against Luther's *Sermon Concerning the New Testament,* and defended the Roman Church in *To the Great Nobles of the German Nation That They Protect the*

Christian Faith Against the Destroyer of Faith Martin Luther, a Seducer of Simple Christians. Apart from Luther's preoccupation with immediate opponents, there were the rejection of the bull *Exsurge Domine*, explanations justifying the burning of papal books at the Elster Gate, and more. Three presses simultaneously were kept busy publishing Luther's writings. The printers could not set type fast enough to keep pace with the volumes of manuscripts that kept pouring forth. As they flowed from the pen, so they went to the type trays; there was no time for editing. Luther worked swiftly with a keen memory. He did not need a long time to think of arguments and to compose and recompose sentences. Arguments and sentences flowed almost automatically from him, giving expression to concepts, applications, and images. Luther's hand betrays no haste. His sentences run in a uniform flourish, slightly slanted to the right, fluid but moderate. The goose quill is applied with equal pressurre across the writing surface in order that it should not spray or stick. There is hardly ever a word crossed out or another word substituted. Writing, the movement of the hand across the paper, must have been enjoyable for him.

Luther fought his enemies, picked apart their arguments, formulated his own thought, sometimes more simply, more apodictically, more penetratingly than at other times. Not the least significantly, he created in his mind, penetrating in its sarcasm, graphic pictures of his opponents: for example, "the goat Emser." These caricatures gained wide recognition. Luther knew how to create stereotypes. He never let this talent be monopolized by the ever-increasing circle of new opponents; he used it not only to rebuff his enemies but also to provide guidance for the common man as to how one should respond—yes, how one, under the circumstances, should espace the snare laid for him. Many in fact did need advice because the papal bull of excommunication had in many parishes led to evil practices that brought the simple believer under severe pressure. The clergy inquired in the confessional concerning the whereabouts of Luther's writings, convinced the penitents to surrender them and burn them, and made absolution contingent upon the willingness of the penitent to distance himself from Luther's teachings. It was necessary to alert the individual and to strengthen his ability to resist. For this purpose Luther composed *A Lesson for the Penitent Concerning Forbidden Books* (WA VII 284-98).

Luther did not spend much time on this treatise on penance. He immediately addressed the practical problem and instructed believers what they should say to the priest in the confessional: "I wish to confess what troubles my conscience. Your office is not to seek to dictate to my conscience; your office is not to inquire after my secrets. You would like to know how much money I have in my purse" (WA VII 291). If the priest would not absolve the penitent, one should then think about the adage: "Where man will not absolve, God will!" And Luther advised further,

When you already have confessed that you have forbidden books, but you do not wish to turn them over and the priest refuses to grant you absolution, you should say: "Dear father, absolve me at my risk. I will not surrender the books, for I would thereby sin against my conscience." If the priest threatens you with the bull, then respond to him in the words of St. Peter, "One must obey God rather than man." (WA VII 294)

At the same time attempts were being made in Worms to draw the emperor to one side or the other without any end in sight of the tug of war. In February Aleander handed the emperor a writing against Luther from the Italian Dominican Ambrosius Catharinus, *Excusatio Disputationis contra Lutherum* (Reason for Disputation Against Luther). At the beginning of March a copy of this tract came to Luther, sent by Wenzel Link. It did not especially impress Luther; it presented no new arguments or thoughts. Erasmus also considered it to be inferior to the writings of Eck and Prierias. But since it had been placed before the emperor, Luther could not completely ignore it. Luther intended to dismiss it with short shrift, but as a matter of fact Luther's response became of much greater importance than he could originally have anticipated.

In his reply Luther devoted only little space to the rebuttal of Catharinus' arguments, but the did present a new expression of his view of the Church. Luther's new presentation was closely linked to the Leipzig disputation, but it added an important element to the thoughts expressed in Leipzig. If in 1519 Luther had derived the essence of the Church fully from faith, now faith assumed a second position and the first place was assigned to the gospel. This was, to be sure, no contradiction of what he had said earlier, but was, in the increased sensitivity of the situation, a precise formulation. From the gospel comes faith; from faith comes everything else. The Church is present wherever the gospel is. And even if everything else is present—baptism, the Eucharist—there is no Church if the gospel is lacking. This was a progressive step, and significant because the word "faith" was always subject to misunderstanding, as if it dealt only with a purely subjective spirit, mind, or level of conscience. With the emphasis on the gospel as the first and fundamental element of the Church, the content of faith is much more fully determined than it previously had been; the criteria of the Church are transferred out of the realm of subjective opinion to the content of an objective message that comes from the outside. The Church is

a unity of spirit, not of place, not of persons, not of things, not of bodies ... because the gospel is—before the bread, before baptism—the single, most certain and most noble symbol of the Church .... Gospel and Church know no jurisdictions, which are nothing but tyrannical inventions of men. Gospel knows only charity and service, not violence and tyranny; therefore, whoever teaches the gospel is pope and succes-

sor of Peter; whoever does not teach the gospel is Judas and betrayer of
Christ. (WA VII 721)

This approach provided a definition not only for the invisible (spiritual)
Church. In the existing confrontational situation of the spring of 1521, Luther defined the Church in terms of clear contrast and not in any other
way. It was much more important to define the true visible Church than to
define the invisible Church, for the true visible Church was not to be confused with the institutional Church, whose officers forbade, suppressed, and
burned Luther's evangelical writings. However, the true Church could be
clearly distinguished from this institutional Church.

In practical application this meant to the reform movement nothing
short of the fact that the true visible Church was recognizable simply by
the evangelical content of the spoken and written word, in sermons and
treatises. This supposition assumed, to be sure, a high degree of sophistica-
tion on the part of every believer: each individual had to use his own judgment.

With respect to theory of revolution, this insistence on personal judgment was related to an important phase of rebellion. The warrant for the
criteria for legitimacy was withdrawn from the historically evolved and
hierachically established authorities. The individual who up to that time
had depended on the word of the established authorities in matters of custom and on the rule of tradition was called on to make his own decision
and declared capable of doing so. Since the essential theological knowledge for making such decisions was lacking, the conscience was triggered,
and ultimately the decision was swayed by public opinion. This public
opinion was developed, despite all countermeasures and contradictory
tendencies, in Luther's favor. Since an idea is always embarrassed when it
embraces personal interest, the results of the many individual decisions ultimately correspond with the prevailing social interests. Wherever theological questions are decided with the healthy, human rationality of a single
individual, the answer is an ideological one corresponding with personal
interest.

Luther's definition of the Church, founded in an observation concerning
the antichrist and concerning the historical position of the Roman Empire
in the divine plan for salvation, was emphatically directed against the papacy. The prophet Daniel served Luther as biblical foil. In the eighth chapter of Daniel, a vision is recorded about a king who, at the end of time, in-
solently and cleverly demolished the chosen people. Luther applied each
aspect of this vision to the pope as the antichrist. But a more important factor appeared in Luther's exegesis. The vision of Daniel provided a sequence of the phases of salvation history, the starting point for the teaching of the four world kingdoms. According to this teaching, four world
kingdoms will succeed one another, and at the end of the fourth kingdom

the antichrist will begin his reign that will endure until he is overthrown by Christ in the parousia. These four world kingdoms in biblical history are Media, Persia, Greece, and Rome. The Roman Empire is the fourth and last world empire. This doctrine of the four world empires was one of the major reasons that, after the fall of the Roman Empire in the storms of the Germanic migration, the need arose to sextend a continued existence to the Roman Empire. In order to provide such a continuation, the popes bestowed the imperial title on the Franks and the Germans. Thus arose the theory concerning the transfer of the empire to the Germans—*translatio imperii ad Germanos*: a fiction to which the feudal German political system of the Middle Ages was indebted for the name "Hole Roman Empire."

It is symptomatic of the growing German consciousness in the Reformation period that Luther saw through this fiction and recognized it as a creation of the popes.

> The Roman Empire is transfered to the Germans only in word while in reality there is no longer an imperium. But at the fall of Rome this man (the pope-antichrist) elevated himself above all kings, all bishops, heaven and earth, and thereby consolidated the empire in his hand, and this lie he reenforced with the forged and clumsy document of the Donation of Constantine. (WA VII 723)

In the *Babylonian Captivity*, which Luther regarded as a prologue of something still greater and as the first part of a "revocation," he called attention to another part of this revocation; this extension Luther now considered to be clarified by the explanation of Daniel (WA VII 777). "You can expect everything from me except flight and revocation; I have no desire to flee, much less change my mind," he had earlier written to Spalatin in December 1520 (WA BR II 243). The revocation, for which the curia so fervently hoped because it would have morally demolished Luther and guaranteed not only a political victory for Rome but also a spiritual one, became for Luther a toy with which to tease his opponent. He sensed his spiritual superiority and was convinced that the lies must be destroyed by the word an not by naked force.

> The pope and his empire (although they fear this with the greatest and most cringing fear) will not be destroyed by the laity, because they don't deserve such a mild punishment, but rather the papal empire will be preserved until the advent of Christ, whose worst enemy is and was the papal empire. Thus will the papal empire be destroyed—who elevates itself against all, not with hands, but with the spirit of Satan, so that spirit will overwhelm spirit and truth will reveal the deception, because to expose the lies means to destroy them. (WA VII 777)

This was apocalyptic sentiment. Luther, like many of his contemporaries, supposed that judgment day was imminent. Luther would gladly recant, but not that which was desired. At this time he was working on nothing else more intensively than on his "revocation," which was formulated in this way: "Earlier I called the pope a vicar of Christ; I now revoke, and I now say that the pope is an enemy of Christ and an apostle of the devil" (WA BR II 293). This was written on Palm Sunday 1521, as the imperial herald already was a good week underway and only a few days from Wittenberg, with an imperial citation and letter of safe conduct for the condemned heretic in his pouch.

The imperial herald, Kaspar Sturm, bore the official title "Germany," a further indication that Germany as an independent political entity within the empire was pressing to the fore, because at that time it was usual for official heralds who were charged with proclaiming the will of an estate or of a prince to bear a title in which the name of the estate or prince was represented. "Germany" led Luther to Worms. The itinerary was like a triumphant march. Aleander blamed the "rascally" herald, who took the greatest pains to bring the heretic in triumph to Worms. Under the protection of "Germany" and the imperial insignia, Luther left Wittenberg on April 2, 1521, for Worms. Nicholaus von Amsdorf, Peter Suaven (the Pomeranian noble who was studying in Wittenberg), and the Augustinian Johann Petzensteiner accompanied him. The goldsmith Christian Döring, provided his carriage, and the university provided twenty gulden for the trip.

In Erfurt the rector and the university senate led Luther in a festive procession into the city. They hosted a banquet for the condemned heretic and invited him to preach in the Augustinian church. Luther preached about work, human laws, and faith. Each person should arrange his work in such a manner that it serves not only himself but also someone else, he urged. "Is he wealthy? Then his goods also should benefit the poor. Is he poor? He should make himself valuable to the wealthy; where there is a farmhand or a maid, his or her work should benefit the master .... Don't worry about me. I know what human laws are. The pope can issue as many laws as he likes, and I will obey them all if I am so inclined." And when it was asked if one should obey human laws, he answered: "When genuine Christian love and faith are present, everything that man does is worthwhile and everyone can do as he wills, but he must not trust in works because they cannot save him" (WA VII 813). Luther's sermon was conservative and mild, without contention and threats, and yet the festive reception had tumultuous results right after his departure. A choirmaster who had greeted Luther had so incensed his narrow-minded colleagues, devotees of the old faith, that they accused him of corrupting himself and exposing himself to the same condemnations imposed on Luther, and they expelled him from their chapter. Revenge followed swiftly. In the same night a restless mob demolished the houses of antireform clerics.

Justus Jonas, born in Nordhausen but the living in Erfurt, joined the little travel group, and, accompanied by his servants, traveled on his horse with Luther. In Gotha and Eisenach Luther again was obliged to preach. Then the same misfortune overtook him that had overtaken him three years earlier on the way to Augsburg: stomach and bowel trouble. He was ill when he arrived on April 14 in Frankfurt, where disturbing correspondence awaited him. The game now seemed to have become too bold for the elector Frederick. He did not believe he could offer Luther adequate protection any longer and thus informed him that it would perhaps be better if he did not come to Worms after all.

The situation was indeed threatening enough. On March 6 the emperor had issued the citation and letter of safe conduct for Luther's summons to Worms, in which no word concerning revocation had appeared except the reference to the diet's desire to be informed by Luther concerning the books that he had published. But then the emperor issued a mandate that confiscated all of Luther's writings. The mandate could only have been meant to intimidate Luther and to cause him to return to Wittenberg. Under these circumstances, could Luther place any confidence at all in the imperial letter of safe conduct, and must he not fear that his fate would be the same as that of Jan Hus in Constance, when the letter of safe conduct for the Bohemian reformer was rescinded in 1415? In the light of the words of this recent mandate, it was a gamble to trust the emperor because a promise did not obligate nor was it honor bound. The heretic was considered in the power of Satan and all means to combat Satan were legitimate. Even God had duped and deceived Satan: since man was too weak to resist the devil, God, in the person of His Son, took on the form of man. The devil could not lay hands on God, but he could seize man. The devil believed Christ to be a man, but in reality the devil laid hands on God when he attacked Jesus. Thus Satan could not retain Christ in the realm of the dead and was forced to surrender Him. At Golgotha the devil was deceived by God. And thus it should and must happen repeatedly for the devil. He must be duped now also, and especially when he slipped inside a person and transformed that person into a heretic. Heretics saw the reverse side of theology, which was satanology. Almost everything that can be attributed to God could also be ascribed to Satan; only the signature need be changed. Thus in order the more to enhance its own power, the Church stoked the fear of the devil.

Luther was aware of satanology, the devil, the councils, and the story of Jan Hus. Nevertheless, despite all the talk about the devil, Luther wanted to proceed to Worms, even if there were as many devils there as there were tiles on the roofs. Thus he wrote to Spalatin from Frankfurt: "We are coming, dear Spalatin, even though Satan has sought to restrain me by more than one illness .... I realize that the imperial mandate was issued in order to intimidate me. But Christ lives, and we will come to Worms despite the gates of hell and the powers of the air" (WA BR II 298).

It was no power of the air but his friend and correspondent, Martin Butzer, who met Luther near Oppenheim on his renewed journey and requested him to come to the Ebernburg. Glapion, the emperor's confessor, was there and wanted to speak to Luther. However, Glapion could as easily talk to him in Worms, Luther thought, and permitted no detour. Luther sensed that Glapion's request was only a subterfuge of the papists to keep him from Worms and by delay and detour consume the time period for which his letter of safe conduct was valid.

On Tuesday, April 16, 1521, in the morning shortly before ten o'clock, Luther and his companions in their little Saxon carriage rolled through Martin's Gate into Worms. The news of Luther's approach had preceded him. Nearly one hundred mounted nobles waited for him miles from the city and provided him escort into the city, an escort which normally was provided only to princes when they came to an imperial diet. Trumpets announced Luther's arrival at Worms. Masses of people lined his way, watched from windows and doorways, stretched and strained to touch his cloak, and every eye sought his gaze. As Luther climbed down from the carriage, a priest embraced him and deported himself, as the infuriated Aleander reported, as if he had touched a holy relic.

Luther lodged in the Johanniter Inn, or the „Hospitaller Hospiz", in a room with the two Saxon nobles, Bernhard von Hirschfeld and Hans Schott von Oberlind. The Johanniter Inn was, like all inns, crowded. Worms at the time, with its normal population of about 7,000, was bursting at the seams. The city could not contain the imperial estates with their retinue and all the motly masses of merchants, street vendors, jugglers, and prostitutes who wanted to make money during the session of the imperial diet. Prices rose sharply. The curious stood before the Johanniter Inn, eager to see and hungry for sensations. With such a tumult it was not advisable for Luther to venture into the streets. Luther, therefore, remained closeted in his quarters, where, nevertheless, he still had difficulty avoiding visitors.

The next day, Wednesday, April 17, 1521, Luther stood before the emperor. The imperial marshal, von Pappenheim, and the imperial herald, "Germany", led him shortly before 4:00 P.M. from his quarters by way of side streets to the episcopal palace in which the emperor had taken lodging and in which the diet also was convened. The direct route from the Johanniter Inn to the episcopal palace through the Kämmererstrasse was blocked with masses of people, and the authorities wished to avoid increasing the popular excitement which had been aroused by Luther's entry into Worms.

The meeting was set for 4:00 P.M., but two hours elapsed before Luther was admitted into the imperial presence. It was an historical spot in which Luther waited. In Roman times on the place where the episcopal palace now stood, the holy temple precinct of the Romans had been marked off.

The Burgundians had erected their royal palace, the palace of the Nibelungen, on the site of the ancient Roman temple precinct. Siegfried, Gunther, Gernot, Giselher, Hagan von Tronje, the figures of the Nibelungen Song had entered and exited here, and, driven here by love, Kriemhild and Brunhild fought their duel to the end. In the Etzel Saga the Huns, at the command of Attila, stormed and destroyed the palace; from here Hagan must have hurried to the nearby Rhine with the Nibelungen treasure in order to bury it for all eternity beneath the river's billows. The Burgundians left Worms after the defeat inflicted by the Huns and moved south to the region around Lake Geneva. The Burgundian realm that was established there bequeathed to that dukedom the name whose titleholder now was none other than Charles V, the emperor who dreamed of resurrecting the Burgundian dukedom. Charlemagne had had an imperial palace here. From here Henry IV had departed for Canossa in 1077, and here, in 1122, the controversy between empire and papacy concerning the investiture of bishops was settled. The old imperial palace had become an episcopal palace, which is no longer standing; the French destroyed it in 1689, in the same campaign in which they destroyed Heidelberg Castle.

Shortly before 6:00 P.M. the imperial marshal and the imperial herald led Luther, followed by several Saxon advisers, into the great hall of the episcopal palace. On his chair surrounded by advisers and the electors sat the emperor, a frail youth of twenty-one years with a protruding lower jaw, the hereditary feature of the Hapsburgs. Luther stood before Charles with slightly bent knee, as court etiquette dictated. There he was only to speak when requested had been communicated to him earlier. The Trier official, Johann von der Ecken, was selected as imperial spokesman. With a brief explanation first in Latin, then in German, von der Ecken opened the proceedings: "His Imperial Majesty has summoned you, Martin Luther, for two reasons: first, to provide an opportunity for you to identify yourself with the books which have been published under your name; second, to determine whether or not you are moved to revoke any of these books or any of the teachings from them." "Read the titles," the Saxon adviser, Doctor Schurff, called out (WA VII 828). This took a little time: about twenty titles were read aloud, and Luther was thereby provided a pause to collect himself. Then he admitted with a soft voice that indeed the books were his, but concerning the matter of revocation he requested time to think. His request was granted, and on the next day at 4:00 P.M. he was to return, prepared to give an oral answer not to be read from a prepared draft. The emperor made a gesture, and Luther was dismissed. Sturm accompanied him back to his lodging.

On that same evening, Luther wrote to the Viennese humanist, Cuspinian that he would not recant. The time to reflect he needed not in order to determine whether or not he would revoke, but carefully to consider

how, in the given forum the long, firmly determined "no" should be uttered. He did not want merely to present a naked "no"; he would rather at
least present his reasons for the "no," and is highest hope was to engage
the opposition in discussion. Doctor Luther had skilled himself in the
hope that the emperor would summon a troop of scholarly persons, doctors, licentiates, and masters to instruct and refute him. At least this is
what Luther wrote a little later to the artist, Lucas Cranach. It was an extremely naive expectation provoked by the lofty fantasy of intellectual self-
assertion that was associated with profound ideas but knew princes only
from afar.

Luther worked the entire Thursday morning on the draft of his speech.
Even if he should not be permitted to read it, nevertheless he would have
it prepared in a written form. The day before, his entire preparation had
consisted in having a new tonsure cut.

On Thursday, April 18, after 4.00 P.M., the imperial herald called for him
again. They took the same route that they had taken on the previous day,
and once again Luther was obliged to wait for two hours. It was growing
dark. Torches were being lighted as Luther finally was summoned into the
great hall of the palace. The hall was packed with people; even some
princes were forced to stand.

Once again the Trier official, von der Ecken, opened the proceedings
with a short introduction in both Latin and German. The time for reflection requested by Luther had now expired and the imperial spokesman
wanted to know whether or not Luther would revoke his books or any
parts of them. Luther answered, first in German, then in Latin. As an introduction, he requested, as custom dictated, to be excused if he out of ignorance should fail to give to each high lord the proper title or if his manner
should be in any other way blameworthy. He was only a monk and not accustomed to or worthy of such company. Then he came to the point. His
books were divided into three categories. First, he had written works of ed-
ification in which even his enemies had taken no offense. Second, he had
written works against the papacy and the papists who were destroying
Christianity with their pernicious teachings. If he should revoke these
books, he would then himself become an instrument of this tyranny. Third,
he had written against individuals. He admitted that often he had been
more aggressive than is fitting for one in his calling. But he, after all, was
no saint. Futhermore, he was not fighting his cause but the cause of Christ.
Therefore, it was not within his power to revoke these writings. By prophetic and evangelical Scriptures he requested to be shown his errors; if he
thereby should be proven wrong, he would be the first to consign his
books to the flames.

That was clearly no revocation but a call for disputation. Should and
could the emperor and empire permit themselves to be drawn into a de-

bate with a monk? On the other hand, Luther had declared himself willing to accept instruction. Could his offer be rejected, and must not the rejection of such an offer provide additional fuel for the unrest among the populace? And again, was it not indeed because of this unrest advisable to strike a hard course and to demand now without further discussion a clear yes or no answer?

A brief conference among the princes ensued. They decided to demand a clear yes or no. Thereupon the Trier official, von der Ecken, in sharp reprimand, declared that Luther had not answered the question. It was not appropriate to discuss here matters that had long since been decided by the councils, von der Ecken contested. "Do not expect a discussion concerning articles of faith that you are unconditionally required to believe. Answer uprightly and honestly, unambigously and without reservation, whether or not you will revoke your books and the errors that they contain."

Luther answered:

Because then Your Imperial Majesty, Electoral and Princely Graces, desire a plain, simple, and truthful answer, I will give it, an answer without horns or teeth, namely this: unless I am persuaded and convinced with testimonies from Holy Scriptures or with obvious, clear, and irrefutable reasons and arguments—because I believe neither the pope nor councils alone, for it is clear that they have often erred and contradicted themselves—I am bound by the Scriptures that I have quoted; my conscience is bound by the Word of God, so that I cannot and I will not revoke because it is neither safe nor sound to act against conscience. I can do nought else; here I stand, God help me, amen. (WA VII 838)

In this Latin form and with its German conclusion the speech was published in Wittenberg at the beginning of May 1521. The protocol of the imperial diet offers the shorter form, concluding with only the "Gold help me, amen." This was the customary manner in which Luther concluded his sermons, and it is probably the more accurate form. The longer conclusion, with its "I can do nought else; here I stand ... ," expresses the mood of the situation so forcefully that, although its authenticity cannot be conclusively confirmed, it has become a familiar quotation permanently linked to "Luther in Worms." It is quite possible that, the imperial protocol notwithstanding, the longer form is the original one or was added later by Luther himself, because the Wittenberg edition which includes it contains several passages in first person singular with Luther as narrator. This point of view suggests that the reporter had worked into his report original scripts from Luther's own hand. At any rate this Wittenberg account is the oldest printed form in which the events at Worms were made available to the public.

After this speech by Luther there was a short exchange with von der Ecken, who zealously insisted that councils had never erred. In reply, Luther offered to demonstrate wherein they had erred, but the emperor made a sign to dismiss. The meeting ended. *Al fuego* (into the fire) was heard in threatening Spanish tones as Luther left the hall. "I came through, I came through," Luther exulted as, throwing his arms high over his head in the gesture of the German foot soldier who has survived battle, he reentered the Johanniter Inn.

On the next day Charles V had his handwritten charge against Luther read. The emperor was determined "to hold fast to everything that had occurred since the Council of Constance. Because it is certain that a single brother errs when he opposes his opinion to the opinion of all of Christendom, since it would also mean that Christendom for a thousand years or more must have erred ... I will not hear him again. He has his safe conduct, but from now on I will consider him a notorious heretic ..." (Wrede II 596).

That was the argument of hereditary power. Oriented toward peace and order, toward conserving the status quo, it raised its one indestructable argument that a single brother in opposition to a thousand years of Christendom must be in error. Error and truth were measured by tradition and custom, by agreement or disagreement with prescribed traditional norms, exactly at a time when a social movement, always expanding and assuming many-sided political aspects, shook the foundation of the established order and permitted itself to be less impressed with nothing than with an appeal to venerable, old, long-approved opinions.

The imperial estates were pleased neither with Luther's "no" nor with the emperor's charge. They were interested in putting the matter amicably to rest but in such a manner that they themselves would appear as arbitors, decision-makers, and authorities in affairs of faith and Church. They wanted Luther to revoke even if only partially, for in that case the reasons for excommunication would have been blunted and possibly the papacy would have seen the necessity of permitting moderation and rescinding the ban entirely, as had been done in the case of Henry IV after his penance at Canossa. That the estates were prepared to continue their front against the papacy they had already revealed in February, as they had done in a similar manner at earlier imperial diets, by bringing up the *Gravamina of the German Nation* against the Holy See. Duke George of Bearded from Albertine Saxony, who since the Leipzig disputation had been a decided opponent of Luther, not only supported the *Gravamina* but even anticipated the other estates in this matter in that he himself drew up a biting *Gravamina*. The attitude of Duke George was a clear sign that the imperial estates did not wish to appease the papal party. Despite the emperor's charge, the estates insisted on further negotiations and hearings so that they might be in a position to persuade Luther to revoke. For the pope's representatives it was very important to achieve the opposite, to conclude the grievous Luther affair now as quietly as possible and in conformity with the imperial charge, because every additional negotiation over this repugnant affair would only damage the already damaged curial prestige.

Thus electoral Saxony, electoral Brandenburg, and the Palatinate intervened with the emperor, who reluctantly granted the estates an extension of three days, within which period they were to persuade the heretic to revoke. The estates also insisted that the ban against Luther, in case it should become unavoidable, should first be published and prosecuted only after he had once again reached sanctuary. A committee made up of all the estates should now take up the Luther affair.

On Wednesday, April 24, 1521, Luther was required to appear at the lodging of the archbishop of Trier. There awaited him the elector of Trier, the elector of Brandenburg, Duke George of Albertine Saxony, the bishop of Augsburg, the bishop of Brandenburg, the German master of the Teutonic order (who administered the property of this order within the empire), Count George of Wertheim, Doctor Bock of Strasbourg and Doctor Peutinger of Augsburg as representatives of the imperial cities, and Doctor Vehus, the chancellor of the margrave of Baden, whom the committee named as spokesman.

The committee did not desire to dispute with Luther, the chancellor of Baden informed him, but rather to graciously admonish and fraternally remind him: he should consider the unity of the Church and not despise the power and authority of councils, even through they could err, for they are, after all, made up only of men. The councils certainly had not contradicted one another; they had not taught anything contrary to law, but had merely formulated interpretations in various ways in consideration of time, person, and place. And if these entreaties could not move him, he should permit his conscience to be moved and not stubbornly insist on his own opinion against the opinion of so many learned people. Luther was obligated by fraternal love to soften his opinions and interpretations, and he should indeed consider the great danger that he could cause.

The chancellor employed every technique of persuasion. He spoke as he would to a headstrong child and included threat and enticement along with friendly admonition; if Luther would not recant, the emperor would continue to proceed against him. Luther had written many worthwhile things: concerning Christian liberty, for instance, and concerning good works and other matters. However, he was putting at risk all his worthwhile writings to be condemned along with his other writings. Nevertheless, if Luther would act responsibly, His Imperial Majesty would preserve the worthwhile writings.

But the chancellor's effort was to no avail. Luther softened neither his opinions nor his interpretations. The arguments presented to him by the committee's spokesman were long familiar to him. Such arguments did not weaken his conviction. On the contrary, they demonstrated to him the strength of his own intellectual position because the arguments from the very start avoided an intellectual discussion and merely made opportunism the reason for agreement, whereas Luther was concerned with truth. Concerning the councils, it did not disturb him that they had arrived at various formulations; what disturbed him was that they had taught doctrine that contradicted the Holy Scriptures. Luther insisted that he had not presented his own arbitrary convictions in his books, for his articles did not originate with him. They came from God and the Holy Scriptures; therefore, he could not disown them. Concerning the offense that he might cause, there were two types of offense: that of love and that of faith. The offense of love one could with good will remove at any time, but not the offense attributed to faith, because faith was anchored in teaching and in the Word of God, and that offense was present unceasingly from the creation to the consummation of the world. Into this offense "the Word of God thrusts great scholars and saints."

The committee requested Luther to withdraw while it deliberated. Once again Luther was summoned into the room; again with great admonition the committee sought in vain to persuade him. He remained confirmed in his convictions. Because the electors and the princely graces would not engage in a disputation with him, he also would not dispute with them. Moreover, he would not permit it to be said later that he did not submit his writings to the judgment of His Imperial Majesty, the electors, and the estates. On the contrary, Luther submitted his writings to the judgment of everyone—with the one proviso that they be judged in conformity with Holy Scriptures.

The margrave of Brandenberg confirmed once again his understanding of Luther's response: "Herr Doctor, as well as I can tell, you have said that you will not change your opinion unless you are persuaded by Holy Scriptures." Luther responded: "Yes, gracious Lord, or by clear reason."

At this the committee adjourned. Only the archbishop of Trier tried once more to influence Luther's opinion. With the archbishop was his official, Johann von der Ecken, whom Luther had already met on the occasion of his two appearances before the emperor. In addition, Doctor Cochläus, Dean of the Chapter House of Our Lady in Frankfurt-am-Main, attended the archbishop. Jerome Schurff and Nicholaus von Amsdorf attended Luther. Von der Ecken, on behalf of the archbishop, sought to persuade Luther to drop his appeal to the Scriptures. It was meaningless to appeal to Scriptures because of the various interpretations and meanings ascribed to them: heresy had always been the result of such an appeal. Without the interpretation of the Holy Father and the councils, it was ridiculous to appeal to Scriptures.

But such an attempt to convince Luther was bound to fail miserably.

Now no one yielded to another. Everyone talked at the same time. The meeting broke up on a note of ill will.

In the afternoon Cochläus went to Luther's lodging. Cochläus wanted to continue the dispute, but alone with Luther. To no avail Cochläus drew Luther aside for private conversation. The estates, despite the evidence, did not want to acknowledge the impasse. Once more they persuaded the emperor to extend the period of Luther's safe conduct for two more days, an extension that was announced on Wednesday evening.

On Thursday, April 25, 1521, the Augsburg city herald, Doctor Konrad Peutinger, and the chancellor from Baden, Doctor Vehus, appeared in the Johanniter Inn. They negotiated through the morning and the afternoon with Luther and believed that they finally had achieved success when Luther declared himself ready to permit selected articles from his writings to be judged by a council. But the joy was short-lived because Luther could not be moved to renounce his addendum to the agreement that the council must be bound by Holy Scriptures and must correct him by arguments based on the Scriptures. Luther would rather die than to profane the Word of God. He remained steadfast in this response as the archbishop of Trier made on final attempt to persuade him: How then did Luther suggest solving this problem? Advice other than that given by Gamaliel, Luther responded, he could not suggest: "For if this counsel or this work be of man, it will come to nought. But if it be of God, ye cannot overthrow it, lest haply yl be found to fight against God" (Acts 5: 38-39).

The imperial estates wanted to treat faith and teaching like any other public affair in which they claimed competence and authority. For example, they wanted to treat religious questions no differently from money matters, taxes, juridical concerns, the militia, and economic laws. In a way the estates were justified in their opinion because, on the one hand, the disputes concerning religious belief disturbed public order, the preservation of which was the responsibility of the estates, and on the other hand, treating ecclesiastical affairs like any other matter would afford the estates the possibility of emphasizing their own *Gravamina* against Rome and of promoting sovereignty for the German nation in church questions. With respect to their political ambitions, the estates were consistently pursuing the right course when they rejected Luther's demand that he should be corrected by the Scriptures, because to recognize God's word as the only criterium for the validity of a doctrine meant nothing other than to surrender the power of decision and to engage in endless discussion—in fact, to cancel the whole history of dogma and to begin again.

Although the imperial estates were inclined to grant Luther concessions and to make matters easier for his conscience by permitting a partial revocation, and as far as possible, helping him save face in any conceivable compromise, it was precisely because of such a posture on their part that they found it necessary to insist that Luther recognize their rightful authority to decide without any ifs, ands, and buts. The rationale of the imperial estates was sound and politically advantageous. Luther frustrated their goals. He would not be bound to any plans. The estates were trying to use him as a pawn. Their plan succeeded only insofar as the estates, for a certain period, could indeed employ Luther's name to place pressure on the emperor. But Luther would not play the game according to the rules set by the estates. Luther would not play at all. On the contrary, he risked his life for his belief.

And Luther's belief was such that no political logic or any other logic for that matter could bind it. In the Heidelberg disputation in April 1518, Luther himself had introduced the statement that faith had no logic; in other words, faith could not be rationally demonstrated. Faith did not pertain to those things that could be proven or disproven, or to those matters concerning which votes and decisions pertained. The lips could be forced to form the word, the ear to hear, the knee to bow; liturgical conformity could be mandated; but what to Luther's understanding truly constituted faith—trust in Christ and in God the Father—could not be imposed.

Shaking their heads in bewilderment at the impasse and angered at such stubbornness, the estates were forced to face the fact that their attempts at negotiating a compromise had failed. Once again Luther received twenty-one days of safe conduct, and he left Worms on April 26 in the morning between nine and ten o'clock.

Once again, as on the trip to Worms, the imperial herald Sturm accompanied him. However, Luther was obliged promptly to find an excuse to free himself from Sturm's company. Even before Luther's departure from Worms, he was informed by the electoral advisors Philipp von Feilitzsch and Frederick von Thun that he must now retreat for a while from the public eye. The elector had ordered that Luther be conducted to a secure sanctuary. "I deferred to his judgment," Luther wrote to Lucas Cranach on the return trip. Thus he dismissed the imperial herald near Friedberg, sent him to back to Worms, and gave him two letters—one to the emperor, one to he imperial estates—in which he once again explained and justified his deportment.

On May 3 Luther left the Saxon carriage. His traveling companions Suaven and Schurff he sent ahead on the most direct route to Wittenberg, and kept only Amsdorf and Petzensteiner with him. Luther let it be known that he wanted to pay a visit to his relatives in Möhra, and spent a night and half a day with his Uncle Heinz in the Luther family house in Möhra. On the renewed trip, late in the afternoon of May 4, the little travel band was apprehended between the castles Altenstein and Liebenstein by the knight Hund von Wenckheim and his squire. Luther was placed on a horse, and his travel companions were permitted to continue their journey.

Late at night, Hund von Wenckheim arrived with his prisoner at the Wartburg. Martin Luther had reached sanctuary.

The news of Luther's disappearance resulted in enormous public excitement. One contradictory rumor followed the other. The papists were deemed well capable of murder. In Worms it was reported that Luther had been stabbed with a dagger and that his body had been discovered in a silver mine. Aleander once again feared for his own life. The artist Albrecht Dürer, who just at the time was on a trip through the Netherlands, noted in his travel diary when the news concerning Luther's disappearance reached him,

> O God, if Luther is dead, who now will explain to us the holy gospel? O God, what could he not have written for us in the next ten or twenty years? O all you pious Christians, join me in bewailing the loss of this God-inspired man and in petitioning God that He send us another enlightened man. O Erasmus of Rotterdam, where are you? ... Hearken, you knight of Christ, ride forth alongside of Christ, rescue truth, gain a martyr's crown. You are already an old man anyway. I have heard that you have given yourself two years of productive activity. Well, spend that time in the gospel and for the good of true Christian faith and be assured that the gates of hell, the Roman See, als Christ says, cannot prevail against you. (Ullmann 94)

After all means of negotiation were exhausted and all attempts had failed, the imperial condemnation of Luther could no longer be avoided; it could only be postponed for a short period until the first storm of resentment aroused by his disappearance would subside and none of the rumors concerning his death would be verified. On May 26, the day after the official adjournment of the imperial diet, Carles V issued against Luther an edict predated to May 8, and had it confirmed by the imperial estates still present in Worms. The Edict of Worms imposed the imperial ban on Luther. No one was permitted to feed, house, host, or provide drink for him. His writings were forbidden, their distribution punishable. It also was forbidden to distribute his picture or to disseminate his opinions or doctrine. All writing was to be subject to strict censorship. Everyone was enjoined to arrest Luther and his supporters or to reveal their place of refuge. Whoever attacked Luther or his supporters should have the right to their property. Luther was declared *Vogelfrei*:

> wild game, unprotected; to kill him was the obligation of those loyal to the emperor. For the rest of his life Luther remained under the imperial ban.

The diet of Worms demonstrated a certain watershed in the course of the early bourgeois revolution. Since the posting of the theses in 1517, increasingly wider circles were drawn step by step into the discussion concerning Luther's ecclesiastical case history. Luther himself had promoted for some years the process of the merging of his own affair with social problems in that from the beginning, but especially since 1520, he linked theological pronouncements to social, political, and economic questions, thus appealing to ever-increasing ranks, classes, and other groups. The logic of his newly discovered and firmly adhered-to fundamental ideas, along with the opposition of opponents and support from various quarters, propelled Luther into the center of events, a position which he at first had not at all sought but which demanded of him the greatest measure of personal involvement. Various groups, which to be sure did not in every case share his theological opinion or who in some cases misunderstood it, proclaimed Luther a hero and in the general unrest and critical mood welcomed his struggle against the papacy.

Thus after 1517 Luther was hailed by a wide variety of opposing forces that had only one thing in common: they all criticized the existing order and considered it in need of reform. They all took the greatest offense at the papacy, but otherwise these discontented forces were quite disparate in their goals, interests, and choice of means. The broad movement to defend Luther against the papacy included representatives of the university intellegentsia; members of the urban bourgeoisie, including patrician circles; a socially heterogeneous, humanistic circle; and some nobles. This movement was also supported generously by a number of princes.

At Worms a decisive situation had arisen for all these groups as well as for Luther. All efforts at compromise had failed: Luther refused to revoke. The imperial proscription had been implemented. No doubt could exist concerning the authenticity and legality of the Edict of Worms, but that did not all mean that the edict would be obeyed. The execution of the edict depended on how well the imperial estates in their several sovereignties were willing to enforce it. Decisive was the fact that the reform movement from then on had to count the emperor as an enemy, and that every confirmation of reformation was exposed to greater risk. Futhermore, the fact was established that Luther, as monk and theologian, had not merely launched a movement and was now borne along by it, but that from now on he would be obliged to make more decisions concerning this movement, be they theological or purely political: there remained little distinction between the two. Luther's theology fell into inner and outer tensions.

For the continued development of the early bourgeois revolution, this phase was most significant in that it linked the Lutheran doctrine of justification by faith alone and the doctrine of the priesthood of all believers with political and social interpretations and interests of a reform ideology. The future fate was dependent on the speed and intensity with which representatives of the various classes and ranks would join in the movement and the enthusiasm with which they would participate, as well as on the goals set for the revolution and the methods chosen to achieve them.

W hen the Edict of Worms appeared, Luther already had his first period of residence at the Wartburg behind him. The transition had not been easy. After the excessive work of the last months, the rigors of the trip to Worms, and the seething masses in the city, now he was surrounded by silence and solitude. Luther was not permitted to identify himself to the other people living at the Wartburg; only the warden of the castle, Hans von Berlepsch, knew Luther's identity. Luther exchanged his cowl for a knight's tunic, concealed his tonsure with a beret, grew a full beard, and slung a sword at his side to complete the transformation. Martin the monk had become Squire George. Instead of the frugal monastic fare to which he had been accustomed for sixteen years, now on the table before him steamed the knights' hearty meals, with large cuts of wild game and domesticated animals, treats which formerly for Luther had been available only at special academic banquets. Hans von Berlepsch did not forego the opportunity to host his guest at table, and Luther was obliged to sit through many a boring hour.

The transition into this new life was not without consequences. Stomach and bowel, which earlier had given him so much trouble on the way to Worms, could not quickly adjust to the new life. Constipation became so severe and unbearable that Luther several times was on the verge, despite all security risks, of traveling to Erfurt to seek medical help. At the beginning of July, for an entire week, he was unable to do anything. Pills sent by Spalatin finally brought him some relief, but his discomfort returned several times. Thus right in the middle of a letter to Amsdorf, Luther interrupted his Latin sentences with a German exclamation expressing his frustration: "My arse is really sore." Pills for the nagging ills of the body, Bible, ink, paper, and pen were Luther's means of consoling the solitary spirit, of compensating for the isolation from friends, and of soothing the rupture with his pressing daily battles.

In his luggage Luther had brought to the Wartburg a copy of Latin Vulgate. This text helped him through the first depressing days. Spiritually oriented to the current of the church calendar as it calls attention to biblical events, Luther selected the texts for the feasts of Easter, Ascension, and

Pentecost, and wrote an esegesis on the sixty-seventh psalm. Thus only three weeks after his arrival at the Wartburg, he sent to Melanchthon a manuscript of over thirty pages, requesting its publication. In the meantime, the long-desired books and parts of his manuscripts completed before his trip to Worms had arrived. Once again Luther was in his element, and he took up the thread of his tought where he had been forced to break it off at the beginning of April: with the homilies and with his explanation of the Magnificat.

But before this, and from time to time in the midst of his work, he relieved himself of the unattractive task of dispensing with an opponent of awkward style. The thirteenth thesis for the Leipzig disputation, Luther's major blow against papal primacy, still pricked pro-Roman enthusiasts to test their pens and prove their church loyalty by attacking him. This time it was one of the Louvain theologians, Jacob Latomus, who presented himself for battle. Even before his Worms journey, Luther had heard of Latomus' writings; in the last days of May, he had received them at the Wartburg. The terrible style annoyed Luther. Such opponents Luther preferred to have others rebuke, but this matter was of such weight that Luther himself took up the pen. By the beginning of July, Luther's reply was in Wittenberg and could go immediately to the printer. In this work Luther once again summarized his doctrine on justification and his argument against papal primacy.

Latomus had cost Luther some time. The theme was, to be sure, explosive and remained so throughout the Reformation, but for Luther it belonged to a previous stage of development in which he had arrived at his conclusions concerning the subject. More pressing now was the fight against the Edict of Worms, which extended and aggravated conditions created by the bull of excommunication. As a result of the promulgation of the imperial ban in conjunction with the ecclesiastical ban, believers in city and country were placed under even stronger pressure of conscience by the clergy. Pressure on the conscience exercised in the confessional became the most important means of combat for the clergy still loyal to the pope, because the Edict of Worms had failed in a political sense to achieve its goal. The reason for the failure was that the emperor and empire had no executive authority over the imperial estates. Decisions, laws, edicts, promulgations, and dispositions of the emperor and the imperial diet were, to be sure, binding and legal, but their execution lay in the hands of the imperial estates. Whether or not and to what extent the edicts were implemented was completely dependent on the will and opinion of the estates: in the princely territories, on the sovereigns; in the imperial cities, on the civic councils. Although the Edict of Worms created a threatening legal predicament for Luther and his followers, in no case was it decisive for the fate of the Reformation in the sense that the Reformation could have been suppressed by simple police power. What had been decided was only that from now on the Reformation must reckon with the opposition of the emperor. Everything else remained tentative and would finally depend on the degree to which the Reformation could be effective in the realm of the imperial estates with or in opposition to the territorial princes and urban councils. The success of the Reformation would be brought about only by an intellectual struggle to gain the assent of each individual, above all the assent of those who possessed decision-making authority, social prestige, economic, financial, or intellectual influence, so that these individuals would attract and lead others, and determine or at least render favorable their attitude toward the Reformation.

In this struggle for each individual, the confessional played a major role. From the pulpit and through the priestly office, the clergy impressed and influenced believers en masse. The priest achieved a great deal through the performance of his office; therein lay the strength of communication in the worship service. However, the individual could submerge himself in the congregation and abandon his personal responsibility to that impersonal body because it was a congregation, possessing specific social attributes, rather than an undefined mass. But in the confessional the priest had each individual before him, without any possibility of the individual's escape into the irresponsible "it." Here the Church played its strongest card, the power of the keys over the conscience. "Whosoever sins ye remit, they are remitted unto them; and whosoever sins ye retain, they are retained" (John 20:23). Here the Church continuously renewed the ethical guarantees for the traditional and cultivated loyalty of believers to the hierarchical authorities. The Church supported itself in the name of tradition and, by appealing to the noblest values in man, entrenched this tradition, simultaneously instilling fear and promising consolation. Without doubt, the secret of the confessional was not always kept.

If the struggle for the individual was to be won for the Reformation, then this instrument of the confessional must be struck from the hand of the ecclesiastical hierarchy. As early as 1517, in the indulgence theses, Luther had placed the confessional under scrutiny. His theology, not least significantly his doctrine on original sin, was wholly committed to releasing the conscience of the individual from the pressure of mandatory confession. For, in fact, if man had inherited his sinful nature and could not completely be liberated from it by either baptism or penance; if he remained a sinner even after having been declared righteous and had to continue to do life-long penance, what was the purpose of repeatedly plaguing the conscience concerning the presence or absence of known or unknown sins? Theologically the course had been set much earlier for Luther to challenge the tyranny of the confessional. However, the use of the confessional to defeat the Reformation now provided an impetus to the challenge that could no longer be postponed. As early as February 1521, in conformity with the need of the hour, Luther has addressed this question and had instructed penitents as to how they were to deport themselves when the confessor pressured them. Now Luther went a step further, not only by giving advice as to how confessional pressure should be thwarted but also by rejecting without qualification every confessional pressure.

To be sure, Luther did not reject auricular confession. He regarded it as good and useful, and he had experienced its salutory effects. But he regarded penance from the view of Christian freedom. The confessional must be employed in freedom, without duress. When you have need, then confess, but do not permit anyone to coerce you into the confessional. Confessions may be heard not only by a smooth-tongued, ordained priest with a bald pate and a long frock; every Christian can hear your confession and grant you remission of sin. Luther entitled his pamphlet *Concerning Confession. Whether or Not the Papal Authority Can Demand It,* and he dedicated it to the gracious and honorable knight, Francis von Sickingen, his special lord and patron, als Luther addressed him. But with this pamphlet the theme was not exhausted nor was the problem solved. Luke 17:11-19 records that Jesus said to the ten lepers who pleaded with Him for help that they should show themselves to the priests as the law of Moses commanded. Defenders of the necessity of auricular confession had held this passage before Duke John as evidence for the fact that the necessity of the confessional was commanded in the Bible. The duke wanted clarity in this matter and had question transmitted to Luther through Hans von Berlepsch. It was an important matter because the question provided an opportunity to convince the future elector, the younger brother of Frederick the Wise, of the validity of Luther's views, to strengthen the influence of the Lutheran party at the electoral court, and to win the ear of the duke from the insinuations of the Romanists.

Luther would have taken up the story of the ten lepers in the homilies even without the request from Weimar, because this story was listed in the text for the sermon on the fourteenth Sunday after Trinity. Thus Luther anticipated the liturgical order of the texts to be promulgated in the homilies by publishing the *Gospel of the Ten Lepers* in advance as an independent pamphlet, thereby drawing off from the postille "(from the middle of the keg as it were) a draft for his dear Germans."

Not the least remarkable characteristic of this work is the transformation of an argument given by Luther's opponents into its opposite. One of the widespread and mischievous arguments of his opponents was that Lutherans agitated against obligatory confession because they themselves did not like to go to confession. The argument was meant to incriminate the Lutherans and to present them as weaklings who had no courage to confess their failings. Far from permitting such an argument to impress him and cause him to search for excuses, Luther, on the contrary, snapped back that it indeed was difficult to confess. Through Luther's wily reply, the doctrine of original sin, which at first glance seemed so dismal and alien, appeared as a theological concept spiced with peasant cunning. Yes, indeed,

> we confess our sin, we are poor sinners who do not like to confess. And it is no wonder, because without God's grace it is not possible that the natural man should like to confess, and thus it is true that we are the enemies of confession not only by the sincere reason of divine law but also from the standpoint of natural frailty. This causes us no special disgrace, because it is a common weakness in all the world. (WA VIII 342)

Luther explained that even the tyrants of the confessional and great saints, who are not like us poor sinners, nevertheless also confess most reluctantly. If we turned the wheel in the opposite direction and we did not have to confess to them but they to us, we should soon see how poorly they would speak of the dear confessional. The fact that they so loved to hear confessions was due to the holy confession fee that filled their bellies and to the stories that titillated their curiosity; it was at the expense of the poor simpletons who had entrusted their secrets to them that the confessors amused themselves at dinner. With the mention of the confession penny which the penitents were obliged to pay, attention was called to that which at least in part motivated the struggle against obligatory confession. This struggle was concerned primarily, though not exclusively, with removing from the hand of the Church this means of communicating, gathering information, and wielding influence; at the same time, it was also somewhat concerned with keeping the penitent's pockets closed and accustoming the masses not to pay for every pastoral service. How the individual was armed against obligatory confession is evident. The doctrine of original sin eased psychological apprehension. It said "yes" to human nature and liberated it from the vain efforts to be more than what it was at birth. "Be a sinner and sin boldly, but believe and rejoice even more boldly in Christ who is the victor over sin, death, and the world," Luther could therefore write on August 1, 1521, from the Wartburg to Melanchthon (WA BR II 372).

Luther dedicated the *Gospel of the Ten Lepers* to Haugold von Einsiedeln. Spalatin added to the dedication the names of Hans von Dolzig and Bernhard von Hirschfeld in order to identify and strengthen those advisors from the Saxon nobility who were in that circle around the elector and his brother and who, because of their opinions, could be considered Lutheran. Luther and Spalatin persistently pursued every line of enlisting, influencing, and gaining benefactors, supporters, and influential advocates in the ranks of those who in the preceding years had been won to the cause. Luther and Spalatin's efforts were expressed in their "politics of dedication."

Spalatin, whom we have already met several times as the mediator between Luther and the elector, held a very influential position. His duties included informing the elector concerning all matters pertaining to the university as well as formulating university recommendations, documents, and regulations. It was primarily Spalatin's responsibility to suggest to the elector various policies that the university might implement and to recommend the most appropriate and plausible. Spalatin was thus a key figure in the complicated network of connections between Luther, university, reformers and their followers, and the elector. Spalatin also was the most influential agent in shaping the political opinions in the prince's circle.

The question which primarily oppressed Luther in his first weeks of solitude at the Wartburg was how the reform movement would proceed in Wittenberg without him. Would his Wittenberg friends become timid and fainthearted? Would they fear the dangers which the Edict of Worms unmistakably conjured up? Luther desired to encourage them and to strengthen their self-confidence, and it was imperative that he do so. He therefore wrote an exposition of the thirty-sixth psalm and presented his interpretation in the form of a letter of consolation for his Wittenberg friends (WA VIII 210-40). The major thought with which he sought to encourage his Wittenberg friends and strengthen his own self-confidence was that, though they be branded heretics, the papists would never be able to make them heretics, for he and his friends were supported by the Holy Scriptures.

Luther's fears concerning Wittenberg proved to be unfounded. Surprising and happy news soon reached him which demonstrated that the Wittenbergers had no intention of becoming dispirited; on the contrary, they gave themselves to implementing what had up to that point been developed in their doctrine, writings, disputations, and sermons. Furthermore, implementation was occurring not only in Wittenberg, and this naturally interested Luther above all. Amidst this joy, however, there were two elements of sadness. First, it was now Karlstadt who set the tone for much that transpired in Wittenberg. This filled Luther with anxiety because, soon after the Leipzig disputation, Luther had sensed in Karlstadt—his fellow disputant who was not very fortunate in opposing Eck at Leipzig—a strain of theological thought which, in its zeal for the law, alerted Luther to caution, for this penchant did not reconcile well with Luther's idea of Christian liberty. Second, Luther was sad that he was unable to be present and that there were circumstances under which he was no longer needed. On second thought, did the Wittenbergers any longer need him at all? Sporadically and suggestively the idea recurred in his correspondence that after his Wartburg exile, which would not last forever, he would not return to Wittenberg and would perhaps seek out a new center for his activities; he especially thought of Erfurt. But then he erased that idea. Luther knew that Melanchthon, in whom he had ever-increasing confidence, was in Wittenberg. *Loci Communes* (Common Places), Melanchthon's newly published work, convinced Luther that his teaching was in good hands. Logically arranged and systematically structured, this dogmatic, doctrinal edifice, which Melanchthon had based on Luther's fundamental ideas, was for students a theological compendium than which no better could be imagined. Luther's ideas, which had blazed a trail by means of his lectures, intensive research, and confrontations, were in the *Loci Communes* structured by steps so that the subject matter was easy to learn and retain.

Luther himself did not need such a written systematic arrangement. He possessed just such an outline within himself, and it consistently provided him, from situation, with correct ideas and useful arguments. Luther could not have written such a *Loci Communes*. His problem-oriented thought centered more on paradoxes of the experiences of faith than in the channels of the dialectic of concepts, although the latter path was not strange to Luther; occasionally, when a worthy opponent presented himself, Luther gladly permitted himself the pleasure—but not without hairsplitting—of a duel about concepts.

Luther received from Karlstadt's writings and, at the beginning of August, from Melanchthon's correspondence, the first signs that the Wittenbergers not only held to the cause but also were willing to press on. The writings of Melanchthon and Karlstadt were concerned with celibacy, vows, and the communion *sub utraque*—the administration of the communion in both kinds. These were problems that Luther earlier in several writings had only touched on but in other writings had treated more comprehensively. The question concerning celibacy, or the right of the clergy to marry, came to a head in the spring of 1521, when some priests actually married and were subjected to reprisals as a result. For example, a priest from the territory of George the Bearded was penalized, as was also a priest under the spiritual authority of Albrecht of Mainz. In a petition, the University of Wittenberg interceded for the victims, and Karlstadt composed a writing in defense of clerical marriage. But Luther, who just one year earlier in his work to the German nobles had demanded the abolition of celibacy as a requirement, nevertheless found Karlstadt's opinion unsatisfactory because it was not sufficiently grounded in Scripture. After it became a serious consideration, the question also became amusing to Luther because the idea was publicly circulated not only that priests in general should be permitted to marry but also that Luther in particular might be expected to take a wife. Luther, who was now approaching his thirty-eighth year, by his entire mode of life, especially by monastic discipline, had unconsciously become a confirmed bachelor. "In any case, they will not hang a wife on me," Luther exclaimed in one of his letters.

With the discussion concerning communion in both kinds, a similar development transpired. Regarding this question also, though he must have agreed in principle with Karlstadt from the very beginning, Luther ultimately was displeased by Karlstadt's arguments. Naturally Luther had no argument against the proposal for communion in both kinds, but he did object to Karlstadt's opinion that the reception of the Eucharist in only one form, that of the bread *(sub una)*, is sin. With this idea Luther could not at all agree, and a significant rupture in their views promptly became apparent. This difference determined the discussion for the following years, and the longer the debate prevailed the more it widened the gap within the Reformation movement. The Eucharist, as with all other matters, Luther insisted, should be received in Christian liberty. The essential is faith. The forms under which the Eucharist are administered are of no importance. He insisted: Do not transform into a new law of bondage what has been freely granted to us! The matters concerning the vows Luther considered so important and pressing that he wished to discuss this question personally with Melanchthon. Luther believed that the question could not be adequately explored by correspondence alone.

Luther's insistence on these particulars is noteworthy and somewhat surprising. Should he not have learned with unequivocal enthusiasm that the Wittenbergers were continuing his work, and, as they thought, were also consolidating it; and was his hesitation only that of one who is absent and, therefore, seeks from a distance to direct, or play a role in determining his position with regard to other more serious questions of principle? The latter is the case. The position which for Luther at this period, under the conditions of confinement at the Wartburg, was most important and which made him sensitive to the slightest nuance of variation was his posture with respect to Christian liberty. This posture determined to a great extent his view of the ways in which the Reformation could progress from doctrine and idea to action and reality.

Certainly one must negotiate; Luther was convinced of that. But negotiations, which had occupied him from the very beginning and in which he was a master, were the written and spoken word and thought. Luther displayed the hesitancy of the intellectual to act before the concept on which the deed is based is fully expressed in words. There might also have been a hesitancy to set upon a less meaningful course of action. Luther had not attacked the fraudulent life of the papists, but he had assaulted their false teaching, as he had explained during the preceding years more than once to clarify his own objective and to allay the rising misunderstanding. Here something of that tension is revealed into which his theology was drawn: the more an ever-growing movement absorbed his theology the more Luther was thereby thrust into public view.

It was not without inner conflict that Luther adapted himself to the transfer of the Reformation from the realm of the spirit and of teaching into the area of specific, visible transformations. He committed himself to the change and mastered the situation by his pen. Luther was obliged to describe in writing his view of what was at stake in the debate. Thus he needed no longer merely to say "yes" to what others said; on the contrary, he could himself teach others. How could he participate in the events taking place in Wittenberg other than by answering and solving the questions and problems that arose there, as he was accustomed to do from the Bible and from his theological insights?

He could and must respond; his commentary was all the more necessary since the problems that arose in Wittenberg became more and more concentrated around the Mass, the center of worship and the most important act pertaining to the duty of the priest. The Mass was the most significant of all sacraments and simultaneously the focus of ecclesiastical activity in faith, teaching, dogma, canon law, hierarchical status, mass communication, mysteries, revenues wealth, and material interests of clergy and laity.

Luther's disappearance after the diet of Worms and his failure to return to Wittenberg, had not at all dampened spirits there even though his absence led to anxious questions regarding his whereabouts. Apparently Luther's Wartburg exile released the energies of others who up to that time had stood in the shadows of the great name and had not achieved recognition. This was true of Luther's Augustinian brothers as well as of his university colleagues. From among the Augustinians, Gabriel Zwilling, born in the German colonized border area of Bohemia, became highly visible. Of frail build, without an especially strong voice but with impressive oratorical skill, he developed in sermons which lasted for hours mocking agitation against private Masses and appealed for the reception of the Eucharist in both kinds. It was rumored that a secret understanding existed between Zwilling and Luther, and that Zwilling preached at Luther's behest and suggestion. Zwilling had not only Augustinians for a congregation; students, faculty, and burghers also came to hear him.

Zwilling did not merely preach about the Mass; he actually changed it. He was able to gain agreement that at the Augustinian church no more private Masses would be celebrated; that is, Masses simply read by a priest with no congregation present and at which there could be no participation in the Eucharist apart from that of the officiating priest, who served himself the host and the wine. From now on among the Wittenberg Augustinians, only congregational Masses were to be celebrated and dispensing of the elements in both kinds was to be obligatory. On September 29, 1521, such a new Mass was for the first time celebrated, no longer merely for the monastic brothers in the monastic chapel of the Augustinians, but in the Wittenberg city church. Melanchthon was present with several of his students, and he received the Eucharist in both kinds.

There was great excitement. This was perceived as an unheard of event, and, indeed, it was. Here now, for the first time, ideas relating to the Eucharist were not only discussed, written about, philosophized on and theologically investigated, mentioned, disputed, proven, and contradicted, but actually acted upon. The greatest excitement was in the theological faculty because something had happened in the city church that pertained to that faculty's realm of competence, and it had occurred without previous consultation with this highly esteemed faculty. Under these conditions, the theological faculty naturally had to form a commission and interrogate the Augustinians. Inquiry was all the more urgent because the Augustinians, shortly after this occurrence, suspended Masses altogether. Since the Augustinian prior, Konrad Helt, had not wanted to assume responsibility for the fact that Mass was no longer read in the prescribed manner, he believed it necessary to accept the lesser of two evils by temporarily suspending Mass altogether, and he issued the necessary instructions to this end. The elector demanded reports; one commission session followed hard on the heels of the other. The accumulated material was sufficient for a series of theses for several disputations by doctoral and licentiate candidates.

The most unperturbed reaction came from the elector and his chancellor, Doctor Brück. As experienced politicians, they were confident that "kitchen and cellar" (food and drink) would bring the monks to reason. It was the Mass benefice that provided for kitchen and cellar. If the Masses were canceled, if the monks did not perform their duties, then kitchen and cellar would soon be empty. Such a prospect would dampen the reform ardor of the monks.

The elector and his chancellor misjudged the matter. Before kitchen and cellar were emptied, the monastery itself was abandoned. On November 12, 1521, thirteen monks left the Wittenberg Augustinian monastery: monks primarily from the Low Countries, as the prior apologetically reported, but no Saxons. This was the first mass exodus from a monastery during the Reformation period: a revolutionary deed, a break with a way of life hallowed by tradition and dogma.

The exodus from the monastery on the part of the Wittenberg Augustinians was of great significance in that it had a lasting effect on the dissemination of the new teaching as well as on the progress and radicalization of the Reformation. There always had been examples of discontened individual monks and nuns who for various motives and reasons had fled their cloisters. Annoyances of this kind could be repaired by capturing the malcontents or, in solitary cases, by absolving them from their vows by special dispensation. A stigma against the recalcitrants restrained the contagion which might have resulted from such examples of defection. But now the situation was fundamentally changed in that the cases multiplied, exodus became a common occurrence, and, above all else, the instances could not be explained solely on the basis of lack of will, unhappiness, lack of personal discipline, or insufficient pastoral skill on the part of the superiors; beyond these explanations, exodus was both a symptom of social crisis and at the same time an instrument for overcoming it. The exodus from the cloisters was a symptom of the crisis insofar as defection demonstrated that the fundamental social value system that had served as the foundation for monasticism had lost its cohesive force. The exodus was an instrument to overcome the crisis insofar as defection was a concrete step toward the transformation of the Church and therewith the purging of one of its most hotly disputed institutions. Sometimes directly influenced by Wittenberg, sometimes independently and even without knowledge of what had taken place in Wittenberg in the late autumn of 1521, monks and nuns in many other places soon began leaving their monasteries and convents.

The monks who left the monasteries were assuming no light burden. In the monastery they enjoyed the security of a regulated life with exact time divisions and assigned tasks that provided a rhythm and purpose to each day. The monastic meals were modest but regular. There was a firmly established hierarchy which protected the individual from insults and contained the inevitable taunts and dissensions of communal life within tolerable boundaries. Ascetic exercises increased the level of enjoyment and sensitized the temperament for the daily small pleasures. Prayer and worship repeatedly focused the life of the soul on the highest imaginable values, inspired meditation, and minimized egocentricity and petty ambition for office. Inhabitants of monasteries were not people who had nothing to lose. The Reformation not only liberated them; it also put them a disadvantage. It deprived them of the security of monastic walls and communal life and thrust them unprotected and unprepared into the secular world. Outside of the monastic walls, deprived of every security, they were forced to develop the highest measure of industry, activity, and ingenuity in order to survive. The world did not welcome them with open arms. They became a burden to relatives and friends. Not infrequently, they had been placed in a monastery or convent in their earliest years in order that they would be cared for and in order that kith and kin would have one less mouth to feed. Monks usually had not learned a trade, and even if they possessed some skills, it did not follow that a guild would have compassion on them and admit them to membership or permit them to practice a trade. They were well equipped for prayer and worship, and already there was a numerous "clerical proletariat" of vicars and priests who bent the knee for modest fees. They were hard put to sustain themselves and in need of everything except new collaegues.

The monks who abandoned their monastery were a challenge to society, especially because they were serious about the new teaching and because now they were heeding the word of all those who had been joking about the monasteries and ridiculing them, mocking the monks and deriding and offending them, and at the same time applauding the new doctrine. Now the monks insisted that their former ciritics implement the reforms for

An den Christli-
chen Adel deutscher Nation
von des Christlichen standes besserung.
D. Martinus Luther

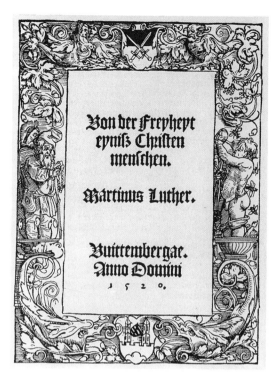

Von der Freyhept
eynis Christen
menschen.

Martinus Luther.

Wittembergae.
Anno Domini
1 5 2 0.

Title page of Luther's pamphlet
"To the Christian Nobility
of the German Nation"
Leipzig 1520

Title page of Luther's pamphlet
"On the Freedom of a Christian"
Wittenberg, 1520

Luther burns
the Bull "Exsurge Domine"
on 10.12.1510
in front of the Elster Gate
in Wittenberg
Coloured woodcut, 1557

Imperial citation to Luther to appear before the Reichstag in Worms, issued on 6 March 1521 and bearing the signature of Charles V

Imperial herald Kaspar Sturm
drawing by Albrecht Dürer

Cardinal legate Hieronymus Aleander
contemporary woodcut

Martin Luther at the Worms Reichstag, 1521
painting by Felix Schwormstädt

Conrad Peutinger
painting by Christoph Amberger, 1543

Johannes Cochläus
woodcut, 16th century

The Wartburg
copperplate from "Topographia" by Matthäus
Merian, Frankfurt/Main, 1690

The Wartburg: front court

Luther's room at the Wartburg

Martin Luther as Squire George
woodcut by Lucas Cranach, 1522

The "Babylonian whore"
woodcut from the September Bible

Augustinian monastery in Wittenberg,
side view (today Luther Hall)
next to the tower with the spiral staircase
Katharina's door

Luther's room in the former
Augustinian monastery

Interior of the City Church. The major's site of Luther's
Wittenberg ministry
In the background the Lucas Cranach altar

"Christ and Antichrist", woodcuts by Lucas Cranach, 1521
Jesus expels the money-changers from the temple—the
pope, out of greed of money, invites them to enter

Caricature of Luther's adversaries: Murner,
Emser in Leipzig, Leo X, Eck in Ingolstadt, and Lemp in Tübingen
one-side print, around 1520

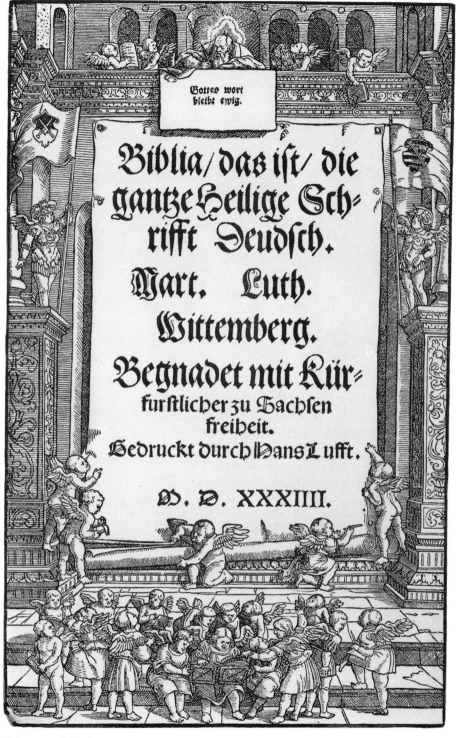

Title page of the first complete edition of Luther's
translation of the bible
Wittenberg, 1534

Illustration from the first complete Luther bible:
God blesses his entire creation with Adam and Eve
in the center

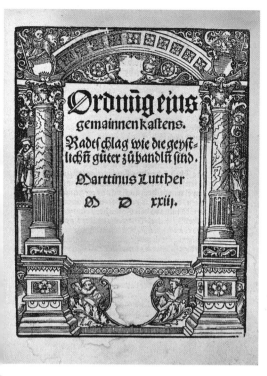

Title page of the Leisnig financial arrangement with letter of introduction by Martin Luther, Wittenberg 1523

Title page of the Large Catechism, 1529

Title page and first page of the evangelical hymn-book published in 1524 (the first one appeared in 1523)

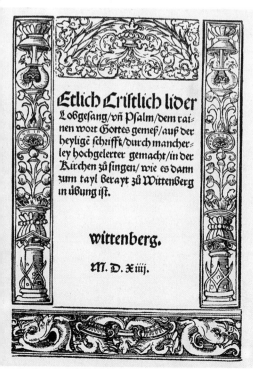

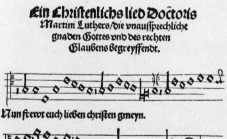

The house in which Luther died

View of altar, pulpit and Luther's grave at the
Castle Church in Wittenberg

which they had been calling. The future of these monks depended on how far the Reformation would progress and whether or not it would be able, at least as it affected the Church, to bring about changes. This question was much more serious for the "liberated" monks that it was for the university theologians in their secure positions, for the civic councilors, or for the knights and nobles, because the monks had risked everything on the success or failure of the Reformation. They were thus the most zealous agitators, preachers, emissaries, organizers, and disseminators of the new teaching. They neither slumbered nor slept, and could not afford to abandon their attempts to ensure that the truth they had recognized and to which they had committed themselves met at least with public tolerance, but preferably with positive acceptance and elevation to the norm, buttressed by resolutions, proclamations, and laws.

At the Wartburg Luther was a great distance from Wittenberg, but he nevertheless bore the full responsibility for what now occurred in the monasteries, because it had been his doctrine of justification by faith alone that had set in motion an intellectual process and had freed the mechanisms of the soul. The effect of Luther's doctrine was finally to cast doubt on monkery as a way of salvation and to encourage the decision to abandon the monastery. Luther dared not leave these monks without recourse, and he did not. Now they were accused of having broken their vows and of having been unfaithful, and such an accusation bore especially heavily on men who for decades had been trained in humility and obedience and whose thought more than that of others was centered in the fundamental ideas of propriety, ethics, and morality rather than in the baseness of material, social, or physical concerns.

More than once at the university there had been disputations concerning vows; Karlstadt and Melanchthon on those occasions had stepped forward with arguments. For disputations on this subject, Luther had sent two sets of theses to Wittenberg in September 1521. The question concerned not only the monk's vow, but also celibacy and to what extent a promise is morally binding and obligatory; it thus pertained to a perennial and fundamental problem for every system of morality, regardless of the spiritual presuppositions or the social conditions under which it had been launched.

The arguments of Karlstadt and Melanchthon seemed to Luther too weak. They tended to discuss the question from the point of view of the lesser of two evils, and to make the keeping or the breaking of vows dependent on whether or not the person had the fortitude to keep the vows, and thus to justifying the breaking of a promise with the excuse of human frailty. Such an explanation based on the Lutheran doctrine of original sin is completely understandable if not completely compelling. Luther sensed that dangers of a primary nature lurked therein, because such a line of argument could offer opponents not only reason to defame the Reformation but also the possibility of avoiding, with reference to human frailty, the binding commands that God gives to Christians.

Nevertheless, the ecclesiastical vows had to be abandoned, and their invalidity demonstrated at all costs. If the accusation of breaking vows could not be disarmed, Lutherans would be threatened with a serious moral defeat and the launching and development of the Reformation would be at high risk. The opponents did not need to be told what had to be said; they would retain their opinion in any case. Luther had to address the monks, friends, and persons sympathetic to reform, as well as the wavering and the undecided.

Luther found a simple solution; celibacy and monastic vows need not be honored because they were invalid from the start and, therefore, could not be binding in any way on the conscience because they were contrary to the Word of God. Marriage was part of the natural order of creation. To remain unmarried was left to a man as his free choice, but no one was subject to a command pertaining to the married or unmarried state. Furthermore, the monastic vow was contrary to the baptismal vow, for in the baptismal vow the Christian already has vowed all that he can vow: namely, to follow Christ. An additional vow could only rest on a whisper from the devil, not from God.

Such an argument can be effective only for the person who, like Luther, has adopted the principle to permit the conscience to be bound only by the Word of God. Furthermore, this argument assumes that questions of conscience are more important than questions of law. But without a priority of conscience over law, revolutions are not possible, because revolution always entails in one manner or another a violation of existing laws and accepted codes. Thus Luther's answer concerning the validity and obligation of vows contains, for his time, the solution for the fundamental moral problem of revolution: namely, that of liberation from the moral pressure of the accepted legal presumption behind which the society now under assault barricades itself. Under the actual historical circumstances of the time, permitting the conscience to be bound only by the Word of God had revolutionary significance. It offered the possibility of freeing the individual from society's persuasion, and of restricting society's claim on the individual initiative, because the conscience is not the voice of the ego; the conscience is to a greater extent the voice of the "neighbor" (superego) which speaks in me. Luther relieves the conscience of its obligation to the prescriptions of canon law. However, if the conscience is no longer bound to canon law but to something else that takes precedence over the acceptable law or sets itself against it, intellectual and spiritual queries about existing conditions increase. The revolutionary appears conscienceless to the apologist and defender of the existing order. Therefore, pride and "consciencelessness" also belong to the standing repertoire of accusations against Luther.

With relish Luther mulled over the various aspects of this problem. Few others were as familiar with it. He knew on which questions the monks and others who had dared to embrace the new, in Wittenberg and elsewhere, most urgently needed exhortation and encouragement.

> How often has my heart foundered, punished me, and reproached me with their (the papists') strongest argument: Are you alone wise? Are all others in error and have they erred for such a long time? What if you are wrong and so many people are led into error who will then be eternally damned? Finally Christ, with his clear and unerring Word, strengthened and confirmed me so that my heart no longer flounders but raises itself against the argument of the papists as a stone levee rises against the waves and mocks their threats and their storms. (WA VIII 483)

Thus Luther described his own experience with the temptation which repeatedly attacked him. He informed his Wittenberg Augustinian brothers of his own experience in order to strengthen them in their struggle against the Mass. Luther entitled the work dedicated to this problem *Concerning the Misuse of the Mass*. It was first composed in Latin and then translated by him into German.

The nagging doubt, "Are you alone wise?" is only to be overcome when the opinion of the entire world is regarded as nothing but chaff and straw. But how is that possible? How can one close one's ears to the taunts of the world? It can be done, even by one weak in faith, but it does not help, because there are still the power of the devil and the judgment of God. The *Anfechtung* (temptation) can be overcome if one holds firmly to the Word of God not only against the devil but also against God's judgment, as Jacob did when he was tempted by God, wrestled with Him, and thus believed God against God. He therefore received the name "Israel": "the man who struggles with God." Thus temptation leads into the deepest paradox of faith: God must be believed against God. Here absolute divine trust in God is demanded, a trust which does not permit itself to be mitigated by anything, but which takes God at His Word and regards nothing else.

Our conscience bites, Luther says, and in many ways makes us sinners before God. Therefore, we must arm ourselves with the Word of God and preserve and protect the conscience with the true Word of God (WA VIII 483).

With this idea, the seminal thought in Luther's theology was brought into focus and found its concluding formulation: *verbo solo*: (by the Word alone). In 1516 Luther had described God's work of salvation as being by grace alone, by faith alone. Therewith he had solved the problem of justification, and now comes the answer to the question concerning the origin of faith in the formulation "faith from hearing" *(fides ex auditu)*. The Word of

God alone makes faith certain and the conscience tranquil. Little else is as representative and as characteristic of his thought patterns as is the use of the little word "alone," which facilitated the expression of Luther's ideas. With this formulation he broke through that assiduous "on the one hand and on the other hand" and that elastic "this as well as that" of scholasticism, of which he himself was a master. It was because of Luther's mastery of the scholastic methods that he could push them aside and leave them behind. *Sola gratia, sola fide,* and *verbo solo:* these were the key elements of his theology, borne of that *Christus solus,* which struck him as he prepared his first lecture on the psalter, and which finally provided the *soli Deo gloria:* to God alone the glory. The essence of the struggle was expressed in these formulations evoked from his being.

The intellectual contents of these formulations were tightly knit and mutually determinative. A new expression did not necessarily represent the addition of an idea that had nod previously been present; the new expression might, on the other hand, clarify and interpret what already had been contemplated. Occasionally, in theory and in practice, the principle of *verbo solo* is expressed long before the Wartburg exile. However, now the principle is implemented, especially in connection with his first attempts in changing the liturgy of the Mass. In this respect, as time went by, it became to an increasing degree the factor that distinguished Luther's theology from contrary or rival interpretations.

Previously, in the writings on the sacraments of the fall of 1519, Luther had presented the view that the Mass was not correctly employed, that its efficacy depended not at all on the number of Masses and the gestures of the priest but simply and solely on the commissioning words of Christ and on the faith of the recipient. In the *Babylonian Captivity,* he had set forth his arguments. Now he introduced another aspect of the problem of the Mass: the essence of the priesthood.

The priest was to offer sacrifice and thereby appease God. He did not offer sacrifice for himself alone, but for all the people. That was the essence of the priesthood in the Old Testament. The priests slaughtered goats, lambs, oxen, pigeons, and other animals, sprinkled the blood on and before the altar, burned certain parts of the sacrifice in the pan, and with the burnt offerings provided a pleasing aroma in order to placate God. The thigh, hind leg, neck, stomach, and other choice pieces the priests devoured themselves. They were supported by what the people offered to God as sacrifice. God received what was considered the seat of life: the blood and the intestines. God's anger was great and not easily appeased, and thus many sacrifices were required. An entire tribe of Israel, that of Levi, was therefore selected to perform the priestly functions.

In the New Testament this outward priesthood was cast away. The New Testament has one single priest: Jesus Christ. With His sacrifice, which can be neither exceeded nor repeated, Christ once and for all placated God's anger and made all Christians righteous priests. Their ordination "makes prayer, access to God, and doctrine (which are proper and appropriate for a priest) common to all people" (WA VIII 487).

When the old priesthood was dissolved, so also was the office of the priest: sacrifice. To perform the Mass as a sacrifice and to enlist shorn priests was a denial of Christ. Sacrificing, anointing men to the priesthood, garbing them in vestments, and shaving their heads could only be from the devil. If, since 1518, Luther had placed the papacy under the suspicion of being the antichrist, now he ascribed the entire priestly vocation to the devil. Priestly acts were to be rejected because priests themselves were to be rejected. With this view an awareness was heightened and touched on something of the social dimension of the priesthood. There came a realization that the papal priests conceived of the Mass as sacrifice so they would have something to do at the altar.

What Luther here said about the priesthood had only one purpose: to make clear that the Mass was no sacrifice. In order to free the consciences of those who no longer permitted Masses as well as the consciences of those who no longer heard them, it was necessary to abandon the concept of the Mass as having a sacrifical character. The suspension of Masses terrified the mind, especially because one feared to kindle God's wrath by discontinuing to offer the sacrifice essential to appease Him. Behind this dread anxiety stood the ancient concept that God must be appeased by some kind of act, best of all by sacrifice. But that ancient concept of God constituted a view which had plagued Luther in his early days in the monastery, had plunged him into anxiety and such deep despair that he had disputed with himself and with God, and had discovered within himself the urge to kill this God. Therefore, in the discussion concerning the character of the Mass, Luther's inner conflict was reawakened and he felt compelled to prevent a misunderstanding to which his doctrine of justification of faith alone was repeatedly subjected: that faith itself was a form of sacrifice that could appease God.

But to perceive of faith as a sacrifice that was able to appease God meant no longer to accept God as the single subject of salvation but to appoint man himself as a coauthor of salvation, thereby endangering the *soli Deo gloria* and the *solus Christus*, and transforming faith into works. In *Concerning Good Works*, Luther did not escape this danger entirely; now he barred the door against such an interpretation. Man's faith did not appease God; it was God alone who reconciled, who turned toward man in grace. Faith could only grasp for the reconciliation that already had been accomplished without any act of man. The concept of reconciliation free of any human act resulted from Luther's ideas on predestination, which, however disturbing, were anything but fatalistic.

As the question concerning the sacrificial character of the Mass was linked with the highly personal experience of Luther, so also was the binding validity of monastic vows. Apart from the fact that he disowned the monastic vows, as already mentioned, with reference to the authority and validity of baptism, he also attacked them on the basis of the commandment to honor father and mother. Here the general struggle against monkery was merged into his personal fate; he had, after all, become a monk against the will and against the protestation of his father. He had himself experienced the father-son conflict. At that time his decision to become a monk also was a decision for self-assertion against the paternal will. Luther had prevailed in the father-son conflict, but the thorns of that conflict continued to prick his conscience. Now Luther resolutely directed those thorns against the defenders of monasticism. It was an injustice to persuade people that the monastic estate should be valued more highly than the obedience that children owed to their parents. The pamphlet *Concerning Monastic Vows (De votis monasticis judicium)* Luther dedicated to his father, Hans Luder.

During Advent Luther could tolerate his Wartburg exile no longer. Regardless of whether the news from Wittenberg was good or bad, he wanted to see for himself what was transpiring. It is impossible to establish how he succeeded in persuading the Wartburg warden to provide him with a horse, and whether the matter was discussed with a third party. In any case Luther rode to Wittenberg. He must have had great confidence in his disguise as Squire George to have interrupted his journey by stopping in Leipzig, but nothing bad came of it. In Wittenberg Luther stayed at the home of his friend, Nicholas Amsdorf, where he was visited by Lucas Cranach and the goldsmith, Christian Döring, who had provided Luther with the carriage for his trip to Worms. Posterity is indebted to this Cranach visit for his painting "Luther as Squire George."

In Wittenberg Luther found that all was going well. No procedural changes against him were indicated. Luther advised that the relics in the Castle Church collected by the elector be placed in a community chest, and that the gold, silver, and jewels be used for the benefit of the community. One omission, however, angered Luther. Spalatin had delayed printing the treatise on monastic vows, the work on the misuse of the Mass, and a pamphlet directed against Archbishop Albrecht. In an irritated tone, Luther wrote Spalatin that he should once and for all stop conducting himself too circumspectly with respect to whatever appeared suspicious. Luther wanted printed what he had written, if not in Wittenberg, then somewhere else. The protest had its desired effect, as the works on monastic vows and on the Mass were soon thereafter delivered to the printer.

Luther remained in Wittenberg only about three days; then he went on his way. He took with him from Wittenberg an important stimulus. In his conversation with his friends, the plan matured to translate the Bible into German. On his journey, a second stimulus came to him. From rumors, he had heard that "many of our people" were rowdy. This report disturbed Luther so that, as soon as he had returned to the Wartburg, he composed *An Earnest Admonition to All Christians to Avoid Riot and Rebellion*, which demonstrated most clearly how Luther conceived of the progress of the Reformation. One should preach and continuously hold the Word of God before the people, but in no case strike with the fist!

Why not strike with the fist? Had Luther himself not dreamed, about one and a half years earlier, of washing his hands in the blood of the Romanists? And now this passivity! Had Luther become timid?

It was not timidity that motivated Luther to warn of unrest and rebellion. He also did not retract what he had said earlier. At that time, in the midsummer of 1520, Luther had appealed to the nobles, kings, and princes to strike with all weapons and to destroy the "plague of the earth." Even now Luther would not have denied that right to them. They were the authorities and should execute their office. However, the common man had been expected to remain patient and passive. Nevertheless, there were indications that this distinction between those in authority and those under it was no longer clearly recognized. Still Luther could give reasons why the common man should take to heart and resist the temptation to threaten with fist and flail: rebellion brought no improvement but only punished the innocent; God had forbidden rebellion; and finally, rebellion was "no doubt the suggestion of the devil."

Luther rejoiced that the papists feared rebellion. He made no pretense about his satisfaction; he could not suppress his joy at the thought, and he fully delighted in the fear of his enemies. Fear should overwhelm them; they should be terrified by a dry leaf falling from the tree. But such a mild punishment as physical insurrection was not sufficient for them. Divine wrath had fallen upon the papacy and punished with the Word. The Word threshed more thoroughly than the flail.

Luther had great confidence in the Word: "As soon as the lies are revealed, no blows are necessary any longer; the papists will fall and disappear in all disgrace as a result of their own acts. For no man is so mad as to follow, rather than to hate, manifest lies and falsehood" (WA VIII 678). This sudden confidence that man was not so mad as to follow the manifest lies did not reconcile easily with Luther's pessimistic anthropology which, five years earlier, had led him to the conclusion that the nature of man was naturally corrupt. Here again we encounter the fundamental contradiction in Luther's concept concerning the path of the Reformation: man is totally depraved, but suddenly he should be able to follow truth.

This contradiction cannot be completely removed as long as we regard it only in the frame of Luther's anthropology. However, it becomes less glaring and more comprehensible when we follow Luther's view that it is, after all, the Word of God that turns man and enables him to recognize truth. Many years later Luther would be confronted with irreconcilable conflicts that developed from this contradiction. But now he was still of a tranquil mind and used himself as an example of how much the Word can do. "Behold, how in these few years that we have pursued and written such truth that the blanket for the papists has become very small and short!" (WA VIII 684). Luther predicted, "and if we can continue our activity for two more years, then you will see what will happen to pope, bishop, cardinal, priest, monk, nun, bells, gates, Mass, vigils, cowls, caps, tonsures, rules, statutes; and the entire abscess and vermin of papal rule, like smoke it will dissipate!" (WA VIII 684).

The confidence in the power of God's Word here became an illusion, and Lutheran theology now began, in addition to mobilizing for the course of the Reformation, to reveal a curbing and an arresting influence and to exhort to patience. This emphasis was associated with, among other things, eschatology: the doctrines concerning final events. Luther was convinced that judgment was imminent. In fact, God's judgment of the papacy had already begun, in that the papacy found itself under the judgment of the Word; Judgment Day and the return of Christ were no longer remote expectations, and Christ would soon completely and absolutely overcome the antichrist. Man should not seek to accelerate this work of redemption by provoking rebellion. Christ already had begun a spiritual revolution. The devil sought to negate Christ's spiritual revolution by provoking a physical rebellion and thereby rescuing the antichrist.

The thought that the devil desired rebellion left room no longer for the consideration that rebellion might also be commanded for a righteous cause. "I hold with and will always hold with those who passively endure rebellion, no matter how unjust matters are, and against those who cause rebellion no matter how justified, because rebellion cannot be engaged without the spilling of innocent blood or the imposition of damages" (WA VIII 680). Riot and rebellion are always wrong regardless of what goals are sought and who promotes them. Naturally Luther knows that in necessity force must be used against the enemies of the gospel, or, as he understood it, against the papists; however, the use of force pertains not to everyone but only to the rulers, "because whatever occurs through the use of authorized force is not to be considered riot and rebellion" (WA VIII 679). The common man is to wait, confess his sins, and pray for deliverance.

In this view lay the strength and weakness of Luther's concept concerning the content and the parth of the Reformation. According to this view, the content of the Reformation must consist primarily of the preaching of God's Word. When God's Word gripped the heart and awakened faith, everything else would naturally flow from that experience, and, insofar as new regulations for harmonious community in the society were necessary, these regulations were to be enacted and implemented by the legal authorities in an orderly manner. The goal and message of the Reformation was not the transformation of society but freedom for the Word of God. Everything else was subservient and must not detract from the most important objective: faith. In the prevailing historical conditions at the end of 1521 and the beginning of 1522, Luther's strength lay in concentrating on the objective. For the future development of the Reformation, however, this concentration grew increasingly weaker since, once faith had been kindled, inevitably a multitude of practical questions arose. To the popular movement, no more than a subordinate role was ascribed. Luther regarded the popular movement with skepticism and open distrust. What we today affirmatively describe as popular movement would have appeared to Luther as pertaining to *Herr Omnes*, or Mr. Everyman. Mr. Everyman has no rational faculty. He cannot distinguish between evil and good people. "He strikes in the crowd at random and he cannot attack injustice without causing great evil" (WA VIII 680). With this statement, a sharp demarcation in Luther's theology is drawn in that it seems to retain a neutral position vis-à-vis those regulations necessary to the ordering of communal authority; in reality, this theology also curtails its own sphere of possible action. The more theology is elevated to axiom, the more easily theology is ensnared by exploitative powers and directed against the revolution.

Whether or not Luther composed *An Earnest Admonition* as a result of direct discussion with the electoral court cannot be demonstrated. From Wittenberg Luther had already informed Spalatin that he intended to write such a piece. In any case, regardless of whether the arguments presented in the work seem valid, the tenor of the writing undeniably corresponded very well with what the court desired to hear and with what the court needed for the support of its own policy, especially in view of what now was taking place in Wittenberg.

On December 3, 1521, students and burghers in Wittenberg had disrupted the Mass in the city church and, with drawn knives, had driven the officiating clergy from the altar. There were loud threats against the Franciscan monastery, so that the city council felt obligated to place a guard there in order to prevent trouble. A few days later, about the time when Luther again left Wittenberg, articles from the community were placed before the city council, demanding that "everyone should be free to preach the Word of God because God's Word should not and will not be bound." All Masses should cease, and all sodalities, or brotherhoods, should be dissolved, and communion should be administered in both kinds. "Beer halls and taprooms, since excessive drinking continues, should be closed, as well as the brothels, of which there are many in the city, regardless of whether they are under the supervision of students, priests, burghers, householders, or the rector or bishop." The civic representatives and some burghers angrily presented these articles to the council and demanded pardons for those who had caused the disruption in the city church.

At that juncture the elector ordered the officials von Belzig and Gräfenhainichen to muster a levy before the city in order to punish the troublemakers. With some difficulty the city council succeeded in mastering the situation and avoiding a confrontation with the elector, its territorial lord. Before the gates of the city, the guard detail was allayed with several kegs of beer; the community assembled in the castle courtyard and turned over to the warden a list of the names of the rebels. There the matter rested. The elector declined to punish the rebels, but he also forbade any alteration in the Mass.

But Wittenberg did not obey the elector's order. Karlstadt, who previously in September and October had hesitantly opposed Gabriel Zwilling, dispensed the Eucharist in both kinds in the city church at Christmas. This was a clear violation of the elector's order. New tensions threatened. Students engaged in pranks, worship services were disrupted, the unrest increased.

On December 27, 1521, three strange characters from Zwickau—clothmakers, Nicholas Storch and Thomas Drechsel, and a student, Marcus Thomae, called Stübner—arrived at Melanchthon's home. The Zwickau city council had expelled them as rabble rousers. Now they hoped to find support in Wittenberg. They surprised Melanchthon with accounts of their rich spiritual life, which caused the young scholar to be very reflective. They claimed in all manner of dreams and visions to have access to God. They also criticized infant baptism. Melanchthon was not capable of resisting the onslaught of these spirits and he felt unsure of himself. Perhaps there was something to what they said? In any case, Melanchthon requested the elector not to proceed against them with force. It would be best to recall Luther to Wittenberg in order that he could test these men. Melanchthon also considered convoking a disputation in order to respond to the questions concerning infant baptism raised by the Zwickau prophets.

But the elector, greatly annoyed, rejected such an idea. The Wittenbergers already had "enough on their ledger." They should have nothing more to do with Storch, Drechsel, and Stübner, and it was too dangerous for Luther to make the journey from the Wartburg to Wittenberg. The three Zwickau prophets soon disappeared from Wittenberg.

Luther was not impressed with spiritual visions. The appeal of the prophets to special revelation meant nothing to him. The spirits must be tested, for God commissions for a ministry only through the ordained or with clear signs. If these prophets had never experienced *Anfechtung* and were as confident of their calling as they pretended to be, such inexperience and overconfidence constituted a sign that they did not possess the true Spirit. Their self-serving, pious, devotional, and religious talk, and their account of how they were caught up into the third heaven, as they claimed, discredited them.

That infants were unable to believe on their own, the major argument presented by the Zwickau prophets against infant baptism—an argument henceforth never to be silenced—impressed Luther not in the least. "How will they prove that children do not believe? By the fact that they do not speak or demonstrate faith? Beautiful! How long, then, are we Christians when we sleep or do other things?" (WA BR II 425). A surprising argument; it sounds almost naive because we unconsciously, like the enemies of infant baptism in the sixteenth century—the Anabaptists or those of similar persuasion—hold faith to be a form of intellectual activity or capability that is dependent on knowledge, recognition, or understanding. But, according to Luther, that is just what faith is not. Earlier, in the Heidelberg theses of April 1518, Luther announced that faith possesses no logic. It is not at all an acquired "achievement" of man, but rather a gift of grace which God plants in the heart. And why should not infants experience this gift of grace? Luther protected faith from reason and brushed aside the arguments of the opponents of infant baptism with a simple wave of the hand.

The brief witness of the "Zwickau zealots" in Wittenberg remained, to be sure, only an episode, but it was symptomatic of the fact that the reformation movement began to diversify and tended to strike paths that no longer necessarily followed Lutheran teaching. In January and February of 1522, even in Wittenberg differences surfaced that Luther considered tolerable and not incompatible with his own views.

After long negotiation, the city of Wittenberg issued an ordinance on January 24, 1522. The sodalities were dissolved. Their private income as well as the wealth realized from benefices and other ecclesiastical holdings were transferred into a community chest and administered by the mayor and those commissioned by the respective urban districts. The community chest was used to purchase a grain and wood supply, to assist the poor and suffering, and to lend money to needy artisans. Beggars and vagabonds were to be expelled from the city. Only those who could sustain themselves "with work and other honest deeds" were tolerated.

This city ordinance proposed a new order for the worship service. The Eucharist should be distributed in both kinds, the words of institution were to be spoken in German, the elevation of the host should be discontinued. The brothels were closed. Pictures and statues were removed from the churches; their removal caused tumultuous scenes.

In these months in which Luther was isolated from the events taking place throughout the land, the reform movement, without his direct action but as a result of the rapid dissemination of his writings, was broadened and deepened. Not only the events in Wittenberg, with which he was confronted at the Wartburg, testify to this. As early as the summer of 1521, in Erfurt, there had been renewed unrest, the so-called priest storms. As already mentioned, in Zwickau a fanatical group had appeared whose views were far more radical than those of the Wittenbergers. But in other areas of the empire also it became clear that, as the Reformation spread, diversification was more clearly defined.

Within its early perimeter, an internationalization of the reform movement may be observed. Not only in the cities on the Baltic coast but also throughout the whole Baltic region, preachers proclaimed the new doctrine. In the Low Countries, even the most rigorous attempts to enforce the Edict of Worms could entirely prevent neither the dissemination of Lutheran writings nor the activity of the Lutheran preachers.

However, it was preeminently in Switzerland that an independent center of the Reformation now began to develop. The leader there was the priest of Zurich Cathedral, Ulrich Zwingli, who, in part stimulated by Luther and in part motivated by his own intellectual development, renounced Church tradition and the Church fathers as the source of correct doctrine, and admitted only the Bible as the source of teaching. With these convictions, Zwingli, like Luther, also came into conflict with traditional ecclesiastical practices. These conflicts became especially inflammatory with respect to whether the command concerning fasting should be observed. The Swiss Reformation very quickly struck its own course, which was similar to the current observed in Wittenberg, especially in Karlstadt's teaching. Thus, for example, the question of images was treated much more radically in Switzerland than in Wittenberg, and in Switzerland the urban authorities, rather than the princes who made the decisions in central Germany, naturally assumed the role of deciding questions of doctrine and the order of divine worship.

Simultaneous with the rapid territorial expansion of the ecclesiastical reform movement was the much slower expansion of a social reform movement. Up to this point the ecclesiastical movement had drawn into question or openly challenged papal primacy and episcopal jurisdiction in spiritual matters. This attack had originated primarily with the lower clergy, monks, students, and the universities. However, now the movement was no longer satisfied with mere preaching; as in Wittenberg, it implemented substantive changes in the worship service and in the use of ecclesiastical wealth. But these reforms affected the immediate interests of the burghers, artisans, craftsmen, shopkeepers, and other groups, thereby expanding the social basis of the movement. Hence both social and ideological or theological uniformity were lost.

To say "yes" to Luther, to criticize Rome, to preach evangelically, to receive the Eucharist in both kinds, to ignore the Edict of Worms, to preach against interest and usury, to provide care for the poor and the sick, to place the commonweal above personal benefit—in brief, to desire reformation—did not mean at this or any later time adopting completely, recognizing, and representing without any deviation Lutheran theology with its "by grace alone" and "by faith alone," its denial of free will, its doctrine of original sin, and the specific arguments against the primacy of the pope. In reality, there grew up a very diversified assortment of theological positions with explicit social and political demands and expectations. Ideologically, these demands and expectations fused mainly in the conviction that only the Bible was to serve as the foundation for theological thought. Consequently, in the wake of the Reformation, many spiritual streams which had appeared earlier in Church history once again welled up spontaneously or were revitalized by the most varied religious writings.

Thus in the Reformation dialectic there surfaced sporadically, along with specific Lutheran theology, rich resources of mystical, apocalyptic, or eschatological thought, and even the peculiarly critical variant (from a social and political perspective) known as chiliasm, the doctrine of the millenium at the end of time. Ideologically the positions were not yet clearly defined; one could not yet speak of denominationalism.

In any case the Reformation was much more than a medieval heresy. Theologically it was brought to a focal point in Luther's doctrine of justification, but it was in no way wholly contained in or limited to that doctrine; it presented a dynamic, ever-expanding synthesis of the potential for protest in the Church, state, and society—a mobilizing ideology, full of contradictions, which awakened hopes and paved the way for revolt, appealed to opposing interests, and was variously interpreted by its supporters. This ideology changed, developed, diversified, and became radical; it was blunted by the social movement which it had brought forth. Through all that transpired, each of the agitating classes, ranks, groups, and parties marked this movement and ideology with its own stamp so indelibly that finally one can justifiably speak of several Reformation ideologies.

As these ideologies begin to emerge in 1521–1522, three groups can be distinguished even though they cannot be sharply differentiated from one another. First, there was the Saxon-Thuringian center, which was personified in Luther. Second, there was a center comprised of parts of Switzerland and southern Germany, which at that time included Alsace. This group was distinguished from the central German Reformation group primarily by the fact that in it the social, political, and ideological middle class influences were more pronounced and that it was the urban authorities with whom or despite whom (as the case might be) the new ideas succeeded. Third, in both areas a social and ideological stream cut its own course left of both Luther and the south German reformers. To be sure, this current, like the others, drew its following from all social classes and ranks, but mainly from the lower urban classes. The third group might therefore be classified as plebeian.

On January 20, 1522, the imperial government in Nuremberg issued a mandate against the novelties in electoral Saxony because they were in open defiance of the Edict of Worms and of the duty of the imperial princes to protect the Church. Elector Joachim of Brandenburg, Duke Heinrich the Younger of Braunschweig, and Duke George of Saxony forbade their subjects to attend the University of Wittenberg. As a result, many students left Wittenberg. The Wittenbergers had gone too far too fast, and hand caused difficulties for the princes. They would have to be brought into line and be forced to accept certain modifications of their civic ordinances. But such restrictions would require Luther's sanction. His Wartburg sojourn was about to end.

Chapter 10

Bible, Congregation, and Civil Authority: Reformation Without Riot and Rebellion March 1522–February 1523

Luther was at peace with himself when, at the end of February 1522, he decided to return to Wittenberg. While translating the New Testament, a work which he had begun after his Wittenberg visit of early December 1521, and which he had quickly completed, there was a pressing need to discuss several difficult passages with his Wittenberg colleagues, especially with Melanchthon. For this purpose Luther had at first wanted to be in Wittenberg by Easter at the latest. As he could perceive from the news from Wittenberg that a certain insecurity was growing and that a certain uneasiness was demonstrated as to the possible course of events, Luther no longer desired to delay his return until the scheduled Easter date. His perception was that unclear spirits had fallen over his flock. In a mildly satirical letter of consolation beginning "Grace and joy from God the Father on the acquisition of a new relic," a reference to the electoral penchant for collecting relics and holy artifacts of every description, he announced to the elector his decision to return early. What had now taken shape in Wittenberg was a relic of a special kind, with nails, spears, and whips. His Electoral Grace need only extend his arms and permit the nails to be driven through his hands; that was the way it must and should be. "His Electoral Grace should not wonder that it is not only Annas and Caiphas who rage but that Judas is also numbered among the apostles and Satan among the children of God" (WA BR II 448). Luther knew these assaults of the devil and did not fear them. He wanted to be back in Wittenberg soon and the elector should not trouble himself too much about Luther.

The elector did not intend to trouble himself with Luther, at any rate not just at that moment and not in any way that might cause the elector unpleasantness. The annoyance of the imperial government was sufficient for Frederick, and his cousin George of Albertine Saxony and the bishop of Meissen had in the last weeks registered their displeasure with him. If Luther's return to Wittenberg could not now be avoided, Frederick wanted to be sure that he could in no way appear responsible for Luther's reappearance there. Frederick sent instructions to his official, Johann Oswald in Eisenach, that he should inform Luther that the elector had supported Luther's cause only in that the elector had favored a hearing for the reformer before the emperor. However, if Luther should now appear in Wittenberg, he should consider that it would be difficult for the elector to ignore a papal or imperial request for Luther's extradition. Of course, if the elector could be certain of God's will in the matter, he would adhere to that will. In addition, another Reichstag was being prepared; Luther should submit his opinion in writing to it. Futhermore, until the convocation of the new Reichstag, he should remain silent.

The instructions to the Eisenach official contained no command to Luther to remain at the Wartburg under all circumstances. The instruction was so framed that the entire responsibility for the decision to remain at the Wartburg or to return to Wittenberg was placed on Luther. Luther desired and needed no more. He left for Wittenberg.

Nevertheless, on his journey from the Wartburg to Wittenberg, he sought anonymity; futhermore, he probably rather enjoyed traveling incognito. In Jena, he stopped at the Black Bear Inn. Two Swiss students who were at supper in the inn and whom Luther hospitably invited to his table were not a little amazed at the educated squire who paged through the Hebrew psalter. The student were on their way to Wittenberg where they hoped to study, and they asked, motivated by strong curiosity, whether anything had been heard from Luther and whether he was once again in Wittenberg. The unknown squire informed the students that he had trustworthy information that Luther was not yet in Wittenberg but that he soon would be there. In case the students should really go to Wittenberg the squire requested them to greet their Swiss countryman there, Jerome Schurff, from one who would soon arrive. The innkeeper, who had heard the conversation, suspected his guest to be Luther himself and motioned to the students that the one seated at the table was indeed the one about whom they had been asking. Luther had enjoyed the game and anonymity and paid for the students' supper.

The nearer Luther approached Wittenberg, the bolder his mood became. From Borna, where with his escort he had stopped briefly at the constable station on Ash Wednesday, he wrote to the elector:

> I do not desire protection from Your Electoral Princely Grace; in fact, I thought to provide Your Grace with more protection than Your Grace could provide for me. If I thought that Your Grace could and would defend me by the sword, I would not come. Our undertaking cannot be accomplished by the sword. God alone must promote our cause without any human concern or activity. Therefore, whoever has the strongest faith can provide the most protection. And because I now sense that Your Electoral Princely Grace is still weak in faith, I can under no circumstances regard Your Electoral Princely Grace as one who could grant me protection and security. (WA BR II 455ff)

Luther's self-confidence had now reached its highest and its boldest at an almost unimaginable peak. He saw himself as the instrument of God. "Your Electoral Princely Grace knows, or if Your Grace does not know, so permit Your Grace to be informed, that I have my gospel not from man but from heaven through our Lord Jesus Christ; that I could have boasted myself (as I will do from now on) a minister and evangelist; that I permitted myself to be summoned to interrogation and judgment was not because I doubted my cause, but out of excessive humility in order to attract others" (WA BR II 455). What Luther had written to Melanchthon just a few weeks earlier concerning the Zwickau prophets had been forgotten along with what he had thought of their suspect and direct communication from God. He denied their claims. Heaven had spoken to him, not to the others. How else could he have reacted since the elector had placed all responsibility on him? He must fail, or in spirit reach for the stars. In the ecstacy of returning home, he saw himself vindicated by divine grace.

On March 6, 1522, Luther reentered Wittenberg. Melanchthon breathed a sigh of relief. The burden had become too heavy for him. The other leaders of the Wittenberg reform movement also were happy to have Luther once again in their midst. They had been the ones who had hoped for and urged his return. However, Luther was forced to bow to the demand of the elector and assume full responsibility for the homecoming. In conformity with the request of the elector, Luther had composed a letter in which he presented his reasons for returning. The elector needed such a letter in order to defend himself from the accusations of those who would blame him for bringing Luther back to Wittenberg. In his original draft, Luther declared that the primary reason for his return was a summons by the Wittenberg congregation, but the elector would not allow that reason to stand. Luther was obliged to revise the letter and to omit any reference to being recalled to Wittenberg by anyone. Instead, in the final draft of the letter, he attributed his return to his concern regarding the general unrest and the threat of rebellion in Germany. Thus Luther's return seemed to be in complete conformity with his pamphlet *An Earnest Admonition to All Christians to Avoid Riot and Rebellion*, which had now been published. The tenor of this writing set the tone for his appearance before the congregation in the city church, where for one week, from March 9–March 16, Luther preached daily. These Lenten sermons, also called "Invocavit" sermons, had a dual purpose. They were designed to consolidate what had been gained and to present those gains as legitimate; at the same time, they were intended to call for moderation, to ease the temporarily strained relations between the territorial lord and his city, and to silence those who resisted the compromise reached with the electoral advisors in Eilenburg in February. Luther's appeal for moderation was directed especially against Karlstadt, who in recent weeks had placed himself in the forefront and had increasingly played a definitive role as a leader in sponsoring innovations.

Without naming Karlstadt, the Lenten sermons in their theological content were directed primarily against him. Luther found himself in a strange, almost paradoxical position. In fact, the Wittenbergers had hardly gone beyond what Luther himself had developed in his writings over the last few years: priests should marry, the Eucharist was to be administered in both kinds, the Mass was not a sacrifice and should therefore be abolished, no obligation was to be attached to auricular confession, and Church wealth should be transferred to the community and used to care for the poor. What could Luther complain about! Only this: that reforms had been introduced too quickly without a careful preparation of the heart and, above all, that his advice had been transformed into rigid, coercive regulations.

The Lenten sermons appear primarily to be directed against the methods of the Wittenberg reforms. However, behind the question of method is concealed also the question of content. Luther never wearies of hammering home to his auditors that evangelical freedom may not be transformed into law. Of course, it is correct to receive communion in both kinds, but the Eucharist is valid only for those who in faith request it. Therefore, consideration should be extended to those who are still weak in faith, and no one should be forced to accept what he is not prepared to accept. Certainly one can take bread and wine from the altar with one's own hands, but this procedure is not strictly commanded. Certainly priests may marry and monks and nuns may leave the cloister, but "may" is not "must." Certainly images are not to be worshipped, but to make and to have them does not necessarily mean to worship them. Luther feared people were being misled by outward reform measures, that they were once again, as under the papacy, hanging their Christianity on the peg of outward ceremonies. Nothing could be gained by such a reform; on the contrary, the devil would thereby triumph, because he desired to draw hearts away from faith and bind the conscience with outward works. Luther feared for the content of the Reformation when changes were implemented too quickly and attempts were made to achieve with laws, regulations, and prescriptions what in his opinion could be achieved only by faith awakened by preaching. What Luther envisioned was the Christian made mature by faith who, according to the strength of his faith, decided for himself such things as when and how often he would attend communion, whether he would receive the Eucharist in one or in two kinds, when and to whom he would confess his sins. To be sure, Luther's approach to reform presupposed a transition period in which no firm or binding rules governing the liturgy could be established; the results could have been, for example, that the Eucharist might be received in one or two kinds, in one congregation in one manner and in another congregation in another manner.

In fact, these undefined, parallel, and confusing liturgical practices occurred repeatedly during the Reformation, but always only for a transitional period, until finally the elementary need for order and regulation prevailed. Luther had an aversion to laws. He desired to see faith develop and given time to mature because he bound everything to faith. *Sola fide* became the goal of the Reformation and the standard for the methods employed to achieve reformation. The decision concerning reformation is sought on the plane of faith and individual consciousness; the transformation of society, on the other hand, comes about incidentally. This social transformation is intrinsically and completely divorced from the concern of faith; social transformation becomes a possible and not undesirable consequence of true faith, but not a valid goal for its quest.

Dressed in his monk's cowl and wearing a freshly cut tonsure, Luther preached his Lenten sermons. He thus demonstrated how little he regarded outward signs. The monk's cowl and tonsure were so unimportant that they could be retained, and did not need to be abolished by force. In the liturgy, outward forms were also so unimportant that customs adhered to up to the present could be retained without any danger to the soul. Therefore, at Easter 1522, the Mass in Wittenberg was again celebrated in the Latin language; only the words of institution were spoken aloud in German. The congregation was informed that the Mass was not a sacrifice but a gift of Christ's grace to believers. The splendidly ornamented priestly vestments could also be retained. By its clerical garb, the clergy could once again be distinguished from the laity, and the clergy were no longer required, as they had been a short time earlier, to perform their office before the altar in the dress of a simple burgher.

Gabriel Zwilling accepted Luther's authority, but Karlstadt protested. Karlstadt was ten years older than Luther. During the critical winter weeks of 1521–1522, while Luther was still at the Wartburg, Karlstadt's opinion had prevailed in Wittenberg against all the doubts of the timid and hesitant; now he held firmly to what he considered correct: the Old Testament regarded the making of images as idolatry.

Karlstadt was forbidden to preach in the city church. Luther had no interest in continuing the quarrel. Vainly Luther admonished Karlstadt not to write against him. However, Karlstadt already had sent to the printer a manuscript justifying his own position and defending the innovations in Wittenberg. The rector of the university had Karlstadt's pamphlet confiscated. In order that the printer would suffer no loss of business, Luther immediately provided the press with one of his own writings. Thus Luther himself, who just a short time earlier had been angered by Spalatin's censorship of his work, began to censor one of his earliest coworkers for reform. The authority which Luther exercised in word and concept grasped for the means of power to forestall criticism. The new doctrine, which now as always had disintegrating and inflammatory impact wherever it encountered resistance, now began, where it found acceptance, to function as a force for conformity.

For the trouble that the dispute with Karlstadt caused him, Luther was richly compensated by the very fruitful cooperation of Melanchthon. Together they read the German text of the New Testament which Luther had brought with him from the Wartburg, corrected it, and polished individual sentences and expressions. For this work Melanchthon's exceptional knowledge of Greek was an invaluable aid. Luther had based his German translation of the New Testament on the 1518 second Strasbourg edition of the 1516 first edition of the New Testament that Erasmus of Rotterdam had published in the original Greek. Luther had compared questionable passages with the Latin Vulgate as well as with another Latin text which had been prepared by Erasmus. Luther did not translate word for word; on the contrary, he sought to tell the biblical story eloquently in the German language. After he had published his translation of the New Testament, Jerome Emser (the mountain goat of Leipzig), Luther's old opponent, was able, without great difficulty, to point out with obvious satisfaction a whole series of translation errors. Emser's critique disturbed Luther hardly at all; Luther quietly corrected the mistakes in new editions. He knew himself superior to all opponents in that he had provided the meaning of the biblical text in the German language, a meaning which for German ears was more concealed than revealed in the Greek text.

In September 1522 the German New Testament appeared, accompanied by Lucas Cranach's woodcuts from the Apocalypse of St.John. The September Testament, as this edition was soon called, was so quickly sold out that in December a slightly revised printing could be published. But only in 1534 was the entire "Luther Bible" completed. The fact that the Old Testament is written in Hebrew, with a few short passages in Aramaic, made translation much more difficult than translating the New Testament had been, and Luther could succeed in producing an Old Testament translation only with the cooperation of a whole team of colleagues.

Luther's September Testament was not the first Bible in the German language. Fourteen German translations of the Bible preceded Luther's, but none of them can be compared in beauty and forceful expression to his. The earlier translations were limited in impact because their language was too closely oriented to local dialects of the various regions where they appeared, and the translators could not free themselves from a literal presentation of the text to capture the meaning behind the words. However, translating the Bible is not just a philological endeavor but also a theological and historical undertaking. Complete comprehension of the biblical text embraces understanding not only the message for the generation in which it was written but also the message for all future generations. Only the rediscovery of the original message made it possible to interpret the total biblical expression from a uniform point of view, thereby gaining liberty in translating the text so that the translation indeed becomes a faithful copy of the original presentation. The Bible can be vital only when this message, delivered in a remote past and under social conditions long since supplanted, is renewed in the language, images, and concepts familiar to those who must now comprehend it. To be sure, a one-hundred-percent guarantee that the meaning is correctly devined, completely understood and accurately translated can never be achieved because the text always passes through the medium of the translator before it meets the eye of the reader. The presupposition and goal of translation is the comprehension of the text. With such a complicated book as the Bible, no translation can be a once and for all occurrence. Translation and comprehension remain ongoing tasks.

Luther sought Christ in the Bible. From this Christocentrism he interpreted the whole Bible. The Christocentricity of the Scriptures, the meaning of the Christ event, Luther found disclosed in the Pauline epistles. Luther's theological accomplishment was to preserve a unified biblical Christocentric point of view, the foundation for his Bible translation and the posture that made possible the specific quality of his translation; for Luther's theological center lends to the material a spiritual sovereignty without which even the most solid philological knowledge is not able to attain the goal. To regard Luther's Bible translation merely or primarily as a linguistic achievement is to misunderstand it. It was an historical achievement in comprehension, an intellectual and spiritual coup which embraced the linguistic achievement but which was not exhausted by it.

Luther could give himself unfettered to his German language translation of the Bible because he was certain of his view based on the centrality of the biblical message, and had long since become convinced that this message could be heard only in the vocabulary of the hearer so that faith could work in the heart. The principles of *sola fide, fides ex auditu,* and *verbo solo* — faith alone, faith from hearing, and by the word alone—provided inner freedom for his singular use of the language. It was precisely because of his inner freedom that Luther's linguistic achievement had such a long term impact.

It was also to his advantage that Luther's German was that of the Saxon-Thuringian region, which had been settled by various German tribes, especially the Saxons, Thuringians, Franks, and Hessians. Thus in this region a form of German developed which incorporated common features from various linguistic areas. The fact that the linguistic border between north and south Germany ran through the Wittenberg area and that immigrants from Flanders had earlier settled in the Wittenberg region also played a role. Although to be sure it was not spoken outside the Saxon-Thuringian region, the German that had developed there was more readily understood outside

its own domain than was, for example, Alemannic outside of Swabia or
Low German outside of north Germany. In addition, the German in the
Meissen chancellery had taken on a literary form that was considered wor-
thy of imitation at many princely courts and in the urban scribal centers.

Luther was not a "creator of language," as is often heard; he did not invent any new language. For centuries the Germans had been speaking
their dialects; what else could they have spoken? Luther was indeed a master of his language, and he did not permit the imposition of restraints by
Latin grammar. The Luther Bible in the succeeding centuries became the
most widely read book in the German language. As a result, it has become
a model and a norm for the German literary language. The Luther Bible
contributed to the cultural independence and uniqueness of Germany and
the Germans.

The fact that the pre-Luther Bible translations had no widespread appeal
was not exclusively due to their inferior linguistic quality or to the limitations imposed by regional and dialectical provinciality. They had missed the
mark because the time was not ripe; society had made no great demand for
the Bible in the German language as it did in the early days of the Reformation. The need for a Bible in German had not necessarily been obvious.
The demand grew out of the social crisis which the Reformation provoked.
Popular attention had focused on the message proclaimed in the Bible, and
the message had become a point of conflict between classes, ranks, levels,
factions, and other groups, thereby inciting a popular demand for the Bible. Turning to the Bible indicated that the class struggle was growing
more acute and demanded a decisive solution of the major problems, and
called attention to the fact that all other sources of information pertaining
to social ills had failed and led to a dead end.

The dead end of thought and action was demonstrated at the turn of the
fifteenth century in many ways. The rebellions and attempted rebellions of
this period could not bring any long-term solutions because, among other
things, they were continuously confined to demanding the abolition of
those annoyances which, at the moment, were considered intolerable, and
which affected the daily life of the common man, such as new taxes, sur-
charges on beer and wine, increases in prices, suspected but not always
substantiated deceptive intrigues in the halls of urban government, increased feudal dues, and ecclesiastical mismanagement. The rebellions
lacked a unifying idea that could provide all individual demands with a
common denominator. The leaders of the rebellions were the spokesmen
of the moment for the discontented masses, rather than ideologues with
powers of motivation for future-oriented action in the interest of society.

As long as the masses, classes, ranks, and various groups attributed their
respective miserable positions to coincidence—derived in part from the
hard-heartedness, cunning, and knavery of those who were the superiors,

masters, landlords, commanders, employers, and lords—and as long as the protests were directed against these coincidences, an opposition pressing for change remained for the most part rigidly grounded in the foundation of the old society and in the pre-ideological stadium of a social movement. However, as soon as such a movement and its leaders instead attempted to view these miserable conditions as the results of an overriding principle applicable to the entire society if not to the whole world, the movement entered the stadium of ideology, thereby gaining motivation to transcend social barriers and developing a potential for binding together alienated classes. The reform movement of any one class or rank thus becomes not only a concern of society as a whole but also, to a certain extent, a social goal.

These relationships, which presently interest us mainly as indicators of the rising need for a German Bible, will be easier to understand through peasant interpretations of the social situation. Under the influence of an increasing goods-money connection, growing dependence on the market, the effects of early capitalism, and the accompanying social differentiation, an increasing number of peasants complained about growing pressure from the lords, mounting fees, higher taxes, and new burdens imposed by feudal obligations. These peasants were undergoing a basis historical experience; they were worse off than their parents and grandparents had been or at least worse off than they themselves had been earlier. They expressed their discontent by public complaints, and, by court proceedings against their respective lords, they defended themselves against what, in their opinion, was unjust. They accused the lords of illegal action and demanded a return to the "good old law." Occurrences of this nature, which are characteristic of the entire feudal period, had multiplied since the last decade of the fifteenth century. These disputes demonstrated that the latent friction between feudal lords and dependent peasants had become more acute. One significant cause of this increased friction was the fact that the feudal lords themselves were caught up in the wake of capitalistic development, had fallen into financial difficulties, and therefore had become more demanding of the peasants. Peasant appeal to law may have succeeded in some individual cases, but isolated successes did not significantly alter the miserable position of the peasants as a class.

Nor did isolated appeals to law significantly alter the position of any other class, rank, or group. In the solution of individual cases nothing was achieved for the improvement of the general lot. But as the idea that more than the individual case must be addressed and that something must be done in the general interest prevailed and found support, the term "common good" became more frequently a basis for argument in publications of the most various kinds, especially in those in which reform plans were discussed. The level of consciousness was raised by these learning experiences. Ever more frequently, experience illustrated that the problem was not caused by the evil of individual lords or by their corrupted morality and ethics, that life offered more than enough reason to complain.

When immorality of the ruling class failed as an explanation of misery, analysts were obliged to look for other explanations. Only the historical process would demonstrate whether this quest promoted more convincing reasons than the discarded ones or simply provided supplemental arguments and new blind alleys. In the Bundschuh conspiracy at the end of the fifteenth and beginning of the sixteenth century, an idea arose elevating the peasant interpretation of the social situation to a new and higher plateau: the demand for "divine law." This demand proposed in essence that a return to the "good old law" was not sufficient, that the life of man must be essentially oriented to the will of God. Hence the situation which was considered to be generally miserable was no longer explained by the coincidences of day to day life but rather by a universal transcendent principle. When reasoning had finally arrived at this plateau, it was not far to the question, Where, when, and how could this divine will be recognized?

Since the Church, with its extensive land holdings, ruled over many peasants as feudal lord and exploiter, and since, for various aforementioned reasons it was plagued by evil abuses and increasing criticism, trust waned in its ability to declare the will of God. As trust waned, the need increased for answers to these vital questions from sources other than the ecclesiastical hierarchy. Thus the knowledge of the Bible became a necessity for those who sought remedies; not just for those who knew Latin, but, to an increasing degree, for those who knew only German.

Eventhough Luther moved primarily in academic circles, concerned himself with the problems formulated in those circles, and added his own, with the translation of the Bible into German, as Friedrich Engels expressed it, Luther placed "a mighty tool in the hand of the plebeian movement" (Marx-Engels Werke, VII 350). The Bible translation was rooted in social interconnections of exceptional intellectual and spiritual intensity. In the same years as those during which social theory regarding oppositional and revolutionary forces began to question "divine right," and was elevated above the bare moral and juridical critique of the existing circumstances, Luther also began, of course because of his profession, to wrestle with the question of God's righteousness. Luther demonstrated that God's rightousness had nothing to do with earthly justice, discarded morality as a criterium for the determination or the understanding of the righteousness of God, and opened with the *sola fide* principle the way to a new interpretation of man's position before God. What most clearly seemed to be the exclusively personal problem of Martin Luther, as such played out only within his breast, was clearly manifested as an element and specific example of a general development.

In scholarly disputes Luther forced the Bible as the rule of authority upon his opponents. Whoever challenged Luther and wanted to be taken seriously was obliged to use arguments based on the Bible. Appeals to conciliar decisions, papal decrees, the great names of the scholastics, even the Church fathers were no longer valid and had argumentive worth only insofar as they were harmonious with the Bible. This biblicism was an expression of a deep-seated crisis of authority. Whatever did not come from the Bible was suspiciously viewed as a human statute and as such not binding on the conscience. At the same time, biblicism was an intellectual anchor in the crisis. But then, if only the Bible was valid, could it be interpreted and who could interpret it correctly? In the history of the Church, bitter battles had been fought over this question, and past authorities, no longer recognized, derived credibility from their answers to this question. Thus the return to the Bible meant that the intellectual struggle whose historical resolution had been discarded must be repeated and once again resolved. The *re-bellare*, the repetition of the battle (of all against all), gives its name to a salient characteristic of revolution: rebellion.

Seen from the perspective of the reform movement, there was no desire for something new at the beginning of the Reformation, but rather the demand for something old and long since disappeared. This demand markedly corresponds to the demands for the "good old law" noted in the peasant movements. It appears indeed to be a fundamental rule of the early phases of revolutionary movements or of early revolutions in general that they seek their ideals primarily in the past. With varying intensity and varied attitudes, specific reference to the past may be observed all the way up to and including the French Revolution of 1789. Furthermore, reference to the past was a contributing factor to the phenomenon that, for approximately three centuries, reformations in the guise of revolutionary movements and revolutions played a great role as the burgher capitalistic society emerged from feudalism through the revolutionary upheavals of the transitional period between the Middle Ages and modern times.

A cycle of reformations began with Hussitism at the beginning of the fifteenth century. The cycle persisted in sixteenth century Germany, where, as a result of a more advanced and, for the first time, widespread genesis of conditions felicitous to capitalism, the cycle took on a new quality of an immature middle-class revolution.

In the wake of the internationalization and differentiation of the Reformation emanating from Germany, the middle-class character of the Reformation was strengthened in Switzerland, the Netherlands, and England. Linked to the war of independence against Spain, the Reformation took on a new revolutionary character in the Low Countries; here the early middle-class revolution was victorious, and there arose inside feudal Europe a middle-class republic.

In the English revolution the ideological function of the Reformation finally exhausted itself, because the middle class and capitalism had reached a higher level of maturity. Thus the Reformation cycle in a certain sense made way for the middle class revolutionary cycle.

In this phase of world history, the progressive part of humanity, with Bible in hand, sought new horizons. Wars of independence and revolutionary uprisings became religious wars. Social movements, as Friedrich Engels expressed it, carried "religious shibboleths" (Marx-Engels Werke VII 343). Consequently, the success of the social movements was the "success of their religious guise" (Marx-Engels Werke XXXIX 483).

In Germany and elsewhere, during the first third of the sixteenth century, biblicism was the expression for that intellectual rebellion which the Reformation and early middle-class revolution had introduced. In Germany biblicism had prepared and intensified this revolution and had contributed to its radicalization; on the other hand, the radicalization of the Reformation drove biblicism to its own singular destiny. Radical Reformation and biblicism went hand in hand. Biblicism did not remain confined to scholarly circles; it penetrated to the people and was given by the populace the powerful impulses that moved the common man.

Luther's opponents took note of the popularity of his Bible translation with increasing bitterness. One of Luther's opponents, Cochläus, with whom Luther in Worms had earlier come into conflict, commented on the effect of Luther's German New Testament with complete contempt. Luther's New Testament, Cochläus contended, was

> so widely distributed by the printers and published in such large numbers that the tailor as well as the shoemaker, even women and other simple people, could take in much of this new Lutheran gospel although they knew only what little German they had learned from reading letters on gingerbread; the people read this Luther New Testament as the spring of all truth and with the greatest desire. Thus within months they acquired so much skill and experience that they were bold enough to dispute about faith and gospel not only with the average lay Catholic but also with priests and monks, indeed with masters and doctors of Holy Scripture …. Thus the Lutheran layman came to the place where he, in meetings and conversation, effortlessly cited more scripture than even Catholic monks and priests. (Cochläus 120 ff)

The impact of the Luther Bible came about mainly because it appeared precisely at the time when the reform movement was rapidly speading to all territories and was becoming socially diversified and radicalized in its demands. The expansion of the movement was a steady process in the development of the Reformation. Its nature was to integrate in increasing numbers new ranks and classes and to unite their respective demands, hopes, and desires in the cause of the Reformation.

The Edict of Worms in its own way helped to accelerate the process. By increasing the risk for those disseminating Luther's writings, doctrines, and ideas, the edict assisted in separating the chaff from the wheat and called attention to the strife even in those places where up to that time the dispute hardly had been noticed. Decisive to the success of the movement, however, was that the cities, especially the imperial cities, adopted the Reformation. Despite the many differences between the cities there was a fundamental common practice that the Church and clergy did not belong to the burgher legal councils which were in charge of privileges and special rights. The Church and clergy were juridically not fully integrated into the city; in brief they constituted their own separate and special status. It was precisely this special status which Luther had placed in question with his doctrine of the priesthood of all believers. Even if his other views did not find unanimous support in all points among the burghers, his doctrine concerning the priesthood of all believers was sufficient to awaken the sympathetic attention of the burghers and to gain a tolerant reception for Lutheran preachers. The step-by-step progress of the Reformation, proceeding in regular cadence in the cities, is evident in the appearance of Lutheran pamphlets, tolerance for Lutheran sermons, distribution of communion in both kinds, the use of the German language in the liturgy of the Mass, strife concerning the appointments to preaching posts, disregard for episcopal commands and prohibitions, deliberations concerning the use of ecclesiastical and monastic income for the communal needs, issue of new directives for a community chest, a new liturgy, and confiscation of Church and monastic property, accompanied or followed by court cases and disputes with the respective presiding abbot or bishop. These reforms corresponded to the interests of the broadest circle of the urban populations, wherein no great difference existed between the concerns of the traditional commercial and guild burghers and those of the middle and smaller business entrepreneurs.

The major question in the urban reform movement was who should sanction liturgical innovations and regulate ecclesiastical income and property. As long as it was only a matter of the dissemination of Lutheran doctrine by word of mouth or by the distribution of pamphlets—thus by preaching or by selling literature—the matter was rather uncomplicated. Of course, every dissemination of Lutheran ideas was a violation of the Edict of Worms, but since the execution of the edict lay in the hands of the imperial estates and there was no imperial executive who supervised compliance, the respective responsible authorities did not take enforcement of the edict too seriously. To ignore the edict was simple for the imperial cities, since they recognized the emperor only as their titular sovereign and in their internal affairs managed matters as they pleased. It was more complicated for those cities integrated into princely territories and subjected to a territorial lord. These cities were obliged to consider to what degree their lord was committed to execute the Edict of Worms.

However, as soon as the reform movement was no longer confined to sermons but had arrived at altering the liturgy itself, a critical point had been reached that demanded increased attention and the intervention of the authorities, because administering the Eucharist in both kinds was only a step away from removing images from the churches, and then another step away from seizing ecclesiastical wealth, collections, and other revenues. At this point the authorities charged with keeping order were challenged, and they were obliged to decide whether they would permit the preachers and evangelists of the new faith to preempt to role of the urban councils or whether the councils themselves would see to order in the Church. This question became acute as, finally, the defenders of the old faith took a decisive stand, matters took a violent turn, and the use of force was threatened. But every appeal to force confronted authorities with the problem of violating the public peace and with the decision of whether or not they should invoke the laws available to them. This decision rested much more heavily than did the question of spiritual disobedience to ecclesiastical hierarchy on the basic question of all social structure: the question of authority and power. The use of force by reform enthusiasts or by the congregations under their influence challenged the monopoly on using force, which in the cities was held traditionally by the urban councils and which in the territories was retained within the rights and duties of the territorial lords. As soon as the Reformation no longer confined itself to preaching and writing but, instead, proceeded to implement changes, a power struggle developed. Under these circumstances, the use of force and the relationship of the reform movement to the authorities became a basic question on which the future fate of the Reformation was decided.

Luther was obliged to ask himself these questions. In principle he had answered them already in his writings from the Wartburg: in mundane matters obedience is owed to the civil authority, but not in questions which concern the salvation of the soul, and the antichrist should be overcome by the Word alone, not by the fist; Christians should avoid riot and rebellion. However, as the reform movement developed further, it repeatedly raised the question concerning the use of force and its relationship to the civil authority under changing conditions. The answer once given demanded new variations and accommodations to the situation. Could Luther expand and vary his answer without contradicting himself?

Since his return from the Wartburg, Luther stood intellectually and by the logic of the situation between two fires; he did not want to surrender what, up to that moment, he had taught, and, in the interest of preserving his identity, he did not dare surrender it; but, at the same time, he was confronted on every side with requests and suggestions which could not be addressed by a simple repetition of what he had already said. Because of the course of events and of his own activities, Luther's role had evolved into that of spiritual and intellectual leader of the Reformation, a leader from whom was expected not only answers to questions relating to faith but also directives and decisions with respect to very practical, political, legal, and administrative questions for which he did not always have the knowledge and experience necessary to provide answers. In such situations he could to some degree perform successfully when he reconsidered these questions from a theological point of view and thus transferred them to a frame of reference in which he was competent and could, in good conscience, give an answer. Although until 1520 or 1521 it had been primarily the attacks of his opponents that had seemed to drive Luther from one position to another as it became necessary more precisely to define his opinions, now problems originated in increasing measure from the ranks of his own followers. In the continuing struggle against Rome, obedience to the ecclesiastical hierarchy was disintegrating under the influence of Luther; but now he must demonstrate to what extent by his influence and discernment he could replace the old with the new.

In his quest for guidelines as to what the new should consist of, he could draw from only three sources: the spontaneous action of the masses, the Bible, and his own imagination. Nevertheless, in every case the solution had to be brought into correspondence with the theological fundamentals of his doctrine: that is, the solution must be biblically based. If Luther had depended on the spontaneity of the masses, he would have been obliged to fall into a rearguard position and relinquish his leadership role. Earlier at the Wartburg such a possibility had caused him no little apprehension. If Luther should look only to the Bible without regard to real life, he could instruct the conscience, to be sure, but he would not be able to address practical questions. If he gave himself to his own imagination, his path might well lead into a sectarian alienation from the world.

In his Lenten sermons, Luther attempted to justify spontaneity and channel it. He praised spontaneity, though not the spontaneity of the masses or of Everyman, but rather the spontaneity of God's Word, which would take its course despite all opposition. But since the Divine Word always and only could be realized in and through people, the application ultimately led to practical results in that the new spontaneity followed upon persistent and thorough preaching of the Word.

The permanent results of the Wittenberg movement were achieved by the initiative of the community. The community, as the basis of mass activity, placed the Reformation action groups in decisive situations: the community placed the city councils under pressure but at the same time offered community support to the councils against imperial officials.

Luther provided the rationale for the community's role. According to

Luther, the community had the right to judge doctrine, elect pastors, and appoint and dismiss teachers. With these privileges Luther had established as a principle of the Reformation the right of the community to make decisions. The political significance of this right consists in the act of placing community privilege above the hereditary and charter rights of the bishops and cathedral chapters, wresting from them the prerogative of ecclesiastical appointments, and thereby putting an end to both the discipline imposed on the lower clergy committed to the Reformation and the lower clergy's social dependence on the hierarchy.

This Christian community was not necessarily identical with the legally constituted burgher community; the two corresponded only partially in membership. The right to participate in civic affairs in the burgher community was reserved to those who were legally recognized as citizens of that community. In principle, in the Christian congregation everyone had a voice. This privilege developed out of the doctrine of the priesthood of all believers, and created for noncitizen classes the right and possibility to speak and act in the Christian congregation. With this privilege the middle-class Reformation was opened downward and leftward to the people. Thus the community principle formed the center of the Reformation movement. Depending on which social forces would come to the force, the movement could slide to the right and be at the service of the authorities, or it could come into very sharp conflict with them.

The community set the platform for the exchange of opinions and for the testing of arguments. The community legitimized action in advance or after the fact. It was the proving ground for the validity of the authority of the preachers, leaders, and spokesmen in their respective roles in the urban debates and later among the rebelling peasants. In the community there existed a natural democracy, nourished by communal traditions, actualized by the political struggle. The community was the primary organization and organ of the masses. That the community understood itself as a Christian community derived from the religious presuppositions of the day, from the religious nature of the Reformation, and, not insignificantly, from the sociological function of the Church as the union of all baptized Christians, regardless of their worldly position. The Christian congregation was at that time a manifestation of what later revolutions would elevate to the principle of popular sovereignty.

Luther had not invented the congregational principle. It simply appeared spontaneously with the progress of the Reformation wherever this progress met with resistance from traditional authority. Luther's acceptance and affirmation of the congregational principle shows the reformer at that juncture at which he was closest to the onward and upward course of the early middle-class revolution, and where he was most receptive to the impulses from the popular movement.

Luther's initiative in establishing the congregational principle was inspired by discussions in Leisnig, a small city on the Freiberg Mulde River in Saxony. These discussions had developed in the fall of 1522 and continued throughout the entire year of 1523. The abbot of the Cistercian monastery at Buch held administrative authority over the parish church of Leisnig; therefore, he could determine who would serve in the church as pastor. The abbot resisted Lutheran preaching and liturgical innovations. Therefore, the Leisnig congregation decided, on its own initiative, to call Lutheran pastors, disregard the patronal rights of the abbot, and compensate the preachers, according to the judgment of the congregation, from ecclesiastical income at the congregation's disposal. In so doing the Leisnig community laid hold of ecclesiastical property. In undertaking these measures, the community appealed to Luther for advice and, finally borrowing from the Wittenberg example, worked out its own financial arrangement.

The Leisnig financial arrangement established that all incomes from parish receipts, altar fees and sodalities, taxes, bridge tolls, cash on hand, provisions and movable goods of the parish together with all deeds pertaining to such were to be placed in the congregational treasury or community chest. Similar regulations were adopted in regard to the artisan guilds. The wealth of the community chest was to be used to compensate pastors, chaplains, sacristans, and teachers, to care for orphans, the ill, the elderly, and the poor, and to provide loans for the needy. It also was to contain a surplus for future emergencies and sufficient funds to provide upkeep of public buldings, churches, parsonages, schools, sacristies, and hospitals. Begging was forbidden. In case the funds proved to be inadequate to accommodate all these needs, the landlords were to be subjected to an annual assessment. The community elected ten elders, who administered the community chest and submitted an annual financial report.

Luther published the Leisnig regulation and introduced it with his own preface. He praised its achievements and generalized it: the public authorities should take over the monasteries and help former monks find sustaining employment in the secular world; for the rest of their lives, provision should be made for elderly monks and nuns who could not survice outside the cloisters; no more novices should be admitted, and the monasteries should be phased out gradually. It would be best to place the wealth of the cloisters in a community chest in order to care for the poor from these resources.

This was secularization and social program of the moderate burghers of the middle class. The paternity of the Wittenberg regulation is unmistakable. The regulation expropriates exclusively ecclesiastical property, of course for the benefit of the community. Thus a line of demarcation was drawn between secular and ecclesiastical feudalism outlining the extent of the assault on ecclesiastical feudalism. This assault was tolerated by the princes. Hence the middle-class moderate revolution reached its goal of destroying ecclesiastical feudalism. Beyond this borderline began the leftist action against secular feudalism. Insofar as the Left exceeded what was possible, we can consider the Lutheran movement as the Center of the middle-class revolution. In part influenced by the Wittenberg and Leisnig example bult also in part independently, a whole series of cities mandated community chests and regulations dealing with poverty: in 1522, Nuremberg; in 1523, Strassburg, Regensburg, Breslau, Augsburg, Constance, Ulm, Nordlingen, Esslingen, Schwabach, and Bremen. By these mandates, the reform movement in the cities surged ahead, accompanied by unrest, tumult, and confrontation. The year 1522 was the high point of such unrest. For the year 1521, riot and rebellion were documented in sixteen cities; in 1522, it occurred in fifty-two cities; in 1523, in forty-four cities; and in 1524, in forty cities. In 1525, the year of the Peasants' Revolt, fifty-one cities were shaken by riot and rebellion.

For the urban upper classes and their organ of authority, the city council, the problem was retaining control of civic affairs and of making the reform movement serve these classes. Precedence assisted the upper urban classes in retaining authority through patronage and investiture rights pertaining to those churches situated in territories subject to urban administration. The income and property of city churches were derived to a great degree from gifts and endowments by citizens on behalf of the dead. The church was obligated on the basis of these bequests to read Masses for the souls of the deceased burghers. The urban councils claimed for themselves the right to be the testators of their deceased fellow citizens. Supported by the position of testator, the urban council even in the pre-Reformation period had assumed control functions vis-à-vis the church. Just as in earlier centuries the noble "proprietors" of churches controlled by noble families or the territorial lords had exercised their rights, in accordance with imperial law, to be patrons and protectors, so the cities, primarily the imperial cities, had certain rights in the affairs of the Church. As for the administration of the income and property of the Church, the Reformation did not introduce anything essentially new; however, it provided an acceptable rationale by which these established rights could be exclusively and rigorously exercised.

Through the liturgy the Reformation introduced a new element into the city-church relationships by emphasizing the inner order of the Church. Councils and urban congregations, now adopting Luther's congregational principle and wherever possible extending it, assumed full responsibility for the order of worship, the installation and dismissal of the pastor, and the regulation of his compensation, as well as deciding whether or not his views were in harmony with the gospel. This meant nor more, no less than that the imperial city authorities—in fact, city authorities in general—

assumed for themselves the rights once reserved for the bishops, the theological faculties, and the pope. This assumption of ecclesiastical authority by urban leaders also provided opportunity, without great internal disturbances, to direct the reform movement from above.

While Luther was decidedly receptive to these movements in the cities, providing them with the congregational principle and, in his preface to the Leisnig community chest regulation, with important guidelines, he assumed a negative, reserved, and alien attitude toward the attempts of Franz von Sickingen to unleash a "war against priests" by his military assault on the archbishop of Trier, Richard von Greiffenklau. Sickingen and other knights, as early as 1520, had informed Luther of their common cause with him and of their willingness to provide him protection. This offer of protection had emboldened Luther in his pamphlet *Address to the Christian Nobility of the German Nation*; nevertheless, Luther recognized their offer only with friendly and grateful words. That was where the matter remained. It was not only his rejection of violent action, on the basis of principle, that determined Luther's attitude in this question, but also his class instinct of the intelligentsia, comprised of the upper middle classes and the territorial prince. The imperial knights whom von Sickingen sought to assemble about him were, from the point of view of the middle-class moderates, unlikely recruits for the causes of the Reformation, for, on the basis of long experience, the urban middle class found them highly suspect. It was, after all, the knights who, with their warlike activities, disturbed the peace and, with their robber-band assaults on traveling merchants, made the highways unsafe.

At the beginning of September 1522, Sickingen opened his campaign against the archbishop of Trier. However, the knight was in for a bitter surprise. Trier did not surrender. The anticipated support from the bands of knights did not materialize, and after one week Sickingen was forced to break off his siege with nothing accomplished. He retreated to his castle fortress in Landstuhl where he in turn was besieged and killed. The Schwabian League, alliance of southwest German territorial forces and urban militia with a combined army of 1,300 infantrymen and 1,500 cavalrymen, overran Sickingen's supporters in June and July of 1523 and razed thirty-two castles belonging to the defeated knights. The "war against the priests" had collapsed. Luther had wisely avoided association with these events. His conduct must be considered sagacious because the anti-Reformation forces would have loved to use this situation—simultaneously with the suppression of the "war against the priests"—to deal the reform movement a blow.

Indications for such a plan are not lacking. The war against Sickingen came at the same time, if not by the same cause, as the new mandates against the dissemination of the Reformation. Duke George the Bearded of

Albertine Saxony forbade, in November 1522, the purchase and sale of the Luther Bible in his territories, and the imperial administration in Nuremberg, in March 1523, issued an edict against all ecclesiastical innovations and the dissemination of Luther's writings.

The most important objective was to secure the welfare of the Ernestine princes under whom Luther served, because each in turn was disturbed about the obvious relationship of the Lutheran movement with popular unrest. To be sure, the Ernestine princes had protected Luther: they did not enforce the Edict of Worms; they permitted the gospel free course. However, it was for these very reasons that they saw themselves confronted with difficulties in the imperial government. Their Albertine cousin, Duke George, assailed them with accusations that they did not fulfill their princely duties and that they tolerated a troublemaker in their dukedom. Luther instructed them that it was not the gospel that caused unrest; on the contrary, the enemies of the gospel were responsible if popular unrest increased. The princes needed to be reassured that the reform movement would be directed not against the secular authorities but exclusively against the evil circumstances in the Church. At the same time, the princes needed to be able to act with a clear conscience when they resisted the imperial directives and refused to suppress the Lutheran movement by force.

Theologically translated, the question was to what extent Jesus' Sermon on the Mount had validity and whether it implied that a Christian under no circumstances could appeal to the sword. If the Sermon on the Mount is interpreted literally and is understood as binding on Christians under all circumstances, even in secular matters, the result is an unconditional obedience vis-à-vis every authority, the ideology of a flock of sheep which passively permits itself to be led to slaughter, as the command, "Whoever demands your coat, give him your cloak also" would seem to indicate. In the history of the Church this problem was solved by ascribing the obligation to fulfill the Sermon on the Mount only to those "evangelical circles" of sanctified Christians, but such a prescription could not be applied to the less sanctified. Thus Christendom could free itself from the position of sacrificial lamb, but the Word of Jesus lost thereby its dignity as irrefutable certainty. The dilemma was perceived as especially sensitive when the Bible alone was regarded as authoritative and the basis for all argument, especially since Luther himself had rejected all distinctions between commands and admonitions as untenable.

Resistance to antireform commands, prohibitions, and measures of the most varied kind was essential and unavoidable. But how could such resistance be justified without violating the Sermon on the Mount? Luther preached on this theme several times in October 1522 at the Weimar court. He summarized his conclusions in the pamphlet *Concerning Secular Authority and How Far One is Obligated to Obey It.* It is not surprising to find here fundamental ideas already enunciated in *On the Freedom of a Christian,* according to which obedience to the secular authority could be required except in matters of consience. In *Concerning Secular Authority* Luther summarized and reformulated views at which he had long ago arrived.

In one connection, however, he now offered a major new concept and development. By distinguishing two divine realms, he solved the dilemma of the Sermon on the Mount and the hard realities of life in which the Christian must sustain himself despite the Sermon on the Mount. Two realms had been ordained by God: "one which makes man righteous before God; the other, the outward, which provides for peace and prevents evil deeds. Both are necessary because without Christ's spiritual rule no one can become just before God; one cannot become just by secular rules. Thus Christ's rule is not over all people, for Christians are always in the minority and always in the midst of non-Christians" (WA XI 252).

The distinction between the two realms is analogous to the distinction between the visible and the invisible Church without, however, being completely parallel. This analogy has its historical precedent in the thought of St. Augustine, who distinguished the city of God from the city of earth. Biblical support is found in the words of Jesus: "My kingdom is not of this world." This support notwithstanding, Luther's concept represents his own unique achievement: the political theory of his Reformation. In Luther's theory of Reformation, the Sermon on the Mount has as much effect on secular life as, in pre-Reformation theory, admonitions have on commands; moreover, Luther's concept escapes the pre-Reformation distinction of admonitions and commands without its weaknesses. Luther's view permits politics to be political and rational while insisting on the validity of God's Word for the conscience. Luther's two-realm theory erects a spiritual dam against that which would transform Christendom into Islam, interpreting the gospel in a fleshly manner, and making the gospel into law. Luther's theory became more and more the basis for the dispute with all those who wanted to achieve more with the Reformation than the liberation of conscience and improvement in ecclesiastical affairs.

Luther certainly was not incontrovertibly opposed to pursuing goals and ambitions, but he firmly rejected every idea that such activity was necessarily derived from the preaching of the gospel. The two-realm theory served as a weapon against the enemies of the Reformation and still more significantly as a barrier against the radicalization of the Reformation that threatened to destroy not only ecclesiastical feudalism but also secular feudalism. Under the prevailing circumstances of 1522 and 1523, the two-realm theory directed its barbs against thos princes and secular authorities who stood in the way of reformation and especially against those who were prohibiting the distribution of the Luther Bible. Luther treatened them:

For there are very few princes who are not regarded as fools or knaves.

So they are, and they demonstrate this truth, so that the common man catches on and recognizes that the princes (who hold God in contempt) are a plague to the masses and to the common man. Furthermore, the common man is concerned that he will be defenseless unless the princes act like princes and again rule with reason and sobriety. We will not, we cannot suffer your tyranny and arrogance any longer. Dear princes and lords, you had better improve. The world is no longer as it used to be when you could hunt and drive the people like beasts. Therefore, abandon your vanity and arrogance, and take care to act correctly and to permit God's Word to have free course, which it will have, must have, and should have, and from which it cannot be restrained. Is heresy abroad? It will be overcome by the Word of God. But if you insist on wielding the sword, look out that one does not come and demand, and not in God's name, that you put up the sword. (WA XI 270)

Chapter 11

With Word and Faith
Against the Rebellious Spirit
"There Must of Necessity Be Sects and Factions ...
But Avoid Violence"
March 1523–August 1524

To obey or not to obey ...

Luther realized that merely preaching and making allowance for the weaker members, in the congregation could not go on forever. Was obedience required in this case? Was obedience required in that case? Just at the time that Luther concluded his writing concerning secular authority and to what degree it must be obeyed, his impatience with the slow development of the Reformation grew. For years he had written, preached, argued, and disputed, and still not even in Wittenberg had he been able to accomplish all that he desired. The canons of All Saints Chapter House resisted him, continued to celebrate Masses, and bristled against the administration of communion in both kinds. The frustrating part of this matter was that All Saints was able to retain the support of the elector. The Roman Mass at All Saints was a clear sign that Luther's influence on the elector was rather limited. The elector tolerated and protected not only him but also the old Catholic believers. With respect to the chapter, Luther saw himself in a fatal situation; every attempt to alter practices there was a disguised struggle with the elector himself. Those who were au courant sensed this. Luther's complaint to Spalatin that the idolatrous practices at All Saints Chapter must be abolished and that no more regard could be had for the weak in faith had little impact. At the beginning of March 1523, Luther threatened the canons that he no longer would consider them Christians if they did not finally give up the Roman Mass and begin to administer communion in both kinds. He threatened in vain; on this point he accomplished nothing.

The now ill elector, who more frequently than ever before retreated to his castle on Lochau Moor, gave no indication that he would comply with all the requests that Luther directed to him through Spalatin. Only a few of these requests personally affected Luther; in most cases they were requests made by strangers who lavished flattery on the reformer while dinning in his ear, not granting him any rest until he wrote a letter to the elector or supported their supplication with a line or at least referred to their petition. A young Bohemian noble sought a position in Electoral Saxony. Luther was requested to plead his cause although Luther promised the petitioner no results. A young girl from Torgau complained about a barber who had promised to marry her but had jilted her. She requested Luther to appeal to the barber's conscience and also to persuade the elector to help her get her man. An old priest, Frederick, requested a benefice; a young priest, Erasmus, wanted a small parish; debtors pleaded for respite. Furthermore, there were always the academic promotions. But what is an academic promotion banquet without wild game? Thus Luther would write to Spalatin presenting the requests and Spalatin would select the opportune moment to present the requests at the next electoral audience. Not for himself personally, yet for his own cause, Luther was obliged to make requests for his monastery. Luther received no salary as did his young friend Melanchthon. Luther's professorship was still listed in the name of the Augustinian order although the order hardly existed any longer in Saxony. Without a regular salary, Luther's livelihood was derived entirely from the monastery and the occasional gifts that the city and other benefactors bestowed on him. But the monastic income was indeed modest and irregular. Everywhere the discussion prevailed as to whether or not the Bible justified the paying of interest and the tithe to ecclesiastical institutions. But it was not yet the peasants who caused difficulty in this matter, at least not in the environs of Wittenberg. Here it was a noble, Günther von Staupitz, who refused to pay.

The Augustinian monastery in Wittenberg derived its income from the village Dabrun, and the monastery had leased lands in and around the village to Günther von Staupitz. However, the lease rent had not been paid for months and the monastery fell into debt. The monastery, which formerly had been a sanctuary and retreat that provided Luther a modest degree of economic security, now became an increasing burden. It was almost empty. Apart from Luther and the old prior, Briesger, there were only a few of the former brothers remaining in the monastery; consequently, Luther himself was obliged to assume the vexing financial affairs. His advice, on the occasion of the publication of the Leisnig community chest regulation, that the civic authority take over the monasteries, was no idea born out of speculation; on the contrary, Luther's own experience had suggested this recommendation in the hope that, as a result, fiscal management would be improved.

In February 1523, Luther offered the elector the monastery's renunciation of its Dabrun income to the benefit of the elector. However, the elector did not accept Luther's suggestion; he ordered rather that Günther von Staupitz pay his rent. Nevertheless, the rent remained unpaid. In October 1523 Luther suggested again to Spalatin that the elector should indeed assume the financial management of the monastery—to no avail.

Thus the intervention of the civic authorities in promoting the development of the Reformation became for Luther himself a problem of daily life; behind the questions of dogma and conscience churned the questions of money, sustenance, and stomach. Luther could not live from his writings. They had made him famous, had filled the cash drawers of printers and itinerant book merchants, but had left his own pockets empty because he received no royalties. The sixteenth century had not discovered that money could be earned by writing. It was also considered not quite proper to demand lecture fees from students because the professors had either their fixed salary or, as a general rule, one or more benefices from which they drew income and which they received as compensation for presenting lectures. Thus the university intelligentsia still lived very much under feudal conditions. From a social point of view, their position was distinguished very little from that of a noble's feudal tenant.

This position was secure and sufficient when the incomes flowed in at a steady pace; regularity, of course, presupposed that the peasant rents from which this feudal-bound intelligentsia lived remained constant. But as the rents were geared to a fluctuating production level, the income of benefice holders also became insecure. This insecurity mounted as the economic goods-money equation prevailed. Under these conditions, the intelligentsia inevitably wanted the authorities to intervene to establish and preserve regular incomes, which could be guaranteed only by territorial authority. A guarantee presupposed that this territorial authority itself would develop a regular financial structure and thereby would take a step beyond purely feudal lordship and administration practices. From benefice holders to salaried officials—that was the perspective which the territorial states offered to the intelligentsia, a perspective which, to be sure, was just evolving, a concept on which the territorial state itself must have stumbled in the sixteenth century, although precedent had been set by the example of a few "salaried" officials in the fifteenth century. The Reformation offered favorable opportunity for this economic development. The intelligentsia took advantage of the economic transition from benefice to salaried position, whereby, we can confidently assume, the Reformers also extended their appeal not only to brain and conscience but also to stomach and reason.

Benefices were a feudal form of payment, a guarantee of a secure social position for receivers of income. The office holder, be he professor, church acolyte, or princely counselor, received no regular monthly salary for his services, which were more or less precisely specified. On the contrary, several farms in a village or in several villages, together with an entire village or villages, were allotted to him and were to supply him with certain products: grain, poultry, eggs, milk, cheese, wood, and other similar items, or, instead of those products, a corresponding money payment. Usually payment was partially in produce and partially in money. The benefice-holder, who provided no service in exchange, was considered a burdensome parasite by the peasants who were forced to nourish themselves by the sweat of their own brow. The exploitation of the peasants by benefice-holders was obvious. The benefice-holder was obliged to concern himself with collection of the incomes from the benefice. The lord (the territorial prince, in the case of the university) was content with this arrangement and had no vital interest in altering the system by erecting an expensive administrative bureaucracy to facilitate collection of payments and incomes to the benefice-holders. The opposite side of the coin was, however, that the treasury of the prince could not reckon with income from those lands which had been bequeathed as benefices, for such income took the form of services rendered to the territorial lord. Because the number of acres which could be granted as benefices was limited and could not be arbitrarily added to or multiplied, a definite limit was placed on the increase in the number of benefice-holders. However, this restriction meant simply a limitation of feudal circumstances, of growth for officialdom and for the intelligentsia; in short, of everything that could be described in modern terms as administrative apparatus or, even more comprehensively, as state apparatus.

If the territorial lord decided, however, not to bequeath any more benefices or grant any more fiefs, and instead to compensate his officials, servants, professors, scribes, and officers with money, the restriction disappeared; the limitation on growth of state bureaucracy gave way to economic clout. To be sure, such a tranformation presopposes a corresponding development of the goods-money economy, in which money as the most general goods equivalent has become the dominating form of social wealth and the dominance of money in turn demands centralization of financial administration. The conditions for such a position were maturing, though unevenly, in the various German territories, under the impact of early capitalistic development at the end of the fifteenth century and into the sixteenth century. At any rate, the demand for centralization of financial administration provided the background for the specific daily problems with which Luther henceforth was obliged to come to grips in the monastery, and suggested the means by which he hoped to solve the problems. The need for centralization was, furthermore, one of the general developments contributing to the continuing support of the Wittenberg reformers for their territorial lord or prince, and consequently for the Saxon territorial state.

The decision to support the prince was surely no simple matter of surrender, blind submission, or silent obedience. On the contrary, it was developed in repeated attempts to influence him and win his favor. The principal attraction was not the territorial lord himself; at least as compelling, though not so understood and not always consciously, was the class or group interest of these reformers.

The territorial state offered security to the intelligentsia, and therefore the intelligentsia supported the territorial state. The intelligentsia was sustained by the state, helped to stabilize it, and served it. The intelligentsia defended the state from foreign and domestic threats. After all, the intelligentsia was not about to saw off the limb on which it sat.

The developmental trend was as unclear to Luther's contemporaries, who could not see the forest for the trees, as it is clear in the light of historical hindsight. What the sixteenth-century person's "objective" might have been is assigned by the modern-day historian. The sixteenth-century person could not have been as disinterested as the twentieth-century historian can be about sixteenth-century concerns. Luther's contemporaries had only their subjectivity at their disposal, and it felt its way cautiously forward. The students sulked when Johannes Bugenhagen, financially hard pressed, found it necessary to demand lecture fees from his auditors because the university could offer him neither a benefice nor an adequate salary, but Bugenhagen was expected to lecture and he desired to do so. The elector, in great need of tranquillity, was disturbed when Spalatin repeatedly brought to his attention university matters and always concluded with a demand for more money for the professors. Luther's continual grumbling about the conditions in the All Saints Chapter displeased the elector. Matters there should remain as they were, the elector instructed his counselors. His forefathers, he himself, and his brother Johann had, in regards to the All Saints Chapter, always acted in good faith, and sometimes in keeping with Luther's advice. Therefore, the elector could not permit innovations.

That the elector spoke of innovations when Luther spoke of consequences produced by the gospel was not a good sign. Innovations were not to be permitted. In this matter, the elector was in unison with the old Catholic believers, but not only with them: that innovations could not lead to any good was the basic conviction of all conservatives. Furthermore, it was the spontaneous platitude of the social consciousness. Luther himself took sincere pains not to permit his designs to appear as innovations, but rather as a return to the pure teaching of apostolic times. However, his posture did not greatly impress the elector. It was the elector's duty as prince to protect his professor. The elector fulfilled that obligation. However, Frederick the Wise did not permit himself to be taken in tow by his professor. Intellectually the elector distanced himself from Luther: from the elector's point of view, there indeed innovations, and to prevent these was the duty of the prince. The elector took this responsibility very seriously, especially after his counselor Hans von Planitz from Nuremberg had informed him that in the imperial chancellery, not merely the usual malicious gossip was circulating concerning him but als the rumor that plans existed to remove him from his imperial suzerainty. No such plans ever materialized, but caution was the rule of the moment for Frederick the Wise. The elector believed his fellow princes capable of such conspiracies.

Thus Luther operated on the border of what was tolerable for his prince. Despite all remonstrances, Luther insisted that he could not refrain from publishing, since neither did his opponents remain silent but continuously heaped abuses upon him. However, the thorn in his relationship with the elector—the All Saints Chapter and the specific command to refrain from all innovations there—could not be blunted. Luther could only let the matter rest for the time being when he could not prevail, because with respect to what the elector preceived as innovations, Frederick would not permit matters simply to run their course, as was his custom. Thus Luther reminded the elector of what he had written to him from Borna as he was returning to Wittenberg from the Wartburg: the elector should not suffer any injury because of Luther. Luther would not spare his own life if, without damaging the gospel, he could avoid involving the prince in is affairs.

Luther was now forty years old. He was no longer as emaciated as Mosellanus four years earlier at the Leipzig debate had described him. Since his return from the Wartburg where he had become accustomed to a somewhat richer diet, Luther had developed a double chin and a pot belly. Despite the workload which he now resumed, the frenzy of the months before the diet of Worms seemed to have subsided. In addition to his sermons and his ongoing translation of the Bible, not only his extensive correspondence cost him much time but also the hosting of many guests who conceived of one reason or another to lay eyes on the famous man. One of these guests, the Catholic Bishop Dantiscus of Ermland, described his visit in Wittenberg with Luther as follows:

> I discovered there some young men, highly skilled in Hebrew, Greek, and Latin, especially Philipp Melanchthon, who is considered the foremost in a thorough knowledge of the scriptures and doctrine, a young man of twenty-six years who, during my three day visit, demonstrated himself to be a man of highest learning and attractive manners. Through Melanchthon, I informed Luther of the reason for my visit in the following manner: "Whoever has not seen the pope in Rome and Luther in Wittenberg has not seen anything." Therefore, I desired to see Luther, to speak with him, and, to ensure that our meeting would not be an annoyance to him, I assured him that I had no design other than to greet him and to wish him well. Not every visitor has access to Luther, but he received me without ado and thus with Melanchthon I went to him near the end of supper, to which he had invited some brothers of his order, who sat dressed in their prescribed white cowls and who were thus easily identifiable as brothers although their hair was cut in the fashion of the peasants. Luther arose, extended his hand somewhat shyly, and bade me be seated. We sat, and for almost four hours, until late into the night we conversed. I found Luther to be a man of understanding, wisdom, and eloquence. H edid not mention anything of great significance ex-

cept in his bitter remarks against the pope, the emperor, and some other princes. If I were to write down all theses remarks, I should need more than a whole day, but the servant who is to carry this letter is now ready to depart. I must be brief. Luther looks like the pictures of himself in his books. His eyes are penetrating, almost with the uncanny sparkle that one sees occasionally in the eyes of the possessed; the king of Denmark has similar eyes and I cannot but conclude that Luther and he were born under the same constellation. Luther's manner of speaking is fervent, filled with allusions and sarcasm. His dress is indistinguishable from that of a courtier. When he goes out of his residence, which was formerly the monastery, he wears, so I am told, the Augustinian cowl. As we sat together, we not only conversed, but in high spirits we also drank wine and beer, as is the custom in Wittenberg. Luther appears to be "a jolly good fellow," as the saying goes, in every sense of the word. His integrity, so highly praised by many, does not set him apart. It is easy to detect Luther's pride an arrogance: he seems to be consumed in ridicule, slander, and sarcasm. His books clearly reflect his other traits. It is said that he is well read and he writes a great deal. Right now he is translating the books of Moses from Hebrew into Latin, a task for which he solicits principally Melanchthon's help. This young man, Melanchthon, pleases me above all the other scholars in Germany. He does not agree with Luther concerning all matters. (Hipler 54 ff.)

At home Luther dressed like a courtier, but when he went out he dressed in the garb of a monk: a minor but by no means a chance observation. In the monastery Luther wore what did not seem appropriate for the place and which flouted convention; on the street he wore a garb which for some time had been considered provocative. His garb provided a not entirely pointless demonstration of what he now assiduously and repeatedly taught and attempted to hammer home on all fronts: outward appearances have no meaning for the Christian. Thereby Luther set himself in conscious opposition to all who, in striving for the Reformation not only in word but also in deed, attached importance to whether or not pictures should hang in the churches; what clothing was appropriate; whether or not priests and monks were permitted to wear what the laity wore; which prayers and hymns could be used in worship and in what order, and whether in German or Latin; when, how frequently, and to whom Holy Communion was to be given; whether the communicant with his own hands could take the cup and the bread or must permit the sacrament to be placed in his mouth by the clergy; whether the priest should follow the usual formula in pronouncing absolution after confession or whether absolution should now be expressed in other words; whether or not the devil must be exorcised before baptism; whether the infant was to be immersed in the baptismal font as in the ancient and Eastern Church or whether the traditional practice of a trickle of water on the head in the form of a cross was sufficient; whether or not the sign of the cross should also be made with oil on the forehead; and whether or not this or that ... .

Luther regarded all these external matters as unworthy of consideration. In Luther's opinion, if only true faith is present, all else will in time rectify itself. But some outward form was indeed necessary. The congregations now desired to ensure that pure doctrine was being preached. And the preachers, acolytes, and ministers were not only to preach better and differently than before; they also were to show and do something better than before. Luther himself had taught that valid works would flow from valid faith. Was valid faith demonstrable only in sermons and did the Reformation have no more effect than to bring about a few new expressions? Thus it was the pressure from the congregations which moved Luther almost against his will to issue some suggestions for the order of worship. Luther explained that there had been abuses in the liturgy. Instead of the preaching of the Word, there was only reading and singing and the telling of unchristian fables and fictions, and such a liturgy was conducted as an endeavor to gain God's grace and blessing. The most important advice that Luther gave against this was that the Christian congregation should meet only when God's Word is to be preached and when prayers are to be offered. As in the apostolic church, congregations should assemble at 4:00 or 5:00 A.M. A student or a priest, it makes no difference which, should read a passage from the Bible, and someone selected for the purpose should step forward and interpret what is read. Afterward, the congregation should thank, praise, and implore God. In addition, hymns might be sung, especially the psalms, which are ideal for such a purpose. In the evening at six o'clock, congregational worship should again take place. In the morning worship, readings should be selected from the Old Testament; in the evening service, from the New Testament. It was not necessary to have the entire congregation assembled at these daily morning and evening services, but preachers and students should conduct the devotions. On Sunday, however, the entire congregation was to assemble, and if anyone desired to receive the sacrament, it should be given to him. However, daily Masses (that is, the celebration of Holy Communion) should cease, because the Word was more important than the sacrament. Yet even with respect to this matter Luther does not want to make an inflexible rule: if anyone desires the sacrament during the week, let it be given to him as time and opportunity permit. The procedure for the administration of the sacrament Luther explained somewhat later in a work dedicated to his Zwickau friend, Nikolaus Hausmann.

Luther provided much more detail concerning baptism. It was important in baptism that the entire liturgy be conducted in the German language because baptism was the initiation ritual into the Christian faith, and all participants should plainly understand what is happening. Luther's baptismal liturgy was very conservative. He merely translated the Wittenberg Latin baptismal service into German, shortened the ritual of exorcism, and, after the formality of breating on the child, the purpose of which was to drive out any impure spirit, and also after the ceremony of stroking the lips of the child with salt, which was to bring him wisdom, he introduced a new prayer concerning the flood. After that prayer, attempts to exorcise the devil were continued: the laying on of hands, the touching of the ears and nose with saliva. On behalf of the child the godparents renounced the devil, the priest dipped the child into the baptismal font, the godparents held the child in the font, the priest made the sign of the cross with holy oil on the child's forehead, lifted the child from the font, and put a cap on its head. The godparents held a lighted candle around which they guardedly closed the infant's hand.

This is the service which the Wittenbergers knew from many years of tradition, except that earlier the priest had conducted the service in Latin. That here and there the service was somewhat abridged and that at once place a new prayer was introduced was hardly noticed by the laity. Luther did not want to be accused of having introduced a new baptism. "So remember that in baptism these outward gestures are of not great significance, but take care that you stand at the font in genuine faith, hear God's Word, and sincerely join in prayers" (WA XII 47).

The sermon stood at the center of the Luther worship service, a consequence of Luther's theological assessment that faith comes from hearing the Word. The worship service was thus a propaganda event, a means for the dissemination and consolidation of the Reformation. Moreover, the entire personal nature of Luther was projected into the liturgy. Luther was first of all a teacher of Holy Scripture and himself preached untiringly. Thus with the dissemination of this worship service there took place something like an objectification of his personality, which was not limited to the new liturgical forms and spoken word but was reflected no less in congregational singing. Luther, who himself loved to sing, also wrote hymns from 1523 on. The first motivation to write a hymn came from the news that on July 1, 1523, in the market place of Brussels, the Lutherans Heinrich Voss and Johann van der Eschen had been burned at the stake. "We sing a new song" begins the twelve verse hymn that Luther composed in tribute to the memory of the first martyrs of the new faith. This first hymn was soon followed by others, some as translations into German of old Latin church songs, some as adaptations of the psalms, some as completely new creations in composition and melody.

Luther was able to capsulize the most complicated theological concepts in easily understood hymns. He put his theology into the song of the people and thus sang his way into their midst. Anyone who wishes quickly to grasp the fundamentals of Luther's doctrine should read Luther's hymns. For example, the idea that sparked his struggle against scholasticism and led him finally to a confrontation with the ecclesiastical hierarchy was that man suffers under the burden of original sin and is unable to achieve anything with free will, an idea repugnant to modern sensitivity. Luther had his congregation sing this doctrine.

> Forlorn and lost in death I lay,
> A captive to the devil,
> My sin lay heavy, night and day,
> For I was born in evil.
> I fell but deeper for my strife,
> There was no good in all my life,
> For sin had all possessed me.
>
> My good works they were worthless quite,
> A mock was all my merit;
> My will hated God's judging light,
> To all good dead and buried.
> E'en to despair me anguish bore,
> That nought but death lay me before;
> To hell I fast was sinking.
>
> (Leupold LIII 219)

These words do not express mere speculation. Here Luther describes his own travail of soul—his "monastic fears"—in his early in the monastery. Luther's doctrine was born of his experience; therefore, he could sing it. At the beginning of 1524 there appeared from the press of the Nuremberg printer, Jobst Gutknecht, a hymnal entitled *Some Christian Hymns of Praise*, which contained eight hymns and therefore was referred to as "The Eight Hymn Book." Four of these hymns were by Luther. A little later on there appeared in Erfurt an *Enchiridion, or a Handbook of Spiritual Songs*, comprised of twenty-five hymns, eigtheen of which came from Luther. A hymnbook published in Wittenberg in 1524, the so-called "Wittenberg Choirbook," contained thirty-two hymns, twenty-four of which were Luther's.

While Luther—cautiously, hesitantly, and perhaps more at the insistence of friends and congregations than as a natural development in the sequential procedures of his own teaching—took the first step toward the revision of the liturgy, the situation in Germany became increasingly critical. It became ever plainer that the longer the reform movement—with its liturgical, ecclesiastical, biblical, and doctrinal questions—was in progress, the more persistently it approached that threshold on which the reformation of the Church revealed its character as a part of the transformation of social conditions. That the Church reformation was a part of a general transformation was obvious wherever community poor chests had been instituted. From 1522 on, this integration was further revealed in the question raised in many places as to how taxes and tithes were to be regulated. An important weapon of the Reformation was the deprivation of the priest of his tithe. If the priest would not preach evangelically, he was no longer worthy of his compensation!

However, the matter was not long limited to the priestly tithe. In Eisenach in the spring of 1523, the local preacher, Jacob Strauss, made a demand of much broader and more radical implication, that interest on loans be abolished. This suggestion was directed against the Augustinian choirmasters at the Mary Chapter in Eisenach, who demanded up to twenty-one percent interest from those indebted to them. Strauss' agitation to abolish interest met with striking success; many citizens refused to pay the interest on their debts. The Weimar court was obliged to intervene, and long and tedious discussions ensued between the electoral counselors and the Eisenach city council. That the interest demands of the Augustinian choirmasters were excessive and constituted an out and out exploitation was clear to everyone. Duke Johann ruled that in the future only five percent interest would be paid. Luther had suggested that amount; nevertheless, that the debtors had on their own initiative simply suspended their interest payments, Luther could not approve, because he saw in such arbitrary action an erosion of public order. Luther rejected completely Strauss' argument that the interest payer violated biblical commands when he submissively paid the usurious interest. From this position the argument was extended to the most fundamental concern. It was no longer merely a question of paying interest but primarily one of the validity of the Mosaic code. In the Old Testament it was forbidden to the Israelites to take interest from their fellow tribesmen. Should this rule also apply to Christians, or were the regulations contained in the Old Testament suspended by the New Testament? Behind this question lay many other concealed problems. Is the gospel, the good news of the New Testament, only for the life of faith, or are there also conclusions to be drawn from it for the correct regulation of secular affairs? In general, how far and in what sense is the Bible at all normative for life?

Luther himself was in no small measure responsible for the fact that the Bible became the generally recognized basis for argument in social disputes. Now the tendency became even stronger to conceive of the Bible as a legal standard and to interpret the gospel in a "fleshly" manner. This radical biblicism was an accompanying feature of the social and political radicalization of the reform movement. Luther had erected with the doctrine of the two realms a wall against taking the Bible too literally and making it too binding for life. Thereby he implemented only what the practical reason of the rulers and of the ruled had agreed on for centuries.

In 1523 and 1524, Luther's doctrine of the two realms assumed growing significance because Duke Johann in Weimar and his son Johann Frederick incresingly requested his advice. The more his illness forced Elector Frederick to retire from his ducal responsibilities, the more the electoral administrative duties were concentrated in the hands of Johann and his son. That the latter two rulers increasingly appealed to Luther was spurred by the fact that it was in the very territories of the Ernestine Thuringia, for which Duke Johann and Duke Johann Frederick were responsible, that those forces arose which desired to push the Reformation beyond the measure circumscribed by Luther. Along with Strauss' activity in Eisenach, it was the activity of Thomas Müntzer in Allstedt and of Andreas Karlstadt in Orlamünde that caused apprehension in the Weimar court. Strauss, Müntzer, and Karlstadt became a problem for the ruling family. The Weimar court approached Luther with the problem.

It was through his preaching activity in Jüterbog in 1519 that Thomas Müntzer first came to Luther's attention. Müntzer also had attended the Leipzig debate. In 1520 Luther had procured a position for him in Zwickau but had then lost sight of him for some time. In April 1521, Müntzer was dismissed from his position in Zwickau by the city council because he had preached against the wealthy cloth merchants and a riot feared. Encouraged by the hope of making common cause with the Hussites and thereby promoting the Reformation from that center, Müntzer went from Zwickau to Prague. Soon disappointed, he was obliged to leave the city.

After short stays in Nordhausen and Glaucha near Halle, at Easter of 1523 Müntzer found a position as preacher in the Johannis Church in Allstedt, Thuringia. With this position, Müntzer finally enjoyed security, an income, and a circle for his activities in which his ideas could be accommodated. However, Müntzer's ideas were by now no longer reconcilable with Luther's teaching. Although in 1519 Müntzer had passed for a Lutheran in the eyes of friend and foe, and although it was to describe Müntzer's anti-Roman Church posture that the word "Lutheran" was first used, now the picture had changed. The incipient Reformation for a time had brought Luther and Müntzer together and had placed them in a common front. The continued progress of the Reformation, its radicalization and differentiation, opened to Luther and Müntzer separate and distinctive paths along which they arrived not simply at divergent positions but finally at irreconcilable opposition.

Protected by the Saxon elector and his advisors, the university professor Luther, whose affairs preoccupied the pope, the emperor, princes, the Reichstag, and the imperial administration, and whose name held the whole educated world at attention, had pondered the degree to which one was to be subject to the civil authority. He had achieved the decisive intellectual breakthrough for putting the Reformation in gear. The movement should proceed without wrecking and breaking, without riot and unproar. What eventually was to be altered in regard to civil laws, orders, and decrees, and whatever reorganization was to take place, should be singularly and exclusively the affair of the responsible governmental authority. Preaching anywhere and, if need be, by anybody, but reforms only from above: that was Luther's creed relating to the political course of the Reformation. The significance of his creed became increasingly clear.

Thomas Müntzer, on the other hand, had adopted an entirely different social milieu. Müntzer, like Luther, had enjoyed a university education, but the possessed no security, no favoritism from the princes, no sympathy from city councils. And even if such privileges had been his, as for example temporarily in Zwickau in 1520, he soon squandered them, not by being abrasive (or at least, not exclusively), but rather by channeling his thought and feeling into an ideological course that, wherever he was, sooner or later ran into conflict with established authority.

Müntzer taught that God still lived. Not only in the Bible had He revealed Himself; God still spoke in the present with quickening voice in the hearts of the faithful. However, the divine voice could be perceived only by those who were not preoccupied with material well-being. Moreover, this was especially true for the poor—not for the poor in spirit but for the materially poor—those at the bottom of the social scale, who were oppressed, exploited, and deceived. This was indeed an entirely different concept of faith from Luther's. First and foremost, Müntzer's concept of faith possessed a social profile.

It is impossible to determine today from exactly which sources this concept of faith was fed. Certainly mystical influences are detectable and, as will be explained in more detail, Old Testament prophecy and apocalyptic passages in a mystical vein: concepts which also were well known to Luther but which, by the Christocentric emphasis in his theology along with his Pauline orientation, had been for the most part held in intellectual restraints. As noticeable as these influences were on Müntzer, the decisive matter was that he independently worked them over. Doubtless his contact with Nikolaus Storch and the other Zwickau prophets, who had excited Melanchthon during their visit in Wittenberg at the end of 1521 and the beginning of 1522, played a certain role. Müntzer had at least one fundamental idea in common with the Zwickau prophets: that God still today revealed Himself to man and that the divine voice could still be heard in visions, dreams, and the responses of the heart.

This concept had far-reaching impact. If God still spoke today in these ways, the significance of the Bible became relativized. It ceased to be the sole source of information concerning the divine will. With this proposition, religious thought struck a new direction in which it freed itself from the authority of established university theologians; scholarly learning was not at all necessary to correctly interpret the Bible, since the possibility must always be considered that God would reveal something new that was not revealed in Scripture. The way of reform was thus thrown open to important innovations. Subjective revelation meant that with its openness to innovations the popular movement could become independent and could liberate itself from the ideological hegemony of the intelligentsia.

For example, Karlstadt, who arrived at ideas similar to those of Müntzer, reported that he stopped uneducated people in the street and asked their opinion about specific Bible passages. Müntzer had advanced so far in rejecting the Bible as the complete and sole revelation that occasionally he hawked the expression, "Bibel, Bubel, Babel," thereby deriding as babbling fools those who believed the Bible to be the only source of revelation and that valid interpretation rested upon intellectual endeavor. Although Müntzer did not entirely reject the Bible, and he did not cease to be a Christian theologian, his view of the Bible was not the one held by Luther. Furthermore, Müntzer espoused a theology different from Luther's. Luther approached the Bible from a Pauline position, but Müntzer interpreted the Bible from the standpoint of the prophets and from the apocalypse. The difference is profound. Paul was the most intellectual among the apostles: scholarly, reflective, entirely concentrated on Christ and faith, and happy to leave mundane things to civil authority because they were really without any significance in the face of the imminent parousia. The prophets, however, demonstrate the most restless element of those whose spirits stamp the Bible. They inspired courage in the people during the Babylonian captivity and admonished them to perservere in faith. The prophets stormed against apostasy, and the prophets did not speak of the will of God and of faith as being set apart from the wordly political order. They were men from among the people, but they did not merely represent popular interests. On the contrary, in preaching to the people, the prophets warned of judgment to come, and they based their authority on divine commission received through voices or visions. Their apocalyptic prophecies are visions of the end of the world, of the judgment day that God will bring to pass at the end of the age, and of the final struggle—preceding or accompanying doomsday—of the elect against evildoers and the damned: scenes of terror, revenge, and hope. Martin Luther was a teacher of Holy Scriptures; Thomas Müntzer was a prophet of a new world. This distinction indicates the difference between their intellectual positions. Luther was a professor at the university of the elector of Saxony; Müntzer was a Thuringian pastor. Luther associated primarily with monks, students, scholars, councilors, and aristocratic court officers, and he correspond with princes. Müntzer spoke to cloth merchants, miners, simple urban inhabitants, common workers, and farmers. Thus the social distinctions between Luther and Müntzer were marked.

The more Luther became integrated into his environment, the more his view adapted to the view from above; the more Müntzer was captivated by his environment, the keener became his insight in viewing matters from below. Luther's name became synonomous with the former view; Müntzer's with the latter. Both views are elements of the early middle-class revolution. Luther had provoked the early middle-class revolution; to that extent he was Müntzer's precursor and he prepared Müntzer's way. After a Luther had spoken, a Müntzer could not remain silent. Thus, the Luther-Müntzer antithesis is not a trivial friend-foe relationship but a genuine historical dialectic. Historically, Luther and Müntzer belong together. One is not possible without the other, especially not at the time in which their antithesis was manifest; furthermore, one is not comprehensible without the other.

Exactly where Luther hesitated in the new formulation of the liturgy, Müntzer in Allstedt proceeded boldly. He abolished Latin from the liturgy and composed a Mass entirely in German. If the Croatians, Armenians, Bohemians, and Russians could conduct the Mass in their respective languages, the Germans should be able to do the same, Müntzer declared in his pamphlet *Order and Justification of the German Mass at Allstedt*. The inner purification of the worshiper was, according to Müntzer, the prerequisite for being open to the will of God and for toppling tyrants. As long as inner purification had not yet occurred, the Reformation was in danger of going astray. Consequently, Müntzer warned the citizens of Stolberg in a circular letter of the summer of 1523 to "avoid unjustified uproar."

However, the period in which Müntzer in tranquillity and in a concentrated fashion could work out his theological fundamentals in Allstedt did not last long. The first conflict arose in the fall of 1523, when Count Ernst of Mansfeld forbade his subjects to attend Müntzer's services in Allstedt. In March 1524 the first violence occured. After one of Müntzer's sermons, his followers destroyed the Mallerbach chapel in the cloister of Naundorf, not far from Allstedt, because idolatry was practiced there with pictures and wax figures. Now the point had been reached from which the electoral authorities could no longer pretend not to notice. From this point on, the situation rapidly grew more critical. Thomas Müntzer established in Allstedt a league of thirty members who ceremoniously entered their names in the membership role at a meeting near the city moat. In june the membership in the league had grown to 500, among them many miners from Mansfeld. Now there was no more talk about avoiding "unjustified uprorar." On the contrary, it was announced that anyone who did not wish to join the league should leave Allstedt.

In this situation, Duke Johann decided to investigate matters in Allstedt for himself. He summoned Müntzer to the Allstedt castle because he wanted to hear Müntzer preach. Müntzer used the opportunity to try to win the duke and his son, Johann Frederick, for the league's cause. It was a bold gamble and it failed. Müntzer announced in the "sermon for the prince" that the collapse of the old order, with its unjust system, was imminent. He confirmed his conviction by a vision from the Book of Daniel in the Old Testament, prophecy concerning the fall of worldly kingdoms and the beginning of the Messianic lordship. Müntzer contended that five world kingdoms had succeeded one another in the course of world history: the first was Babylon, the second was the kingdom of Medea and Persia, the third was Greece, the fourth was Rome. The fifth was the Holy Roman Empire of the German Nation, ruled by filth and full of hypocrisy "that slithered and crawled across the whole earth" (Müntzer 64). The ecclesiastical and secular lords copulated in a pile like serpents and eels. The stone had been cut out of the mountain and was about to smash this empire. The princes had been summoned to seize the sword against this empire. But if they should fail to do so, God would take the sword from them and give it to the common people.

This message was anything but music to the ears of the princes. Now they knew where Müntzer stood. "He was a foolhardy person," Johann Frederick commented WA BR III 311). Even before the preaching of the sermon for the princes, Luther had been informed concerning Müntzer's impact on Allstedt. In March Luther had written to his friend Hausmann in Zwickau that the spirit of Nikolaus Storch prevailed in Allstedt and Orlamünde. However, on June 18 Luther advised the electoral prince? Johann Frederick, that the "Satan of Allstedt" should be sent to Wittenberg to face interrogation. Before the congregation and indeed before the whole world Müntzer was prepared to defend his doctrine, but he would not submit his teaching to the Wittenberg scholar's corner. Müntzer did not recognize the Wittenbergers as authorities; indeed, despite their common paths from 1519 to 1520, it might be doubted that there really had been a parallel development, in the full sense of the term, between the thinking of Luther and that of Müntzer.

Luther saw that the time was ripe to oppose the Allstedt group openly. He directed to the territorial rulers his *Letter to the Saxon Princes Concerning the Spirit of Riot and Rebellion,* one of the sharpest works he ever penned. For Luther there was no doubt that the devil was loose in Allstedt. Therefore, the epistle begins with a history of the devil and his work. The devil first attacks with the fist and then with cunning and deception. At first he makes martyrs of Christians, then he summons false spirits and false prophets and fills the world with sects and heretics all the way up to the pope. This has been his technique in the past and it is still his technique today. The Allstedter spirit wishes to cancel Scripture and to destroy the spoken Word of God, the Eucharist, and baptism, and to lead us into a frame of mind in which we tempt God with our own works and free will, where we determine for Him His time, place, and measure with respect to how He should work with us. Destroying objects of wood and stone is the fruit of such belief, but not joy, peace, patience, or any of the other fruits that the Holy Spirit gives. Let the Allstedters preach, because

sects must exist, and the Word of God must be battle ready and must fight. Let the spirits wrestle with one another. If some will be deceived thereby, no matter, that is the normal course of battle. Wherever there is a battle, some will be killed and some will be wounded. Nevertheless, he who fights bravely will be crowned. But where one wants to fight with more than the Word, where on also wants to break and strike with the fist, there Your Princely Grace must intervene, no matter whether it be against us or them, and those pugnacious ones must be expelled from the land and told, "We will gladly stand by and suffer that you fight with the Word so that right doctrine will prevail, but because the fist pertains to our office, restrain from using the fist, or else leave the dukedom." (WA XV 218-19)

"Or else leave the dukedom": that was Luther's ultimatum, which was in accordance with the expectations of the princes. In addition to the devil's work that he scented in Müntzer, what especially infuriated Luther was Müntzer's incitement of riot in electoral Saxony, which provided protection and security for the Reformation, while avoiding and leaving undisturbed the territory of George the Bearded in Albertine Saxony, where every Lutheran sermon was rigorously suppressed. Luther interpreted the unrest in electoral Saxony as opposed to the tranquillity in Albertine Saxony in his own unique manner. In Duke George the Bearded's territory God's Word was lacking: the devil had nothing to do there. However, where God's Word was preached, as in electoral Saxony, there the devil attempted to intrude. Therefore, expel the devil!

To get rid of Müntzer did not demand much effort on the part of the Ernestine princes. They summoned him to an interrogation in Weimar on August 1, 1524. Then they ordered his print shop closed. Müntzer got no support from the Allstedt city council. Thus his sojourn in the city could not be extended. Sometime during the late hours of August 7 or the early hours of August 8, Müntzer left Allstedt and sought refuge in the free imperial city of Mühlhausen in Thuringia. Here, in the hard struggle of intramural polemics, Müntzer developed into the ideologue of a radical plebeian faction.

Johann Frederick had earlier conceived of a plan whereby Luther would travel through Thuringia to instruct the preachers and, with the help of the civil authority, dismiss those preachers who were not capable. Hardly anything makes clearer Luther's transition with respect to social position. In this assignment, what he had done about nine years earlier, commissioned by his Augustinian order as district vicar, he was now to do by commission of the prince, on whose authority he was equipped with plenipotentiary power in an increasingly dangerous situation, and instructed to exercise that power in the suspect parishes. Earlier, his commission had been to maintain discipline and enforce the monastic rules in the monasteries. Now more was at stake: obedience to the civil authorities and the avoidance of violent uproar, which could result only too quickly from ideological aberrations, especially since, even without an excuse for an uprising, a disquietude among the masses could be sensed. Nine years earlier Luther had been responsible for order in the monasteries; now he was to be keeper of order in the entire dukedom. That he was ready to assume this role, indeed that he more or less had grown into it and had identified himself with it, he expressed very confidently in a pamphlet directed against the Edict of Worms:

> Now dear Princes and Lords, you are hastening some poor souls along with me almost to our death, and our demise will be your gain. But if you have ears to hear, I would like to tell you something surprising. If the life of Luther were not so precious in God's sight and Luther lived no more, none of you could be sure of his own life or lordship, and Luther's death would be your personal loss. (WA XV 254)

The transition from monastery overseer to proctor of the dukedom did not occur abruptly. Luther had not sought the job. On the contrary, as he coped with difficult struggles and serious dangers, the responsibility was gradually imposed on him until his new role, with little change in specifications but with a clarification as to social position and function, was urged on him.

In the middle of August Luther began his visitation tour. Not Müntzer but Karlstadt was now the problem: Müntzer was no longer in the dukedom. In 1523, after many quarrels and confrontations in Wittenberg, Karlstadt had withdrawn to his benefice in Orlamünde where, far from Wittenberg and its governance, he had developed his reforms pertaining to the use of images in worship. It was this question that had brought him into difficulty with the elector and into confrontation with Luther.

In Orlamünde images disappeared from the church. Had not God in the Old Testament strictly forbidden His people to make likenesses or to worship them? Thus away with this idolatry! Naturally the obligation to dispense the Eucharist under both bread and wine was observed. Moreover, in still another matter Karlstadt went further than the Wittenbergers: he stopped baptizing children, thereby clearly indicating that his concept of faith was different from Luther's and that they disagreed, therefore, on the fundamental issue of the new doctrine. For Luther faith was a divine gift which everyone, even children, could be granted; therefore, Luther believed it acceptable to baptize children who had not yet achieved the age of understanding, because faith is not dependent on understanding or reason but rather on its own nature. Reason may occasionally serve faith, but faith does not use reason as a crutch.

Karlstadt also believed that faith was a gift of grace. However, as a former Thomist, it was quite clear to him that faith and reason belonged together and that reason was necessary to gain faith, to preserve it, and to bring to fruition. Children were unable to exercise reason in this capacity; therefore, it was meaningless to baptize them. In matters of faith, Karlstadt was not able to free himself from reason. In this matter, he remained arrested by the *via antiqua*, the old path of scholasticism, which he had taught and which was so despised by Luther. Karlstadt's conversion to Luther's thought had occurred too quickly—spontaneously, and almost overnight; thus his former thought patterns stubbornly persisted as he pressed forcibly forward and wanted radically to break with tradition. The dialectic of these intellectual interconnections was of such a nature that, during the very years when the Reformation was being transformed from idea to deed and when Luther was penetrating to the idea of "evangelical liberty," Karlstadt was reaching far beyond Paul into Mosaic law. Luther, who earlier at the Wartburg had sensed this tendency in his former cohort of the Leipzig debate, sarcastically ridiculed him, saying that Karlstadt would yet have himself circumcised.

Furthermore, another disagreement separated the former allies. Before he had gone to Orlamünde, Karlstadt had spent some time in Wörlitz. He lived there as a farmer, did not wish to be addressed with his doctor's title, and requested his neighbors to call him "Brother Endres." Certainly his dour experience with his university colleagues was reflected in his conduct, but the roots went deeper, touching on those ideas by which Thomas Müntzer was also led: the common man was nearer and dearer to God than are scholars, powerful lords, and the rich. The emotional agitation contingent on these ideas led to identifying with the common man, but, in association with strict Mosaic legalism, could easily give rise to a sect.

For Luther it was plain that the same spirit that prevailed in Allstedt prevailed in Orlamünde. He threw Müntzer and Karlstadt, without distinction, into the same pot. Up to a certain degree and seen from his standpoint, Luther's evaluation was not entirely unjustifiable, because both men appeared to aim at the same goal: rebellion against authority and thereby endangerment of the peaceful progress of reformation.

Müntzer also sensed Karlstadt's kindred spirit; yet Müntzer's attempts to effect a closer relationship and, where possible, a league between Allstedt and Orlamünde remained without success. Despite all the beliefs that the Orlamünde followers of Karlstadt and the Allstedt followers of Müntzer held in common, with respect to one question the Orlamünders diverged: they rejected the use of violence and they vehemently warned Müntzer in a letter not to undertake any course of violence.

Thus Karlstadt was infuriated when he heard Luther, on his visitation trip, preach in Jena, where, without calling Karlstadt by name, Luther aimed at him when he raved against Müntzer. Later, after the sermon, Karlstadt challenged Luther in the Black Bear Inn. Luther did not avoid the challenge. Luther's inner resentment against Karlstadt and the spirit that moved him were so strong that he refused to speak with Karlstadt privately. Karlstadt was forced to confront Luther in the presence of the guests about the table. If Luther's words in the sermon had not been without spite, now his words at the table were not without ridicule. That struck dogs yelp was the thrust of Luther's answer to Karlstadt's complaints. The two men became embroiled in argument. Not long before, Luther had not wished to provide the enemies of the Reformation with a manifestation of the quarrel that persisted within the ranks of the movement between himself and Karlstadt. In 1522 Luther had requested Karlstadt not to write against him. This former position was now forgotten. The contradictions could no longer be swept under the rug! They must be aired. As a sign that Karlstadt might now write against him, Luther presented to Karlstadt a gold gulden. Karlstadt accepted it. The custom in the sixteenth century was to place a gold coin in the hand of the mercenary soldier. By accepting the coin, the mercenary bound himself to participate in the approaching battle. By presenting Karlstadt with a gold gulden, Luther employed this custom as a provocation. Thus with a coin, the rupture between the two former allies and colleagues was acknowledged.

Two days later, on August 24, 1524, Luther entered Orlamünde. The court preacher from Weimar, Wolfgang Stein, accompanied him. In a letter the city council had requested Luther to visit Orlamünde and not unjustly to accuse or suspect the Orlamünde congregation of false teaching. At Luther's arrival in Orlamünde, it was necessary to summon the members of the city council from the fields where they were at their daily chores. A rather vehement argument took place between Luther, a cobbler, and a tailor, concerning the question of images in the church. Luther's argument that the use of images made no difference so long as they were not woshipped was not convincing to his antagonists. The Orlamünders reminded him that the bride must finally disrobe and come naked into the bridegroom's bed. This surprising logic caught the monk Martin off guard. Only months later, as he was writing his essay *Against the Heavenly Prophets*, did an answer occur to him: But what if the bride prefers to wear her nightgown? Mating is not thereby prohibited!

Karlstadt had not been able to participate in the conversation. Luther had resolutely insisted on Karlstadt's absence from the discussion. Even so, nothing was accomplished by the discussion. Luther instructed that his wagon should be made ready for departure, and he must have been happy to have taken leave of Orlamünde without being stoned or spattered with mud by the iconoclasts—the opponents of images and nightgowns. Luther's gift for convincing and instructing others had failed him in this instance. Now the civil authority would have to perform its office. Despite the pleas of the Orlamünde city council to consider the fact that Karlstadt's wife was in a state of advanced pregnancy and that she and her husband already had a small child to care for, Duke Johann ordered the apostate Wittenberg professor and now preacher in Orlamünde, Andreas Bodenstein von Karlstadt, to depart from his dukedom.

Chapter 12

With the Civil Authority Against Riot:
The Victory of Class Instinct
Over the Good Intentions of Faith
Fall 1524–Spring 1525

Müntzer and Karlstadt were driven out of electoral Saxony. However, neither Luther nor his prince could breathe easily. Reformation without riot and rebellion, which Luther dreamed of and which his territorial lords would gladly have tolerated, remained a fiction, a pious wish swept away by primitive force. In the same weeks in which it had been possible to avoid the worst consequences (from the Ernestine point of view) in Allstedt and Orlamünde, the Peasants' War broke out in the southwest portion of the empire. In the area of Lake Constance and the Black Forest peasants rose in revolt; armed with scythes and flails they attacked the manor houses, and, in their initial assaults, gained widespread acceptance of their demands. A reduction of burdens and tithes; a reduction of feudal services; a return of the common lands and forests (the *Allmende*) to the village communities; a recognition of the rights of peasant ownership; the right to fish, hunt, gather wood, and many other privileges: these demands were met in full or in part, depending on the locality. The shocked feudal lords wavered, resorted to delaying stratagems, and made hasty concessions in order to pacify the aroused peasants and gain time. Lutheran preachers sided with the peasants, preached to them, wrote pamphlets for them, provided them with Bible quotations which justified their cause, and encouraged them to believe that now, with the Reformation, a serious attempt at reform was finally to be made.

It was easy for the Romanists to demonstrate that this violent course was the fruit of the Lutheran seed. Were the Romanists completely wrong in this appraisal? To be sure, Luther had warned against riot and rebellion and had passionately fought against any attempt to interpret the gospel and Christian freedom in a fleshly manner. But how could he prevent such a fleshly interpretation, and how could be prevent people from reading into "Christian liberty" their own needs and aspirations? Furthermore, deriving from his personal struggle courage and confidence that more was to be achieved in and with the Reformation than thus far had been?

Goethe's *Zauberlehrling* is suggested: the magician's apprentice who, seeking to imitate his absent master, conjured up the spirits but then discovered to his consternation that he had not learned the incantation with which to bridle them. Luther had indeed conjured up the spirits, but not the ones which now came. What now occurred did not depend on what Luther had thought, said, written, preached, or rejected. Once the Reformation was set on course, it followed its own laws, those of revolution: from an apparent modest initiative, a movement that spread over the whole society was unleashed, seized upon one social class or group after another, absorbed the aspirations, demands, desires, and grievances of every group, gained the impetus of historical necessity, and flamed up against the established system of political power and social conditions. If there was any doubt in the first year of the Reformation that this movement could be described as a revolution, the outbreak of the Peasants' War removed it.

The violent revolutionary outbreak of 1524-1526 demonstrated in many ways that the Reformation was the springboard and framework for the early middle-class revolution. Peasant revolts and riots, even widespread peasant wars, were not new. They broke out repeatedly in feudal society: sometimes here, sometimes there, with more or less violence, and with more or less impact. These uprisings were the expression of the fundamental contraposition, in the feudal society, of the ruling feudal class to the dependent peasants. This contraposition, furthermore, contributed to provoking the Peasants' War of 1524–1525 but was not the only cause of that war. What distinguished the German Peasants' War from medieval peasant uprisings was its central position in a large social movement in which the most varied inconsistencies crisscrossed. Within this context, the Reformation and Peasants' War joined hands in a revolutionary assault of a new quality, an attack in which each—first ideologically, then progressively also socially and politically—occupied itself not only with the old contrapositions of feudal society but also with the new conflicts arising out of the goods-money economy of early capitalism.

The German Peasants' War came directly out of the reform movement and, to a certain extent, in the agrarian regions was identical with the radical form of the Reformation assumed there. This union between reform and revolt was the result of an ideological and historical process. The reform movement led inevitably and everywhere to the question as to how the social and political life could be made to correspond to God's will, the Bible, and the gospel.

In the cities this problem of the transformation of the church had found solutions in the establishment of community chests, begging orders, and all matters pertaining to them. Luther found it necessary repeatedly to address social problems. The problems concerned usury; lack of care for the poor, the aged, and the ill; unfair prices and compensation; inflation; ostentatious dress; "license in gluttonous eating and drinking"; and, last but not least, the inequitable and unjust distribution of wealth.

Thus the Reformation as an ideological movement absorbed and pondered all the social problems and ills and at the same time raised expectations for solving them. In order to bring to public attention their special interest and to represent it as part of the general good, the various classes, ranks, and groups readily employed slogans made popular by the Reformation.

Since 1521 pamphlet literature had been increasingly preoccupied with the peasant and his problems. Until then, the peasant often had been caricaturized as blockheaded, avaricious, crude, and ignorant; now he appeared as an inquisitive conversationalist who even knew his Bible and who must be restrained from striking with his flail a path for the Reformation. In 1523 Balthasar Stanberger wrote in a *Dialogue between Peter and a Peasant* that "the peasant must once again become judge and lord in the house, make the priest also accept the flail so that he has to nourish his own children. Then Karstans and Flegelhans also will come with their indulgences and forgive the clergy their sins. May God hasten that day" (Lenk 177).

Concerns of the Reformation invaded the village, overshadowing parishes, monks, and merchants, and finally influencing to no insignificant extent market relations and also the conduct of the nobles. It did not arrive there full blown, however, nor did it immediately address all questions. As in the city, here the Reformation proceded in stages until it joined force with the fundamental matters that characterized peasant existence.

At first the Reformation in the countryside was also a matter of preaching. With due consideration to how the noble patron of the particular parish regarded the evangelical preaching of the individual clergy, it was necessary, when the pastor was in conflict with the patron, for the peasants to decide whether they should distance themselves from the pastor or whether they should protect him from possible reprisal and remain loyal to him. In not a few cases, as, for example, in the spring of 1525 in the Thuringian forest, such gave occasion for unrest that in a very short time developed into a rebellion. However, if evangelical preaching was approved and permitted to continue uninterruptedly, the peasants, in addition to demanding the gospel of salvation from their ministers, eventually demanded to know what all these new and beautiful words had to say about home and hearth, material well-being, and the peasants' relationship with their feudal lords, and whether, apart from Germans songs at Mass and the Eucharist in both kinds, everything was to continue as usual.

The questions forming the decisive links between reform preaching and the socio-political problems of the peasants were the tithe and the free selection of the pastor. These two questions were closely connected and presented two sides of the same coin.

The tithe was a church tax. It was not earmarked for the pastor; he usually lived on the income from a modest benefice. The church tax went to a noble who possessed the jurisdiction over the church: that is, he exercised a certain guardianship over it. The same demand for a communal use of church income was heard in the country that had been heard and acted upon in the urban centers. In the village as in the city, the demand for community chests was realized, and in the village as in the city, the call was heard to channel the tithe not to unknown clergy, beneficiaries, or other parasites, in unknown faraway places, but to the local clergy and the village poor.

Furthermore, since Luther had agreed with the community principle in granting the community the right to install and to dismiss teachers, pastors, and church wardens according to communal will, it followed that the village community also had the right to elect its own pastor. Thus the village community possessed an instrument either to protect the pastor from the reprisals of an anti-reform bishop or itself to put pressure on the pastor in the event he did not preach, write, or act in accordance with community expectations.

Therefore free election of the pastor appertained to the fundamental demands of the rebellious peasants as did also their expressed purpose to abolish all that was contrary to the gospel while retaining all that was founded on the Bible. Biblicism, in vogue since the publication of Luther's translation, now made its stamp on the peasants.

To be sure, in the peasant village communities as in the urban middle-class communities, the final outcome depended on who had the last word. Authority resided not with the cottagers, stallkeepers, tenants, and owners of small tracts of land, but with the owners of large tracts and the owners of teams of horses. The owners of large tracts and teams made the decisions in the community, and community decision and reaction depended on them. This fact is of great importance for the fate of the Reformation in rural areas as well as for the historical function of the Peasants' War.

As long as only the peasants who owned little or no land, cottagers, and other villagers of low esteem expressed discontent, any movement representing them would have small chance of spreading because it was difficult enough for such people to be heard even in the village council. There were many reasons why the Reformation became a peasants' war in the rural regions. The masses of peasants were no longer willing to bear the rapidly increasing feudal burdens. The fact that the village leadership adopted radical reform demands and sought by force to implement them was of decisive significance. The village councils employed reform slogans in order to consolidate their own positions, arouse the entire community, unite with neighboring communities in forming armed companies, and strike an alliance based on generally accepted articles, plans for mobilization, and the election of commanders.

The village leadership corps was made up of people who had market connections, to some degree exercised functions in the transport of goods, played the role of middlemen, and not infrequently were mill owners or innkeepers. These people were able to enlist the pastor since he already was accustomed to saying what was expected at weddings, baptism, burials, or at the pig-slaughtering festival, and to receiving a nice cut for his services as well as for his usual duties of composing letters and petitions and of performing other secretarial chores. In English a scribe is still designated as a "clerk," which is of the same derivation as "clergy."

It was in those rural regions where the feudal burdens were most oppressive, the urban-rural interdependencies closest, the market ties tightest, and the territorial decentralization and the multiplicity of small political entities most pronounced that the Reformation became the Peasants' War. That is, the Peasants' War erupted where, on the one hand, the goods-money economy with its early capitalistic elements most decisively dominated the rural regions, and, on the other hand, the feudal domains were smallest, the political decentralization greatest, and hence the ability of the ruling feudal class to take action or to organize was at a minimum. Since the uprising brought not only local but also far-reaching inconsistencies to the fore, it could in no way be limited to peasant groups; it also included plebeian circles, miners, even some individual nobles, and it rapidly spread from its place of origin.

After the first wave of uprisings in the southwest, the movement temporarily subsided in the following months. In the spring of 1525, the movement flared up again and within fourteen days suddenly had spread over all south Germany except Bavaria. It engulfed the Neckar valley, the Oden forest, the Rhine-Main region, and Franconia, and it burst into Thuringia. Between Easter and Whitsuntide 1525, the whole area from Lake Constance and Alsace all the way to Thuringia was in broad rebellion.

The rebels in upper Swabia had compressed their demands into "Twelve Articles." Of the learned men whose names the rebels listed as mediators in the "Memmingen Confederation" and whose word they would trust, Luther's name stood at the top of the list. No one enjoyed greater authority than Luther. Müntzer's name was not included in this list of mediators. Outside of Thuringia Müntzer was unknown among the rebelling masses.

Luther was confronted with a strange mediatory task. No one would really take his advice because class wars are not settled by arbitors, and certainly not when the opponents are already in the field. Luther tried to adopt a neutral position, and he urged moderation on both sides. He issued a stern warning to the princes. Even more severe were his words for the peasants. He wrote to the princes in his *Admonition to Peace, Concerning the Twelve Articles of the Swabian Peasants*, "It is not the peasants, dear Lords, who set themselves against you. It is God Himself who resists you in order to punish your tyranny" (WA XVIII 295). Luther sensed that he now indeed could be the feather that tipped the scale: "And if I wanted to take revenge on you, I could laugh up my sleeve and stand on the sidelines to watch the peasants, or I could even join them and thus make the matter for you much worse than it already is" (WA XVIII 296). But Luther did not pursue this option. He did not go over to the peasants' side, nor did he stand on the sidelines. To be sure, he advised the princes to make concessions to the peasants, but earlier in the *Admonition to Peace*, he had bluntly called the peasants robbers and highwaymen who misused and disgraced God's name. The rulers unjustly take your property; on the other hand you take from them "their authority in which their whole property and life and being consists; therefore, you are much greater robbers than the princes and you intend to do worse things that they have done" (WA XVIII 305). Luther did not hesitate to describe the peasants' demand for the abolition of serfdom as unchristian. Such a demand was completely opposed to the gospel and rapacious because each serf thereby robbed from his lord the services due him. A serf could be a Christian and possess Christian liberty just as a prisoner or a ill person could be a Christian and possess Christian liberty but still not be free. This article would make all people equal and transform the spiritual realm into a worldly one; such a transformation was impossible, "because the worldly realm cannot exist where there is no distinction among persons: for example, some free, some prisoners, some lords, some subjects." The other articles concerning hunting and fishing privileges, services, and taxes, Luther leaves to the legal experts, "because it is not proper for me as a theologian to judge and decide such matters. I am to instruct the consciences as to what corresponds to the divine and Christian matters" (WA XVIII 327). In no case would Luther tolerate the peasants adorning their demands with the name "Christian." If they insisted on doing so, he would consider them his enemis. Luther knew, of course, that he would be branded a hypocrite and a lackey of the princes, but he would not permit such pejorative titles to bother him.

The *Admonition to Peace* was only superficially directed against both sides; in subject and content it was an appeal to the rebels to lay down their arms. The pamphlet was in defense of secular authority. What Luther thought about the beneficial unity to which he summoned the parties is revealed in his enthusiastic approval of the Treaty of Weingarten. The army of the Swabian League, a union of lords and cities of southern Germany, confronted the well-armed masses of peasants in the Lake Constance region on April 15, 1525. George Truchsess of Waldburg, commander of the Swabian League, did not risk an attack on the peasants; he drew them into negotiations and tricked them into agreeing to lay down their arms and return home. He guaranteed them amnesty and promised to establish a judicial council to hear their complaints. But as the peasants disbanded and made their way home, Truchsess attacked and annihilated them. Luther had quickly published the text of the Weingarten treaty and had urged its imitation.

In the second half of April 1525, Luther undertook a fact finding trip through Mansfeld and the Thuringian centers of rebellion. He traveled to Eisleben, Stolberg, Nordhausen, Weimar, Wallhausen and once again to Nordhausen, but in vain. He found no hearing. The reformer Luther demonstrated personal courage, braced himself against rebellion, and experienced open enmity and threats to his person. Everywhere the spirit of Thomas Müntzer confronted him. What we consider the hot breath of revolution appeared to Luther to be hell itself. His hatred boiled over. It seemed to him that Germany was threatened with destruction in blood and fire and was on the verge of becoming a colossal grave. Everywhere and repeatedly Luther encountered the impact of Thomas Müntzer, "the Satan of Allstedt," who now pursued his course in Mühlhausen. From Müntzer Luther could expect no mercy. "I would like to smell you roasted; you have such a tender jackass' flesh," Müntzer had written to Luther (Müntzer 161).

The impressions gained from his fact finding mission did not depress Luther regardless of how destructive they were to his previous hopes for a peaceful course for the Reformation. After this trip no admonition to keep the peace or to extend grace and mercy was valid any longer. Now the message was:

> Thereford dear lords, liberate, preserve, help, have mercy on the poor victims, stab, strike, strangle where you can … because rebellion is not simply murder but, like a great fire that ignites and consumes a land, rebellion produces a land filled with murder and bloodshed and makes widows and orphans, and like the greatest calamity, destroys everything before it. Therefore, whoever can do so should smite, strangle, stab, secretly or openly, wherever possible, remembering that nothing can be more poisonous, damaging, disgraceful, satanic than a rebel. Just like the mad dog that must be killed, the rebel will attack you and the whole country if you do not attack him first. (WA XVIII 361; 358)

Luther conveyed this message in *Against the Robbing and Murderous Hordes of Peasants*, a pamphlet that summoned the lords to put down the rebellion. The lords needed no encouragement. They had already decided to act. On May 15, 1525, the Thuringian peasant army was destroyed near Frankenhausen. Six thousand peasants were slaughtered. Thomas Müntzer was captured and tortured in Heldrungen (probably in the tower) and, on May 27, decapitated near Mühlhausen.

As a teacher of Holy Scriptures, Luther should not have responded as he did. He could have left his position stand as it was expressed in *Admonition to Peace*. Luther was no Müntzer and could not have become one. Did temper temporarily conquer him? At most, in the selection of his words but not in fact. That Luther opposed rebellion he had written four years earlier. Luther's perspective of the Peasants' War was quite different from our retrospective view.

"Mercy" here, "mercy" there .... I am not interested in your plea for mercy, but rather in respect for what God's Word demands; therefore, my pamphlet is appropriate and remains so even if it offends the whole world. What do I care if the pamphlet displeases you as long as it pleases God? ... Is it not proper to keep one's mouth closed when one has heard what God says and desires? Or is God obliged to impart to such unworthy mouths reasons and justifications for why He will have it so? (WA XVIII 386)

Angrily, violently, caustically, Luther attacked on all fronts and defended his severe pamphlet against the peasants. God must sustain him and lend His Word to Luther's anger. Luther's class position, as he had said of faith, was not derived from his intellect. Class position and faith do not depend on intellect but determine intellect, as they do not permit themselves to be comprehended in morality but rather subject morality to themselves. This moral attitude toward power and property demonstrates the subjection of morality. Power and property cannot be dispensed with because there must be inequality among people; otherwise, no worldly power can exist.

Thomas Müntzer seized upon these aspects—which he had perceived in the new pope of Wittenberg, as Luther was now occasionally called—when, in the fall of 1524 he wrote against Luther:

Behold, our lords the princes, they are the cesspool of usury, of theft, and of robbery; they claim all creation as their property: the fish in the water, the birds in the air, the vegetation of the earth must all belong to them. Thus they remind the poor that God has commanded, thou shalt not steal, but that commandment does not apply to the lords and the princes. The lords and princes cause the people—the poor peasant, the poor artisan, and others—to live in misery and poverty, and when a poor man offers the slightest resistance, he must be hanged. And to all this Dr. Lügner (Liar) says amen. The lords themselves have caused the common man to be their enemy. If the lords do not wish to do away with the cause of rebellion, how can matters turn out well in the long run? If when I proclaim such a message, I am considered rebellious, so be it. (Müntzer 149)

Because he proclaimed this message, it was necessary that Müntzer be counted rebellious, and when Luther heard this message, he was obliged to proceed forcibly against it. This was not a matter of theological dispute; on the contrary, it was a critical question concerning the character of the movement. Luther and Müntzer granted each other no concessions. They forgave nothing; the battle must be fought to the bitter end. "Therefore, strike, stab, strangle, whoever can," Luther vehemently urged his class. "On, on, on, while the first is still hot. Don't permit your sword to grow cold; let it not grow faint! Forge blow upon blow upon the anvil of Nimrod; topple their tower! As long as they live, it is impossible for you to be free of fear. You cannot hear God's Word as long as they reign over you. On, on, as long as it is day, God leads the way, follow Him!" Thus Müntzer incited his followers. The first German revolution was anything but tame. "There was a time when Germany produced characters who could be compared with the best revolutionaries of other countries, when the German people had developed an endurance and energy that in a united nation would have had marvelous results, a time in which German peasants and plebeians were pregnant with ideas and plans by which their posterity often enough was repulsed in horror" (*Marx-Engels-Werke* VII 329). This was the leitmotif for the book on the German peasant war written by Friedrich Engels in 1850. The rebelling masses of the first German revolution were more merciful than they should have been. Instead of striking off the heads of their masters, the peasants trustingly handed them the pen for a quick signing of agreements which no prince honored longer than was necessary. Vainly Müntzer had warned, "My greatest concern is that foolish peasants will agree to a false truce because they do not realize the danger" (Müntzer 257).

Although the rioting peasants were moderate, the princes and lords struck and failed not to repay the peasants in double coinage. Luther parroted only what the lords thought, and for that the hypocritical lords and ladies blamed him. Even more loudly than from the ranks of the defeated, martyred, and slaughtered peasants who now knew how they stood with Luther and who no longer wanted even to hear his name, grumbling, complaints, and false accusations concerning Luther's lack of compassion came from the councils, officials, lackeys, and the loudmouths from the very circles that had put down the peasants or, in their hour of danger, had denied them any assistance. These groups were really no different from Luther as far as their attitude was concerned. On the contrary, while Luther was content to react against the peasants in writing and preaching, the councils and their lackeys took physical action against the peasants: the councils collected all types of weapons, powder, lead, food, and money for a militia; enlisted, equipped, and financed the defense force; strengthened fortifications; placed garrisons in the castles; drafted the enfeoffed knights; enlisted mercenaries; and in the ranks of the peasants placed spies who diligently gathered intelligence, hurrying to and fro, riding, running, writing, scrawling, lying, and petitioning. The councils sent executioners to the scenes of battle and paid them promptly for their services. Luther had provided this treachery with a good conscience. Now he exploded.

Luther, shaking with rage, accused the councils and lackies of hypocrisy. Yes, they say we do not agree with the peasants and we do not object to the punishment they receive, but it appears unjust to us that you teach that no mercy should be extended to the poor peasants, for you say that they should be killed without mercy. Answer: If that is your accusation, I am innocent of the charge. This is all a cover for your bloodthirsty wantonness and the fact that the peasants' state pleases you secretly. Where have I ever taught that mercy should never be extended? Is there not in the same pamphlet my plea to the authorities to accept in mercy those who surrender? Why don't you open your eyes and read those passages? ... It is quite apparent that you are a spider which sucks poison even from roses. (WA XVIII 388 ff.)

How can a battle be fought if there is no stabbing, striking, and strangling? The tone of the accusation displeased Luther. It presented to him very clearly his position and the position of his class, and it evoked his written response to the situation.

On May 30, 1525, Luther wrote to his brother-in-law Johann Rühel, who had transmitted to Luther news concerning Müntzer and at the same time had informed Luther that *Against the Robbing and Murdering Hordes of Peasants*, had aroused shock requiring an explantation. "That I am called a hypocrite is fine, and I am glad to hear the accusation. Do not be surprised; for some years now, you have been hearing me blamed for and accused of many things, but with time the accusations have dissipated or have been proven false. I would need much leather indeed to muzzle the mouths of all my critics" (WA BR III 515). To strangle without mercy could only produce martyrs, and in Leipzig it was openly reported that, now that Frederick the Wise was dead, Luther feared for his own hide and sought to dupe Duke George into approving Luther's action.

Luther's reaction to Rühel's assessment is still tainted by the bitterness of the battle. "The peasants should eat straw. They do not heed the word and they are mad; thus they must hear the musket and it servers them right. We should pray that they learn to obey, but if they do not, mercy cannot be extended. Let the muskets subdue them; otherwise, they will make things a thousand times worse" (WA BR III 515).

If we wish correctly to evaluate Luther's position in the early middle-class revolution, especially as reflected in this critical passage, we must first ask with what social class or group Luther identified himself, in the interest of what social class he was spokesman, and by which social forces his activities were directed. Here is the place correctly to assess and to summarize what we have learned of Luther's social origins and of the social status that he finally achieved, and above all else to understand how he pursued his profession and how he assumed class indentification through these means.

Luther's parents already had completed the transition from agrarian life with its many feudal ties, to entrepreneurship in mining, thereby turning to a life more and more dependent on early capitalism and suffering the unavoidable consequences regarding their manner of thinking, feeling, and acting. At the same time this new way of life meant abandoning the village and commitment to the city, resulting in the urbanization of a previously peasant farm family.

Martin Luther was the grandchild of peasant farmers as well as the son of a miner, through whom he peasant link, which Luther later occasionally mentioned in his *Table Talks*, began to fade at least for two reasons. Unlike many village children, Luther had not lived under the same roof as his peasant grandparents; furthermore, the social climb of his parents by hard work was possible only because they had abandoned the village. The peasant components in Luther's character, on which an emphasis in popular presentations not so long ago was still in vogue, were probably exaggerated in the accounts of an aging Luther as recorded in *Table Talks*. Nevertheless, these peasant components had nothing to do with Luther's class position, or, if something, a negative influence reflected in the many derogatory remarks by Luther concerning the peasants. He accuses them of being miserly, dishonest, dull, and concerned only with their own advantage, and as far as the Christian faith was concerned, not very mature. Of course, these remarks should not be taken too seriously, because Luther never minced words in criticizing any other social group, and he had laid down the law to each in its turn; furthermore, we should not forget that Luther's view of the peasant was obviously stamped by the common platitudes of humanistic literature.

Hans Luder's goal of assisting his son to an elevated and respected position in the society of the day by the sudy of law was an ambition typical of the social class in which he was working his way up. Already in his imagination Hans Luder could see his firstborn as a judge, counselor, or official in a princely court. Such ambitions were realistic expectations of the early middle-class entrepreneurs. To consolidate and secure his position, the petty entrepreneur of the early bourgeois society needed good relations with the urban and territorial authorities, because these authorities not only guaranteed tranquillity but, under favorable conditions, could also help the social order to improve. Finally, the secular authorities, especially the princes, guaranteed the political and legal framework for the whole society. It was particularly important for capitalistic enterprise in mining that the princes held authority over the mining operation. Although conflicts occasionally arose, control by the princes was initially advantageous to all.

Luther's family heritage illustrates the gradual development of a class position, a connection to the representatives of the then-most modern means of production, and an orientation to higher socio-economic achievement through dependence on those in positions of authority. However, Luther broke away from the course prescribed by his father; he enterred the monastery and became a monk and a priest.

With respect to his class position, entering the monastery was a step toward fundamental change, because monastery and Church knew no classes. Every baptized Christian belonged to the Church regardless of his position in the society, and in the monastery members of all classes and groups were accepted. Furthermore, whoever was admitted to the monastery or was ordained a priest—as was Luther two years after his admittance to the monastery—became estranged from his original social milieu.

Luther adjusted to a status within the feudal society which temporarily liberated him from the immediate ties to social classes and groups. He was not a burgher, farmer, or noble; not a feudal lord, serf, or peasant; not a manufacturer or early capitalist entrepreneur; not a knight, soldier, or member of the city council. He was obliged to study, pass examinations, and climb the academic ladder; after a few year he became a university professor and theologian. Furthermore, as professor-theologian, he found himself after a few years once again caught up in historical currents as he engaged in subversive and revolutionary activity. It is under the specific historical conditions of the sixteenth century that we encounter Luther the intellectual.

The sixteenth-century ingelligentsia, who cannot be measured by today's yardstick, were dependent on individuals or organizations for their livelihood. The intellectuals were concentrated at universities, at princely courts, in urban councils, and last but not least in ecclesiastical office. The intelligentsia were dependent on patronage, especially when they sought independence and not to be in someone else's service; when it was not possible to find a patron, however, they endeavored to establish themselves at some university. With the development of the printing press there was already a quickly expanding book market, but no intellectual could earn his living solely by writing because the concept of copyright did not exist, reprints were in vogue, and honorariums were rarely paid. Gifts and contributions from persons in high positions substituted for honorariums, and the most secure means of gaining a livelihood was still through a Church benefice. Indeed, the universities themselves to a great degree were established on ecclesiastical benefices.

Coming from all sections of the society, this heterogeneous intelligentsia lived in the tension between Church, secular authority, and public opinion. This intelligentsia was a major force in formulating public opinion critical of Church and society and thereby in creating that necessary arena in which ideological discussion of the broadest spectrum could be conducted.

Luther was a typical example of this intelligentsia. His activity in ecclesiastical service and in his teaching office at the university led him into deep intellectual conflict with scholastic theology and the Church hierarchy, a conflict which threatened his life and from which he was at last rescued by his prince, who offered Luther social and political asylum.

However, his respect for secular authority is not by any means an opportunism born of the circumstances that understandably could have led Luther to increasing orientation toward princely domination. In Luther's orientation is reflected, on the contrary, the political rationale of the entire group to which he belonged as well as that of the early rising capitalistic circles from which he came. The sixteenth-century intelligentsia served the territorial princes and their rule; the intelligentsia helped to erect the territorial state; the intelligentsia drew its living mainly from the princely territorial state, was supported by it, and defended it from all assaults from within and without.

Luther's attitude toward the territorial state is not unusual. On the contrary, his attitude represents the rule rather than the exception. The territorial state lies on the line of progress in the centralization of the state apparatus, a line originating in the feudal system. In western Europe there developed on the foundation of the league between king and burgher strong feudal monarchies that tended toward absolutism. However, in Germany a strong central authority was lacking. Furthermore, the emperor at the very beginning of the Reformation had decided against it. Under these circumstances, it was the princely dominion that provided the centralization indispensible to the middle class and the intelligentsia. However, the German princes did not contribute to centralization on a national scale, as the kings of France and England has done; on the contrary, they centralized within the context of each of the innumerable separate sovereignties of the splintered Holy Roman Empire of the German Nation. In brief, Luther's class position was such that, by his place in the division of labor that marked his society, his entire personal development, his posture, and his impact on the class struggle, he had become a representative of the intelligentsia that was closely affiliated with the middle class and dependent on the territorial prince. Furthermore, his class position explains his attitude toward the Peasants' War.

The Peasants' War brought no new transition in Luther's position. It simply clarified his consistent stance in class struggles: with the majority of the burghers, on the side of the rising electoral territorial state, against the papacy and the Roman curia. But the reform movement and the class struggle that accompanied it had struck a course which Luther no longer wished to pursue and indeed could not pursue without breaking with the very class into which he was firmly integrated. Luther was not capable of such a radical rupture. To be sure, he had shed his cowl, but not his class, which, on the contrary, he defended tenaciously and inflexibly without regard to the consequences.

According to Karl Marx, the Peasants' War was "the most radical act in German history" (*Marx-Engels Werke* II 386). The Peasants' War bore the stamp of the revolutionary-democratic traditions henceforth pursued by the German people. Before the revolution of 1848, Germany had experienced no other popular uprising of such vehemence as was seen in the German Peasants' War.

By giving precedence over all religious and theological questions to the fundamental question of power, as it relates to the ruling and the ruled and to social organization as well as to revolution, the Peasants' War sharply interrupted the course of the Reformation and the entire revolutionary movement. In the regions where the rebellion broke out, the power of the rules was temporarily paralysed and the establishment of a new authority was begun—though not completed, for at an early stage it was destroyed by fire and sword. Nevertheless, for a brief moment in the middle of the Peasants' War, a historical alternative had flashed across the scene as the rebellious peasants had begun to organize themselves regionally in the pattern of the Swiss cantons.

To be sure, we must be cautious not to strain the "What if?" However, it is a justified question, and it must be asked repeatedly because it alone opens a window on the uniqueness of the historical moment, without which historical reflection is boring, loses its drama, and hardly promotes more than a burden on the memory. "What if?", more than any other consideration, opens the moment toward the future. The openness, to be sure, is not without obstruction, but it continuously offers more than a single possibility of action. Everything that happens does not necessarily have to happen in the way it transpires. History occurs according to certain objective rules, but these rules emanate from the subjective activity of man, and they continuously include a broad dialectic of possibility and reality. The objective course of history is determined by plotting a line of realities across a plane of possibilities. Politics must recognize, create, and realize the possibilities.

From a social and economic point of view, it becomes clear from the specific actions of the peasants and especially from their demands that a military victory, if they had won, would in no way have resulted in the complete destruction of the ruling noble class nor of the breakup of large estates. Nevertheless, it would have resulted in considerable relief for the peasant economy from feudal payments of various kinds and therewith advantageous conditions for agrarian capitalistic development. Beyond that, demands like those of the so-called Heilbronn program for a unified currency, measure, and weight system provided greater opportunities for the development of the middle class and for a national market.

Such conclusions are not merely speculative; they simply describe what the rebellious peasants had already accomplished but could no longer perpetuate after their defeat.

Of course, another question is how long, in the case of a peasant victory, the results would have remained unchanged, or what direction would have been taken. This question cannot be answered. One can only suppose, based on indications, that the most advanced countries of Europe would have proceeded more quickly toward capitalistic development and that such a development would have determined the direction of the entire continent.

Thus the defeat of the peasants determined that no fundamental changes in the balance of power between the ruler and the ruled would take place. However, lack of change meant that those social and political forces that in the historical forefront of the Reformation had set the tone in economical and political affairs continued to do so, and would determine what Germany would derive from the Reformation and from the entire middle-class revolution. Those social and political forces were vested in the territorial lords and that part of the middle class allied with them.

The revolutionary course, which finally channeled itself into a powerful anti-feudal popular uprising, had been given decisive impetus by Luther; all who wanted to promote reform in some manner had appealed to him. Luther's tragedy, as well as the tragedy of that particular historical hour, was that his class position led him to side with ruling authorities, thereby inevitably bringing him into opposition with the natural consequences of his own movement.

Chapter 13

"The Word Abides":
Marriage and the Eucharist Controversy
Summer 1525–Fall 1529

Luther exulted with the victors. He appeared to have been caught up in the intoxication of the bloodbath. But he did not wholly belong to the victors; he was only half theirs. The other half of him belonged to those to whom the victory of the princes offered no benefits and even threatened their position. There were doubts about the strength of the Lutheran movement. What was openly proclaimed in Leipzig was rumored in other places. The doubt concerning Luther's position was not entirely unfounded, because it was during those days, when the fate of the peasants was being decided and Luther's class position was becoming clearly manifested, that the elector Frederick the Wise died. With Frederick's death on May 5, 1525, the question was brought into sharp focus as to whether Luther's expressed views had been patronized exclusively by this man or whether his reforme movement was in fact politically and economically supported by some of the other imperial estates. In essence it was a matter of whether Luther's position in the battles of the early middle-class revolution was solely determined by the coincidence of his particular situation in Wittenberg, or whether he represented the interests of distant social and political groups, for only if the interests of such social and political groups were represented could the Reformation, at least in Germany, mature. Doubtlessly the realm of the possible was drastically reduced after the end of the Peasants' War, but what remained did not preclude significant decisions. For instance, it was not at all clear which of those interests and needs of the ruling authorities that supported the Reformation would prevail. Would the attempts to endorse the Reformation only to the extent that it would expand the territorial authority of the princes prevail, or would the cities and their urban middle class succeed in expanding their own area of influence through the Reformation? The socio-political aspect of the reform movement had already indicated these possibilities. On the other hand, a very dangerous test of power was still to be addressed: the imperial or Hapsburg-Roman counterattack. In contemporary terms we might say that this test was the unavoidable confrontation with the counterrevolution. This confrontation had great significance, and not only for Germany, because the outcome would decide whether the Reformation would be sustained and would continue to develop in the land of its origin. Ongoing reform depended ultimately on whether the Reformation, under the secular authority of the princes or of the cities and their urban middle class, would be able in the future to provide ideological stimulus and support for progress. In Germany the continued future development of the European Reformation cycle was at risk.

The death of the elector, temporizing and good old Frederick, whose nickname "the Wise" Luther gladly acknowledged, deeply affected him and caused him grave concern. The news of the elector's death reached Luther in early May in Weimar, as he continued his preaching tour through the regions troubled by the Peasants' War. The news caused him to break off his itinerary and hurry back to Wittenberg.

Arming and enlisting were occurring at fever pitch, and troops were being assembled at staging areas. Frederick's funeral, regardless of all expense and genuine piety, became a telling test of the influence that Luther enjoyed at court and of the extent to which his advice would be heeded in this situation. During his life Frederick had carefully avoided any personal contact with Luther or granting him an audience. Only once had Frederick seen Luther in close proximity: in Worms at the imperial diet. Whatever had to be arranged between Luther and the elector was done through Spalatin and was accomplished through correspondence. In the matter of introducing a new liturgy for All Saints Church in Wittenberg, Luther could make no headway with the elector. The elector held a protective hand over the Catholic canons of All Saints Chapter, Luther's obstinate opponents. The elector was to be buried in All Saints Church, otherwise known as the Castle Church. Was he to have a Catholic funeral? What a remarkable set of circumstances: while rebellion raged in the dukedom and castles, palaces and monasteries were put to the torch, and the fate of the dukedom itself seemed to hang by a thread, the court, and Luther also, agonized over what kind of burial to provide for the elector. This scene was not as strange as it might appear, for now it was most important to provide a sign and to give attention symbol. Thus it was a relief for Luther and his Wittenberg friends that the elector Frederick at least on his death bed had received the Eucharist in both kinds.

As was the custom at the death of great leaders, the burial was to be conducted with pomp and ceremony: a procession which the common people came out to meet and then joined; bell-tolling; the bearing of the casket by eight pallbearers, all knights and nobles; the accompaniment of the casket by the common folk in the funeral procession through cities and boroughs; the poor, candles in hand, wailing in grief at the casket. Luther had no objection to these procedures. However, to the proposals that "a bishop or a high ranking prelate was to celebrate Mass," that two separate Masses were to be celebrated, that four offerings were to be made, and that a general offering was to be collected, Luther responded, *Non placet* (This has no place here; it does not please me). Luther also considered it a spectacle barbaric and ridiculous for his century "that steeds be drawn up around the altar," and that a lance be broken. However, he did not object "that a sword be buried" *ut ex more* (according to custom) with the body of the elector (WA BR III 488). The sword pertained to the office of the Saxon elector because he was at the same time duke of Saxony and imperial vicar. During the period when the imperial throne was vacant between the death of one emperor and the election of another, the elector of Saxony was the imperial head of the empire and commander of the imperial forces, which, of course, existed only on paper. The evening before the burial, on May 10, Philipp Melanchthon gave an eulogy in the Latin language and Luther preached in German. On May 11, at the burial service, Luther preached again in German.

He had passed the test. He had been given a sign. However, the test and sign were valid only for electoral Saxony. How would the other lords react? It was not so evident that matters would proceed as they had up to the death of Frederick the Wise, because even those who wished Luther well and secretly rejoiced that he had caused the Roman curia so much difficulty could not completely dismiss the idea that Luther's undertaking, despite all counterprotestations, had played a role in provoking the Peasants' War, the greatest danger to the status quo of the power structure. The temptation was at hand to wipe the slate clean and return to the Roman Church and the good old times when the guidelines were simple and clear. Was the Reformation to collapse along with the Peasants' War? The peasants were severely punished. But would it be wise to strain the bow too much, to destroy everything that had been accomplished in the last few years, and thus to provoke still another rebellion? Both possibilities appeared conceivable and had to be weighed.

A third possibility finally prevailed in the wisdom of the hour. The old Church had been seriously damaged by the Peasants' War. Many monasteries had been laid waste and the monks driven off. Many of the clergy had been forced to seek refuge with the princes; the power of the knights already had been broken in 1523 with the defeat of Franz von Sickingen. In the face of general insecurity the territorial lords had demonstrated themselves to be the most reliable forces for order; the urban middle class, especially the oligarchical city councils, had gained the support of the princes against the threats of the lower classes. The endangered nobles had been forced to appeal to the princes for help. The princes joined forces and, without imperial help, put down the rebellion by their own might. The princes were masters of the situation. Should they now agree to full restoration of the pre-Reformation privileges of the Roman curia, and permit once again in German affairs an interference that the princes had bitterly resented for years and that now had significantly weakened? Under these conditions, it was advantageous for the princes to pursue their respective religious policies as they had begun to do in recent years in the lands which had remained Catholic as well as in those in which the Reformation prevailed. Of course, current policies would change, in that the princely hand would rest more firmly on the Church and clergy in order to exercise the strongest control and to drive from office all those who had made common cause with the rebellious peasants, had hesitated in taking sides, or had in any way made themselves suspicious. The weight of the Reformation in this power constellation, and the form that it would assume under the new arrangement, remained to be demonstrated.

With unfailing instinct Luther had sensed this tendency of the time, and since the summer of 1524, if not earlier, had been doing whatever he could do, at least in electoral Saxony, to promote the influence of the Reformation. Luther was well aware that the princes, by their united action against the peasants, had drawn closer together. Although Luther earlier, in his first pamphlet concerning the Peasants' War in which he appealed for peace, had directed part of his criticism to the princes—including the Catholic princes, of course, and especially the Catholic duke, George the Bearded—now he considered it advisable cautiously to feel out those princes against whom, up to that time, in various ways, he had demonstrated a certain disrespect—not without just cause. Luther would exercise caution in his relations with such a powerful potentate as Henry VIII of England; his old enemy Duke George; and last but not least the archbishop of Mainz, Albrecht of Hohenzollern, whose indulgence trade eight years earlier had incited the entire controversy. Luther's correspondence with these potentates was not totally successful, but it did contribute to minimizing the differences that existed between him and these rulers. The correspondence provided both sides the opportunity for reconciliation and repeated expressions of good will.

Until 1525 the Reformation had been firmly established only in electoral Saxony, Hesse, the county of Mansfeld, the majority of the imperial cities, and a variety of smaller provinces. In many cases the reformed areas lay interspersed with Catholic regions. Furthermore the new ecclesiastical regulations were still tentative, and it was difficult to specify whether in any given region Catholic or Reformation ecclesiastical forms prevailed. Therefore, after the Peasants' War and with it the "Reformation from below" were lost, it was very important for the continuation of the Reformation that its political base be expanded. Luther had grasped this essential truth and had sought personally or through friends to win as many authorities as possible, both inside and outside the empire, to his teaching.

The most interesting attempt in this direction was the attempt to persuade Albrecht of Mainz to marry so that his ecclesiastical properties would be transformed into a secular dukedom. Even though this attempt failed, it was not built on sand. It was known that Albrecht enjoyed liaisons with many women. Albrecht interpreted celibacy not as an exercise in asceticism but rather as license to satisfy his natural desires without burdening himself with the duties of marriage. In addition, Albrecht was a worldly person, a patron of the arts who had made the Moritzburg in Halle into a center for the arts and who had enlisted the service of Matthias Grünewald. But above all else Albrecht was a Hohenzollern, and it was with another Hohenzollern, also named Albrecht, that Luther achieved in those weeks of the Peasants' War his greatest political success: the transformation of the territory of the Teutonic order into the secular dukedom of Prussia. To be sure, that Albrecht who was the master of the Teutonic order belonged to the Franconian rather than to the Brandenburg line of the Hohenzollern house. But what difference did that make? It was a political maxim and well understood that the dynasties, despite their separation into various lines, when at all possible pursued common interests and, despite all family rivalries, practiced a policy beneficial for the entire house.

What Luther could not have known in 1525 proved to be exceptionally important in the future history of Germany: in 1618 Poland, which possessed feudal suzerainty over Prussia, would enfeoff the Hohenzollern elector, Johann Sigismund of Brandenburg, with the dukedom of Prussia. This union between Brandenburg and the dukedom of Prussia in the person of Johann Sigismund would give rise to Brandenburg-Prussia. The decisive precondition for such a formation was the victory of the Reformation in the former ecclesiastical territory of the Teutonic order and its transformation into a secular dukedom. Since 1523 Luther had corresponded concerning this matter with the grand master of the Teutonic knights, and as early as 1523, he had advised the grand master, Albrecht, to transform his ecclesiastical province into a secular dukedom. Could the achievement in Prussia be repeated in Mainz? What would happen if a spiritual elector, the chairman of the imperial collegium and the chancellor of the empire, should embrace the Reformation? If this goal could have been achieved, Luther would have accomplished more with a good word than the unfortunate Franz von Sickingen had been able to accomplish with drawn sword and cavalry charge.

Luther's plans and deliberations were in no sense timid or modest. What appears to us by historical hindsight to have been a missed opportunity and fills us with bitterness in the light of the slaughter of the rebellious masses, Luther did not regard as the end of an old hope but rather as the beginning of a new one, a confirmation of what he believed to have always known: the devil wills to destroy evangelical reform, but hell is unsuccessful in its compaign. God's Word triumphs over the devil's efforts. This attitude on Luther's part was only a logical conclusion because he had never, not even for a moment, toyed with the idea of using the Peasants' War to promote the Reformation. That is why Luther's letters and writings reveal no particular depression during this period. On the contrary, Luther gloried in what he had done, disavowed nothing, and made no excuses. The struggles, however, had cost him strength. Luther viewed them in an apocalyptic dimension, but he had survived. Now he would sever the last papal tie. He would marry.

Luther frequently had advised others to marry, but always he had laughingly declined when it was suggested that he do so. Now he took the step. For three years he had been acquainted with a Cistercian nun, Katharina von Bora, now twenty-six years old, who came from an impoverished noble house and who, in April 1523, with eight other nuns, had escaped from the convent of Nimbschen near Grimma. Luther had played a personal role in arranging for the escape; the merchant, Leonhard Koppe, from Torgau, had arranged the details for the flight and had carried it off successfully. On Easter night the nine nuns had secretly left the convent. The story that they were smuggled out of the convent in herring barrels is apocryphal. We can be certain only that Koppe drove them to Wittenberg in a wagon. The arrival of the nuns in Wittenberg caused a sensation and much gossip, derision, and crude humor. It was not so much freedom as a husband that the nuns sought, the popular gossip had it: all of the nuns were under fifty years of age. The gossip, derisive as it was, hit the nail on the head, because for clergy, monks, and nuns to be allowed, able, and willing to marry, and to have a suitor or a spouse was, under the terms of the Reformation, the most significant realization of what they conceived Christian liberty to be and of what they could do with it. It testifies to the significance of Christian liberty as now employed by monks and nuns that the general society laughingly gave its approval and left in their corners the killjoy grumblers who were shocked by such marriages.

While students gave free rein to pornographic humor, Luther wrote one letter after another begging for at least a few gulden so that the escaped nuns would have something to eat and be able to exchange their convent habits for discreet secular clothing. Some of the nuns were soon picked up by their families. Others married. Three remained to be cared for: Margarete and Ave von Schönfeld and Käthe von Bora. These nuns could not return to their families because the families lived in the territory of Duke George the Bearded, and he took a dim view of the defection of nuns from their convent. Duke George had Heinrich Kelner, a citizen from Mittweida, summarily decapitated in Dresden for assisting a nun to escape her convent.

If Luther had wanted to marry at that time, he would have chose Ave von Schönfeld, not Katharina von Bora, whom he considered too proud. However, Luther procrastinated and Ave married another, a young pharmacist by the name of Basilius Axt, who supervised Lucas Cranach's apothecary. Käthe was taken in by Master Reichenbach and his family on Bürgermeister Street. Reichenbach was a jurist, a city scribe, and later also served as mayor of Wittenberg. Käthe made herself useful and became friendly with Barbara Cranach, the wife of Lucas Cranach, the famous artist, book merchant, and pharmacist, as well as Wittenberg's richest citizen and several times its mayor. Käthe desired to marry, but not just anybody. In her first weeks in Wittenberg she fell in love with Jerome Baumgärtner, just one year older than she and the son of a Nuremberg patrician family. Happiness and hope blossomed, but only briefly. Baumgärtner returned to Nuremberg and Käthe never heard from him again. She became ill from sadness and disappointment. Apparently the Baumgärtners rejected this misalliance of their son with an escaped nun. Even though Käthe came from a noble house, such an alliance was not acceptable to the proud patrician family.

As with Luther vis-à-vis the idea of divine election through grace ten years earlier, so it was with Luther vis-à-vis Käthe. He did not really want her, but took her because marrying her was the most satisfactory solution to the problem. Abandoned by Baumgärtner, Käthe finally overcame her sorrow and considered other possible suitors. Luther helped her to select suitable candidates and wanted to get her married. He recommended Nicholas Amsdorf, whom she would have accepted, but Amsdorf did not wish to marry. The rector of the university, Kaspar Glatz, demonstrated interest. In vain Luther urged Käthe to accept Glatz's proposal; Käthe found the old miser repulsive.

As circumstances would have it, Glatz, after the expiration of his term as rector, took over Karlstadt's Orlamünde pulpit that had just become vacant, not, however, without becoming involved in financial quarrels like his contentious predecessor Karlstadt. Luther tried one last time to divert the fate that was overtaking him. He wrote to Baumgärtner. Baumgärtner would have to decide; otherwise, it was quite possible that Käthe would be taken by another. Baumgärtner did not reply to Luther's letter. In the spring of 1525, Luther wore the monk's cowl for the last time; henceforth, the burgher's breeches and jacket and the professor's gown constituted his wardrobe. In thinking of Käthe, he must have smiled to himself frequently. The idea of marriage preoccupied him and others also, even though they did not necessarily think of Käthe when they urged Luther to marry. Luther regarded the prospect of marriage humorously and indicated ot Spalatin that there were surprises in store for him.

I have had three wives simultaneously and loved them so much that I have lost two who are taking other husbands. The third I can hardly hold with my left arm, and she too will probably be snatched away from me. But you are a sluggish lover who does not dare to become the husband of even one woman. Watch out that I, who have no thought of marriage at all, do not overtake you, you too eager suitor, just as God does those things that you least expect. (WA III 474ff.)

During his preaching tour through regions ravaged by the Peasants' War, Luther visited his father in Mansfeld. The father desired to see Luther's children before going to his grave. His desire would be fulfilled. Luther granted the pleasure to his father—a pleasure long overdue because, first, it is natural for a son to fulfill paternal hopes, and second, twenty years earlier the young Luther, with his thunderbolt-speaked decision to become a monk, had grieved his father and bitterly disappointed paternal hopes. Now, when time was of the essence, when momentous events were occurring, when even all that which was sensed rather than read in the apocalypse seemed to be transpiring, when the end remained uncertain, when perhaps Luther had not much longer to live, marriage was brought into the arena. Luther wanted to defy the devil once again. "If I am able to spite the devil, I will marry my Käthe before I die, though I hear that the peasants continue. I hope that they will not steal my courage and joy. Their own god, and no one else, may believe their statement that they are not like Müntzer" (WA BR III 482). The recipient of this letter, Johann Rühel, counselor to Count Albrecht of Mansfeld, must not be intimidated by those whom Luther would not permit to deprive him of his joy, those whom he held to be "Müntzerish"—the rebellious peasants.

Since Luther so certainly and naturally spoke of "my Käthe," he must have had an understanding with her; at least he must have been confident that she would not reject his proposal. Luther could be certain of Käthe, for even in the autumn of 1524, when Glatz was courting her and Luther was encouraging the courtship, the annoyed Käthe had appealed to Amsdorf and had complained that Luther was seeking to force Glatz upon her. In her complaint, Käthe had added that she would be prepared gladly to accept "Herr Doctor," as she called Luther, or Herr Amsdorf, if one of them would have her. Amsdorf held firm in his decision not to be married and to remain a bachelor throughout his life, but now Luther was ready to marry and Käthe accepted him.

On June 13, 1525, Bugenhagen married Luther and Käthe in the monastery. Witnessess were Lucas Cranach and his wife, who had in the interval taken Käthe into their home; the canon Johann Apel, who himself had married a former nun; and Justus Jonas, the provost of All Saints Chapter House. After the ceremony, the married couple lay next to each other on the bed, in symbolic fulfillment of the nuptial act, in the presence of witnesses. In the marriage ceremony, form and custom were followed, but after the decision to marry had been made, Luther had advanced the date to the earliest possible time in order to preclude unwanted advice and to silence evil gossip.

Käthe was twenty-six, Luther forty-two. The marriage went well. People had something to gossip about, and they relished the subject of the marriage of a monk and a nun. At the very moment when the whole world groaned under the catastrophe of the Peasants' War, did this wretched monk have nothing better to do that to woo a wayward nun into his bed? Even Melanchthon was perplexed, but he consoled himself with the thought that Luther would at least forego the buffoonery that accompanied wedding ceremonies, "which we often have criticized," and that Luther's new estate would enhance his honor. "The man is exceedingly gracious, and the nuns have employed all their arts in order to ensnare him. Perhaps his many contacts with the nuns, despite his noble nature and grandeur of soul, have weakened and inflamed him. In this way, he apparently has been brought to change his life style at a very late age. However, the gossip that he bedded her before their marriage is an outright lie" (Stupperich VII/I 288ff.).

According to custom, the marriage ceremony and the symbolic nuptials before witnesses were to be followed by the couple's public appearance in church, and finally by a reception. The married couple were united with respect to Church, table, and bed. Luther postponed the reception for fourteen days to June 27 so that his parents, who must journey from Mansfeld, and his close friends who must come from greater distances, could be present: Amsdorf from Magdeburg, Link from Altenburg, Spalatin and the court marshal Dolzig from Torgau and Lochau, the counselors Rühel, Thür, and Müller from Mansfeld, and of course Leonhard Koppe, Käthe's liberator from Torgau, without whose daring deed there would have been no wedding.

The invitations everywhere were received with wry amusement. Luther himself still could not believe what had happened. "It is without doubt an adventurous occasion to which I invite you as I am to become a bridegroom. How strange that idea is to me! I still can hardly believe it, but the compunction is so strong that I must believe that I am to serve and honor it," Luther wrote to the Saxon Court Marshal Dolzig and requested game for the wedding reception (WA BR III 537ff.). Wild game requests are characteristic of Luther's court correspondence and provide insight. In the case of Leonhard Koppe, Luther assumes in his letter to Dolzig that Koppe already knows "what has happened to me and how I have become captivated by Käthe's charm. God enjoys performing miracles, to make me and the world appear as fools and apes. Greet your Audi from me, and take care when I host the lunch that you help my wife, and be sure to tell her what a fine man I am" (WA BR III 534). Luther continued his letter to Dolzig with a request for a keg of the best Torgau beer, "and be warned if the beer is not good, you will be obligated to drain the keg yourself" (WA BR III 539). Dolzig also was requested to bring Gabriel Zwilling with him.

Among his Wittenberg colleagues and friends, Cranach, Bugenhagen,

Melanchthon, Schurff, and Jonas attended the wedding reception. If the list of invited guests is reviewed, it will be noticed that with the exception of Luther's parents and the bride's parents, the guest list constitutes the original "Luther group," those friends who had stood with him through thick and thin: Spalatin and Amsdorf, who had supported Luther from the very first disputation; Schurff and Jonas, who, like Spalatin and Amsdorf, had attended Luther at Worms (Jonas was also the colleague who had held at bay Luther's opponents at All Saints Chapter House); Bugenhagen, who had secured positions in Wittenberg church circles; Cranach, who had influenced the Wittenberg city council in favor of the Reformation; the court marshal, Dolzig, who, like Spalatin, had had the ear of the recently deceased elector and who was thoroughly familiar with the organs of government; and Melanchthon, who, as a scholar, had so many wide and advantageous connections with the humanistic world. Also in attendance at the wedding reception and somewhat distinguished from the guests already listed were the city councilmen from Mansfeld, old friends from home who had helped to secure the Mansfeld territory against Thomas Müntzer. In addition, there was Wenzel Link, the former general vicar of the Augustinian order and the successor to Staupitz in that position. Link had protected Luther inside the Augustinian order and was himself now married. He held high the Reformation flag in Altenburg. In attendance also was Gabriel Zwilling, the glib German-Bohemian and satirizing agitator who had begun the campaign against the Roman Mass, had incited rebellion among the monks, and in his radicalism had perhaps exceeded even Karlstadt, although Zwilling had never severed himself from Luther.

Furthermore, one other guest was present, to whom no invitation had been sent but who had come anyway. Although he was temporarily residing in Luther's house, he could not be publicly introduced because he was obliged to maintain a low profile. It was under great duress that Karlstadt had fled from the ravages of the Peasants' War and, having no other place to go, had petitioned Luther for help and lodging. Luther had granted both; he was not petty or vengeful. After all, they had been colleagues, they had stood together against Eck in Leipzig, and they were both of the same profession, both university scholars. Despite the vitriolic exchanges of recent months, these ties bound them together.

Luther's marriage was the most decisive step in his personal life since his entrance into the monastery. His haste and impulsiveness upon embracing monasticism were perhaps matched by his hesitance and deliberate effort in gradually liberating himself from it. From the very beginning of his monastic life he had taken very seriously his Augustinian obligations. It was not indolence or negligence that had brought him into conflict with monasticism; on the contrary, the conflict was engendered by his conception of the path to salvation, as opposed to the merely contemplative life by which one could retreat from worldly problems and perhaps at the same time enjoy a modest security. Luther had embarked on the path of salvation. His concept of monasticism did not obstruct his spiritual development as he followed this path; on the contrary, monasticism provided direction, a goal and a dynamic to his spiritual development. First and foremost was the fact that he persistently kept vigils and engaged in daily Bible reading, which according to the Augustinian rule was an obligation. His persistent observance of the liturgical hours indoctrinated him indelibly in the piety of the psalms; the Bible took complete possession of him, especially after he was charged in his profession with interpreting Scripture; hence, a special place was determined for him in the social division of labor. Luther completely fulfilled his task as Bible interpreter and gave to society what it demanded, a biblically founded answer to the question concerning God's righteousness. The *justitia Dei passiva*, the suffering righteousness of God, once discoverd, rendered the monastic path to salvation questionable and finally erroneous. The monastic exercises and rules lost their meaning, but they had become so habitual that they could not quickly be abandoned. It was the monastic ideal of righteousness attained through good works that gradually expired in Luther; then he abandoned the vigils and Staupitz released him from monastic obedience; finally the pope excommunicated him. Luther could have left the monastery long ago as many of his fellow Augustinians had done, but where should he go? He held a professorship, and therewith his professional standing, from the Augustinian order. The material benefits and status provided something like tenure. Luther's living came from the monastery directly, for he received no other salary. And the struggle against the fleshly interpretation of the gospel and against the tendency to rebind Christian liberty to outward manifestations, thereby reducing this liberty to a new legalism, now incited Luther to stroll the alleys and streets in a monk's cowl and tonsure, thereby demonstrating the inconsequential nature of monasticism and all the outward gestures for procuring salvation.

Luther's monastic life was ascetic and celibacy a matter of course. Celibacy was no particular challenge for him. The temptations of the flesh, which occasionally presented themselves, Luther conceived to be entirely natural impulse and to be taken for granted. Celibacy was much less frequently violated in the monasteries than the malicious gossip and the pornographic cartoonists would suggest. Since man in Luther's view was by nature a sinner before God and should not seek to achieve sinless perfection, because man thereby would rob God of His honor, it was entirely natural and according to divine will that man employ his reproductive organs for the purpose for which they were intended. Since the beginning of the 1520s, Luther had written a whole series of pamphlets against celibacy and concerning marriage. The major idea in these pamphlets is consistently that marriage and cohabitation between man and woman was provided for at creation and that this provision should not be resisted. To place man and woman together and expect that they should not desire each other was just as irrational as placing fire and straw together and expecting no combustion. Luther repeatedly presented this idea in various ways. Of course he could not free himself from the idea that, as far as sexual activity was concerned, special conditions prevailed and that those who abstained from sexual union must possess a special grace. However, such a grace was given only to the few, and it was better for whoever did not possess it to marry rather than to wage continuous warfare with nature. The advice to marry was applicable for the majority. Luther thus made a major contribution toward easing the inhibitions, unknown to the ancient world, that had filtered into Christianity, principally although not exclusively through monasticism. Furthermore, that Martin Luther had personally experienced the monastic life, had thought it through, and had essentially overcome it, is an emancipating achievement of the first order.

Luther's marriage finally spelled the end of his monasticism. He now took leave of the monastic life and entered the secular world. The most important precondition for this transition was not only that he begin a civil marriage but also that he maintain it by the realignement of his material support. As an unpaid professor Luther did not derive from the monastery gifts and contributions sufficient to support a family or maintain a household. From the date of his marriage Luther received an annual salary of 200 gulden from the electoral treasury, exactly the amount received by Melanchthon, the highest paid professor at Wittenberg. In addition, the new elector, Johann, presented Luther and Käthe a wedding gift of 100 gulden, and even Albrecht of Mainz, not wishing to miss an oppurtunity to make a gesture of good will, sent his emissary to Wittenberg with a gift of 20 gulden. Luther refused to accept the gift from Albrecht, but Käthe, more practical than her husband, had no scruples about pocketing the money. Käthe was more practical than her husband. Managing the household fell to Käthe, for Luther understood precious little about day-to-day management because he could never quite overcome his monastic indifference to earning his daily bread. Wherever he could, he helped, even though he possessed no surplus. Several times he was in financial straits because he had vouched for people with no steady income. Käthe, whom Luther in playful criticism of her resolute character nicknamed "My Lord Käthe" early in their marriage, was not alone in pointing out that Luther was too generous and too casual in helping others. Lucas Cranach and the goldsmith, Christian Döring, who were among the supervisors of the Wittenberg community chest, finally forbade Luther as well as Melanchthon to serve as guarantors for those seeking loans. Luther was often perplexed by the peculiarities of his remarkable economy wherein, after tallying the income from his various positions, he discoverd that he had spent more than he had earned. Despite Luther's lack of skill in managing his finances, gradually, due to Käthe's thrift and supervision, a small surplus was established. Several rooms of the former monastery, which was now Luther and Käthe's dwelling, were used as a brewery. A poultry yard also was provided. The monastery garden, where Luther liked to walk, also provided vegetables and herbs. Luther knew how to graft fruit trees, and he marveled that such a small twig might prescribe the fruit for the entire tree, whereas it would seem that the opposite should be true. Luther the bookworm now felt the need to try his hand at other crafts. He attempted to repair a clock, and he actually succeeded in setting the casters to work once again, an accomplishment that gave him much satisfaction. He also tried his hand at wood lathing and at spinning. His success at these skills is not recorded. He pursued such activities for relaxation rather than to perfect a skill. In any case, Luther could not have devoted much time to crafts because the demands on him for lectures, correspondence, sermons, polemical writings, and the preparation of book manuscripts continued. Nevertheless there was a new impulse and a new order in his life. Earlier, when not at his lectern or in the pulpit, he had been at his desk from morning until night. In the evening, he had sunk dead tired into the same humps and bumps of the straw mattress that he had abandoned at the first cock's crow. Such housekeeping, or lack of it, was now at an end. Käthe was a very German housewife; that meant made-up beds, sparkling kitchen utensils, clean rooms, and no odds and ends left lying around the rooms. It is fortunate that Käthe did not reign over Luther's tower study, from which he had launched his first assaults against the papacy and where pamphlets, letters, papers, books, and manuscripts were piled not exactly in neat fashion. Also cluttering the study were quills, inkwells, and all those things that one needs when one has a doctorate. Within a year Käthe bore their first son, who was given the name Hans in honor of Luther's father.

In the autumn of 1525, when Käthe was looking forward to the birth of their first child, Luther addressed a necessary task that he had already postponed for a year, partly because he wanted to complete other work or because of pressing interruptions, but primarily because the subject of this necessary task—the long overdue confrontation based on differences with Erasmus of Rotterdam that had augmented over the years—was psychologically unpleasant. Käthe is said to have urged him to the task lest it be thought that Luther's respect for the great name of Erasmus was excessive and that Luther was therefore reluctant to challenge the renowned humanist. In fact Luther would have liked to challenge Erasmus earlier: it was not consideration for his renown that had given Luther pause but the obvious political expediency of not offending a friend of the Reformation. Luther realized that he and Erasmus were of different spirits, and Luther occasionally referred to their differences in his correspondence to friends. However, Luther also knew that enmity and suspicion were directed at Erasmus from the same circles from which the Edict of Worms had emanated. In view of this consideration, Luther had avoided polemics against Erasmus.

It was Erasmus who finally issued the challenge. For a long time Erasmus had resisted the request of highly placed persons to write against Luther, but now, in order to demonstrate his loyalty to the Roman Church, he took up his pen. Henry VIII of England desired such an Erasmian polemic and the emperor Charles V expected it. In the autumn of 1524, Erasmus bowed to pressure, while at that historically strategic moment Charles V, by the Edict of Burgos, forbade the convocation of the planned German National Council called for November 10. The imperial estates sympathetic to the Reformation (and not only the estates) had placed great hope in the council. After the diet of Worms in 1521, at which the Edict of Worms was issued, the two Nuremberg diets of 1522 and 1523-1524 succeeded in hampering measures and decisions that would have implemented the Edict of Worms against Luther and the Reformation. Especially the representatives of the imperial cities used their influence to this end. Pope Hadrian VI (1522-1523), who wore the papal tiara after the death of Leo X in 1521 and who earlier had been the tutor of the young emperor, was a Dutchman, the last non-Italian on the papal throne until the 1978 election of Karol Wojtyla as John Paul II. Hadrian VI wanted to take the wind out of the sails of the Reformation by having his nuncio Chieregati read in Nuremberg a confession concerning papal failures, by promising to redress the *Gravamina*, and by demanding at the same that the Edict of Worms be enforced. Hadrian did not consider his program merely a diplomatic check; he had the much more serious intent of restoring to the Catholic Church obedience and discipline while sharply attacking ecclesiastical abuses and encouraging reforms. But because Hadrian VI died in 1523, his attempts remained merely an interlude without long-range effect. Hadrian had also urged Erasmus to write against Luther. The imperial estates took notice of Hadrian's admission of papal failures without responding with any major concessions. The imperial estates stood firm by their demands: redress of the *Gravamina*, and then they would see how matters developed. As early as 1520, Luther had called for the convoking of a German National Council. In fact, his pamphlet *Address to the Christian Nobility of the German Nation Concerning the Improvement of the Christian Estate* had been conceived and written as the program for such a council. This subject was to be the council's fundamental consideration. That the National Council was ready to convene and had been summoned to convene on Luther's forty-first birthday was not without symbolic significance. The success of Luther's entire Reformation program seemed within grasp. However, at a stroke of the imperial pen, the imperial estates submitted. They did not dare to summon a national council in opposition to the declared will of the emperor. Perhaps the first shock waves in the wake of the Peasants' War, which rocked the ruling classes, made them more willing to submit to the emperor's will. Erasmus' attack on Luther at this historically strategic moment must have appeared especially treacherous.

Erasmus entitled his anti-Luther pamphlet *Diatribe Concerning Free Will.* Once again the first and fundamental questions—disputed in 1516 and 1517 and again in Heidelberg in April of 1518—with which Luther had opened the assault on scholastic theology, were debated. Luther was glad to take up the theme of this debate. "You alone among all the others have recognized the key question, and you do not bore me with the papacy, purgatory, indulgences, and similar nonsense .... You and you alone have identified that on which all else hinges and you have put the razor to the throat and for that I thank your heartily" (WA XVIII 786). Thus Luther evaluated the subject. And Erasmus commented on the significance of their engagement in battle in his own style: "Perhaps an Erasmus who writes against you will do more for the gospel than certain dunderheads who support you" (WA BR III 285).

Humanistic thinking will never consent to the doctrine of original sin, based as it is on the concept that human nature is totally depraved and of itself not capable of any good will, and that apart from grace alone, free will is nothing, can do nothing, does nothing except depraved deeds. Even though these pronouncements are biblically based and may be acceptable within an exclusively theological system, they do not appear reconcilable with the dignity of man. Catholic semi-Pelagianism, with all its emphasis on the role of prevenient grace, finally views free will as the decisive factor in attaining salvation, thereby conceptualizing "free will" as similar to "a healthy human understanding"—for how can a person be responsible for his deeds if he possesses no free will? How can he decide between good and evil? So reasoned Erasmus.

Such arguments, long known to Luther and many times presented to him, impressed him not in the least. God alone is salvation. God alone measures guilt. He alone condemns. He alone grants grace, justifies, and saves when He will and whom He will. Man can do nothing against this divine prerogative. Man can only accept the divine judgment. This is in fact best, and it is by the divine prerogative that man is well provided for, for God alone is infallible and His Being is grace and mercy. This concept that man is divinely elected to salvation or to damnation is the center of the predestination dogma that later the Geneva reformer Calvin made the center of his teaching, and that subsequently, under other historical preconditions and circumstances, could be linked closely with a prosperous middle class in the Netherlands and in England. Certainly Lutheranism was more hesitant than Calvinism in identifying the elect with any given class. But from a purely theological perspective Luther had already presented in his polemic against Erasmus' predestination ideas with such penetration that even Calvin later could not have formulated any stronger. That this formulation of Luther's predestination doctrine occured in his debate with Erasmus is not at all coninincidental; it was here once again a matter of the absolute defense of the unconditional liberation of the conscience from ties to old hierarchical prescriptions.

Therefore, Luther did not accept rational arguments against predestination doctrine. Such arguments, on the contrary, necessarily appeared to Luther, given his theological orientation, as suspicious from the very start because they originated from human nature which exalted itself against God. The "whore, reason," prefers to submit to the devil, adjusts to all situations, and proves everything that is demanded of her. Human nature does not possess free will. It is like a horse, ridden by God or the devil. The rider possesses the will, the horse obeys.

This was not just empty speculation on Luther's part, nor was it derived simply from a list of selected premises. Experience and observation lay behind Luther's predestination theory. His view was not based on "pure" theology, despite its formal presentation. In Luther's predestination theory unique psychological tendency and life experience were revealed. It is not coincidental that these revelations were penned by Luther a few months after the conclusion of the bloody Peasants' War.

Erasmus believed that he could find his most effective arguments against Luther by calling attention to the many contradictions in the Bible, for he had concluded that no definite answers and no absolute certainties could be derived from the Bible. Among scholastic theologians, the listing of "yes" and "no" answers had been a favorite exercise, in which the powers of discernment and the art of synthesizing could be tested. That Erasmus employed this method with veiled cynicism and haughty skepticism confirmed Luther's long-held suspicion that Erasmus belonged "with Lukian and others to the Epicurean pigsty, who, since they themselves do not believe in God, ridicule as irrational and ignorant all who believe and confess God" (WA XVIII 605). Luther found Erasmus' entire method of reasoning intolerable. Here once again everything depended on the "meat of the nut," as he already had learned in his Erfurt years: was it philosophy or theology that led to God? Erasmus' skepticism could not be tolerated because it undermined everything and rendered laughable the spiritual essence of the Reformation. If in matters concerning the Christian faith no certain and firm assertions could be made, as Erasmus would have it, then there was no point in challenging the papacy; then the entire adventure— all the battles engaged in and all the dangers endured by Luther and so many others—was worth nothing and was a farce. Actually Erasmus came to agree that the adventure was counterproductive. Repulsed by the day-to-day occurrences, he withdrew, weary and resigned, to his Basel study. Other humanists who at the beginning had placed great hopes in the Reformation came to the same conclusion. They were disappointed and preferred to return to the bosom of the Roman Church rather than to pursue a hopeless cause, which did not improve people after all and only provoked an even greater decline of morals, education, and scholarship. Against this assertion Luther declared: "Take away the firm statements of the biblical revelation and you do away with Christianity." And again: "The Holy Spirit is not a skeptic. He does not inscribe doubt or idle teaching in our hearts, but assertions that are more certain and firm than life itself and all experience" (WA XVIII 605). Luther insisted on this conviction, and he had to insist on it, for otherwise how could he persevere?

The pamphlet against Erasmus was the decisive defense of the fundamental intellectual positions of the Lutheran Reformation in the face of the rising Catholic counterthrust. From this moment on, Rome could, in its countermeasures against Luther, appeal with justification to Erasmus. To be sure, Erasmus, like many other humanists, had in his fashion prepared the way for the reformation of the Church. However, even now Erasmus was anything but an ardent defender of Rome. Erasmus' position was based rather on scholarly skepticism regarding the revolutionary storm and those whom he suspected of having incited it. But it was noteworthy enough that the rising Catholic counterrevolution spoke of human freedom and sowed doubt and skepticism while the Reformation as a progressive movement defended a deterministic world view according to which what occurred in the world was not dependent on human goals. The Reformation rejected skepticism and adhered firmly to clear, scriptural statements even when such statements were vehemently challenged, and even when the attack came from great intellectuals whom one would prefer to have on one's side. Luther entitled his pamphlet against Erasmus *The Bondage of the Will*. In reference to God this pamphlet brings into focus something of a concept long perceptible in Luther's thought: that of *Deus absconditus*, or the hidden God. It is in this same pamphlet that he defends the clarity and splendor of the Holy Spirit as well as the certainty and reassurance which are to be gained from the Bible. He also emphasizes again that anger belongs no less to the nature of God than do grace and mercy. This point had already been made in Luther's lectures on Paul's epistle to the Romans. But there is something gloomy about the concept of the hidden God even though it is not lacking in significance. The hidden God and the revealed God are one and the same. It is the same God who reveals Himself and remains at the same time concealed. This idea goes beyond the observation that God does not permit man to know all that He plans for the race. On the contrary, the disturbing conclusion drawn from this concept is that God engages in pantomime, concealing His Being: His power in impotence, His love in anger, His "yes" in "no." Because He loves, the Father is angry and His love is demonstrated by the very fact of His anger. The significance of this concept of the hidden God is that it makes faith in God possible where none of His love but only His anger is felt. It is noteworthy that this pamphlet was written while the excitement of the Peasants' War still stirred within him. The same conviction expressed in a confession of faith is inherent in the undaunted ability of Lutheran thought intellectually to confront and silence the voice of resignation in the face of the Peasants' War. His battle cry of "despite everything" and "now really in earnest" reveals Luther's inclination to believe God against God, or something of that ancient spectacle of man wrestling with God, which the Bible describes in the tale of Jacob, who wrestled with God and was henceforth called Israel.

Take God at His Word, trust His Word, and hold fast to Him: that was the kernel of Luther's particular piety, which stamped his character and by which his personality was molded from within. This tenacity in Luther's character was demonstrated by a debate, one which seems to us today to be meaningless and unproductive because long ago we broke with its prerequisite: the debate concerning the Lord's Supper, initiated by Karlstadt in 1524, which soon drew Luther into the arena against the South Germans and the Swiss. Many who partake of the Eucharist today probably do so simply as a matter of course, with an inclination to participate in an established tradition tasting those elements of a particular culture that make its religious customs meaningful. The participant today may regard partaking of the Eucharist as an act that serves to call to mind the memory of Jesus Christ and that should symbolize communal life. According to this view, in the Eucharist Christ can be present only in the mind of the communicant. Thus, at best, the communicant follows the path of Karlstadt and Zwingli, not of Luther; moreover, the communicant's rationale reproduces that of Karlstadt and Zwingli; indeed, the communicant is yoked with them. In fact, in regarding the Eucharist as a memorial only, the modern-day communicant even exceeds Karlstadt and Zwingly. The man who vehemently opposed these rational ideas, who rejected them completely, and who would deny their credibility, was born 500 years ago.

We must be cautious to recognize the frame of reference and the historical remoteness that distance the sixteenth from the twentieth century, lest we, in tracing the threads of the fabric of that society, unconsciously ascribe our value judgments to that period. With regard to the sixteenth century, all the interlacements were traced frequently by Luther and the other reformers in the questions that they raised, which were entirely different from those that directly interest modern man. Luther dealt with commerce and usury; the thought about these subjects, expressed his rage, and made suggestions as to how commerce could be more fairly conducted and how money could be made available in a more Christian manner, but decisions commerce and interest-taking he left to the authorities. Care concerning for the poor, the aged, and the infirm and ill, as well as care for children, were natural concerns of Christian charity, and were also praised as virtues and required as duties by other civlized religions. One of the requirements for knighthood was to serve as protector for widows and orphans. The *ora et labora* (pray and work) ethic was prescribed by the earliest monastic rules. To deny a worker his fair wages was considered, in the casuistry of the sacrament of penance to which Luther no longer held, "a sin crying out to heaven."

With respect to these concerns, Luther's positions did not differ from that of the other reformers, and he could easily agree with them on such matters. The strong similarity of their positions was due to the fact that these problems arose out of the immediate environment. It was not regarding the socioeconomic questions that reformers opposed one another in irreconcilable fashion, but rather concerning what occured on the altar. In this question the significance of their profession as theologians was concentrated. They understood more of chalice and pall (the covering for the chalice), pulpit and desk, than of middle class activities in commerce and trade, not to speak of farming; the reformers, however, were experienced in diplomatic matters and they could be employed in politics. The reformers were better at declining nouns and conjugating verbs than they were at measuring, counting, and computing. They solved their problems with grammar, logic, rhetoric, and quotations, not with the hammer, chisel, weapon, or hoe. The reformers were priests and scholars, not merchants, artisans, soldiers, or farmers. What already has been demonstrated concerning Luther's personal career was generally true for all the reformers: the division of labor in the society of their day had assigned them a definite place. Their workplace stamped its image upon them, and they carried out the office in which they found themselves.

On this very academic-clerical plane, and on no other, the problem concerning the Eucharist developed. Later middle-class revolutions would be led by an ideological and political leadership elite which no longer was materially dependent on the Church. The position of the later middle-class revolutionary elite no longer rested primarily on ecclesiastical titles and benefices and did not find it necessary to argue about ecclesiastical liturgical order. Therefore, in the Reformation period, the struggle for position and leadership of the revolutionary party was carried out primarily in the realm of dogmatics.

Nevertheless, these dogmatic struggles reflected in a certain sense those other questions of social and political controversy that lay at the foundation of the contention between the reform camp and its opponents. In his critical position of 1525 and 1526, Luther looked for new alliances and political forces with whom and by whom his teaching could be promoted and protected. Finally he found such allies in the Ernestine Wettin line and in the landgrave of Hesse; from other quarters also princely patrons were attracted to the Reformation. In Switzerland, however, where Ulrich Zwingli had carried on reform since 1521, there was no constellation of princely support. There, where the Reformation was dependent on the urban element and, in an emergency, on a wealthy agrarian nobility that also constituted a civil jurisdiction, it was necessary that reform be supported by these constituted authorities. This fact explains Zwingli's influence on the reformers in the South German imperial cities. Within the reform camp, the question remained as to whether the middle-German course and Swiss-South German course would find a common denominator or in what manner they would distinguish themselves from each other. The longer the answer was deferred the more pressing it became. After the severing of ties with Müntzer, the eucharistic controversy was, for Luther and the Wittenberg theologians, the most important ideological and political round of Luther's disagreement. Luther did not take the course of compromise but rather that of separation, whereby the German Reformation was finally uncoupled from the Swiss.

The eucharistic controversy was not the cause of the uncoupling. The reasons lay in the individual loyalties of the quarreling theological parties, adhering to entirely different social and political power structures. The theological controversy, however, articulated, clarified, and confessionalized differences. If the debate concerning the Eucharist had not brought about the anticipated division, other controversies would have pointed to the various reform routes, which would have been followed without the eucharistic argument.

Nevertheless, for all that, the strife pressed against nerve endings because the question concerned what the sacrament of the altar really was or might be and what should be understood by the presence of Christ in the form of wine and bread on the altar. For every concept, these question touched on the central nervous system of the Church.

In order to understand the theological positions in this matter, we must once again look back briefly to the debate, in the spring of 1522, between Luther and Karlstadt, in which the eucharistic question had played a role. Karlstadt tended to conceive of the "presence of Christ," who was not recognizable through the senses, as merely symbolic, or as a name for something that did not actually exist. Coming from Thomist realism, which saw reality in concept, Karlstadt turned to nominalism in the course of the radicalization of his views in order to rationalize the far-reaching changes in the outward appearance of the Church. Nominalism placed the concept in the symbol. Thus Karlstadt, from a modern point of view, was on an acceptable route. He therefore rejected the real presence of Christ in the Eucharist. This explains why he reacted so strongly, as in February 1522, after the Eilenburger negotiations, and especially after Luther's Lenten sermons in conjunction with which the elevation of the Host was restored to the Wittenberg service. Since in reality only simple bread was present in the Eucharist and not Christ, the elevation of the Host appeared to Karlstadt as idolatry. He believed that he would never be able to accept such a teaching and therefor he prepared to fight it.

In the Eucharist, Karlstadt recognized bread and wine and nothing else. In this view, when Jesus spoke the words of institution, "This is my body," he did not point to the bread and wine, but to his own body. In order to demonstrate his belief—for belief is all that it could be since Karlstadt had not been present at the Last Supper, nor had any of his contemporaries who were wrestling with the problem—Karlstadt went to the trouble of making use of Greek grammar and pointed to the distinction in gender of the Greek words for bread and body. Karlstadt believed that at one point and by one letter he had discovered certain proof that Jesus had begun a completeley new thought when, after the words of institution, he said, "Take, eat." These grammatical arguments Luther easily and laughingly discredited. However, the entire grammatical argument was meaningless anyway because Jesus spoke Aramaic, not Greek. Only if Jesus' Aramaic words were known would an argument concerning grammar—Aramaic grammar, not Greek—have any significance. Aramaic understands itself, not Greek. The aramaic wording can be reconstructed, but only on the basis of the Greek text, so that the arguments pursue each other.

From 1527, Zwingli entered the arena and struck with a keener sword than Karlstadt had wielded against the physical presence of Christ in the Eucharist. That the flesh profited nothing, Zwingli found in John 6:63. A body can be only flesh and not spirit. Thus, since the ascension, the true body of Christ sits at the right hand of God and can never be present on earth in the Eucharist. Jesus had instructed His disciples only to eat the bread and drink the wine in memory of Him. Oecolampadius shared Zwingli's view and used the same arguments. From Oecolampadius, who had written on this question even before Zwingli had expressed his views on the Eucharist, Zwingli borrowed his most famous and most characteristic argument that Jesus and the evangelists had used *alloiosis*: that is, the alternating sense of the same words whereby the word is used in its literal and symbolic meanings alternately. Zwingli would therefore contend that sometimes Jesus used the word "body" to signify His divine nature, sometimes His human nature. His human nature was completely bound to the flesh and, since the ascension, was no longer on earth; but the divine nature, free from this limitation, can unite with faith to be efficacious in the Eucharist. With good intentions, Zwingli made these arguments known to

Luther in an appeal to Luther's willingness to admit his own fallibilty. Luther was amused because he himself would never have arrived at such clever ideas. Seizing upon Zwingli's symbolic interpretation, Luther thought that insofar as a figure of speech could help clarify the explantation, the synecdoche—by which a part is named to suggest the whole—would be helpful. For instance, in modern times, when a hospital patient has an appendectomy, the staff may refer to him not as the patient Mr. Jones but as "the appendix case." By employing the synecdoche in reference to the person of Christ, Luther scores a great victory. Christ is God and man simultaneously. The human and divine natures are inseparably linked in Him. Not only in His human nature did Christ suffer and die, and not only in His divine nature was He resurrected, but both natures participated in His death and in His resurrection. Consequently, God is capable not only of suffering but also of dying, at least in the person of the Son of God. This idea, making an advance toward materialism, injects an awesome element into theological thought. The focus of Luther's lectures on Paul's epistle to the Romans—that is, the advice that exclusively the humanity of Christ be contemplated first, and that afterward only, attention be fixed on His deity—is again brought to attention at a hardly anticipated juncture in the sublimest mystery of faith. Therefore, this advice belongs not to the fleeting moment but to the fundamental substance of what Luther wishes to say. From this position, Luther rejects Zwingli's assertion, "the flesh profiteth nothing." Since Christ freely gave Himself for the forgiveness of sins and sealed His sacrifice with His word, He is completely present in the bread and wine. To be sure, bread and wine are seen, but when faith perceives Christ, then teeth also bite and chew Him. When faith is present, it overwhelms senses and is content with the Word. That is the meaning of Luther's sacramental realism. Certain experiences and observations must have laid the foundation for Luther's view of the Eucharist just as in a similar fashion his own unique experiences and observations had shaped his view of man as a horse saddled by an alien will.

When it comes to matters of faith, proof, by the very of faith, has no application. Proof is always directed toward reason and misses the essence of faith, which is to fill the vacuum where understanding and reason do not avail. This is not merely Luther's view. *Et si sensus difficit, ad firmandum cor sincerum sola fides sufficit* (If reason does not comprehend, that which faith imparts is sufficient for the pure heart), Thomas Aquinas had the faithful sing in the thirteenth century during the Corpus Christi procession.* "The more unprovable the more stubborn" applies to arguments of this nature. Is their persistence not obvious from the history of the Church, especially

---

* From the hymn *Pange Lingua*, of which the second part, the *Tantum ergo*, is employed by the Roman Church during sacramental benediction at the conclusion of the Mass.

from the manner in which dogma was established at councils, from the development of heresy and the fight to suppress them, from discrimination and suppression? If not, the course of the eucharistic controversy would abundantly demonstrate their perseverance.

From the beginning it was clear to Luther that nothing about the presence of Christ in the Eucharist was to be proved, only believed, and that other views were to be rejected. Luther picked apart his opponents' arguments not in order to set up counterevidence but merely to demonstrate the essential insignificance of those arguments and thus to fall back upon the simple words of institution. It was in accordance with this line of perseverance that Luther had his congregation sing *The Word Stands As It Is.*

Luther firmly insisted on "the Word as it is" because it served two purposes: that of political proponent of his own Reformation, and that of representing him as a theologian of grace accompanied by the Word. It becomes clear, in observing Luther's stages of development, that it is the last point that led him ever deeper into conflict with the Church authority. Luther constantly bombarded those around him and the general public with his basic ideas, from which he never digressed; he held to them to the end of his life. As a result, problems to which solutions had long since been found surfaced anew; theodicy gave rein to capering ideas which he brought to tow with formulations that shocked his students because of their apparent contradictions. The apparent digression will be discussed later.

The fact that Luther did not waver in his dogma enabled him to be a stabilizing force in political life and to have a personal political influence. Since the beginning of the indulgence controversy, Luther had had a voice in politics; on the one hand, by crystalizing in his reform efforts the social concerns from wide problem areas and diveregent interests, and, on the other hand, by opening and defining new fronts, he had promoted the Reformation. For some, Luther was a stumbling block and a rock of offense because he could not be won for every cause; for others, he was the cornerstone (see I Peter 2:6-8). In theology as well in politics, Luther was single-minded, not as pliant as the scholastics and not as tolerant as the humanists; his single-mindedness was his strength. The princes who wished to exploit him as a puppet had to learn at Worms and once again in the eucharistic controversy that Luther was indeed not a "lackey of the princes," as he has been called, since the Peasants' War, by the Catholics, thought not only by them.

In 1524 political leagues to oppose or to promote the Reformation began to appear, sponsored by the princes. In Regensburg a group of South German princes joined ranks with the Catholic Hapsburgs. Duke of Albertine Saxony, the elector of Brandenburg, the elector of Mainz, and the duke of Braunschweig-Wolfenbüttel created a league of Catholic princes for central and northern regions of Germany, while Landgrave Philipp of Hesse and Duke John of electoral Saxony entered a covenant in Torgau and Gotha in 1526 to protect the Reformation. Although Protestant princes derived advantages from the Reformation, with their pro-reform posture they also ran the risk of calling down upon themselves the wrath of the strong Hapsburg house, and with it the wrath of the emperor. The young and energetic Landgrave Philipp of Hesse early saw in the Reformation the opportunity to strengthen his political rule. It was Philipp of Hesse who put out feelers in Switzerland, hoping, in the event of a military confrontation with the Hapsburgs, to enlist the help of battle-tested allies, for the Swiss foot soldiers, still the most desired on all battlefields, possessed the highest esprit de corps. To be sure, electoral Saxony responded with reservations to these broad alliance plans: electoral Saxony always had to reckon with the possibility that Albertine Saxony, under the ardent Catholic George the Bearded, would take advantage of any war between electoral Saxony and the Hapsburgs by attacking electroal Saxony in the flank. Many years later, in the Schmalkaldic War, this apprehension proved to be justified.

In the face of the strong power constellation arryed against the Reformation, Philipp of Hesse found the eucharistic quarrel between Luther and Zwingli most annoying; indeed, it interfered with Philipp's plans, and he desired to see it put to rest. Therefore Philipp urged a meeting between Luther and Zwingli, at which they should reconcile their differences and, without losing face, strike a compromise.

For Luther, however, the question was more than a mere quarrel with Zwingli, and Luther could not accommodate Zwingli's position merely for the sake of a diplomatic checkmate. The argument had first erupted between Luther and Karlstadt, not Zwingli, indeed at the onset of the Peasants' War and as a result of the differences between Luther and Karlstadt manifested in the events in Wittenberg during the winter of 1521 to 1522. Since his expulsion from electoral Saxony, Karlstadt had disturbed the otherwise tranquil progress of the Reformation by zealously agitating against Luther in southern Germany and especially in Strasbourg. The Strasbourg reformers contacted Luther regarding the question of the Eucharist, and Luther prepared his answer, *To the Christians at Strasbourg*, in the form of a general epistle, deliberately employing the style of Paul in his address to the congregations in Asia Minor, Thessalonica, Rome, and elsewhere. By employing the Pauline form, Luther wished to demonstrate his claim to leadership of the Reformation. It was this claim to ledership that Luther saw challenged in the activities of Karlstadt.

In the meantime Karlstadt had surrendered and revoked his earlier position. Only as human fallible opinion, not as divine doctrine, would Karlstadt henceforth consider the arguments that he had employed against Luther in the eucharistic controversy. At first, Luther housed Karlstadt in his own home and then procured from the elector permission for Karlstadt to live in Kemberg near Wittenberg. Karlstadt promised not to publish. He could not keep his promise. How could he, as a university professor and preacher, lay down his pen forever and keep his opinion to himself concerning the events that transpired around him? Thus, in 1528, Karlstadt was forced to leave electoral Saxony once again, this time forever.

However, the problem lay not in the personality of Karlstadt, Zwingli, Oecolampadius, or others, but in the self-replenishing current and spiritual force that from time to time still issued forth, which Luther was convinced was at heart destructive and had in fact nourished or even given rise to those attitudes that had incited the Peasants' War. Seeking for arguments and reasons where faith alone sufficed could only draw a Christian away from that which makes a Christian a Christian, entangle him once again in the law, and psychologically lead him back to the papacy, which in reality was far from having been overcome. Luther was completely convinced of this position, and he wrote in pronounced clarity an elucidation of his view. As strange as it may seem, Luther regarded the papacy and the Peasants' War as being, in the last analysis, on the same plane, and the "sacramentarians," as he called those opposed to him with respect to the eucharistic question, as trailblazers to both the papacy and the Peasants' War. By accusing the sacramentarians, Luther used exactly the same technique that his Catholic opponents had employed when they accused him of being the cause of the Peasants' War and when they described the Peasants' War as "fruit of the Lutheran seed." At the same time, Luther not only distinguished theologically his German Reformation from the Swiss Reformation, but also mitigated the force of a societal support base as an impetus for change and thereby narrowed the latitude of his own reformation.

While the reformers established their position in the Reformation by doing what they did best—developing dogma—on the imperial level an unrelenting diplomatic struggle concerning the validity of the Edict of Worms was in progress. At the diet of Speyer in 1526, it was agreed that each imperial estate should conduct itself in the manner that it believed justifiable before God and the emperor. This Solomonic resolution expressed the reality that no uniform policy concerning the execution of the Edict of Worms was possible; the resolution merely gave expression to what in fact had been practiced all along. Luther could be well content with such a state of affairs. So long as such a principle retained its validity and was realizable, there was good hope not only that the Reformation could not be entirely suppressed by the empire but also that by preaching, agitating, and, last but not least, influencing and converting the princes, the reformers would continue to expand the borders of the Reformation. It must have seemed most important to the Hapsburgs and to the Catholic party to end this state of uncertainty and to achieve a legal basis for their initiatives. In a subsequent imperial diet convoked in Speyer in 1529, the Catholic estates pushed through and documented in the protocol a decision obligating all estates to execute the Edict of Worms. Some imperial estates, four princes, and fourteen cities raised protest against this decision. Matters of faith cannot be decided by majority opinion. Since this protest at the diet of Speyer in 1529, the supporters of the Reformation have been described as Protestants.

With this confrontation at Speyer, the situation grew more intense; as a result, the Protestants sought allies and political unity among themselves. The elector of Saxony could no longer ignore Philipp of Hesse's insistence on reaching an agreement with Swiss Protestants. Thus the meeting between the Swiss Protestants and the South German and Alsatian reformers, so desired by Philipp of Hesse, finally took place in Marburg in October of 1529. The purpose of the meeting was to clarify points of doctrinal strife in order to facilitate a political alliance. Agreement was reached on fourteen points, but not on the question concerning whether or not and, if so, in what sense, Christ was present in the Eucharist. This problem could by no means be resolved, not even for the sake of political accomodation. Each side retained its own opinion and declared itself the winner of the argument.

Chapter 14

The Preaching of Law:
For Law and Order in Society and Church
1526–1537

The princes remained princes, and they became even more princely than before; the Reformation afforded them the opportunity to increase their authority. They did not remain exactly what they had been before the challenge of peasant demands. The Reformation had incited Karsthans (Hans the hoer) to reach for the flail in order to hasten the kingdom of God on earth, which Müntzer was already prophecying. Furthermore, the peasants wanted not only to elect their own preachers but also demanded that forest, stream, and meadow be returned to them and that serfdom be abolished. Moreover, they believed that the realization of these reforms constituted the true Reformation.

The revolutionary intensity of the Reformation gradually abated; However, "Müntzerization" persisted for years to come. But indeed, as for what could not be checked, the longer it endured the more it was given practical application to whatever extent it could be implemented. From Luther's impetus and ideas a work had developed, partially his own, but to a greater extent belonging to those who engaged in reform with him because, although they were not dominated by the same faith that impelled Luther, they wanted to seize the opportunities along the way. Increasingly, the work possessed Luther more than he possessed the work.

Luther and the princes were agreed that Müntzerization should no longer be tolerated. But how were such ideas to be circumvented, since "there must be sects," as Luther had read in Paul's writings and as Luther had grimly commented when he had first heard from the regions that supported Müntzer, and since Judas also must be numbered among the apostles? The theologian of grace, which comes from the Word, acted in the same manner as those Church fathers of the same persuasion, among them Augustine, who, more than 1,000 years earlier, had approved the state censorship of the Circumcellions and other heretics. Of course, there will always be sects, but they must be suppressed because they are evil, and in order to punish evil, God sanctioned the use of the sword by the state. The sects reject instruction and thereby demonstrate themselves to be ruled by evil. That is how Luther saw it.

Müntzer was dead, but not his spirit. In the Peasants' War this spirit had made a bold attempt. However, all hopes were dashed with the defeat of the peasants. But should the supporters of the popular movement give up because of Müntzer's defeat? As earlier, when after the exposure of the Bundschuh conspiracies some of those who had barely escaped—especially Joss Fritz, the "exemplary conspirator," as Friedrich Engels called him—continued to bear the standard and indefatigably sought to reestablish a new Bundschuh, so also after the Peasants' War there were men who survived the shock of defeat, reflected on what they had heard, hoped, and experienced, and formulated those reflections into a new aspiration. The Bundschuh conspiracies, to be sure, arose in a period of developing and deepening crises, and they had contributed to the accentuation of every situation of revolutionary potential. The conspiracies merged in the revolutionary movement attendant upon the Reformation and were propelled by it. Now decisive defeat was meted "the Reformation from below." However, Müntzer's spirit prevailed in the Anabaptist sect, a domain different from that of the rebellious peasant bands. Imperial law imposed the death penalty on Anabaptists, and the authorities did not hesitate to invoke the law. Luther did not object to the imposition of this penalty, but he felt sorry for the Anabaptist, the poor devils.

Luther was now primarily continually concerned with discovering what course the Church should follow. That this question could be addressed only in relationship to the secular authority and under its protection, he did not doubt, even though he had misgivings that the secular authority might overstep its province and once again interfere with doctrine. In 1523, Luther, in parrying ecclesiastical and political reprisal, had approved the spontaneous practice of the congregation to judge doctrine and to call and dismiss ministers. However, only one year later Luther rejected the argument of those at Orlamünde who claimed that Karlstadt had been elected by the congregation. Had the Orlamünders done anything other than that which Luther himself had praised the Leisnig congregation for doing? However, because the Orlamünders had selected a *Schwärmer* (fanatic), Luther criticized the election and the electors. Luther evaluated the person elected in terms of his credentials for office and the spirit he manifested; he was not concerned with the principle or the method of election. The method he regarded as secondary, and he left such matters to the peculiar circumstances.

Luther, in opposition to Eck, had championed the idea, in the dispute concerning papal primacy, that the true Church was invisible. He did not now need to revoke this idea because it was not the true and invisible Church that had become corrupt and needed correction but rather the visible Church; it was in the visible Church that the sheep and goats must be distinguished. It was the visible Church that needed to be strengthened by prayer and proper worship. Thus in 1525-1526, Luther was considering the possibility of composing a list of the most trustworthy people, convening them for intensive training, strengthening them with prayer and special worship services, and sending out this little select band to work as leaven, reconvening them at regular intervals to restrengthen and instruct and thus create a firm and reliable kernel fot the re-creation of the visible Church. Luther entertained this idea during the period of the struggle against the "fanatics," a word that Luther now applied, among others, to Müntzer, Karlstadt, and even Zwingli. It was the period in which Luther addressed several circular letters to cities and congregations because he now saw himself more than ever before as the new apostle Paul. A "church within the Church" *(ecclesiola in ecclesia)* suggested itself to him. Of such an idea, orders and sects are born. The rationale which underlies this idea had in the course of not many generations permitted the Roman priestly Church to evolve from the apostolic congregation and the congregations later added by Paul. The cunning of history placed before practical problems the man who wanted to hold only to faith, grace, and the Word, burdened him with responsibility, and directed him contrarily once again into those paths from which he had desired to liberate himself once and for all.

Luther soon gave up his idea of a list. Regulating such a church would have required his personal ecclesiastical administrative apparatus, which he did not possess and with he did not need to encumber himself, because such an apparatus already existed. For instance, throughout the country there were parishes staffed with clergy and there was a secular administrative apparatus which not only exhorted the clergymen to fulfill their official duties but also threatened them with removal from office for failing to do so. The admonitions and threats were all the more effective after many of the pastors who had invoked Christian liberty had married and therefore could not accept as easily as could a celibate preacher the economic insecurity that removal from office entailed.

But lists of a different kind were compiled. There are shelves of them in the archives: protocols from the so-called visitations that on the advice of Luther and Melanchthon were conducted, sporadically from 1526 and systematically from 1528. Village after village, congregation after congregation, city after city were visited by a commission of electoral officials and appointees. The commissions were assembled to provide jurists and people with administrative or financial experience who would concern themselves with the income of the clergy and the legal status of the parishes in regard to feudal and benefice rights, while the theologians on the commission inspected and took special interest in whether the clergy understood Lutheran doctrine, whether they administered communion in both kinds and admonished their congregations to be obedient to secular authority, and whether they espoused ideas of the papacy or Müntzer.

The visitations were not entirely in the interest of the prince. Zwickau preacher Nicholas Hausmann, Luther, and Melanchthon found it necessary to urge several times that Elector Johann order visitation. The visitations were primarily concerned with the specific social and economic interests of the lower clergy: the ministers, preachers, and teachers. Before the Reformation these groups had certainly not enjoyed a high income, but at least they had received a secure and generally constant income. However, now all was chaos. Ecclesiastical wealth from which the lower clergy derived its living had been expropriated on the one hand by communities and city councils and on the other hand by the nobility. New prerogatives governed the use of the wealth, and no thought was given, or at least no priority was given, as to how the lower clergy to whom it had once belonged could sustain itself. Luther watched with growing displeasure as the nobility allowed itself free license with the expropriated wealth. The school system collapsed, along with pastoral care. Teachers and preachers were forced to take on additional jobs in order to sustain themselves. Parental desire to send children to school flagged. Children were better employed watching flocks in the meadow and performing household chores. To become a minister was no tempting perspective. Thus the stimulus to study also disappeared. And why learn Latin since the Mass now was read also in German and Latin no longer maintained its earlier monopoly? Only the prince was in a position to restrain and discipline the nobles, and to guarantee to minister and teacher an income which would permit them to nourish their families. The individual congregations could not perform this task as well as the prince. Of primary interest to the lower clergy was not communalization but regionalization. The congregational principle of 1523 had been a weapon against the bishops; the regional principle constituted a hope for the Lutheran clergy. The congregational principle had liberated the clergy from the chains of the Roman hierarchy. With the territorial-regional principles, the clergy, after surviving the battle and realizing penurious gains, erected for itself a new house. The urban councils as the administrative and executive councils of the community chest were immediately at hand, whereas the prince was remote. In the narrow streets of the little cities anti-intellectualism flourished, but princes established universities. There were reasons why a statute of the University of Wittenberg reminded the rector and the deans not to be seen too frequently on the streets and, when walking the streets, always to be accompanied. Cities and communities were middles class, thrifty, and stingy; princes were feudal, generous, and wasteful. The citizen, the guild master, the artisan, the merchant, and the dairyman were independent. Each lived from wages received from orders and from what he could sell at nearby markets. The clergyman, minister, preacher, teacher could only imagine himself independent. He had nothing to sell, and no ordered anything from him except rhymes to be read at guild or family celebration, or the administration of the Eucharist, baptism, or marriage, and the final benediction at the grave. The clergy earlier had earned money from such requests, but Luther had ruined their business. Socially dependent, this class, to a much greater extent than were the others, was obliged to lean on the authorities. And that dependence prompted a certain good conduct, discipline, and obedience in all outward matters.

This also was what the clergy was expected to teach the people: good conduct, discipline, and obedience; the *Instruction for the Visitation Commissioners to the Clergy in Electoral Saxony* had expressed this line and enjoined remarkable exposition.

Howewer, since some believe that nothing should be taught except faith and that penance follows from and after faith, and because critics must not be allowed to charge that we have abandoned our former teaching, it must be remembered that repentance and law belong to the same faith. Therefore, belief that it is God who threatens, commands, terrifies, etc. is prerequisite. Thus for the common unschooled person such an approach to faith may be expressed in terms of repentance, commandment, law, fear, etc., in order that he better distinguish and understand the faith in Christ which the apostles called *justificantem fidem*: faith which justifies and takes away sin. However, it is faith in Christ that justifies; faith in the commandment and repentance do not provide justification. If an approach to justifying faith is not facilitated for the common man, he will raise unprofitable questions about the word "faith" and become confused. (WA XXVI 202 ff.)

The first one of those who turned away from the respected scholastic theology and turned against the deceivers of the people in the indulgence controversy was none other than D. Martin Luther. Where was his *sola fide* now? The common unschooled person was not to ask unprofitable questions.

The *sola fide* did not possess the rationale necessary to an institution, which the new doctrine now deeded. *Sola fide* at first had served to appease Luther's predestination fears in the monastic cell; then it became the beacon for the widespread anti-Rome movement. *Sola fide* was a convincing and valuable argument against the Roman hierarchy. To be sure, the struggle against Rome was not entirely over, but the need for ideological argument began slowly to change. "Free will" again demonstrated a usefulness for the intellectual mechanism of social attitude: whoever is disobedient and is punished may not blame the punishment and its cause—that is, his transgression—on fate or on some hidden god. Furthermore, the secular authority must be able to hold the individual accountable, but accountability is possible only when free will is ascribed and hence the ability to choose between obedience and disobedience may be assumed. Free will is a postulate of the individual's possibility of being guilty, a presupposition that pertains to jurisprudence, not to Lutheran evangelical theology: God does not grant free will for the salvation of souls, but jurisprudence presupposes free will as justification for judgment. Painstakingly, Luther had maneuvered free will out of theology; now, by the instruction of electoral counselors, free will found its way back in.

> Man has freedom of the will to perform or not to perform, on his own initiative, external works, regulated by law and punishment. Therefore, man is able to achieve a wordly righteousness and to do good works by his own strength, given and sustained by God for this purpose. Hence, Paul describes as the "righteousness of the flesh" that which the flesh or person is able to do by his own power. If man, however, by his own power can achieve righteousness, he then has a choice and freedom to flee evil and to do good. (WA XXVI 226)

Has Luther so completely forgotten himself? Not quite. The words quoted are not his but Melanchthon's. The commission's work of investigating and reporting to the elector had transpired and its findings were reflected in the *Instruction*. Luther satisfied himself with writing a preface for it. Melanchthon was more familiar with the commission's work. His stature had increased, and he no longer resided in Luther's shadow. Was Melanchthon now permitted to write what Luther had not tolerated from any cardinal and which not many years ago he had criticized in the writings of Erasmus? To save face, a watershed had been provided. In *The Bondage of the Will* Luther had observed off-handedly that this point was not man's inability to choose to do this or that but rather his lack of freedom before God to do anything for or against salvation. In the *Instruction*, a few lines after the Melanchthon quote cited above, the idea is pursued: "But this freedom is hindered by the devil," and "On the other hand, man cannot by his power purify his heart and work godly works." Thus it appears that Luther could without reservation accept the *Instruction* and provide a preface for it. But the center of gravity for preaching and teaching had markedly shifted since the early years of the Reformation. Because the commissioners were required to solve practical problems that with faith alone they could not solve, it became necessary to prevent violation of law. Judicial thinking was blended once again with theology, borrowed theological vocabulary, and became oriented toward practical application; theology was not permitted to serve matters of faith alone.

The law now appealed to Luther. His understanding of it was different from that of the jurists. They understood by the term the law and decrees issued and executed by secular authority, or the regulations by which the jurists were required to conduct their office. On the other hand, Luther understood law as the law of God as manifested in the order of creation and as given to Moses on Mount Sinai. But the word "law" was used for the jurists' concept and for Luther's concept. Would the common unschooled man be able to distinguish the subtle differences in the use of the word?

The law of God and the secular law were for the tribes of Israel, of course, one and the same during the wilderness wandering, during the conquest of the Promised Land, and until the division of the kingdom (circa 922 B.C.) into the northern kingdom of Israel and the southern kingdom of Judah. By adhering to the taboos and hallowed norms of community life, the will of God was performed and the law given by Moses was fulfilled. Priests and prophets saw to it that judges, kings, and the people honored the law. Beginning with the division of the nation, or at the latest with the Babylonian conquest of Judea (597 B.C.) and the subsequent deportation to Babylon and Babylonian captivity (596–539 B.C.), the natural assumption that the law of God and the secular law were one and the same ended. The secular law of Babylon was obviously quite different from those sacred laws transmitted by hallowed tradition. Returning from the Babylonian captivity, the Jews under Ezra and Nehemiah rebuilt the temple and the Jerusalem wall. The laws were now reorganized, edited, and codified in the fifth book of Moses, called Deuteronomy, a "reissue of the law." For the internal communal life of the gradually evolving history of Judaism, the divine law and secular law once again were almost one and the same, but they did not become completely identical, because a complete political independence was never again to be achieved by the Jewish nation. As foreign governors, armies of occupation, and alien religions dominated Palestine, secular law could no longer be regarded as divine law. It was now necessary to distinguish what originated with God from what originated with man. It was necessary to distinguish "the law" (the Torah) from laws. Both codes were to be obeyed, but the commitment differed. Compliance and consent were sufficient for the secular laws, but the law of God went beyond to faith and was linked to the promise of "redemption." Works were demanded in order to fulfill the Mosaic law, and faith was necessary in order to believe in the redemption of the promise. This redemption was envisioned in terms of the historical reality of the centuries immediately before Christ. Mainly in a materialistic sense, through the reestablishment of political independence, redemption was viewed on the one hand as something totally transcendent and not to be comprehended by the mind; on the other hand, as something which already was established in the world but which only the heart comprehended, which pacified the heart and reconciled it with God. However, in either case redemption was associated with the appearance of a messiah or redeemer. The gospel, the good news that the redeemer would come or, unbeknownst, had already come, was from the very beginning most intensively associated with Mosaic law. The less strict adherence to Mosaic law was efficacious in changing political and social circumstances or at least in pacifying the heart, the more compelling became the gospel. Law and gospel are dialectically coupled; they reciprocally determine each other. The one presupposes the other and logically follows it. Consequently, without knowledge of the law no understanding of the gospel can be achieved, and without knowledge of the gospel no understanding of the role of law can be realized. But the individual process of arriving at an understanding of this reciprocity is only a logical, abbreviated recapitulation of what took place as social ideological process at the great historical transition periods in which Christianity participated, whether in the formation and rise of Christianity during the first century A.D., or in the Constantinian transition extending to the fall of Rome (475 A.D.) and the beginning of feudalism, or in the early middle-class revolution—with which we are here concerned—during the transition from the Middle Ages to modern times. This transition was characterized by the decline of feudalism and the corresponding rise of capitalism. "Law and gospel" are, in this historical context, theological concepts of the problem-circle of reality and illusion, reality and utopia, what is and what should be, institution and ideology. Thus it is not surprising that Luther seized upon the gospel (Christ alone, grace alone, faith alone) when he was fighting against the legalistic "salvation by works" of monasticism, that he thereby preserved the distinction between law and gospel, that he clung to the gospel and employed it against ecclesiastical hierarchy torpid with scholastic legalism. While Luther clung to the gospel and worked for its revival and dissemination, he deepened knowledge and understanding of the reciprocity of law and gospel and came unwittingly to a new respect for law.

The path to this respect for law was not direct and unobstructed; on the contrary, it was difficult, and for many of those who had originally cheered him and in those early years had desired him to go even further, the point at which he had arrived was vexatious.

The old Luther became conservative. His conservatism was demonstrated in the increasing agreement of his teaching with the new institutionalization of the Church and in the congruence of his doctrinal tendencies with the declining revolutionary curve. But the reasons for his conservatism were not that he had abandoned the ideals of his youth or had betrayed the gospel. On the contrary, his conservatism is explicable exactly in the fact that the did not abandon the ideas of his youth or betray either his friends, himself, or he gospel. The old Luther was the consequence of the young Luther, the logical and historical consequence of an integrated personality. The old Luther, especially in those matters that constituted his essential achievements, was a reflection of the young Luther, not a correction. However, circumstances had so changed that, although the rhetoric for the most part had remained the same, its social function had changed. The young Luther was a rebel in a monk's cowl, pouring oil on the fire. The old Luther was a preserver of order in the professor's gown, calming the waves. For the most part, his words were the same and their meaning was the same, but in the course of time they sounded another ring, which caused his followers and disciples to raise the question of inconsistency.

There was no direct and unobstructed path to respect for law, but the tensions between the classes necessitated that a way be found. It must lead not only to recognition of the law but, most significantly in the changing situation, to an acceptance of the law and to a long-overdue emphasis on the law as necessary to preserve the identity and original intent of reform. In the struggle against scholasticism and hierarchy, the law was at first absorbed in the gospel or concealed behind the gospel; then, in the *Sermon on Good Works*, the Decalogue was reclaimed for the gospel. The writings of 1519 on the sacraments are stamped with the obligatory nature and the irrevocable rejection of ceremonial law. Furthermore, the debate with Karlstadt, Strauss, Müntzer, and the "fanatics," concerning the validity of Mosaic law, leads to another posture of determinative discovery: not only ceremonial law, but all that Mosaic law contains by way of concrete legal prescriptions is nonobligatory on Christians because this law is valid only for Jews. In order to gain clarity on the subject, Luther studied the explicit discussions of Deuteronomy and lectured on this book. Studying the Bible and seeking counsel from it was his method of drawing on the earliest practical application for the solution of contemporary problems. Furthermore, with the Mosaic law in his sights, he targeted the Decalogue. The Decalogue has validity; we should honor it, but not because it was revealed to Moses. The revelation of the Decalogue is only to the Jews; it was proclaimed to them, not to us. The Decalogue's validity for us exists in that at creation it was written by God into the heart of man. The Decalogue is "natural law" that all possess and that all may apply, even the heathen, and by "heathen" Luther means all non-Jews. Thus, in the struggle against Karlstadt's concept of law, Luther presses his concept of "natural law," one of the more important ideological platforms for subsequent maturing bourgeois revolutions.

However, precisely at the juncture at which divine law is divested of its historical materialization as Mosaic law and is declared no longer binding, the dialectic reverses itself. Mosaic law unloads the past and loads the present. It is not by accident that fanatics and rebellious peasants helped set the law in place, for God in righteous indignation ordained that the law be preached to them in order that they be torn from the devil and become ripe for the gospel. With "faith" Luther had attacked the hierarchy; it was the "law" with which he confronted rebellion, tumult, and the common people. Luther was obliged to defend his actions; therefore, he delved more and more deeply into law.

Natural law was written in the heart by God, even without the Word on which "faith alone" was dependent and whence it proceeded; consequently, man had a natural tendency to do what was just and good, or what was commanded in the Decalogue. Therefore, man's nature, despite original sin, could no longer seem so corrupt as it had appeared to Luther before and during the period of the indulgence controversy. As a result, compromises were possible, and Melanchthon could use language which, when used by Erasmus, had infuriated Luther. Luther also defended Melanchthon against the Eisleben preacher, Johann Agricola (1499-1566), one of Luther's young enthusiastic admirers, who had read Luther's writing carefully and understood them thoroughly and who, desiring only to hold fast to the pur evangelical truth learned from Luther, was anything but a fanatic. Not until ten years later did the final break come between Agricola and Luther. Gradually Luther accommodated himself to the rationality of what he at one time had bitterly contested. He proceeded deliberately and slid into channels that he earlier had abandoned with fanfare. There are two explanations. First, the theological categorical pairs—between whose poles at any given time or from time to time his thought hovers—are coupled and inevitably point back to the opposite pole whenever they are questioned concerning their existential foundation. It is, therefore, not because the intellectual process is flawed or the character weak that problems solved long ago reoccur; rather, holding firm to the once-discovered solution leads back again to the starting point. Under different conditions and with enriched experience, one rediscovers the starting point on a higher plane, even though it may not be recognized and accepted as such. It is a well known Hegelian spiral, the negation of the negation, which results.

Second, long-solved problems out of a more vibrant set of circumstances reemerge somewhat transformed, because the social movement, like the ideological process founded on it and with which it is dialectically coupled, is successful—but after 1525, only in that exact measure permitted by the prevailing power structure and necessitated by the social, political, and social-positional interests of the forces now directing the movement. In this context, the outcome of the movement is a new or transformed institution. The movement alters the prevailing condition; the institution maintains what is achieved. When the movement has been victorious, it must with commandment and law secure discipline and order. When this step is not yet or perhaps never will be possible, and when the movement must remain more or less in opposition, it must persevere in faith against commands, prescriptions, and laws. As an opposition movement it makes use of faith; as a stabilized order and institution it makes use of the law. But the function of faith is thereby altered to a certain degree. Whereas in the struggle against the Roman hierarchy faith was and remained *crimen divisionis*, now in the Protestant areas it became increasingly a criterium of inner intellectual conformity with the prevailing order. Against Rome faith was the gesture of defiance, but vis-à-vis one's own secular authority, the gesture of submission. As a criterion for conformity, faith can no longer exclusively be based on the Bible; on the contrary, what each one must know, say, and confess must now be precisely prescribed. Confessional statements are necessary short formulas to which one can hold, which can be learned by heart, recited, exhibited, tested, queried, and heard. Thus confessionalism began. Faith became objectified in doctrine. Faith could now be learned from doctrine and doctrine cited as evidence that one possessed faith.

In the history of the Church all this had already once taken place. The classical result of that first confessional movement in Christendom was the Nicene Creed, adopted at the council of Nicaea in 325; simple and clear, it was to be recited like a prayer. Since the adoption of the Nicene Creed, 1,200 years had elapsed. Society had become much more complicated; also more complicated were the varied ideas expressed in aphorisms, doctrinal splinters, dogmatic minutiae, and intellectual snares to be considered in conveying as concisely and as unmistakably as possible what was believed and what was not believed. Furthermore, the end result of the development of the Lutheran confession of faith was much more restrictive and rigid than was the simple Nicene Creed. During Luther's lilfe the *Book of Concord*, a collection of Lutheran confessional statements, had not yet appeared; it did not until thirty-two years after his death.

However, Luther did not undertake this development with the intention of binding others by his formulas—a gradual and unforeseen eventuality not necessarily desired by Luther—but for the purpose of the preventing others from endorsing their opinions with his name. In connection with the Eucharist strife and at the time of the visitations, Luther summarized in a few pages what he considered absolutely essential, first in the conclusion of his pamphlet *Concerning the Eucharist, Confession*, and later in the so-called Schwabach Articles, which he had composed in preparation for the Marburg Colloquy. It is noteworthy that in this context his summaries reject those compromises on free will that characterize the *Instruction to the Clergy in Electoral Saxony of the Visitation Commissioners* and that now, as before, the gospel and the doctrine of original sin are preeminent, thereby emphasizing the significance of the law. A quiet struggle between Luther, Melanchthon, and the commissioners can be sensed. Luther appreciated their pragmatic approach, but he was unwilling to conform to it.

Doctrine must be clearly and simply expressed. The expediency of clarity and simplicity repeatedly came to the attention of the visitation commissioners as they traversed the parishes throughout electoral Saxony. It was clear that a beginning must be made with the training of children and the instruction of youth. Before the Peasants' War Luther had written a pamphlet *To the Councilmen of All German Cities that They Should Build and Maintain Christian Schools.* The *Instruction* once again emphasized this idea and provided a curriculum plan for the classes, divided into *Haufen* (ranks), as school classes were at that time described. Specific suggestions were made as to the sequence of texts for the learning of Latin and as to which subjects were to be taught in the morning and which in the afternoon. Memorization was the major method of learning. Furthermore, certain psalms were assigned for memorization. The psalms selected were those which venerated family life, praised God, and exalted the king. No psalms dealing with revenge were included.

To prescribe clearly and simply what is to be recited necessitates a catechism. Luther composed one, simultaneously in two forms: small and large. They were composed in a popular pedagogical format so that, if philosophical speculation was not indulged, hardly anything remained unclear. Philosophical speculation was just what the common man was to avoid. Luther's Small Catechism is an unmatched masterpiece in its genre. The Ten Commandments, the Apostles' Creed, the Lord's Prayer, and a definition of the sacraments of baptism and the Eucharist were recited in answer to the simplest formulation of the matching question: What is it? Explanation consists of only a few sentences, and the commentaries on faith conclude each response with the assertion, "forsooth."

The Small Catechism appeared in January 1529, three weeks before the Large Catechism, although it had been finished last. In the Large Catechism, Luther's definition of God is presented:

What does it mean to have a God or What is God?

Answer: God is that Being to whom one should pledge himself, in whom one finds all good and refuge in time of need. Thus to have a God means to trust Him completely and to have faith in Him. As I have often said, it is complete faith that creates both God and whatever idol is worshipped. If you have true trust and faith, you possess the true God, but when trust and faith reflect idolatry, the true God is not present, because the two belong together—faith and God. In whatever you place your heart and trust, I say to you, that is really your god. (WA XXXI 133)

That was certainly true within the framework of Luther's theological questioning—which, beginning with his earliest lectures, had indicated his orientation toward regarding God and man together, deriving his view of God from Jesus (that is, from the incarnation), grasping the meaning of the humanity of Jesus and seeking thence to penetrate the mystery of His deity. To remain true to this starting point and to follow it to its logical conclusions, Luther was dialectically driven to the juncture at which the incarnation concept became its opposite. Three centuries later, Luther's definition of God prompted Ludwig Feuerbach to probe deeper philosophically and to convert Luther's idea of God as the creator of man. According to Feuerbach, it was not God who had become incarnate in human flesh, but man who assigned to God a spiritual likeness of himself. The scholastics, who had always insisted upon the *aseitas* of God, or the autonomy of God—a view of God without any reference to man—must have had their reasons not to permit themselves to be converted by Luther.

To proceed without reference to man was Luther's natural inclination, but was no longer in every case demanded. The more the Reformation became consolidated, the more it became a force for order that was obliged to learn to cooperate with other systems of order. It was most necessary that the Protestant princes be cautious, especially, of course, in their relationship to the emperor, but also in their relationship to the papal hierarchy. The emperor continued to insist on the execution of the Edict of Worms, but he was simultaneously preoccupied on so many political fronts that he himself was forced into negotiations, delay, and temporization. After the diet of Worms in 1521, Charles V obliged to leave Germany precipitously. In Spain a popular uprising (the comuneros) of the cities and provinces raged against him, an uproar that the Spanish grandees sought to exploit in their own interest by curbing the royal power of their king. No sooner was the unrest in Spain addressed than it became necessary to resume the struggle against the French king, Francis I, in northern Italy. In February 1525, German foot soldiers of the imperial army defeated a French Army near Pavia and took Francis I prisoner. Even this impressive victory, about which Luther refused to rejoice, brought Charles V no long term solution but only a temporary breathing spell. The peace terms to which the French king was forced to agree, after his release from captivity, declared null and void by him and the French estates general. The pope gave his blessing to the nullification and switched sides; Henry VIII of England joined the anti-Hapsburg coalition, and the war for the hegemony over northern Italy flared up again. The events on the battlefield depended as much if not more on the economic strength of the belligerents as on strategical deployment, tactics, and offensive. Having served for months without pay, the German and Spanish footsoldiers in Charles' army mutinied in May 1527. They marched on Rome and compensated themselves by mercilessly plundering the Eternal City in the so-called *sacco di Roma* (*sacco*, a very picturesque Italian word for "plunder," literally means "sack"), thereby bringing the glory of the Roman Renaissance finally to an end. After the imperial and French sides were both financially exhausted, peace was concluded in 1529 without bringing any real advantages to either side. The conclusion of peace was imperative in the light of the growing Turkish threat. In 1526, at Mohacs, the Turks had destroyed a Hungarian-Bohemian army. King Louis of Hungary-Bohemia fell in the battle. On the basis of hereditary agreements between the Hapsburg and Hungarian-Bohemian royal house, Ferdinand, the brother of Charles V, was elected king of Hungary-Bohemia. Bohemia and

Hungary were now added to the Hapsburg Austrian hegemony that was to be of long duration. The foundation for the future European power basis of Austria was therewith laid.

Since the battle of Mohacs, fear of the Turk had preoccupied Europe. There was no doubt that the Turk constituted a serious threat to Europe. The Turk was depicted as a divine scourge and rod. In the face of this danger, Luther composed from Psalm 46 the hymn *A Mighty Fortress Is Our God*. Luther set the Germans to singing about what Albrecht Dürer had captured in his graphic *The Knight Despite Death and Devil*, the paean of praise of a life that, through faith in God and in the final divine victory, in its way gave expression to a spirit that centuries later was expressed in words giving an opposite meaning: "No higher Being saves us, no god, no emperor, no tribune; we alone can save ourselves from misery" (the *International*, the hymn of international communism). The famous chorale from the very beginning served as a battle hymn for Protestants. Its symbolism far transcended the immediate purpose for which it was written. Borrowing from Heinrich Heine, Friedrich Engels called *A mighty Fortress Is Our God* the *Marseillaise* of the sixteenth century.

The thought that a higher power could rescue Europe from the Turk or, on the other hand, that a higher power desired the Turk to punish and chasten land and people for sin, misdeeds, lack of faith—that was the thought that preoccupied many and lamed their decisiveness. In Moravia, which bordered on Hungary, and where, after 1526, the threat that the scimitar would soon fall over cities and villages had to be reckoned with daily, the imminent danger incited among the Anabaptists a major controversy as to how the situation should be assessed from a religious point of view and what response should be made to the Turkish threat. Was it permitted with weapon in hand to resist the Turk if he was indeed the rod of God's anger, or by the "divine rod" was it to be understood that God wanted to test man, to see if he were prepared to risk his life in the cause of true faith against the enemy of Christendom? Driven by the desire to submit themselves without reservation to the teaching of Christ, to take literally the Sermon on the Mount, and to interpret it as binding law valid for all times and places, an entire group arrived at the conviction that one must not take up arms and that the most that one can do is to take up one's staff and migrate out of the path of evil. This group therefore was called "Staffers." This is a tragic example of Christian pacifism born of a literal interpretation of the idea of following Christ; therewith a new law was derived from the gospel, a law detrimental to the country. No responsible secular power, no matter how kindly disposed, can tolerate a movement that allows such a conviction to be implemented.

Martin Luther, although no less committed to Christ than were the Anabaptists, was immune to their unhealthy interpretation of the situation because of his theory of the two realms. Even though Luther spoke of the Turk as the divine scourge and rod of divine wrath, there was never the slightest doubt for Luther that the Turk must be met with violent military force. At the same time Luther rejected all suggestions of a "holy war." Luther desired to strengthen the will, and therefore he criticized the lack of preparation on the part of the military leaders, which in his view was due to the fact that the Germans underestimated the greatness, skill, and obedience of the Turks. Luther well knew that no undisciplined horde would attack, but a battle-tested, well-organized, well-disciplined, and masterfully equipped army. Luther emphasized that the German forces was too small and that there were insufficient reserves. Instead of pursuing the enemy after a victory, the Germans were wont to call a halt, relax, and fall prey to gluttony until the next emergency.

In order to resist the Turk, it would be necessary that all of Germany be mobilized. The nobility would bear a special responsibility, for the nobles would bear the sword in order to preserve society. The nobility had indulged itself in gluttony and had robbed artisans and peasants long enough. Now out of the spoils the nobility must provide for the common foot soldier, Brother Veit, upon whom the hope of the country depended. Let the Turk spread fear and terror as far as he will, Luther remarked. Let no one be terrified by the brutality with which the Turk wages war, but rather let his brutality provoke our rage. Not one inch of land is to be surrendered without a fight to the Turk, and nothing whole is to be left for him; everything that must be abandoned must be destroyed; if we must retreat, then the enemy should inherit only a desert. Better to die with weapon in hand than be taken prisoner. No one should suppose that he will survice captivity because, as a prisoner, his life will be reduced to that of cattle or swine. But if one should be taken prisoner, he must hold fast to faith, for everything depends on maintaining faith. In the eventuality that he be taken prisoner, the soldier should memorize the major articles of the Christian faith: the Commandments, the Lord's Prayer, and the Apostles' Creed, because in the empire of the Turks he will find no schools or teachers who will be able to instruct him in such matters. Luther also offers very practical advice as to how, under the conditions of captivity, one can remain constant in faith: whether on his cot or at work, the prisoner must not lose sight of his faith. He should make a sign with the hand or the foot; for example, he might press the finger with the thumb as he thinks of Jesus and imagines how He must look.

Luther warned of the danger of being attracted to Turkish-Islamic culture. The Turks appear to be holy; they pray frequently, refrain from wine, make pious gestures in their worship, and lead a serious and strict life, but in all of this apparent piety there is not true holiness before God; apart from Christ there is no salvation.

Should become a prisoner, the Christian must practice patience. The Christian should not seek to escape and should not give himself over to intoxication because his Turkish master has now a property claim on him. Perhaps the Christian prisoner by his example will convert many of his captors. In his great plight there is one solace: the devil there—the Turk—does not proceed against the Christian with such rage as does the devil at home—that is, the pope—because the Turk coerces no one to adopt his religion and to deny Christ. However, submission as a prisoner of the Turk has its limits. The Christian prisoner of war held by the Turk must not permit himself to be enlisted to fight against fellow Christians. Should Christian prisoners of war be impressed into military service against other Christians, the Christian prisoner must prefer to die rather than render such service.

Luther distinguishes between Christian duty and civic duty. As a Christian the individual must accept the suffering and punishment that God imposes through the Turks, but as citizen and subject the Christian must defend his home, hearth, and family. However, victory cannot be gained by might alone; the Spirit must assist our efforts. First, Allah, the god and devil of the Turks, must be defeated; otherwise the victory of our arms will have little consequence. In 1529 the Turks besieged Vienna, but they were unable to break the heroic resistance of the defenders and were forced to lift the siege and withdraw.

Peace in Italy and the Turkish retreat from Vienna: now the emperor could concern himself once again with German affairs and address the annoying religious question. In preparation, Charles V summoned an imperial diet in 1530 at Augsburg where the Protestants were to submit their views. Luther, who was still excommunicated and under imperial ban—as he would be for the rest of his life—was not permitted to attend the diet. For several weeks he resided at the Coburg Castle in the most southerly part of electoral Saxony, and from this refuge he followed events in Augsburg. Now Melanchthon assumed the role that had fallen to Luther at the imperial diet in Worms in 1521. However, the situation in the meantime had been fundamentally altered. In 1521 the emperor had demanded an answer without "horns or teeth," to be given orally, not in writing; now the Protestants were permitted to present a long written statement. Melanchthon had composed it. It came to be known as the Augsburg Confession, or, in Latin, Confessio Augustana.

Everything that should be included is included, and in such a mild form that one could hope that a Catholic Majesty would listen to it. The confession affirmed belief in the Triune God and original sin, addressed what free will was able to achieve in mundane matters, stipulated that free will was not sufficient to achieve salvation, and asserted that Lutherans in no way taught that secular law should be despised but that, on the contrary, it should be obeyed. Anabaptists, Arians, Manichaeans, and oll others who had been condemned by the Church were likewise condemned by Lutherans, and the teachings of these sects were declared false and corrupt. The Augsburg Confession is characterized by the effort to create an atmosphere for dialogue between Catholics and Lutherans; thus each page reflects great pains to promote conversation with the Catholic side and to avoid anything that could offend the Catholic mind while preserving the Lutheran position and, above all else, clearly distinguishing Lutherans from Anabaptists and from every association that in any way could link them to Müntzer or rebellion. The Augsburg Confession is Melanchthon's masterpiece. Luther could well be content, and he found nothing to criticize. But he could not resist commenting, "I cannot tread so softly."

The impatience that Luther felt from having to observe at a distance how others represented the work that he had begun is suggested in this mild gibe. Once again, as nine years earlier in his Wartburg exile, Luther saw himself excluded from events and complained bitterly to his friends that he was furnished only with lean reports from Augsburg. Much at the Coburg Castle reminded him of his Wartburg sojourn. To be sure, he did not now need to disguise himself as the bearded Squire George, and he need not grow a beard, and he had long since grown accustomed to a bountiful table. Nevertheless, his stay at the Coburg was a period of enforced inactivity and separation from friends. Once again he found himself, as on the lofty Wartburg heights, "in the realm of the birds and breezes," from where he could survey the whole countryside, and where he, as in his monastic garden, was liberated from books. The birds intrigued Luther. He liked to observe them. They reminded him so much of the human species, and they seemed to imitate human political activity. Before his window at the Coburg, there was a bush. Luther wrote to friends in Wittenberg that

the jackdaws and crows have convoked a diet there; there is such coming and going, such noise day and night without pause, as though they were all drunk and mad; there young and old flit about to the extent that I marvel how they can maintain their voice and breath. And I would like to know whether such noble and lusty travelers also are in Wittenberg. It appears to me that they must all have congregated at Coburg Castle.
I have not yet seen the emperor of the jackdaws and crows, but his nobles and lords constantly fly around, not very elegantly dressed, but all in black, all gray-eyed; they all sing the same song, but with a pleasant distinction between youth and age and between little ones and big ones. They do not marvel at the great palace and hall because their hall is arched by the beautiful clouds of a broad heaven and their estate is the open fields, covered with pretty green things, so that the walls of their castle are as wide as the world. They also care not for steeds or harness. Furthermore, they possess feathered wheels whereby they elude the bul-

let and imminent danger. They are indeed powerful lords, but what they conclude at their diet, I known not.

But what I have been able to learn from an interpreter ist that they have prepared themselves for a mighty campaign and battle against wheat, barley, oats, malt, and all kinds of corn and grain, and many aspire to become knights to perform great deeds.

Thus in the diet we see, hear, and observe, with great interest and love, how the princes together with the other estates of the empire sing so happily and live so well. However, it gives us special joy when we observe how knightly they swarm, sharpen the beak, and ready the arms in order that they may conquer the corn and the malt and thereby gain fame. We wish them success and health that all together they may be skewed on one fence picket. (WA BR V 294)

The crows and jackdaws skewed on a picket! Luther thought of the diet of Augsburg in this wry fashion. Actually, Luther liked birds and did not approve of their being netted or traped. Wolfgang Sieberger, a former theology student, who since 1519 had served as an assistant to Luther and whom Luther occasionally accused of not being very ambitious, spent time trapping birds. Luther considered such activity as ignoble and wrote a *Complaint of the Birds* against it. Whether or not Luther's pamphlet had any effect on restraining the lazy Wolfgang from his hobby we do not know, as, unfortunately, we do not know what the assistant Wolfgang thought of his master.

Nine years earlier Luther had taken advantage of his exile at the Wartburg to translate the New Testament into German. Now he desired finally to complete the great task of translating the Bible. Following the great success of the September Testament of 1522, by July 1523 he had completed the translation of the Mosaic Pentateuch, the first five books of the Old Testament. There followed, in 1524, a translation of the historical books from Joshua to Esther; then from 1526 to 1528, he translated the so-called minor prophets Jonah, Habakkuk, and Zachariah; in 1528, he also translated Isaiah, in the first translation of one of the major prophets to be completed by him; in 1529, he translated Proverbs; and in 1530, the Book of Daniel. However, Ezekiel, Jeremiah, and the rest of the minor prophets still awaited translation. Although translating these books into German was Luther's intent while at the Coburg Castle, he nevertheless was unable to complete this task there; not until one-and-one-half years after his return to Wittenberg was the translation of the Old Testament books completed, with the help of Melanchthon, Aurogallus, and Caspar Cruziger.

That the translation of the Old Testament took so long was embarrassing to Luther and his friends because their business interests as well as their reputations were at stake. The German Bible was not only an intellectual and spiritual achievement of the highest conceivable order; it was also a very profitable item. In consideration of sales, the New Testament translation completed at the Wartburg and printed in Wittenberg was kept secret until the Leipzig fair, and thereby achieved a surprising success in the autumn of 1522. Beginning in 1522 a rivalry developed to determine who would be the first to publish the entire Bible, Old and New Testament, in the German language.

Luther lost this competition in 1529, a year before his sojourn at the Coburg Castle. Everywhere people were waiting impatiently for the translation of the entire Bible into the German language, and it was expected that such a work would come from Luther. However, after 1525 it was clear that the work of translating in Wittenberg had hit a snag. Others then seized the initiative and took up the translation of the remaining books. In 1527, for example, the leaders of the Anabaptists Ludwig Hätzer and Hans Denck published in Worms a German translation of the prophets. In Zurich Zwingli revised Luther's Bible translation and gave it a Swiss Alemannian tone. Zwingli's colleague and successor, Leo Jud, translated the Apocrypha, those books of the Old Testament that the ancient Jews did not regard as canonical but that, nevertheless, were considered biblical by the Roman Church. In 1529, the Zurich printer, Christoph Froschauer, published a Swiss Bible. This translation was based primarily on Luther's translation of the New Testament and on those sections of the Old Testament that he had already translated and published, but the Swiss Bible departed so radically from Luther's language that it was distinctive.

In still another way the printer in Worms, Peter Schöffer, exploited the situation. He united in one edition the Zurich edition of the New Testament, the prophets, and the Apocrypha, with those Old Testament books already translated by Luther, Wolfgang Capito (Köpfel) of Strasbourg followed a similar procedure. Capito took from Luther the German New Testament, those translated sections of the Old Testament that had appeared in 1523–1524, and the translation of the prophets Isaiah, Jonah, Habakkuk, and Zachariah; to these passages he added the other prophetic books from Hätzer and Denk, and he completed the edition with the Apocrypha from Leo Jud. These other translations in no way detracted from Luther's work, but it was in fact vexing that others harvested where Luther had plowed and sown. However, he was prepared to accept the exploitation of his labor because he wanted the Bible to be disseminated among the common people, and in consideration of this goal Luther could only be pleased that many printers took over his various biblical translations and reprinted them many times. The Wittenberg printers were at a disadvantage. They found it necessary to proceed with caution and to ensure that their printing costs were covered. With the translation of the complete Bible in Zurich, Worms, and Strasbourg, strong competition threatened them, especially for the South German market. In addition, the market for the new Testament had become surprisingly competitive and not without devious dealings: Jerome Emser, the mountain goat, was greatly disturbed by Luther's fame as translator; consequently, in 1527 Emser published his own translation of the New Testament. However, it soon became clear that Emser's translation was simply a plagiarism of Luther's.

Luther resolved never again to mention Emser's name in his writings. Emser himself did not have long to enjoy his coup; he died in 1527, the year his New Testament translation was published. Henceforth, whenever Luther could not avoid referring to Emser, he referred to him merely as the "Dresden scribbler." With respect to Luther's New Testament in German and Emser's plagiarization of it, Luther could only laugh at the great wisdom that "had so scathingly blasphemed, condemned, and forbidden because it appeared under my name, but now it must be read because it appears under another name" (WA XXXII 634).

Now that the completion of the translation of the Bible was in sight at the Coburg Castle, it seemed to Luther that the time also had arrived to deal with those know-it-all scholars who whined, taunted, found fault, and above all else could not emphasize strongly enough that Luther's fundamental principle, *sola fide*, by faith alone, obviously was based on an error in translating, because this *sola* was not to be found in the Latin text of Paul's epistle to the Romans (Romans 3:28). Luther considered these critics jackasses because they did not understand the peculiar characteristic of the German language, and they saw the four letters of the word *sola* as cow sees a new gate. It was true that the word *sola* was not in the Latin text, but it belonged in the German text because "we must not ask the letters of the Latin language how German should be spoken, as these jackasses do, but we must ask the mother in the house, the children in the street, the common man at the market, read from their lips, and then translate; then they will understand and realize that we are speaking German to them" (WA XXXII 637).

The more his critics hacked away at the word *sola*, the more it appealed to Luther. The usage pertained not only to the fundamental principle of the translating art and to the uniqueness of Luther's theological thinking concerning the freedom that exists in being bound to the Word, but also to his personal integrity, especially his confidence in his claim to have satisfied the art of translating. The rank, honor, and title of his critics did not impress Luther in the least.

Are they doctors? So am I. Are they scholars? So am I. Are they preachers? So am I. Are they theologians? So am I. Are they disputants? So am I. Are they philosophers? So am I. Are they dialecticians? So am I. Are they lecturers? So am I. Are they authors? So am I.

And I will praise myself further. I can interpret the Psalms and the prophets. They cannot. I can translate. They cannot. I can read the Holy Scriptures. They cannot. I can pray. They cannot. And why should I submit to them? Why, I know all their dialectics and philosophy better than they themselves. (WA XXXII 635)

Whithout such self-confidence Luther long ago would have failed. We, like his opponents, may consider this attitude intellectual pride, but without such an absolute conviction no one who has achieved great things in history would have been able to do so. This conviction belongs to that strength of character that is indispensable if a new trail is to be blazed.

After the Coburg sojourn a few years were still to elapse before, finally in 1534, Luther's *Bible: the Entire Holy Scriptures in the German Language* was completed. Hans Lufft published it in Wittenberg. This Bible translation received the official endorsement of electoral Saxony: that meant that the elector John Frederick (his father John the Steadfast had died in 1532 and had been buried next to Frederick the Wise in the Castle Church in Wittenberg) had granted inside electoral Saxony the exclusive distribution right that protected this publication of the Bible from being copied. This Bible translation was not Luther's work alone. Melanchthon, Aurogallus, and Cruziger had assisted in translating difficult passages, and, because illness several times had caused long interruptions in his work, Luther, to avoid further delay, had assigned to them exclusively the translation of the Apocrypha. Shortly before the complete Luther Bible appeared in Wittenberg, the Bugenhagen Low German translation, based on Luther's, was published in Lübeck.

Although Luther's life did not end in 1534 with the completion and publication of the Bible translation, the most important part of his life's work had been concluded. Five years later, together with his colleagues, he took up the work of revising the entire translation from beginning to end, sentence by sentence, to refine, polish, and as nearly as possible provide the exact meaning of the text. The revision took almost three years, and even after its completion Luther continued for the rest of his life to make notes and jot suggestions which a future new edition of the translation should incorporate.

Ever since his entry into the monastery, when Luther was presented a Bible with the stipulation that he read it daily, this book had been more than his life's companion: it had drawn him, body and soul, into its path, had turned him away from Aristotle and philosophy, had provided answers to the questions that the Bible itself posed, and had led him to the juncture where all life and doctrine were scrutinized by Scripture. That this book had been kept from him in his childhood and youth Luther considered a grave deprivation. Now every house, every family should have the Bible, and how the Bible was to be employed in the home Luther demonstrated in his own home. Each morning he prayed the Lord's Prayer with his wife, children, and household, recited the Apostles' Creed, and read a psalm. Beginning in 1532, every Sunday morning he chose a biblical passage, interpreted it, and presented a brief homily for his family. From the collection of these sermons arose the domestic homilies.

Luther presided over a large household, or rather Käthe presided over a large household and managed affairs, but it was "Herr Doctor" around whom all things revolved. The Black Cloister had become Luther's residence; In 1532 the property was legally assigned to him. Where monks earlier had prayed at the liturgical hours and had pursued their silent obligations, children now boisterously played, and from time to time when the noise became intolerable, the reverend doctor mildly scolded. Six children were born to Luther and Käthe: three boys and three girls. All were born in the first nine years of the marriage. Pregnancy followed pregnancy, as was usual for the time, and fertility was considered a gift of God. On June 7, 1526, Hans Luther was born; on December 10, 1527, Elizabeth; on May 4, 1529, Magdalene; on November 9, 1531, Martin; on June 28, 1533, Paul; and on December 17, 1534, Margarete. Martin and Käthe were not spared grief. Elizabeth, not yet one year old, died on August 3, 1528, and Magdalene, whom the parents loved with special tenderness because they interpreted her birth as a consolation for the death of the little girl taken from them so quickly, died on September 20, 1542, at the age of thirteen.

Relatives from far and near appealed to Luther for help in promoting their own careers, because now he was not only the most famous bearer of the Luther name but also the family patriarch. During his stay at the Coburg Castle he had received the news of the death of his father, and Martin was now what his father had been, the "elder" Luther; as such, according to the custom of that day, he had a patriarchal responsibility to be father, lord, and helper to the younger Luthers. In the course of the years, no less than eleven nephews, and nieces enjoyed hospitality in his home. They expected to be accommodated, fed, cared for, aided in finding a mate, and provided with continued assistance. Not only members of Luther's family found their way to Wittenberg but also members of Käthe's family, including Magdalene von Bora, Käthe's "Aunt Lene," a former nun, who greatly assisted in the household chores, in the kitchen, and in rearing the children. She died in 1537.

Furthermore, Martin Luther kept a boardinghouse, a "Burse," which he named "Porse," for small groups of regular boarders—mostly students although some were beyond their student years—who paid for their meals. At that time university professors provided meals for guests of this category not only in order to supplement the professor's salary but also to attract a circle of supporters and thus establish a following. It was a great honor to belong to Luther's table companions. Luther's mostly light, humorous, or reflective table talk was for the guests more important than soup, fish, and vegetables. It soon became customary to write down his observations immediately after the meal. Of course, some could not resist bringing pen and paper to the table and immediately writing down the Master's every word. In good humor, Luther tolerated the zeal of his scribes. Thus the famous "Table Talks" came into existence. The meal was begun in silence. Sometimes Luther retained a monastic silence for the course of the entire meal, and no one was bold enough to break that silence even though he might regret that he had not quite received his money's worth. But usually, after a period of silence, Luther would lift his eyes and ask, "What's new?" Still no one dared to speak. Only after Luther had issued the invitation several times, "Now, my prelates, what is new," did the older guests report this or that, while the younger ones listened with reverent attention. It never occurred to a younger guest to speak without being directly requested to do so. This practice was not confined to Luther's table and did not rest completely on the unchallenged authority that Luther exercised in this circle. It was merely the custom of the day. In every farmhouse the practice was the same; the only difference was that nobody was taking notes in the farmer's cottage when the farmer permitted the foreman to speak.

Luther also finally acquired a farmhouse in 1540, when he inherited the small estate of Zülsdorf near Leipzig. In 1531 he had bought a small garden in Wittenberg, and in 1532 he had bought another. In addition, in 1541 he purchased a small house, and in 1544 a hops garden and still another garden. Together with the former monastery building, Luther owned a respectable amount of property beyond that of which most universitiy professors could boast. From the emaciated monk whose every rib could be counted, as he had appeared at the time of the Leipzig debate in 1519, he had become an indulged middle class burgher with a double chin and a pot belly.

It was not monastic fears that now plagued him but circulatory problems and kidney stones. The spirit of Luther as expressed in the reform movement had prepared the way for the middle class, and now his surroundings assumed characteristics of material ease without suggesting a greedy appetite for acquisition. Luther still accepted no honorarium for his writings, although honorariums were now offered to him; instead, he received, in addition to his salary and gifts from his elector, donations, especially from the princes of Anhalt, the duke of Prussia, and the king of Denmark. The English king, Henry VIII, who had once personally sought to refute Luther's pamphlet on *The Babylonian Captivity of the Church*, now sent him greetings and dispatched emissaries to Wittenberg. Vergerio, a papal legate, who was to select a city in Germany for a future council, did not fail to visit Wittenberg and to dine with the excommunicated heretic in the castle. Princes, marshals, royal chancellors, and counselors served as godparents for the children of Luther and Käthe.

—

Chapter 15

"I Will Be Sustained; They Will Perish"
1537–1546

Luther and his Reformation had become a power, and it necessary that the power express itself politically and be consolidated. From the beginning of the 1530s, the need for consolidation became increasingly urgent. The Augsburg diet of 1530 had ended on no comforting note. To be sure, the Lutheran Confession composed by Melanchthon had indeed been read and heard; the Catholic side had responded to the Augsburg Confession with a confession of its own: *Confutatio*, or the Confutation, to which Melanchthon then replied with the *Apologia*, but the Emperor remained firm in his opposition to Protestantism. He announced that the Lutherans had been refuted and that he was determined to execute the Edict of Worms.

Luther responded to the threats emanating from Augsburg with his pamphlet *A Warning to His Beloved Germans*. Do the imperial forces and the papists threaten us and desire to do us evil? Let them try:

> But the evil that they propose against us I will turn against them with greater vehemence and even if they believe their heads to be hard, my head will prove to be much harder. If in addition to Emperor Charles they had the Turkish sultan on their side, that still would not dismay or terrify me. From now on they must give place to me. I will not submit to them. I will be sustained, they will perish. Their errors are too many. My life will be their executioner; my death their devil. This and nothing else will be their lot, even though they now comfort themselves by laughing at my warning. (WA XXX III 280)

Bold thunder, certainly, but well justified and necessary to encourage his followers, because Melanchthon's irenic formulations had led to no softening of the imperial or papal position, and, to make matters worse, the Roman party reared its head in an even bolder manner. By summoning his followers to resistance, Luther now tried to please Landgrave Phillip of Hesse, whose desire for an overture to the Swiss before the and of the year Luther had regarded skeptically. Finally in 1531, the Lutherans, after much indecision and preliminary discussion, formed in Schmalkalden the Schmalkaldic League. What the Protestant princes and their counselors agreed on was to remain united, even if that meant forming a league against the emperor and other imperial estates that favored executing the

Edict of Worms or for some other reason were motivated to make common cause with the emperor. Such resistance was politically necessary, and lay in the interest of protecting those goals achieved by the Reformation, but resistance to the emperor did raise a very burning and judicial-political question; in searching for a solution jurists and theologians could test their skills in formulating and arguing. Since they were his subjects, was it at all permissible that the German Protestant princes and imperial estates offer resistance to the emperor? And in case a possibility was discovered to answer this question affirmatively in the interest of political advantage, how was such a possibility to be reconciled with the obligation of obedience on the part of the subject to his lord, and could not then a justification be established for condoning the resistance that the peasants a short time earlier had demonstrated against their lords? In the question of peasant resistance, there was quick agreement to the adage *Quod licet jovi, non licet bovi* (What is appropriate for the gods is not appropriate for the oxen), but, after all, what's good for the goos is good for the gander!

Luther was not competent to deal with this complicated legal question. Furthermore, no one involved him or seriously consulted with him, but understandably his name was invoked in support of the politics of the Protestant princes. The question of resistance to the emperor was difficult for Luther, and his first suggestions, had they been implemented even by one of the princes, would have had disastrous consequences. Luther reasoned that, since the princes were subjects of the emperor, they were obligated under all circumstances to open their land to the emperor. Anyone whose faith was threatened by the emperor could evade imperial suppression be emigration. Moreover, one must be prepared to accept every hardship for the cause of faith and to entrust the matter to God.

This attitude, of course, precluded politics. The jurists had great difficulty in persuading Luther to abandon this nonsense. Even the *vim vi repellere* (to counter force with force), which is the foundation of Roman law, Luther admitted only for antagonists of equal rank but not as a right of princes vis-à-vis the emperor. Luther the politician was unable to suppress Luther the theologian. In order to avoid mischief, the princes wisely refrained from disseminating some of Luther's opinions in this matter and from permitting them to be publicly known. Luther feared a reversion to the barbarism of everybody against everybody else in a struggle for naked power if the principle were accepted that the subject had the right to resist his lord. But was the emperor really the lord over the princes in the same sense that the princes were lords over the inhabitants of their respective territories? Finally the jurists were able to convince Luther of the distinction between the two positions. The princes were not appointed by the emperor; on the contrary, the emperor was elected by the princes. This fact allowed for the remedy: an emperor who violated his office could be re-

moved. With respect to this problem, Luther had provided many years earlier in his theory of the two realms a foundation for a solution that permitted politics to remain politics and at the same time did not impinge on his
position. But in the meantime, since the publication of his two-realm
theory, Luther had been preoccupied with natural law and considered himself competent in that realm; now, he was tempted to describe political
questions theologically, and it was difficult for him to sympathize with a
right to resist in secular matters. In intellectual and in ecclesiastical matters, Luther had himself practiced resistance of the most determined kind
against all who sought by hierarchical fiat to impose on him a view that the
considered unacceptable. However, in secular matters, such an approach
was not valid.

Theologically or legally—how would the right of Protestant princes to
resist the emperor be justified? The debate dragged on, but the Protestant
princes could not fold their hands in their laps and wait, doing nothing,
until the emperor had suppressed them, when the theologians had already
pointed out that resistance was justifiable in cases of self-preservation. In
any case, it was necessary that the Protestant princes be prepared for all
eventualities. Luther could understand that argument. Military preparations were already underway anyway, although Luther had not been consulted, and to begin such preparations had been a good decision. Furthermore, even if Luther could not now provide the rhetoric essential to the
politics of the Protestant princes, others could. In this regard, Bugenhagen
proved himself to be much more aggressive and much less inhibited than
was his great example, Luther. Without hesitation, Bugenhagen had already explained point blank in a response to the first query from the
princely court at Torgau that the achievements of the Reformation in case
of necessity must of course be defended with sword in hand against all
parties, and even, if necessary, against the emperor. Note was taken at
court of Bugenhagen's position, and it became the rule when advice was
needed from Wittenberg always to request three opinions: Luther's, Melanchthon's, and Bugenhagen's. To obtain support for the rationale of
court politics, the rider who brought the requests to Wittenberg from the
court was instructed to indicate what response would be appropriate and
what the court would like to hear. Otherwise, what was the point in having
a university? Certainly not to create problems, which arose without provocation. On the contrary, the university was established for practical reasons, to enhance the reputation of the dukedom, and to support political
goals. The university and Luther's association with it was a part of the territorial superstructure. This relationship made easier the further development of the two-realm theory. Finally, Luther drew his conclusions from
the consideration on which he had based his theory and on which his great
Italian contemporary, the first classicist of political thought, Niccolò Ma-

chiavelli (1469-1527), in his reflections on the topic, had always made his point of origin: namely, that politics is an independent realm with its own unique rules where biblical propositions, to be sure, should be considered but may not be interpreted as binding directives. For this reason, the politician or the prince felt all the greater need for spiritual encouragement. Such spiritual encouragement Luther supplied generously. Luther explained that the question of the right to resist belonged to the secular realm and thus was a matter for jurists alone. However, he maintained that, as far as theology was concerned, the "right to resist" could not appeal to the Bible.

Such an explanation was sufficient to justify a policy that was prepared at the first opportune moment to enlist military force for the extension of the Reformation. However, Luther strongly advised against engaging in preventive hostilities against the emperor because, apart from all other considerations, such preventive measures would cost the Lutheran princes their reputation. Public opinion must be taken into consideration. A favorable opportunity for a preventive strike against the emperor presented itself in 1534, when the emperor had his hands full in repulsing the assaults of the Corsar fleet under Chaired-din Barbarossa on Charles's southern Italian territories in the western Mediterranean. Landgrave Philipp of Hesse, an energetic person who was interested in theological questions, possessed faith but took care that faith did not possess him, and adroitly employed his faith politically. In a decisive coup, he restored Duke Ulrich of Württemberg to power from which the duke had been driven by his estates and the Swabian League in 1519, and which since then had been administered by Hapsburgs, who then compensated the Swabian League for the cost of the war against Duke Ulrich. The Hapsburgs were obliged to agree in the treaty of Kaaden to Duke Ulrich's restoration to the dukedom of Württemberg. In Württemberg, where the inhabitants for a long time had sometimes secretly and sometimes openly sympathized with the reform movement, the Reformation was now introduced by secular authority from above. In like manner, it was by secular authority that the Reformation came to Albertine Saxony after the death of Duke George the Bearded in 1539 and the assumption of political authority in that dukedom by his brother, Heinrich. Heinrich required that ecclesiastical and monastic property be registered, and he sequesterd it. Part of the property he expropriated for his treasury, part of it he sold, and part of it he used to enfeoff his friends.

As the Reformation made progress, it enjoyed its greatest success in the northern and northwestern territories. In 1534 the duke of Pomerania accepted the Eucharist in both kinds. Furthermore, in the same year, the prince of Anhalt introduced the cup for the laity. In 1535 Joachim I of Brandenburg died. His successor, Joachim II, commissioned Melanchthon, in 1539, to draw up a new liturgy, and thus in Brandenburg also the Reformation, under the influence of the duke, was standardized by secular authority. From 1537 Bugenhagen spent two years in Denmark and drew up liturgies for the Lutheran Church there. Sweden, which at that time included what is now Finland, had in 1527, at the diet of Västeros, officially embraced the Reformation. The motives of the princes in adopting the Reformation were not exclusively of a material nature. Certainly it was tempting to expropriate ecclesiastical property for the princely treasury, but the profit or increase of income was not always the deciding factor. In addition, political motives played a role; however, the simple conviction that Luther's teaching provided a better guide for Christian life must not be excluded. Significant in this regard are the facts that in many cases it was the wives of princes who first secretly received both bread and wine in the Eucharist and that it was often a change in rulers that provided an opportunity for introducing the Reformation. Nevertheless, the Reformation also continued as a popular movement, especially in the cities, where once again those radical tendencies were demonstrated that had formerly been characteristic of the development in the first half of the 1520s and which had ultimately peaked in the Peasants' War. But the most radical stage of the Peasants' War was never reached again, first, because the secular authorities were now much more alert and had learned from the early Reformation and the Peasants' War, and second, because in the northern and northwestern regions to which the center of gravity for the Reformation from below had shifted, the peasant's agrarian position, and thereby his social as well as his political-legal position, was different from what it had been in Southwest Germany and Thuringia, where the Peasant's War had originally broken out. There would be only one more popular uprising and serious threat to the imperial estates, and that would come in Münster, where in 1534–1535 Anabaptists held the power.

In its historical significance, what the Anabaptist kingdom in Münster undertook extended far beyond the sixteenth century. The penalty for rebaptism was death. Everywhere the Anabaptists were rigorously persecuted. They could not reckon on mercy; each Anabaptist knew that. And despite the severity with which they were treated, there were men and women from every class who still embraced anabaptism, risked their lives, lost house, hearth, and goods, were driven from place to place as refugees, and preferred martyrdom to recantation. Anabaptists were as bold and as heroic as the martyrs of early Christendom.

The Anabaptists wanted to realize the visible kingdom of God on earth. Totally committed to Christ, they believed in political, legal, and social equality for all people, and the imminent second advent of Christ and Judgment Day. They deliberately segregated themselves from the surrounding society, opposed it, and desired to replace it with a radical new order.

The Anabaptists were torn. Should one wait passively until the hour of Christ's second advent strikes, or should one strike the blow "to purify the temple," to destroy the godless in an armed struggle, and thereby to establish the conditions on which a kingdom or at least a community of Christ could arise? There was a stormy debate among Anabaptists as to which of the two courses should be pursued. Moravia became a refuge for those Anabaptists driven from Switzerland, South Germany, Austria, and Thuringia, who desired patiently to await Christ's second advent. In the Low Countries and in Westphalia, a radical activist tendency among the Anabaptists prevailed. In February 1534, radical Anabaptists seized power in Münster and against superior enemy forces retained control of that city for sixteen months until, weakened by hunger, they were overwhelmed and slaughtered by the mercenaries of the bishop of Münster.

The social and political transformation which the Anabaptists had begun in Münster appeared terrifying to their contemporaries. The Anabaptists confiscated the property of every citizen who fled or who was expelled from the city, dissolved the guilds, abolished money, and stored the grain supply in a central granary. They forbade the citizens to lock their doors, proclaimed a community of goods, introduced polygamy, obligated men to sire and women to bear children, permitted women to choose and divorce husbands, and punished women by imprisonment or death for refusing connubial relations. They proclaimed the tailor, Jan Bokelson from Leiden, as king, in imitation of the Old Testament Davidic kingship, abolished the Church, and declared the Bible no longer valid because with the advent of Christ's kingdom the Church age had ended.

Under the conditions of the sixteenth century, the Anabaptist kingdom at Münster remained a bold experiment stamped by its sectarian origins. That the revolutionary potential of the popular movement was once again fomenting was evidenced in the Anabaptist kingdom at Münster, but its force immediately fizzled and was emptied into the anticipatory, utopian, and sectarian. The experience of the rebellious Anabaptists in Münster was tragic. It was the tragedy of a historically necessary illusion, which strove for the impossible and thereby prepared the way for the possible. The Anabaptist kingdom of Münster was the tragedy of revolutionary religious visionaries. With a high degree of intensity, Luther approved and supported the progress of the Reformation by secular authority and its expansion by preaching; nevertheless, with an equally high degree of decisiveness, Luther distinguished his position from that of the Anabaptist kingdom of Münster. The easy confusion of "Müntzer" with "Münster" was not needed to convince Luther that in Münster the spirit of his antagonist, Thomas Müntzer, whom Luther could not drive from his memory, was at work.

It was not without satisfaction and pleasure that Luther's old and new Catholic opponents called attention to the contradictions and dissensions within the Reformation. Luther's opponents drew up whole catalogues of what Luther had once said and what he now in fact did. The favorite theme of Luther's opponents was his betrayal of the peasants. With the critical vision of hatred, Luther's opponents mercilessly exposed everything and invented more of their own which could illustrate and confirm their major thesis that every departure from what the Roman Church had approved led to death and murder in the last analysis among the masses, and eventually to anarchy. Luther's opponents marshaled arguments to fortify their own perseverence and to re-energize themselves, and they were eager to examine the weakness of the opposition. Not the least of their desires was—and in this they were strongly supported and encouraged by imperial diplomacy—to engage the reformers in long discussion, dialogues, and theological debates that could only serve the purpose of exposing the fact that religious prestige was no longer unchallenged in the ranks of the reformers, that their commitment to principle was suspect, and that they were too ready to compromise.

The first move was that of Pope Paul III (1534-1549). In 1537 he summoned a general council, at first at Mantua, but it was postponed several times. Luther immediately recognized the danger posed by a general council. Now it was important not to budge an inch with respect to fundamental doctrines. Especially during the long years of controversy and in association with the South Germans, the inflexible posture had proven to be correct and had paid dividends. Zwingli, as chaplain in the campaign against the Catholic cantons of Switzerland, had fallen in the battle of Kappel in 1531. Zwingli's death caused a leadership crisis among the South Germans and Alsatians, who, with respect to many questions, tended more toward Switzerland than toward Luther. Zwingli's death now caused the South German reformers to seek stronger association with Luther. The South German and Swiss reformers hoped for concessions from Luther because they also were obliged to protect their reputation before the world and to consider their standing before their own followers. But Luther was resolute. What good was a doctrine that allowed the disposition of claims to truth? The efforts to achieve agreement between Luther and the South German reformers went on for years. Martin Butzer (1491-1551) energetically worked for this agreement. Luther remained resolute. The South German Reformers, Butzer from Strasbourg among them, were obliged to go to Wittenberg to demonstrate in personal conversation that they preached the true faith. They journeyed as far as Saalfeld, where they waited, hoping that Luther would come from Wittenberg to meet them there. Luther remained in Wittenberg; at that time he was ill and could not travel. Luther had the South German reformers and Butzer continue their journey to Wittenberg. In Wittenberg he had them sign the Wittenberg Concord, which espouses the Luther position as the foundation for agreement.

Ulrich von Hutten
woodcut from "Phalarism", 1517

Franz von Sickingen, woodcut by Hieronymus
Hopfer, first half of the 16th century

Erasmus of Rotterdam
copperplate by Albrecht Dürer, 1526

Three armed peasants
copperplate by Albrecht Dürer, 1497/1498

Title page of the "Twelve Articles"
of the Swabian peasants
printed by Jörg Gastel in Zwickau in 1525

Rebellious peasants on their way into battle
woodcut, 16th century

Thomas Müntzer
copperplate by Thomas Sichem, 17th century

TOMAS MVNCER PREDIGER ZV ALSTET IN DVRINGEN.

Title pages of Müntzer's pamphlets "Auslegung des andern unterschyds Danielis" and "Hochverursachte Schutzrede und antwwort wider das Gaistlosse und Sanfft lebende fleysch zu Wittenberg … both 1524

Außlegung des andern vnter schyds Danielis deß propheten geprediget auffm schloß zu Alstet vor den tetigen thewren Hertzcogen vnd vorsteßern zu Sachßen durcß Thomã Müntzer Diener des wordt gottes.

Alstedt

M. D. XXiiij.

Hoch verursachte Schutzrede vnd antwwort/wider das Gaistlose Sanfft lebende fleysch zu Wittenberg/welches mit verkärter weyße / durch den Diepstal der heiligen schrift die erbärmbliche Christenheit/also gätz jämerlichen Besüdelt hat.

Thomas Müntzer Alstedter.

Auß der hölen Helie/ welches ernst niemant verschonet.iij.Regũ.xviij.Matthei.xvij. Luce.j.Apocali.Vndecimo.

Anno. M. D. XXiiij.

O deus redime me a calumnijs hoim : vt custodiã mãdata tua. Annũciemqz veritatẽ in filio tuo recõ ditam:ne technæ malignantiũ amplius perseuerent.

Breaking on the wheel
and executing
with the sword
woodcut from the
Bamberg criminal court
order 1507

Landgrave Philipp von Hessen
painting by Hans Krell, around 1530

Title page of Luther's pamphlet "Against the Robbing
and Murderous Hordes of the Peasants"
Nuremberg 1525

Martin Luther and his wife Katharina von Bora
painting by Lucas Cranach, 1526

Johannes Bugenhagen
detail from a painting by Lucas Cranach the younger
in the Wittenberg city church

Philipp Melanchthon
copperplate by Albrecht Dürer, 1526

Nicolaus von Amsdorf
copperplate, 16th century

Justus Jonas
woodcut, 16th century

Andreas Bodenstein, called Karlstadt
woodcut, first half of the 16th century

IOHANNES· AGRICOLA·
DOCTOR· EISLEBEN
GENANT· DESS· CH/
VRFVRTN PREDICANT
3V·CÖLN AN·DER
SPRE·IM· THVM·ſeliger

1·5 6·5
B: 1:

Die ſünden ſein kranck
ſach an der oder ſchen
wider mich geſchriben
von hoh vn volwerend
kreit der werck· So
kenne ich keinen
keiligen der ſo geiſt

VIL·SPRICHWÖRTER·HAB·ICH·ENTECKT
DISELBEN·GAR·SCHÖN·AVSGELEGT
AVF·DAS·DAS·BÖS·SOLT·WERDN·VERMID
DOCH·HALF·ICH·DAS·INTERIM·SCHMID
WART·ABR·IM·GEIST·WIDRVM·SO·STARK
THET·DBEST·PREDIGTE·IN·DER·MARCK
2364

Johann Agricola
woodcut, 16th century

Willibald Pirckheimer
copperplate by Albrecht Dürer, 1520

Disputation between Luther and Zwingli during the Marburg
colloquy; on the right Philip von Hessen
lithograph, 19th century

The Augsburg Reichstag 1530 (plenary session)
copperplate, 16th century

Veste Coburg
detail from the epitaph of the Meienburg mayor
painting by Lucas Cranach the younger, 1558

Now, in confronting the papists, Luther had to remain resolute; from the outset, there had been no reason to anticipate that they would make any concession on his opinion. In any event, rather, that Luther it would be Melanchthon, Butzer, and others who would be involved in negotiations with the papists. Despite all possible compromises that political pressure exerted by the princes might coerce others to make, Luther was determined to preserve for posterity his true doctrine, from which he would not depart and to which he would firmly adhere under all circumstances. With this in mind, Luther composed a confession that has become known as the Schmalkaldic Articles, which act as a corrective to the Augsburg Confession. They are not geared toward reconciliation or union but rather toward distinction and separation.

During his sojourn in Schmalkalden in 1537, when he composed the Schmalkaldic Articles, he experienced one of the most critical physical crises of his life. For years Luther had been plagued with kidney stones. In Schmalkalden the pain became so severe that he thought that he would die. None of the medications prescribed by his physicians brought him relief. During the return trip to Wittenberg Luther was jostled about as the wagon in which he was lying rolled over bumpy roads. The rough ride caused the kidney stones to be jolted into a different position. Finally, in the inn at Saalfeld, the stone was passed in a stream of blood and urine that erupted from the ureter. Faint, exhausted, barely able to retain consciousness, and bathed in a cold sweat, the fifty-four-year-old Luther was obliged to remain in bed until he was able to continue his journey.

Some of Luther's followers believed that the older he became, the more he contradicted his earlier teaching. This suspicion was reflected in the disputations conducted from the middle of the 1530s in Wittenberg. Young people persistently asked why there was now so much talk of law when Luther himself had clearly and most convincingly taught that salvation depended on faith alone, that salvation was bestowed by grace, and that the law, which drove men only to works, was not important. The representatives of this opinion were called antinomists, those who oppose law (*nomos* = law). Interestingly enough, the debates had begun not as an attack on Luther but rather as a criticism of Melanchthon. Melanchthon was recognized as Luther's disciple and was more sensitive and more easily wounded than Luther, who, it was now whispered, was a new pope in Wittenberg. The attack was directed against Melanchthon, but Luther was the real target. Luther sensed that the criticism was aimed at him. He also sensed that these were imponderables difficult to define in the game of rivalry with the somewhat younger generation, that the entire quarrel had something to do with competition due to the generation gap, and that what for Luther had been a question of life and death was for the younger generation a question of winnig a debate. The youth were seeking to play

Luther against Luther; they desired to be more Lutheran than Melanchthon and, where possible, Luther himself. The hidden intellectual problem was all too well known to Luther. Many years earlier, when, as a young instructor confronted with the necessity of giving a voice to the spirit of the biblical text, he had been forced to wrestle with the dialectic of spirit and letter, he, who had metamorphosed the letter into spirit and for that reason had come to hold fast to the simple meaning of the text, was now "metamorphosed into letter" by his students because they had not yet experienced that the Word remains spirit only when it is lettered in fresh expressions. Luther, to be sure, could not tread as softly as Melanchthon, but he could think as acutely and bite even harder. Luther did not dream of permitting the enthusiastic new literalists to present a show in which Luther, the teacher, appeared alienated from his best student, Melanchthon, even tough Luther knew that Melanchthon himself, by one or another vulnerable formulation, had provided the provocation and probably even stood in secret rivalry with Luther.

The antinomist strife broke out in full fury after Luther returned from Schmalkalden in 1537. As with every intellectual struggle, the matter did not revolve around ideas and dogmas alone, but primarily around personalities and personal ambitions. The zealot who started the whole unpleasant affair was Johann Agricola of Eisleben who had goaded Melanchthon.

Agricola belonged to that younger generation that, from the start, had received its Lutheran doctrine directly from the lectern, had assiduously copied what was said in the lecture hall, and had assimilated the teaching through memorization. However, they had never been forced to confront the intellectual and spiritual challenge of a well-developed non-Lutheran theology, and therefore had never learned to completely comprehend and assimilate Lutheran doctrine, thereby achieving an inner freedom and sovereignty over it.

In 1519 Agricola attended the Leipzig debate. He graduated with Melanchthon in 1519 from Wittenberg with the degree of *Baccalaureus biblicus*, and married in 1520, about the same time that Melanchthon married. The two scholars were bound together in a friendly union which also included their families. After concluding his studies at Wittenberg, which he had pursued there since 1516, Agricola, to sustain his family, was employed for two years as a surgeon. His wife, however, opposed his surgical profession and wanted him to remain in a profession associated with the Holy Scriptures. Luther, to whom Agricola, in April 1523, communicated his difficult decision to become a theologian, announced abruptly from the pulpit, without consulting with Agricola, "Tomorrow, Master Eisleben (as Agricola was also called) will preach." At that time, Agricola also was presenting lectures at the philosophical and theological faculties in Wittenberg. In 1525 Agricola went to Eisleben to become school director.

Agricola's concept of the Lutheran teaching of justification by faith was not the result of an inner transforming and purging process. From Luther Agricola had learned that the gospel liberates from the law. Luther laid the foundation for evangelical freedom from the law by repeatedly preaching law, thereby ever renewing the peculiar preparedness of his auditors to receive the gospel. It was different for Agricola. He did not return from the gospel to law; on the contrary, he took the gospel of the forgiveness of sins as the new absolute starting point and thence continuously extended the realm of liberty. Luther sensed a libertine tendency in Agricola's approach. Even though such a tendency could only be suspected and not confirmed, it nevertheless became obvious in Agricola's supporters. Somehow this inclination reminded Luther of the Anabaptists, and he suspected Agricola of "masked Müntzerism". In Agricola's thought there was a disposition toward "a second Reformation," toward a posture of not wanting to remain at the status quo of what had been achieved, toward a desire for ongoing development in the reform movement.

Luther suppressed his own suspicions concerning Agricola for a long time. He did not want to believe that Agricola, whom he liked to nickname "Grickel," had taken up a cause that was most despised by Luther. Indeed, Luther, at the end of 1536, had provided that a teaching position at Wittenberg University be open to Agricola, who until then was still in Eisleben and still involved in many quarrels there. At Luther's first suggestion of a teaching post, Agricola packed up kith and kin, bag and baggage, and hurried to Wittenberg. Luther provided accommodations in his own home for Agricola, his wife, and their nine children. Furthermore, as Luther prepared to leave for Schmalkalden, he left his house, family, and pulpit in Agricola's care. Agricola thus occupied a position of trust that not even Melanchthon had enjoyed and that only occasionally had been entrusted to Bugenhagen. At this juncture, Agricola lost his sense of propriety with respect to what is or is not acceptable in the circle of the established old masters of new doctrine.

That Agricola in his preaching made so much of the gospel of the forgiveness of sins—a doctrine that for a long time the Wittenbergers had well understood—could be tolerated and even smiled upon, but that before long he began to sprinkle his remarks with such thought as "Luther contradicts himself and is not consequential enough" not only challenged what Luther taught but also inevitably aroused the suspicion that Agricola was laying claim to a leadership role in the circle of the reformers. A complete rupture between Luther and Agricola took place when it became known that a group of followers had begun to form around Agricola and had prepared theological theses enunciating their own theological positions. Now Luther acted.

The theses of the Agricola group may not have been prepared by Agricola personally, but there was no doubt that they breathed his spirit. Luther felt especially challenged. Not the least significant reason was that the antinomian theses cited his lectures on Isaiah and on Paul's epistle to the Galations, by which the antinomians wished to demonstrate that Luther himself had represented but had not retained antinomian positions, and that he had slipped into unsound concepts. Therefore Luther published the antinomian theses, commented on them, and inaugurated at the university a disputation directed against the antinomians.

Weimar intervened. The elector wanted to know what was going on in Wittenberg and insisted that the reformers there come to an agreement. He was not particularly interested in the theological substance of the quarrel. The elector regarded matters primarily in a political light; he suspected that certain people in Wittenberg, encouraged by Luther's serious illness at Schmalkalden, secretly reckoned with Luther's approaching death and were already posturing for the leadership role. Thus the struggles for Luther's successor as leader had already begun. Luther was informed of the elector's view of the matter. Nevertheless Luther did not permit himself to be pressured into an emotional, irrational response. To provoke an intriguer, as Luther now regarded Agricola, was no great achievement. However, the problem caused by Agricola was not a simple one to solve. Agricola would have to be defeated by sound argument. Neverthless, the victory over the antinomians could not be realized merely by declaring their teachings as erroneous, especially since Luther himself had made many of the same statements that Master Eisleben now publicized so persistently.

In contrast to the youth who believed that they correctly represented a doctrine when they studiously repeated unaltered its fundamental premises and seminal ideas, Luther had learned long ago to regard its own teaching within that context determined by the specific historical circumstances. Luther would not permit himself to be defeated by his own past, but he also would not deny what he had once promulgated; on the contrary, he explained what the question seventeen to twenty years earlier had been and what purpose his teaching at that earlier date had been required to serve. "That I at first spoke and wrote so vehemently against law in my teaching was due to the fact that the Christian Church at that time was entirely overwhelmed by and burdened with so much superstition and ignorance that Christ was entirely eclipsed and buried. I desired, by the Word of the gospel, to liberate pious, God-fearing souls from such slavery of conscience. But I never rejected the law" (WA TR III 485).

For Luther this may indeed have represented his true position, and was not necessarily the projection of his later years onto an earlier scenario. But what should others do if the conscience, despite the ongoing Reformation, were still bound by some fetter, whether because of a constitution different from that of Luther, or because the Reformation had not met the particular need? Indeed, Luther's experience would not necessarily have been the same as that of his fellow reformers.

Both Agricola and Luther wanted to liberate the conscience. Furthermore, both were agreed that such liberation could come only from Christ, as gospel, as grace, as faith. The argument between the two men was not about this fundamental assertion. The difference lay in the estimation of what God's Word was. For Agricola, God's Word was the gospel alone, not the law. Agricola believed that Christ had put an end to the law; the law was no longer valid. The task of the law had been to provide a criterion by which sin might be recognized; hence, sin had been a breaking of the law. Now, however, since Christ had appeared, sin was no longer a breaking of the law but contempt for the gospel.

Here was the vital point. With this thought Agricola transfered the task of the law to the gospel; he made the gospel into a new law. Such a perception was totally unacceptable to Luther. With respect to this question, there could be no compromise. To interpret the gospel as law meant to make Christ the taskmaster of the conscience rather than its liberator. On the contrary, Christ as liberator had been Luther's early religious experience; he had experienced Christ as the one who had eradicated his fear and hod overcome hell in his behalf. Should Luther now permit Christ to become a new hell?

It was this line of reasoning that so many years ago had prompted Luther so resolutely to take up the struggle against everyone who, he believed, wanted to interpret the gospel according to the flesh. Let us observe once again that there was indeed an aspect of this struggle that had to do with Luther's class position, with his concept of secular authority, and with the paths of reformation; nevertheless, it cannot be ignored that the impetus for Luther's struggle was primarily religious. Moreover, this religious stimulus retained its full force through all the years of the changing struggle.

Christ was no less the focal point of thought and feeling for the old professor than for the young rebellious monk. Christ was for Luther not only the end of the law but also its fulfillment, as Luther had read in Paul. For Luther Christ was preexistent; therefore, Luther had sought Christ in the psalms and was fully convinced that in them he found the doctrine of the Trinity. Consequently, for Luther, an abnegation of the law as God's Word, which Agricola's works were beginning to suggest, was inconceivable.

The distinction between law and gospel belong to the fundamental principles of Luther's thought, but distinction does not mean absolute separation and rigid juxtapositon of irreconcilable giants. Where does the law not need the gospel, and where is the gospel that does not originate in the law, and where is the God whose grace cannot also appear in anger and indeed must appear in anger because grace otherwise would not be power and love but weakness and a betrayal of itself? Luther played off against the antinomians something that they could not possess: the experience of survival in a life and death struggle in which anger and love are expressions of one and the same power. Whoever cannot become angry also cannot love; whoever avoids the law has no good news to preach; whoever does not use force betrays the freedom that force is intended to protect. Therein lies the meaning and the relevance of the antinomian strife.

The antinomian strife ended with a public reconciliation between Luther and Agricola. However, the reconciliation remained a gesture only; the rupture was irreparable. Luther had personally pursued the contest because he knew that not only in Wittenberg, but also in Freiberg and Lüneburg, antinomian positions were represented, and that the freshets of an antinomian current had begun to ripple in the Reformation. Therefore Master Eisleben's views could not be dismissed as if they represented merely a means to achieve personal recognition.

Because Luther had opened his heart to Agricola, the quarrel entailed much more personal suffering for Luther than did all the arguments that he had had with the papacy or with Thomas Müntzer. Now Luther was so bitterly disappointed that he believed that by befriending Agricola he had nourished a serpent in his own bosom. The situation that now had become intolerable both for Luther and Agricola found a solution in 1540, when Agricola departed Wittenberg to become court preacher and general superintendent in Berlin. In the future, Luther would refer to Agricola only with the greatest contempt, and years later, when Agricola's wife occasionally visited Wittenberg, she would not be invited to Luther's home because her visit could only have served to remind him of his painful disappointment in his former friend.

The young Luther had fought against the established authority of a hierarchy that with its regulations bound the conscience. Under such circumstances Luther's theology had been destined to have an antinomian emphasis. The *sola fide* itself opened the way to antinomianism: the work of the law accomplished nothing, but faith alone justifies the sinner before God. From this conviction Luther's entire struggle against the righteousness of works was born, a struggle that had begun with the indulgence controversy.

In one connection Luther always had held firmly to the law. It is the law that leads the sinner to the recognition of sin. On the other hand, Luther's concept of sin was bound not only to law but stemmed from his anthropology. Man is by nature a sinner and remains a sinner even after he is declared justified. Justification is not exhausted in the act of forgiving sin but consists in the fact that man is regarded in grace by God and while still in sin is accepted by Him. Man always remains *simul justus et peccator*: simultaneously justified and a sinner.

However, for the problem provoked by antinomianism, this meant that Luther's fundamental teaching of Christ alone, grace alone, faith alone had not been completely integrated into the dialectic of "law-gospel"; therefore, Luther had been unable to lay the question to rest. Luther reckoned that grace would always exceed divine anger revealed in the law; at Golgotha, however, he saw not only paternal love at work but also divine anger that exceeded all human measure. Law and gospel were not for Luther, as for the antinomians, two chronologically successive stages in the divine plan of salvation, whereby the gospel as the later and higher stage to a certain degree corrects the blunder that had been made earlier with the law. For Luther law and gospel form simultaneously two avenues of divine activity, which are always current and continuously complementary, somewhat in the manner of demand and consolation. The content of the law in this sense is not limited to the prescriptions provided to Moses on Mount Sinai; it is extended to the sovereign will of God, and that will is active not only in the old covenant but also in the new.

On the other hand, guaranteed by the preexistence of Christ, the gospel is found not only in the New Testament; it is also present in the Old Testament. Thus the tendencies toward antinomianism, which are easily demonstrated in the young Luther and to which the antinomians, in 1536-1537, thought they could appeal, Luther had effectively suppressed by his paradoxical view of God and man; by holding firm to the doctrine of the Trinity; and by his method of exegesis, which had the most enduring effect: namely, to regard the entire Bible, Old and New Testament, as one, and to seek God in His triune personality and in His one sovereign and salutary will in the entire Bible.

In this connection it is probably not without significance that the old Luther in the last years of his life specifically chose Genesis as his lecture theme, dealt in detail with the story of creation, and in the midst of the creation story discovered the redeemer.

For the history of the concept of God, full acceptance of the creation story and its connection with the accounts of Abraham, Isaac, and Jacob, the sojourn in Egypt and the Exodus, the Reed Sea miracle, revelation and Sinai, and the conquest of Canaan all had decisive significance. It was this acceptance that first made of Jahweh the sole God beside whom there was no other. Jahweh had been one of the many popular tribal gods, who had been obliged to get along as well as he could with his co-deities and to respect their bailiwicks.

With the acceptance of the creation myth, the worship of God by the Israelites became monotheism. Significantly, this adoption of the myth and the establishment of monotheism took place in all probability during the period of the Babylonian Captivity (597-539 B.C.) after the independence of Judah as well as that of Israel had decisively ended. The breakthrough to complete monotheism was the defiant compensatory reaction of a people determined to survive, a people whose self-awareness in the face of indescribable political misery crested toward the cosmic as the God of Judah, who had lost His domestic altars, was abruptly transformed into the creator of the world. With the coming of monotheism, reverence for God struck the course to universal religious worship, or at least pointed in the direction. However, from now on monotheism posed the riddle of theodicy. Why had God, who had created all things and who was defined as good, also created evil, for where else could evil have originated except with God himself, since no creator exists other than God? Now lightning was dancing about the old Luther, this time flashing through the creation scene—the idea complex in which the breakthrough experiences of his early years were embedded—and giving his spirit no rest.

Once again the question concerning the nature of man arose: if and to what extent he had been corrupted by the fall of Adam and Eve, and what since the fall man can do on his own in order to procure salvation—thus, to what extent, after the fall, man is still God's creation, and what his true condition is. What was to be disputed was *de homine:* concerning man. In consideration of the institutionalization of the Reformation as well as of the growing independence of a new generation, it was necessary to follow the course and retrace the development of ideas that had been established in the series of debates concerning fundamental theological questions in which Luther had engaged from about 1516 to 1518 (that is, from his lecture on Paul's epistle to the Romans to the Heidelberg disputation).

Even now Luther was holding fast to the gospel, and so far all was going well; furthermore, the longer all would go well under his supervision the longer all would go well even without him. There came a time when there was little that be could add. Those who sought advice from Luther were not enemies. They sought advice in order to strengthen their own reformation convictions, not to evade reformation. To dispel doubt, to dismiss scruble, to dismiss fear, to encourage—that was, after all, the purpose of the gospel and also the understanding of Scripture that Luther projected in his correspondence. In his sermons, of course, the same care for souls was reflected; however, he did not now preach as frequently as formerly. After all, Bugenhagen was in Wittenberg when he did not happen to be elsewhere establishing a liturgical order. Luther dedicated himself to explaining the gospel in his lectures and at disputations. Now Luther continued to write letters, to spend more time in presentation than in preparation of lectures, to chair disputations, to mediate quarrels, to calm the waves, and with caustic pen to attack all perceived scoundrels and rogues, which as a favorite activity from which he could not refrain; as caustic critic, more than as celebrant before the altar, he was in his element. For a long time now he had not celebrated Mass or kept the liturgical hours; however, what had been engrained in him since his earliest years remained deeply rooted and reawakened out of his subconscious. He sought forcefully to suppress spiritual resistance, seeking to tear it out of his soul rather than allowing it to die out by accommodating indifference. When was the last time he had heard confession and granted absolution? And why did the Eucharist quarrel erupt just at the time when the celebration of Mass had been abandoned?

The priesthood, Luther had explained, is a vocation like any other vocation. Thus there is no indelible characteristic; on the contrary, every believer by the power of baptism is a participant in the priesthood of Jesus Christ. For a long time participation in priesthood had been Luther's heartfelt conviction, but it was recent personal experience that prompted him to explain the concept in writing. Luther had wanted to confess to all that everyone is a priest. Now he revised this teaching, not in word, for the teaching remained the same, but in practice. In the early years of the Reformation, there was no alternative to permitting the congregations to elect ministers and preachers if such clergy were to be evangelical, because the bishops, who according to canonical law had the authority to call and invest the clerics, supported the Edict of Worms in conformity with their hierarchical position. The right of each congregation to elect its own minister would have opened the door to the followers of Müntzer, Karlstadt, and the radical spiritualists; in addition, it would have freed the way for others. In order to restrain the radicals and to hold the Reformation firmly on course for that group that saw Luther a their man or wanted to make him their man, there was no choice but to examine the clerical candidates by secular authority in order to establish their fitness. Luther had made suggestions as to how such examinations might be administered. Furthermore, on behalf of those candidates who had requested his recommendation to a post, he intervened zealously with Spalatin, Chancellor Brück, and other highly placed persons.

The high point of such activity, which to a certain extent marked the culmination of Luther's career, was reached in 1524, twenty-two years after he had proclaimed the universal priesthood of all believers. In Naumburg Luther consecrated his old friend and drinking companion Nicolas Amsdorf, a former fellow Augustinian monk, as a bishop; Amsdorf had almost been a rival for the hand of Katharine von Bora. Not Amsdorf but another candidate had been elected by the Naumburg Cathedral Chapter. Notwithstanding, Elector Johann Frederick of Saxony rode with a company of 300 into Naumburg, which at that time was not clearly designated as being within electoral Saxony, and the elector declared that Amsdorf was the right person for the bishop's chair. The presence of 300 Saxon cavalrymen facilitated the espousal of the elector's opinion by the cathedral chapter and the setting aside of the results of the previously held election. Twenty years earlier Luther had fought against bishops; now he installed one. According to the Concordat of Worms (1122), bishops were invested with their secular goods by the emperor, with their spiritual office by the pope or his legate. Amsdorf received his secular investment from Elector Johann Frederick; his spiritual dignity was bequeathed by Luther. For the territory that this investure embraced, Johann Frederick had assumed the function reserved to the emperor in the Concordat of Worms, and Luther had preempted the function reserved for the pope. Like the universality of the empire with the imperial office as the ornamental head in the secular realm, so also the Roman universality in the spiritual realm was forced to give place and to wane before the rising independence of the German states.

The many expectations that the high lords now laid before the highly regarded Luther did not always work to his advantage. Luther did not always resist the temptation to concede on decisions that were in fact against his will, and to condone actions for political reasons; such compromises could hardly be reconciled with his doctrine. Thus Philipp of Hesse even dared request Luther to issue a theological opinion that bigamy was not forbidden by the Bible and that the landgrave might therefore, without dissolving his first marriage, take a second wife. Since Landgrave Philipp was not merely an ordinary person who could be summarily dismissed for making such a demand, but was a prince who was needed in the conflict against Catholic opponents, Luther permitted himself to be persuaded, and he secretly provided "confessional" advice that the second marriage be concluded, and that, if the matter should become known, Philipp should simply issue a denial that any second marriage had ever take place. The matter became known. Not everyone believed the denial. Luther had publicly discredited himself, and the landgrave was obliged to be extremely cautious in his conduct toward the emperor because the penalty for bigamy in the empire was death and the emperor held in his hand the authority to execute the law. So many lies were told about Luther and his opponents so habitually doused him with buckets of filth that it was not very remarkable that one of the lies turned out to be true after all. Anyway, rumors were believed only by those who wanted to believe them. For once Luther had wanted to do what he good naturedly had accused Melanchthon of doing at the Augsburg diet in 1530: to tread softly. It backfired.

Luther as the new pope! This was certainly a spiteful rumor that was designed to denigrate and defame the entire Reformation. But despite all the evil and spiteful intent that unmistakably accompanied such stories, this figure of Luther as the new pope hit the nail on the head, in a sense, as Luther was in fact pushed into a position of high authority with respect to religious matters, a position that paralleled that of the pope. The impression that Luther actually was becoming a new pope was strengthened by the observation that he soon learned to manipulate censorship against displeasing dissidents in his own ranks no less vigorously and unscrupulously than had the hated Romanists. Censorship corresponded neither with Luther's natural tendencies nor with his teaching nor with his purpose. It was rooted in the necessity to arrive at a unified opinion and binding solutions with respect to a whole series of practical questions.

As for what he taught, which was essentially his interpretation of the Bible, he had from the beginning fought without compromise to establish his own teaching and to secure for his own opinion the sole claim to truth. Any "democratic freedom of opinion" was for Luther in this matter completely alien. Of course, he knew from his own experience how difficult it was to capture the meaning of a biblical passage, but he had no doubt that there was a fundamental and clear meaning. Convinced that such a meaning could be discovered, Luther's thought followed an impetus that finally was characterized by extreme intolerance, since he in a matter in which so many other opinions could be supplied sought and demanded truth, a truth that could not be decided by vote and in which his opinion was distinguished from false interpretations as fire is from water. In this most sublime of all thought motifs, Luther was not different from the papacy; thus he faced from the beginning the temptation of making himself a new pope, even though subjectively such a thought may have appeared unpleasant to him, because he himself sensed that unintentionally growing into this role was a threatening possibility. In view of the huge correspondence that came to him concerning a wide variety of questions, especially concerning marriage, liturgical matters, and more or less important questions of doctrine, Luther easily could have employed many scribes had he not reasoned that by so doing a papacy would evolve.

However, what Luther himself did not want to do—namely, to set up a chancellery that would supervise ministers and other Church officers and that would take over many of the functions that earlier had pertained to ecclesiastical jurisdiction—the elector finally did in 1539 when he erected a consistory: that is, a standing commission of jurists and theologians who where charged with the administration of the marriage courts, the inspection of clergy, and the maintenance of Church discipline. The establishment of the consistory by the elector marked the definitive end of congregational sovereignty in ecclesiastical affairs, a sovereignty that the Reformation had brought forth and that just sixteen years earlier had been so enthusiastically supported by Luther himself.

The end of congregational sovereignty and the establishment of consistories did not in all points correspond with Luther's ideas, even though such a transition brought him a certain personal relief since he now no longer was summoned to counsel uninspiring marriage disputes. At least with respect to one of the more important questions of Church discipline—the question of excommunication: the prohibition to participate in

the Eucharist, or expulsion from divine worship—Luther, despite his recognition of the prince's supervisory authority, wanted to leave decisions
to the congregations. Even though Luther himself had been excommunicated and had many years earlier vehemently raged against papal excommunication, the fact that in the second half of the 1530s the application of
excommunication had once again become a problem in the Church, and
that Luther himself persistently demanded its use against people who had
conducted themselves dishonorably in relationship to the Christian faith,
demonstrates to what extent the situation had changed for him in particular and for the Reformation in general. As the Reformation was still developing and its representatives were happy if they were merely tolerated
rather than prosecuted by all available legal means, excommunication was
not practiced and would have been considered presumptuous. But now a
new ecclesiastical essence had developed out of the reform movement and
had begun to function as a part of the social order. Now excommunication
was once more legitimate.

Excommunication is a form of the exercise of power and as such neither
good nor bad; its effect and moral dignity is dependent on who exercises
this power against whom and under what circumstances. The papacy had
employed excommunication to exlude divisive sect leaders from the
Church, to subdue individualistic and enthusiastic innovators, and especially to suppress heresies. By the too frequent use of excommunication in
trifling cases and in matters more obviously connected with the purse than
with salvation or the preservation of correct doctrine, excommunication
lost much of its original terrifying effect, and the more it was used the
duller its edge became. The rebels used the "secular ban" in the Peasants'
War in order to isolate and to put under pressure those who would not
join the rebellion and who preferred to remain peacefully at home and
wait to see how the rebellion would turn out. A measure of revolutionary
power was demonstrated in the practice of driving a stake in front of the
house of whoever was marked by the "secular ban," as a sign that no one
should any longer associate with him.

Luther did not want to drive stakes in front of houses, but he indeed desired to expose before the assembled congregation and to force to a gesture of humility those seductive spirits with their loose tongues, who not
infrequently, albeit unintentionally, had struck upon the irrational core of
his new teaching and had pointed out supressed characteristics in his
thought which harked back to Roman ecclesiastical practices. Luther desired to oppose the seducers not out of a pure quest for power but because
the identity of an ecclesiastical community can be preserved in the long
run only when violations against the sacred criteria of conformity do not
remain unpunished. In reality, under the changed conditions of the institutionalized Reformation, Luther consequently continued to use only those

battle tactics of which he had earlier made use when the reform movement was differentiating and radicalizing; then his purpose had been to hinder the fleshly interpretation of the gospel and the rebellion against secular authority. However, the standards had now changed: trifles were now sufficient to cause recourse to big sticks. A girl who poked fun at the Eucharist and the clergy was punished with imprisonment. Unbelieving persons were to be buried in the knackers's yard. A minister who inadvertently dropped the Eucharistic host was arrested. Pre-Reformation days had not been more narrow-minded.

Luther's reputation as a "new pope," the increased use of the ban, the impatience with dissent from his teaching as well as his sharply antagonistic reaction when his own teachings were occasionally used against him, adherence to a strict segregation from the Roman Church, and the intransigence toward the South German reformers characterized the old Luther as a man who, under the existing conditions of his time, achieved his goals. Therewith Luther realized from the German early middle-class revolution an essential positive significant result in Europe: the irreparable transition in the ideological superstructure of society which could not be rescinded by the Counter-Reformation. This revolution was not expressly pro-capitalist or pro-feudal. On the contrary, it was invisibly and unabrasively woven into the fabric of the absolutism of the many German states. If Luther's ideas at the beginning of his public ministry had not accommodated the new circumstances and the minor shifts in emphasis, the revolution could not have been achieved. During his early ministry Luther had been on the attack; now he found himself on the defensive. And now ideas crept into his thinking that earlier he would not have entertained. Luther held firmly to all his teaching and repeated everything he formerly had said on the theme of salvation; nevertheless, a thought that heretofore was only occasionally inferred, and only in parenthetical phrases, was now stated explicitly: God desires man's cooperation in those matters which lead to salvation. Twenty years earlier Luther had not wanted to hear of such an idea. The notion of cooperation, of human contribution, or of the collaboration of man and God, despite all the securities that Luther had built into his system thought, was in reality a path at the and of which nothing could stand other than the solution reached by the Catholic Church after reworking the Augustinian as well as the Pelagian heritage at the Council of Chalcedon in 451: semi-Pelagianism. Semi-Pelagianism held that man should do whatever was in his power; God would then grant him what he still lacked, and man could cooperate because all his efforts were continuously preceded by the grace of God. With the admission that God required man's cooperation, Luther would say in somewhat different words to his inquiring students what his teachers had said to him. Philosophy once again gently interlaced itself with theology. Melanchthon and with him the humanistic heritage were advancing in the Reformation.

On the other side, Catholicism was also advancing—just at that time after the initial shock of the Reformation and when the might of the Reformation as a popular movement was waning. The rising Counter-Reformation also was conceived as the activity of secular authority. In the Jesuit order, which had just been established and was still seeking the full recognition of the papacy, were found the intellectual elite and shock troops that concentrated on and specialized in acquiring the tutelage of young princes, thereby exercising influence over those men who one day would hold the reins of power. The Roman Church developed a strategy for the long run and broad view in its struggle against the Reformation. The Church had already experienced and survived many heresies and threats. It made its Petrine claim: To Peter—not to Paul, from whom Luther had gained the understanding of the gospel—had Jesus said that he (Peter) was the rock on whom Christ would build His Church and against which Church the gates of hell would not prevail (Matthew 16:17–19). By placing the Counter-Reformation on an intellectual plane, this teaching provided the Roman Church with a breadth that enabled it in full confidence to man the entire battlefront for the regaining of lost territories. This broad dimension included what was lacking in the concealed Father God of Luther, and what eventually through worship, liturgy, and popular preaching, could not entirely fail in its impact on the masses, who had expected more of the Reformation that what now was revealed: a mother goddess, Mary, the mother of God, the "Mother of Wisdom" on whose hymn of praise, the Magnificat, Luther himself had written an exegesis, but whom he no longer desired to see venerated. The Counter-Reformation consciously aimed its attack at the gaps that Luther had torn in the piety of the waning Middle Ages; it nourished itself on the successes of the Reformation, and, not less significantly, learned from the insufficiencies and the mistakes. Mary, unlike the Father God, neither became angry when she loved nor used the devil to bring men back to the paths of righteousness. She was simply the mother, concerned for her children. She stood outside the concepts of theodicy. It is no wonder that she became the figure with whom all simple Catholics could identify—simple Catholics who left the cup to the priests and who did not care a thing about free will and grace, because the world must be accepted as it was and because apart from affliction and toil nothing was to be expected. With a combination of such resignation and an apolitical posture on the part of the laity, with the expectation of providing individualized pastoral care in conjunction with the most strenuous activity on the part of the clergy, the Roman Church anchored its position where the Reformation had not penetrated and was able to extend its influence as the Reformation was growing weak.

Luther's motto against the papacy was "Dont't surrender; don't retreat one step." Despite the ready acceptance, in the internal disputations at his own university, of those theories that naturally led to self-awareness and to the establishment of positions permitting his own supporters, through intellectual exercises, partially to reestablish conclusions long since vindicated through disputation, Luther was obliged to fight hard against all that was Roman and therefore from the devil. It seemed the groundwork was providing a compensatory mechanism. The greater Luther's unconscious rapprochement to the posture of his opponents, the louder became his repudiation; it raged in blasphemous expressions and cursing, and it rose to a crescendo of lewdeness. Luther's wonderfully crude pamphlet *Against Hans Worst*, which was directed against Duke Heinrich of Braunschweig-Wolfenbüttel, should be read; reeking of belching, drunkenness, vagabondage, and filthiness, it is truly a masterpiece. Barrages of the crudest castigation which every complaining Wittenberg market woman would have envied marked Luther's pornographic salvos. In pamphlets of this kind, to take every word seriously would be more than ridiculous. These pamphlets are too well organized and dramatically composed to be mere outbursts of rage; they constitute their own genre, born of taking delight in castigating and sharply criticizing the opponent as well as in his destruction, for which purposes the author gives rein to his winged horse. In this genre truth is not at all the matter of concern; on the contrary, the unique purpose is the humiliation of the opponent targeted by the author.

With approaching old age Luther manifested outbursts of rage and long-lasting ill humor that could not be ignored. Physically he was obese, but mentally he was not phlegmatic; he was obviously a hot-tempered person with flashing eyes. He was between five feet two inches and five feet four inches tall (of "medium height," as Mosellanus reports), solid, sturdy, and of square build. Even the shorter measurement could have been classified as "medium," since, formerly, as has been observed in many museums, the knight's armor display of „medium lenght" does not fully correspond to what we today describe as "medium." In portraits from Lucas Cranach's atelier, the old Luther is depicted as compact, rather stout, upright, not bowed, having a short neck, a double chin sagging from the chin bone to the base of the throat, flabby cheeks, dark brown eyes with a yellow glow, and hair covering the ears. The wax impression of Luther's hand, taken immediately after his death and housed in the Luther Museum in Wittenberg, is that of a scholar's hand: small, slender, and with neatly trimmed nails.

With increasing peevishness, age made itself dominant over youth. Youthful styles appeared to the old Luther as too daring and immodest. Skirts were too short: the girls even exposed their ankles. The students were indolent, insolent, slovenly, and ungifted. Luther vented his rancor in criticism. Youth should honor gray heads; he regretted in his old age having to witness so much indiscreet conduct. He had preached the gospel all his life, and had always respected the proprieties and upheld moral virtue, and now he was obliged to witness how little influence his example had exerted. He was so disgusted with the city of Wittenberg that be could hardly tolerate it. On a trip to Thuringia, he resolved not to return to Wittenberg. The city council and the rector of the university sent a delegation to Thuringia to remind Luther of the disgrace that would be brought upon Wittenberg and the university and of what the public might think if he should choose to settle somewhere else. Protesting and complaining, Luther permitted himself to be persuaded to return, not to the Wittenbergers or to his colleagues but to his Käthe.

However, once he had returned, Luther collected himself, reached for his pen, and attacked new opponents, real and imagined. He perceived only enemies everywhere, and in his writing he unburdened his soul. Luther wanted to attack the kingdom of the devil as long as his hand could wield the pen. Increasingly Luther integrated events into his concept of the kingdom of Satan. Twenty or thirty years ago the kingdom of Satan had been identified only with the papacy. Later the kingdom of Satan subsumed also the Turks and then finnally the Jews, and was viewed as the scourge and rod of divine discipline. Luther's writings expanded on this view. Melanchthon, shaking his head in disbelief, exclaimed to his friends concerning Luther's pamphlet on the Jews: "Look at what he is doing now."

Depression of old age? Not exclusively. The explanation is not so simple. It was not the first time that Luther had occupied himself with the Jews. For the biblical exegete who was distinguishing between law and gospel, continuous concern with the Jewish theme was inescapable. In 1523, at forty years of age, Luther had composed his first pamphlet on the Jews, *Judenschrift*, at the time when the discussion concerning the validity of the Mosaic law arose. The pamphlet is entitled, *Dass Jesus Christus ein geborener Jude sei* (That Jesus Christ Was Born a Jew). The content and goal of the pamphlet is exactly the opposite of that of the pamphlet that Luther wrote in 1543 at the age of sixty, which developed ideas that he had openly espoused a few years earlier. At age forty, Luther had thought of Jesus as being born a Jew. To the Jews the promise of salvation had been given and then only through them to all other people. The Jews are the firstborn, the true heirs of what God hod promised and revealed to Abraham, Isaac, and Jacob. We are, in contrast to them, heathen, and we participate in the promise of salvation only through them. Only by faith can we become what they already are by seed and flesh, even when, as is obviously the case, they do not share our faith in Jesus Christ. This can only mean that we all the more loyally and unfailingly must hold by faith to Christ Jesus, to permit faith to work so strongly in us that it will bring forth fruit so convincing that even the Jews must be persuaded that until now they have erred concerning Christ. Luther lists a catalogue of reasons and arguments that would affect such a change of opinion among the Jews. The baptism of a single Jew had been sufficient to cause Luther enthusiastically to pen the missionary pamphlet. But the seed for what was to erupt twenty years later already had been sown: the Jews are the true heirs; we are the stepchildren. That which nourished this seed comes from the seemingly unrelated subtleties of the arguments concerning the nature of the Eucharist and the other sacraments. These arguments perpetuate among other pursuits a continuous debate about the relationship between the testator and his heirs. Who is the true heir, the one who does the work of the law or the one who believes the word of the testator? Furthermore, still another complexity is included: that it was the Jews whom God had selected as the elect people obviously evokes the predestination question that had disquieted Luther until he disposed of the idea of freedom of the will. His anxiety was clearly evidenced after 1516 and persisted until 1523. However, his solution was no longer unconditional at the end of the 1530s after Luther had put the antinomian strife behind him. Now free will once again was given a place—though a very modest one—and it was permissible to look askance at predestination. From this position it was only a very small step, given an appropriate occasion, to a stance from which envy of predestined Jewish heirship is permitted to flame up. The anti-Judaism of Luther's pamphlets on the Jews did not arise—as did its more narrow-minded, secularized twin, anti-Semitism—from a prejudiced ethnic nationalism, but rather from the most subtle priestly mentality.

Luther's anti-Judaism was only the special case of a much broader phenomenon, the roots of which permeate the entire history of the Middle Ages. With the victory of Christianity, the coexistence of various religions in the Roman Empire was at an end. Disregarding the many persecutions to which the early Church had been subjected, the Church now increasingly turned its acquired power against other religions. With the ascendency of Christianity the position of the Jews, who had been scattered throughout the entire Roman Empire since the abortive revolt of Simon bar Kochba in 132 A.D., was fundamentally changed. In the pagan Roman Empire, the Jews had constituted one of many religious groups, but now they were regarded as being without honor, for they had caused the Savior of the world to be crucified. All "honorable" professions were forbidden to Jews; they were permitted to practice only "dishonorable" professions, such as that of executioner, barber, actor, and moneylender. In cities the Jews were forced to live in ghettos, those areas set aside for them by Christians, where they could pursue other vocations but only to meet the needs of the ghettos.

Of special significance for Jews and their future fate was the circumstance that the canon law prohibition of earning interest on money did not apply to them. The Jews were thus officially permitted a practice prohibited for Christians yet economically indispensable: the taking of interest. Moral discrimination was juxtaposed with an economic privilege practiced within narrow limitation and locale. The entire social milieu therefore forced the Jew into the role of financier and moneylender. Marriage between Christians and Jews was strictly forbidden by both religions. Thus the Jews became in the countries of Europe a religious, cultural, and ethnic minority to whom the possibility of assimilation was denied. In addition the Jew in the ghetto was stamped not only by a specific mentality but also by a sharp intra-ghetto Jewish social control that on its own behalf, prompted by religious motives, resisted any assimilation. Life in the ghetto was poor, provincial, and circumscribed.

For feudal societies, this Jewish minority constantly provided a scapegoat that, in the light of its lack of legal protection, could be made responsible for everything possible or impossible and against which pent up aggressions could be unleashed. As the development of the goods-money economy advanced, the distance between a majority and a minority, which is usually more or less clear and, in addition, is respected not only by the minority but also by the majority, could—in the case of the Jews, as a result of their historically ascribed role in societyless easily be preserved. A rising hatred of the Jew resulted. The more elements of a budding capitalism spread through the feudal society and the more the social tensions and strife increased, the greater the antipathy toward the Jews became. Luther was not exempt from this trend.

At age sixty in the year 1543, sensing that his end was approaching, Luther no longer addressed missionary pamphlets to the Jews in an effort to presuade them. Weary of debating and pleading for conversion, Luther was now quick to judge the Jews. He found them stubborn and of evil intent with respect to the Christian faith; therefore, they belonged to the realm of Satan. Consequently his cry was to burn their books, demolish their synagogues, and expel them from the land! Not even Pfefferkorn, Hoogstraeten, and the Cologne Dominicans, who had been so spitefully ridiculed as the "obscure men," had gone that far. Reuchlin, the granduncle of Melanchthon and the father of Hebrew language study in Germany, had not been enthusiasitc about the Reformation and had insulated himself against it. Had not his premonitions been confirmed? Luther's advice to the duke of Saxony with respect to Thomas Müntzer and his followers at Allstedt had been to expel the rebels from the dukedom.In 1524 and 1525 Luther had been in full possession of his virile powers, but they had been subjugated by his strong will to the monastic vow of chastity. Youthful virility he possessed no longer in 1543. He apologized to Käthe for his impotence. The spirit was willing but the flesh was weak. Luther, feeble and unmanned, did not personally expel any Jews from anywhere; others expelled them, especially in 1542 and 1543, though primarily from Moravia, not Saxony.

The early middle-class revolution had not been completed and remained suspended; the Reformation, to be sure, continued to make progress after the defeat of the peasants, but it did not regain its impetus as a revolutionary component. Disappointment and disenchantment were widespread, and Luther himself was not immune. The hopelessness of fulfillment made him irritable, aggravated his physical ailments, and was expressed in outward aggression indiscriminately against anyone whom he fancied his enemy. The revolutionary impetus existed far and near, but, reduced to reformation alone, the movement became constricted and atrophic. Luther became blind in his left eye. Reading became difficult, and he experienced hardening of the arteries, but the hand kept writing for almost three more years. Finally, Luther penned his last lines: "We are beggars, forsooth."

Life had run its course and had come full circle to its source. In Eisleben, where he had been born, Luther died. His last undertaking was a peace mission. He sought to reconcile two quarreling brothers, the counts of Mansfeld. To fulfill this mission, Luther braved the severe winter weather of February 1546 to travel from Wittenberg to Eisleben. On the evening of February 17, in the city scribe's home where he had taken lodging not more that 200 meters from the house in which he had been born, Luther was overtaken with faintness. During that night, a cold perspiration dampened his brow. To those anxious friends standing about his bed, who assured him that the cause was only a fever, Luther replied, "It is the cold sweat of death." Before sunrise on February 18, Luther died.

The last piece that Luther had written two days earlier contained the following:

No one can understand Virgil in his work *Bucolics* unless he has been a shepherd for five years. No one can understand him in his work *Georgics* unless he has been a farmer for five years. No one can understand the epistles of Cicero unless he has been engaged in public affairs of some consequence for twenty-five years. Let not one suppose that he has sufficiently tasted of the Holy Scriptures unless, for a hundred years, he has—in the manner of the prophets Elijah and Elisha, of John the Baptist, of Christ, and of the apostles—governed the congregations. Lay not your hand on this divine Aeneid but bow before it; adore its every trace! We are beggars, forsooth. (WA TR V 5677)

Epilogue

—

VIVIT (He lives): Luther had had these words, the most succinct expression of his confession and the antithesis of the apparent pessimistic resignation of his last words, engraved on his coat of arms. This confession and conviction, "He lives," had driven Luther into battles and *Anfechtungen* in which he had gained an identity that was confirmed in changing situations. This identity pertains to its own set of circumstances, and it may not be assumed that the young Luther can be recognized in the old, or that in the young Luther the old Luther can be anticipated. Developmental changes and transformations lie between youth and age; contradictions become recognizable. It was not always the worst people who eventually became disappointed with Luther because they expected him to do something quite different from what he actually did. Luther had a strong effect: he attracted and he also repulsed. He has gone down in history, which brought him forth and which he has left behind, as offense and hope.

Many of Luther's ideas others had long ago conceived, preached, and inscribed without causing the impact that accompanied his appearance on the historical stage. As a teacher of Holy Scripture, Luther found it necessary to interpret the text that stemmed not from his own time but from a much earlier period. Insofar as he was teacher of Holy Scripture, Luther was lifted out of his time and place and was translated to the transcendental realm of humanity, whose existential problems and solutions exceeded the temporary present. However, at the same time he also read the biblical text with a view conditioned by his own time, and he interpreted the text in such a way that it addressed itself to his contemporaries and fellow countrymen. Thus Luther opened the historical context of the Bible for himself and his age, and he was entirely caught up in the problems of his society. Individual, social, temporal, and transcendental were all synthesized in Luther. This peculiar complexity elevated Luther above his contemporaries and made him a great historical person. The tension of the historical bow, arching through social crisis, Reformation, the Peasants' War, the continuation of the Reformation after the Peasants' War, the historical process of development, and the culmination and the subsiding of the early middle-class revolution determined the orbit of Luther's life in its quadrants, segments, and degrees, just as Luther, conversely, greatly influenced the events and unleashed the driving forces.

In the period of social crisis Luther matured as an independent actor. Fixing his gaze on Christ on the cross helped him to overcome his own fears, to persevere through the paradoxes of the views of God, to overcome the limitations of the monastic route to salvation, and to achieve inner freedom for a struggle against apparently overwhelming forces to which each individual and the society as a whole were exposed. Thus, unintentionally and surprisingly even to Luther himself, he set loose with the posting of his Ninety-Five Theses the social movement of the Reformation and with it the early middle-class revolution. Luther took inspiration from the Reformation, experienced the reaction to what he himself on his own initiative had unleashed, and saw himself bound to warn against, to protest, and to resist those forces that invoked his name for the pursuit of goals of which he did not approve. The social movement read into Luther more than he was willing to grant, and the movement interpreted from the most diverse points of view the essence of his thought.

For a short period of perhaps four or five years, from about the time of the posting of the theses (October 31, 1517) to his Wartburg sojourn (May 1521–March 1522), Luther was one with those who cheered him, but then the paths diverged. The different classes, ranks, and groups synthesized their own interests, aspirations, and ambitions with the expectations that Luther had given. In this situation, all elements involved in the class struggle became oriented, thanks to the overwhelming influence that he had gained, to his personal opinions, explanations, and decisions. More and more it became evident that Luther's activities corresponded primarily with the interests of the early capitalistic burgher circles and of the aristocratic circles, which were sustained by the existing secular authorities, especially the German princes.

In the Peasants' War this constellation demonstrated the tragic consequence that the man with whose name the hope of the masses had been linked for years turned against the popular rebellion with unmerciful vigor. Here we may—in fact, we must speak of two aspects of Luther's personality. From the point of view of his class association, Luther's attitude toward the rebellion is completely clear, consequent, and intelligible. During the Peasants' War Luther acted as a prop and representative of the interests of the German territorial estates and of the burgher class oriented toward the princes. In the decisive moment of German history in the sixteenth century, Luther's class orientation proved to be stronger than the gospel for whose pure preaching he originally had begun his struggle. Theology was not able to take precedence over the class struggles; it had to nail its colors to the mast, revealing thereby that it was a form of ideology.

As uniform as Luther's theology may seem to be as long as we fix our gaze on its central principles of Christ alone, grace alone, faith alone, it becomes clear from Luther's political activity that his evangelical theology was placed under the pressure of a secular authoritative ideology. Two concepts—perhaps, indeed, two forms of piety—lie side by side in quiet contradiction in Luther's thought. The one concept concerns itself with individual salvation, is oriented toward Jesus, and operates by grace alone and faith alone. The other concept concerns itself with society, is oriented toward the princes, and warns against rebellion and riot. The first concept transcends every world authority; the second concept pays homage to secular rule. The tension between the two determines Luther's view concerning Christian freedom, the two realms, and secular authority.

In the early years of his struggle Luther followed more consistently the individualistic anti-authoritative impulse; the older he became and the more responsibility he was forced to assume, and therefore the more he was obliged to think in broader social parameters, the more obvious it became that his thoughts and actions were stimulated by the latter impulse to maintain social stability, although of course he did not completely suppress the earlier impulse to seek individual salvation. Thus the old Luther is distinguished from the young Luther. The differences are not simply rooted in biological age; on the contrary, they are intertwined with the fate of the movement inaugurated by him.

This movement in its historical essence is an early form of the middle-class revolution. Triggered by Luther's Wittenberg theses of 1517, it began as a movement to reform the Church, encompassed in increasing number various elements of society, identified itself with the problems, aspirations, and demands of the masses, and thereby extended far beyond ecclesiastical borders. It became a movement for the transformation of ecclesiastical, social, economic, and political conditions. The movement diversified and radicalized, and in the Peasants' War attacked with revolutionary fury the foundation of the feudal order. In the failure of the Peasants' War, the movement suffered a defeat and was reduced to that measure of change and progress that the princes would tolerate and that the upper middle-class and the aristocratic circles would support. After the Peasants' War the Reformation slipped increasingly under the influence of the princes. It was unable to develop again into a full-fledged middle-class revolution; insted, it became institutionalized and subsided.

Luther's part in this movement is important but limited. He neither desired nor brought about a middle-class social revolution, but in the socially critical situation of that period, he unintentionally provided the initial impulse. Luther did bring about a theological revolution, the hallmark of which is his rebellious appeal to Paul. The social impact of this theological revolution derives from the fact that it could become the starting point and catalyst of a reform ideology.

The revolutionary aspect of Luther's theology in challenging the right of the feudal authority to judge in matters of faith. This challenge opened the way for uniting with the new theology the interests of forces opposing the established authority. Luther wanted to disseminate his ideas by preaching and writing, thereby promoting the Reformation, but he warned against rebellion. Luther's thinking did not overstep the boundary of reformation; he cried halt to rebellion. This line of demarcation is indicative of his class association.

Luther's attitude is in accordance with the fact that from the depth of his personality he was not critical of social conditions as an opposing or progressive burgher might be; he attacked what in his opinion was false teaching in the Church. His ideas, to be sure, touched upon many social problems, but Luther viewed them only from a given point of view and with limited perception. Luther's achievement in theology was sufficient to trigger and to set on course the reform movement, but not to serve or to justify its most radical ideological consequences. Thus Luther's theology corresponded with his class association.

However, the thoughts and actions of others went past the line at which Luther cried halt. After a Luther had spoken, a Müntzer could not remain silent. The operative phenomenon here was not merely a friend-foe antithesis but a genuine historical dialectic. Although a Luther had blazed the trail for progress toward a middle-class, capitalistic society, it was a Müntzer who boldly reached beyond Luther and that world, and thereby made manifest the limitations of Luther's historical achievement.

Martin Luther's historical achievements consist of the following: with his Ninety-Five Theses he triggered the Reformation and thereby also the early middle-class revolution; he refused to revoke his ideas; he exposed the decadence of the papal Church and undermined papal authority; he defended the theological impulses for a middle-class emancipation ideology; he theologically justified the attack on Church property and thereby legitimized the transfer of ecclesiastical property to the benefit of the middle-class and the nobility; with the doctrine of justification by faith alone, the teaching of the priesthood of all believers, the acceptance of the gravamina, and the establishment of the congregational principle, he created a reform ideology that corresponded to the interests of the middle-class, the humanists, the lower clergy, and some of the nobles and princes, and that for a while favored the development of a popular reform movement; with the translation of the Bible into German, Luther gave the popular movement a mighty idelogical weapon and promoted the formation of a national literary German language; he provided sustained motivation for the development of the educational system, for care of the poor, and for the work ethic.

Luther's historical confines are expressed in the following: he limited himself essentially to the struggle against ecclesiastical feudalism, especially against the papacy; he resisted the formation of radical reform movements; he rejected popular uprising against secular feudalism and turned against the rebellious masses in the Peasants' War. After the failure of the Peasants' War, Luther's historical function consisted of defending ideologically the middle-class moderate Reformation and its alliance with the princes. Thus the chasm between Luther and the popular movement became wider, and his dependence on the German princes increased. However, Luther's amicable relationship with the German princes provided for the erection of a barrier against a complete re-Catholicizing of Germany, for the basis of further development of the Reformation in Europe, and thereby for new thrusts in the middle-class struggle for emancipation.

Martin Luther, thought fettered by the inconsistencies of his age, was an activating agent in the process of the early middle-class revolution. As such he not only achieved greatness with respect to the historical development of Germany but also attained universal significance.

Works Cited

WA = *D. Martin Luthers Werke*. Kritische Gesamtausgabe. Weimar: 1883-.
WA BR = *D. Martin Luthers Werke: Briefwechsel*. Weimar: 1930-.
WATR = *D. Martin Luthers Werke: Tischreden*. Weimar: 1912-1921.
Cochlaeus, Johannes. *Historia Martin Lutheri*. Trans. C. Hueber. Ingolstadt: 1582.
Hipler, Franz. *Nikolaus Kopernikus und Martin Luther*. Braunsberg: 1868.
Kalkoff, Paul. *Die Depeschen des Nuntius Aleander vom Wormser Reichstage 1521*. 2nd ed. Halle: 1897.
Lenk, Werner. *Die Reformation im Zeitgenössischen Dialog. 12 Texte aus den Jahren 1520-1525*. Berlin: 1968.
Leupold, Ulrich S., ed. *Liturgy and Hymns*. Vol. LIII of *Luther's Works*, ed. Jaroslav Pelikan and Helmut T. Lehrmann. Philadelphia: 1965.
Marx-Engels Werke. 43 vols. Institut für Marxismus-Leninismus beim ZK der SED. East Berlin: 1960-1970.
Mettka, Heinz, ed. *Ulrich von Hutten: Deutsche Schriften*. Vol.1. Leipzig: 1972.
Müntzer, Thomas. *Politische Schriften, Manifeste, Briefe, 1524/1525*. Ed. Manfred Bensing and Bernd Rüdiger. Leipzig: 1973.
Stupperich, Robert, ed. *Philipp Melanchthon's Werke in Auswahl*. Vol. VII, pt.1. Gütersloh: 1951.
Thulin, Oskar. *Martin Luther: Sein Leben in Bildern und Zeitdokumenten*. Berlin: 1969.
Ullmann, Ernst, ed. *Albrecht Dürer: Schriften und Briefe*. Leipzig: 1973.
Vogelsang, Erich, trans. *Luthers Hebräerbrief-Vorlesung von 1517-1518*. Berlin-Leipzig: 1970.
Walch, Johann Georg, ed. *D. Martin Luthers Sämtliche Schriften*. 24 vols. 1st ed. Halle: 1740ff.
Wilckens, Ulrich, trans. *Das neue Testament*. Berlin: 1979.
Wrede, Adolf, ed. *Deutsche Reichstagsakten unter Karl V*. Vol.II. Gotha: 1896.

Abbreviations

Cochläus	= Johannes Cochlaeus: Historia Martini Lutheri ..., German ed. C. Hueber, Ingolstadt 1852
Hipler	= Franz Hipler: Nikolaus Kopernikus und Martin Luther, Braunsberg 1868
Kalkoff	= Paul Kalkoff: Die Depeschen des Nuntius Alexander vom Wormser Reichstage 1521, 2nd ed., Halle 1897
Leupold	= Luther's Works, ed. by Ulrich S. Leupold, Vol. 53, Fortress Press 1964
Marx-Engels-Werke	= Karl Marx, Friedrich Engels. Werke, Berlin 1956 ff.
Mettke	= Ulrich von Hutten: Deutsche Schriften, ed. by Heinz Mettke, 3 vol., Leipzig 1972-1974
Müntzer	= Thomas Müntzer: Politische Schriften, Manifeste, Briefe 1524/25, ed. by Manfred Bensing and Bernd Rüdiger, Leipzig 1973
Thulin	= Oskar Thulin: Martin Luther. Sein Leben in Bildern und Zeitdokumenten, Berlin 1969
Ullmann	= Albrecht Dürer: Schriften und Briefe, ed. by Ernst Ullmann, Leipzig 1973
Vogelsang	= Luthers Hebräerbrief-Vorlesung von 1517/18, ed. by Erich Vogelsang, Berlin—Leipzig 1930
WA	= D. Martin Luthers Werke. Kritische Gesamtausgabe, Weimar 1883 ff.
WA BR	= D. Martin Luthers Werke. Kritische Gesamtausgabe. Briefwechsel, Vol. 1-15, Weimar 1930-1978
WA TR	= D. Martin Luthers Werke. Kritische Gesamtausgabe. Tischreden, Vol. 1-6, Weimar 1912—1929
Walch	= D. Martin Luthers Sämtliche Schriften, ed. by J. G. Walch, Halle 1745
Wilckens	= Das Neue Testament, ed. by Ulrich Wilckens, Berlin 1979
Wrede	= Deutsche Reichstagsakten unter Kaiser Karl V., vol. 2, ed. by Adolf Wrede, Gotha 1896

Index